Excommunication in the Middle Ages

Elisabeth Vodola

Excommunication in the Middle Ages

University of California Press

BERKELEY / LOS ANGELES / LONDON

University of California Press
Berkeley and Los Angeles, California

University of California Press, Ltd.
London, England

© 1986 by
The Regents of the University of California

Library of Congress Cataloging in Publication Data
Vodola, Elisabeth.
　　Excommunication in the Middle Ages.

　　Bibliography: p.
　　Includes index.
　　1. Excommunication—History.　I. Title.
　　BX2275.V63　1986　　262.9′2　84-24103
　　ISBN 0-520-04999-3

Printed in the United States of America
1　2　3　4　5　6　7　8　9

Contents

Preface

"I cordially agree with the teaching of the Church of England in most respects, but she says one thing and does another, and until excommunication—yes, and wholesale excommunication—is resorted to, I cannot call her a Christian institution." So Ernest Pontifex, the character whom Samuel Butler wishes to shut the door on so many unwholesome aspects of the past, expresses his nostalgia for the institution of excommunication. Its obsolescence, Ernest sees, signals the passage of a phenomenon alien to modern society, the ritual pruning of unfit members to ensure survival of the group.

The chapters that follow will trace excommunication from its fragmentary origins in biblical times to its entrenchment in the religious and social institutions of the middle ages. The times are fraught with dangers for such a book on medieval legal history. A half-dozen of my protagonists—including Bracton, Gratian, and Alexander III—have undergone identity crises since I began, and lesser figures have been shedding their personalities like moths. Attributions undisturbed for six hundred years—sigla scratched in the puckering margins of parchment folios—are suddenly being ardently pursued, now that we have a machine, the computer, that can accommodate the dynamic and ephemeral quality of medieval juristic literature.

Only gradually have I come to realize that my topic is as unstable as my sources. That one speaks in the singular of "excommunication" says more about the limits of human judgment and discourse than about historical reality. Freud said only the human mind keeps the old furniture around along with the new that should replace it, but that is not so. Cargo from all their many ports freight great historical institutions like excommunication.

Fortunately, a number of excellent scholars have turned their attention to this topic, and I have benefited from many of their works. For the early church, I have drawn heavily on Doskocil's *Der Bann in der Urkirche*, Hein's *Eucharist and Excommunication*, and, still incomparable after a century, Hinschius's *Kirchenrecht*. H. C. Lea's works, many of them relevant to excommunication, likewise remain classics. For the high middle ages, the meticulous studies of Huizing and Zeliauskas on canonical doctrine have been invaluable. Professor Donald Logan's *Excommunication and the Secular Arm* is full of insights and information, not only on medieval England but also on excommunication in general; I have also learned a good deal over the years from discussions with the author. I was lucky enough to read E. Eichmann's *Acht und Bann* for the first time in the early years of my graduate research; going back to it often, I have never failed to learn something new.

For the sake of brevity I have largely avoided quoting from printed books, many of which are now available in reprints. I have tried to ease the way back to these texts by making references as exact as possible, sometimes sacrificing uniformity to accommodate the peculiarities of early printed books. All the manuscripts are Latin, so I have eliminated "lat." from citations. Most are from the Vatican Library, and I have shortened citations of manuscripts in the Vaticani fond by letting a single "Vat." serve for location and fond. Quotations of substantial length I have confirmed from at least two manuscripts, though I have noted variants only in the appendixes; even there, variants are limited to those that might affect interpretation. Texts in both the notes and the appendixes are simply transcribed, not edited; apart from adding minimal punctuation and capitalization, I have followed manuscript usages in preference to standardizing them. Square brackets enclose explanatory or supplementary information; pointed brackets, my own suppletions. Lemmata are taken from the commentaries themselves and often vary slightly from the standard editions of the texts.

Since my sources are mostly cryptic commentaries on texts well known to their medieval audience, literal translations would occasionally be unintelligible, and I have sometimes used the device of paraphrasing without quotation marks. Bibliographical references are abbreviated in the footnotes. I have usually cited only the most recent works, where references to earlier ones can be found. Where I repeatedly cite a source, it is in some proportion an indication of my indebtedness. Latin biblical texts are quoted from the Vulgate unless otherwise noted; English translations are from the King James Version.

In its present form this book was begun in the late 1970s, but its origins lie in a dissertation finished in the summer of 1975 under the direction of the late Professor Walter Ullmann of Trinity College, Cambridge. Many of its ideas go back to his inspired and unsparing teaching: writing the final draft, I often had an uncanny feeling that I now understood for the first time things he told me.

For gifts of intellectual liberation I am also particularly indebted to Professor Ellen Stone Haring, who directed my undergraduate thesis on Thomistic metaphysics at Wellesley College, and to Dr. Marie Battle Singer of Cambridge University.

Many people have contributed to this book with friendship and advice. Most of all, Sandy Zabell, whose unshakable confidence carried me over many obstacles. Editors at the University of California Press showed me at several crucial points ways I could make the book better and generously and patiently gave me time to do so. Dr. Karen Reeds, as friend and editor, encouraged and advised me in the early stages of transforming manuscript into book. Mr. William McClung has given much expert advice and help. Dr. Marilyn Schwartz's vigorous editorial analysis freed the final draft from many encumbrances. As editor for the Press, Mr. Paul Psoinos read the manuscript, including the Latin texts, with great care and made many excellent suggestions for corrections and improvements. Among the many whose support encouraged me over the years, I want to thank especially professors Thomas Bisson and David Daube.

I also profited from suggestions from several Press readers—professors Joseph Strayer, Elisabeth Gleason, and Richard Helmholz, whose article "Excommunication as a Legal Sanction: The Attitudes of the Medieval Canonists" (*ZRG Kan. Abt.* 68 [1982]) unfortunately came too late for me to incorporate its insights.

Working since 1975 at the Institute of Medieval Canon Law in Berkeley, I have had the privilege of access to one of the best research facilities available in medieval legal scholarship, assembled and generously shared by Professor Stephan Kuttner. I would also like to thank Kristin England for help with typing and Michael S. Kerekes for organizing the last stages of computer production. Finally, I am grateful to Rose Vekony, from the Press, for careful editorial work on the proofs and indexes.

Sigla and Abbreviations
of Frequently Cited Works

Legal citations are in the usual form: Dig., Cod., and Nov. for the
Corpus iuris civilis; D.1 c.1, C.1 q.1 c.1, *de poen.* D.1 c.1, *de cons.* D.1
c.1 for Gratian's Decretum; X for the Liber Extra, VI for the Sextus,
Clem. for the Clementines, and Extrav. Jo. XXII or Extrav. Comm.
for the later compilations. Innocent IV's *novellae* are cited by incipit,
followed where possible by a citation in the Sextus.

Abb. Ant.	Abbas Antiquus
App.	*Apparatus*
BMCL	*Bulletin of Medieval Canon Law*, new series
Bracton	*Bracton. De legibus et consuetudinibus Angliae*, ed. G. E. Woodbine, rev. and trans. S. E. Thorne
CCL	*Corpus Christianorum, Series Latina*
CCLM	*Corpus Christianorum, Continuatio medievalis*
CDI	*Collection de documents inédits sur l'histoire de France publiés par les soins du ministre de l'instruction publique*
COD	*Conciliorum oecumenicorum decreta*, ed. J. Alberigo et al., 3d ed. (Bologna 1973)
Comm.	*Commentaria*
Comp.	Compilationes 1–5, ed. E. Friedberg, *Quinque compilationes antiquae* (Leipzig 1882)
CRR	*Curia Regis Rolls*, ed. Public Record Office, 16 vols. (London 1922–)
CT	*Theodosiani libri XVI cum Constitutionibus Sirimondianis et Leges novellae ad Theodosianum pertinentes*, ed. T. Mommsen and P. M. Meyer, 2 vols. in 3 (Berlin 1905)
DDC	*Dictionnaire de droit canonique*

Dur., *Spec.* Guliellmus Duranti, *Speculi pars prima (–quarta)*, 4 vols. in 3 (Lyon 1543)

Friedberg E. Friedberg, ed., *Corpus iuris canonici*, 2 vols. (Leipzig 1879–81; repr. Graz 1959)

Glos. ord. *Glossa ordinaria.* See bibliography under *Corpus iuris canonici* and *Corpus iuris civilis*

Goff. Tr. Goffredus de Trano

Host., *App.* [*Apparatus in novellas constitutiones Innocentii IV*], in *Lect.*, vol. 2, part 2

Host., *Lect.* Hostiensis, *In primum (–quintum) Decretalium librum commentaria.* [*Lectura*] (Venice 1581; repr. Turin 1965)

Host., *Sum.* Hostiensis, *Summa aurea* (Venice 1574; repr., with preface by O. Vighetti, Turin 1963)

Hug., *Sum.* Huguccio, *Summa* (see manuscripts list)

Inn. IV, *App.* Innocent IV, *In V libros Decretalium commentaria.* [*Apparatus*] (Venice 1570)

J. *Journal*

JE, JK, JL Jaffé, P., ed., *Regesta pontificum Romanorum*, 2d ed., S. Loewenfeld (ao. 882–1198), F. Kaltenbrunner (–590), and P. Ewald (590–882), 2 vols. (Leipzig 1885–88; repr. Graz 1956–57)

Jo. An., *Comm.* Iohannes Andreae, *In Sextum Decretalium librum novella commentaria* (Venice 1581; repr. Turin 1966)

Jo. An., *Nov.* Iohannes Andreae, *In quinque Decretalium libros novella commentaria* (Venice 1581; repr. in 4 vols., with preface by S. Kuttner, Turin 1963)

Jo. Teut. Johannes Teutonicus

KB King's Bench

Lect. *Lectura*

Maitland, *History* F. Pollock and F. W. Maitland, *The History of English Law*, 2 vols., 2d ed. (Cambridge 1898; repr. 1968)

Mansi J. D. Mansi, *Sacrorum conciliorum nova et amplissima collectio*, 53 vols. (Florence and Venice 1758–98; repr. Paris 1901–27)

MGH *Monumenta Germaniae historica*
  Capit.   *Capitularia*

	Conc. *Concilia*
	Const. *Constitutiones*
	Epp. *Epistolae*
	Epp. Sel. *Epistolae selectae*
	LL. *Leges* (in folio)
MIC	*Monumenta iuris canonici*, Series A (Glosses), B (Canonical collections), and C (Congress proceedings)
NB	*Bracton's Notebook*, ed. F. W. Maitland, 3 vols. (London 1887)
Olim	*Les Olim, ou registres des arrêts rendus par la cour du roi*, ed. A. Beugnot, 3 vols. in 4 (Paris 1839–48)
PG	J. P. Migne, ed., *Patrologiae cursus completus*, Series Graeca, 161 vols. (Turnhout 1857–66)
PL	———, ed., *Patrologiae cursus completus*, Series Latina, 221 vols. (Paris 1844–64)
Pl. Ab.	*Placitorum in domo capitulari Westmonasteriensi asservatorum abbreviatio* (London 1811)
R.	*Review, Revue*, etc.
Raym. Peñaf., *Sum.*	*Summa Sancti Raymundi de Peniafort . . . cum glossis Ioannis de Friburgo* (Rome 1603; repr. Farnborough 1967)
RDC	*Revue de droit canonique*
RHDFE	*Revue historique de droit français et étranger*
RHE	*Revue d'histoire ecclésiastique*
RS	Rolls Series
SS	Selden Society
St.	*Studies, Studia*, etc.
Sum.	*Summa*
TUI	*Tractatus universi iuris*, 18 vols. in 25, and 3 index vols. (Venice 1584)
Vinc. Hisp.	Vincentius Hispanus
YB	Yearbook
Z.	*Zeitschrift*
ZRG Kan. Abt.	*Zeitschrift der Savigny-Stiftung für Rechtsgeschichte, Kanonistische Abteilung*

I

Historical Introduction

"I recently gave a sermon on excommunication, denouncing the tyranny and ignorance of the whole base mob of officials and commissaries and vicars," Luther wrote to his friend Wenceslaus Link in July 1518.[1] "Everyone was amazed: they had never heard anything like it. Now we're all waiting to see what new evil the future holds for me. I've kindled a new fire!"

Luther was right: reports of the sermon led to his summons to Augsburg for interrogation by Cardinal Cajetan a few months later.[2] But a casual reading of the sermon reveals little to offend. On the contrary, it is punctuated with pious injunctions that seem like the preacher's public acknowledgment of the dangers of his own position: excommunication, the sermon says, is like the discipline of a conscientious parent, harmful only to the child who angrily rebels.[3] The only bitter note is Luther's repeated reference to popular deceptions fostered by church officials who hold the faithful in thrall by encouraging them to believe that excommunication will deliver their souls

---

[1] J. K. F. Knaake et al., eds., *D. Martin Luthers Werke* (Weimar 1883–), *Briefwechsel* I (1930) 185–86.

[2] In letters to Spalatin (31 Aug. 1518) and Johann von Staupitz (1 Sept.), Luther said that he had already published the sermon because it had been misrepresented by his opponents (Knaake, *Werke* I 191–95).

[3] "Sermo de virtute excommunicationis," Knaake, *Werke* I 641.

to Satan in permanent damnation, whereas the Scriptures make it clear that Satan's punishments are harnessed to the goal of salvation.[4] Had not a constitution of Pope Innocent IV (1243–54) pronounced excommunication medicinal for those who submitted to it with humility?[5] Why would the pope not have described the sanction as destructive and murderous of the soul if the fears of its desperate victims, fanned by tyrannical officials, were correct?

Orthodox as it was, Luther's sermon underscored some of the tensions inherent in excommunication itself, contradictions that might as easily have arisen from a sincere examination of the sources as from the dishonest persuasions of ecclesiastical officials. For the sanction incorporated, without unifying, many different theological and legal elements.[6] The most primitive was the curse, which existed in all the cultures that contributed to the Bible.[7] The curse entailed social exclusion or even death—of course, in a community whose members depended on one another for the necessities of life, social ostracism might itself mean death. The pagan ritual of *devotio*, in which those guilty of grave crimes were sacrificed to the gods, also influenced excommunication in its earliest stages.[8] Criminals destined for this fate became *sacer*, separated from the profane world and possessed of

---

[4] Ibid. 640.

[5] Ibid., referring to *Cum medicinalis* (VI 5.11.1), further discussed in Chapter 6 at n. 48 and passim. Shortly thereafter, Luther alluded to the "butchering" of church officials bearing excommunications by people who had been misled thus (ibid. 641).

[6] My interpretation of biblical passages on excommunication is especially indebted to two excellent studies: W. Doskocil, *Der Bann in der Urkirche, eine rechtsgeschichtliche Untersuchung* (Munich 1958), and K. Hein, *Eucharist and Excommunication. A Study in Early Christian Doctrine and Discipline* (Frankfurt am Main 1973). Other useful studies on excommunication in the early church include: O. D. Watkins, *A History of Penance* (London 1920) I passim; P. Hinschius, *System des katholischen Kirchenrechts* (Berlin 1869–97; repr. Graz 1959) IV 691–864 and V 1–492 passim; J. Dauvillier, *Les Temps apostoliques, Ier siècle* (Paris 1970) 581–88; F. Kober, *Der Kirchenbann nach den Grundsätzen des canonischen Rechts*, 2d ed. (Tübingen 1863) 382–412; and H. C. Lea, "Excommunication," *Studies in Church History*, 2d ed. (Philadelphia 1883) 235–521.

[7] See Doskocil, *Bann* 5–18, and Hein, *Eucharist* 4–17, on curses in the cultures that contributed to biblical sources. As Doskocil (p. 5) points out, death was the inevitable result of a curse leading to social exclusion in a society in which the community is needed for sustenance. But equally important, if harder to assess, are the psychological effects of exclusion. See W. B. Cannon, "'Voodoo' Death," *American Anthropologist* 44 (1942) 169–81, esp. 174, on "mourning" rituals preceding a victim's death, some of which resemble penitential rites.

[8] H. J. Rose, *Religion in Greece and Rome* (New York 1959) 230.

magical powers mingling consecration and execration.[9] Greek and Roman societies also used curses in legal transactions to supplement a system of executions that remained weak even in the developed law.[10] Surviving in inscriptions, these Greek and Roman curses seem to be echoed in the rhythms of medieval formulas of anathema.[11]

Only gradually were the magical effects of the curse transformed into theological concepts; the stages can be traced at many points in

[9] Festus, *De verborum significatu quae supersunt cum Pauli Epitome*, ed. W. M. Lindsay (Leipzig 1913), s.v. *Sacer mons*, p. 424. See also W. W. Fowler, "The Original Meaning of the Word *Sacer*," *J. of Roman St.* 1 (1911) 57–63; and G. Dumézil, *Archaic Roman Religion*, trans. P. Krapp (Chicago and London 1970) I 129–31; and, on similar words in a different culture, E. E. Evans-Pritchard, *Nuer Religion* (New York and Oxford 1956) 171 and 209. Cf. A. van Gennep, *The Rites of Passage*, trans. M. B. Vizedom and G. L. Caffee (Chicago 1960), introducing the concept of the "pivoting of the sacred," the shifting of borders separating individuals undergoing transformation from one social status to another, as seen from the stable perspective of the "profane" world (esp. pp. 12–13, 113–14, and 168; I am indebted to Professor Eugene Irschick for suggesting that I read this illuminating book). Rituals involving spitting might be an important symbol of this ambivalence in excommunication. Although spitting usually betokens incorporation rather than exclusion (van Gennep 98; cf. Evans-Pritchard 171) it was used in some medieval rituals of excommunication, e.g., that prescribed by the eleventh-century manual for parish priests by John Myrc (*Instructions for Parish Priests*, ed. F. Peacock [London 1868] 24).

[10] On curses as sanctions in Roman law see A. Watson, *Roman Private Law around 200 BC* (Edinburgh 1971) 55; on the persistent weakness of execution in Roman law see J. M. Kelly, *Roman Litigation* (Oxford 1966).

[11] Compare, on the one hand, the ancient curses translated by R. Lattimore, *Themes in Greek and Latin Epitaphs* (Urbana, Ill., 1962) 117, or, for an English example, A. R. Burn, *The Romans in Britain. An Anthology of Inscriptions*, 2d ed. (Columbia, S.C., 1969) 44–45, and, on the other hand, the medieval anathema formulas that became standard in canon law, in Regino of Prüm, *Libri duo de synodalibus causis*, ed. F. G. A. Wasserschleben (Leipzig 1840; repr. Graz 1964) 2.412–19, pp. 369–76. These were excerpted in Burchard of Worms, *Decretum* 11.2–8, *PL* 140.856–61; and in *Le Pontifical romano-germanique du dixième siècle*, ed. C. Vogel and R. Elze (Vatican City 1963–72) cc.85–89, vol. 1, pp. 308–17; and later, more briefly, in Gratian, C.11 q.3 cc.106–8. For further evidence of their use see also R. Schieffer, *Die Entstehung des päpstlichen Investiturverbots für den deutschen König* (Stuttgart 1981) 68 n. 96. The canons are attributed to several still-unidentified French councils, most prominently a council of Rouen. The 567 Council of Tours, under Archbishop Praetextatus of Rouen, might be investigated as a source. Reference is made to a curse against sacrilegious theft, which might have been quoted in some transmissions of the canons (C. de Clercq, ed., *Concilia Galliae A. 511–A. 695, CCL* 148A.175–99 at 192–93). Moreover, one canon in the series (Reg. 2.416 = Burch., *Decr.* 11.6, *PL* 140.859–60) is actually attributed to an unidentified council of Tours. L. K. Little, "La Morphologie des malédictions monastiques," *Annales. Economies, sociétés, civilisations* 34 (1979) 43–60, discusses several early medieval curses, including a ninth-century formula quite possibly from Rouen (pp. 45–46); cf., by the same

the New Testament as well as the Old.[12] Jewish theology had already portrayed God as executor of the curse, as, for example, in the garden of Eden.[13] But in many New Testament passages the curse still worked its effects directly: Ananias and his wife, Sapphira, were immediately struck dead by Peter's words (Acts 5), Ananias for withholding money from communal funds and his wife for lying to protect him.[14] Even the Eucharist could be a medium for the curse, causing sickness and death to those who took it with a guilty conscience.[15] No doubt partly because of this biblical verification, the curse remained among the concepts and customs that periodically reinvigorated medieval excommunication.

In some Old Testament passages exile had already replaced death as the effect of the curse. Jews who married heathens during the Babylonian captivity were exiled; the confiscation of their property might have been a vestige of the death penalty.[16] But the New Testament continued to portray death as a frequent effect of the curse, striking sometimes the enemies of Christ and sometimes Christians themselves.[17]

Christian redemption took root in the Jewish concept of death as atonement for sin: Christ redeemed his followers by "becoming a curse himself" (Gal. 3.10–13).[18] Death of the body sometimes fore-

---

author, "Formules monastiques de malédiction aux IXe et Xe siècles," *R. Mabillon* 58 (1975) 377–99.

[12] On classification see van Gennep, *Rites* 7–8 and 13.

[13] Gen. 3; see Doskocil, *Bann* 14.

[14] Hein, *Eucharist* 78–79; Doskocil, *Bann* 46–49 and passim for other New Testament examples of the curse. Of special interest is Christ's injunction to the apostles to "shake the dust off your feet" in communities where their message was not welcome (Matt. 10.14, etc.). This, as Doskocil observes (p. 29), is close to the Jewish curse formula. Might the foot stamping that sometimes concludes anathema ceremonies bear vestiges? (e.g., C.11 q.3 c.106).

[15] 1 Cor. 11.27–30, on which see Hein, *Eucharist* 62 and 101–3, and Doskocil, *Bann* 71–72. The "True Vine" in John 15 might also be a symbol of the Eucharist (Hein 36–37).

[16] Ezra 10.8; see Doskocil, *Bann* 16–18.

[17] E.g., in Gal. 1.8–9 Paul inflicts on false preachers a curse that Doskocil (*Bann* 55) interprets as annihilation. In Rom. 9.3 Paul imagines a self-curse for Jews who refuse to accept Christ (cf. Doskocil 54). But in John 16.2, Christ warns the disciples that they might eventually be killed "in the name of God." Again, the Jews who conspire to murder Paul bind themselves on pain of the curse (Acts 23.12; cf. Doskocil 40–42 and 54).

[18] Doskocil, *Bann* 59; Hein, *Eucharist* 106–7.

boded but at other times prevented death of the soul.[19] Satan might execute the curse, but by punishing he sometimes helped to redeem. Nor were his punishments confined to the next world. The Corinthian man who slept with his father's wife was delivered to Satan and (most probably) to death to accomplish his salvation.[20] But the heretics Hymenaeus and Alexander were given to Satan "so that they may learn not to blaspheme" in this world.[21] Medieval excommunication drew great strength from the limber biblical interplay of symbol and reality.

Early Christian discipline was probably also derived partly from contemporary Jewish institutions. The last decades before the birth of Christ saw the origins of the synagogue ban, excluding heretics—rebels against rabbinical authority—from all community life and ordinary sinners from all social contacts, except with family members, for three days.[22] The banned had to conduct themselves as mourners.[23] Since, according to the Gospel of John, Christians were banned from synagogues, this Jewish form of excommunication probably directly influenced the Christian.[24]

But words attributed to Christ himself by the Gospel of Matthew were the direct source of Christian excommunication. The passage concerned the Christian duty of fraternal correction: a Christian must admonish a sinning brother first privately, then before two or three witnesses, and finally, if necessary, before the whole church

[19] E.g., in John 15.1–6, the death by burning inflicted on those who do not cling to the "True Vine" seems to presage eternal death (Doskocil, *Bann* 43), whereas for the incestuous Corinthian death serves as partial atonement (1 Cor. 5.1–5).

[20] 1 Cor. 5.1–5. See Doskocil, *Bann* 62–64, and Hein, *Eucharist* 92–96, stressing the distinction between possession by Satan and mere affliction by Satan. (The tradition upheld, for example, by Origen that the sinner absolved by Paul in 2 Cor. 2.5–11 was the same man [B. Poschmann, *Paenitentia secunda. Die kirchliche Busse im ältesten Christentum bis Cyprian und Origenes* (Bonn 1940; repr. 1964) 445; cf. Watkins, *Penance* I 19–21] is refuted by Doskocil, *Bann* 76–80.) Again, in Acts 8.20–24, Peter's curse kills Simon Magus, but Peter's own injunction to "repent" and Simon's petition for Peter's prayers imply that the death is not necessarily eternal (Doskocil, *Bann* 50–51).

[21] 1 Tim. 1.20; cf. Doskocil, *Bann* 84–87; Hein, *Eucharist* 121–22; Watkins, *Penance* I 22–23.

[22] Doskocil, *Bann* 18–24; Hein, *Eucharist* 6–12. See also Theodor Reik, *Ritual. Psycho-Analytic Studies*, 2d ed., trans. Douglas Bryan (New York 1946) 232–33.

[23] See van Gennep, *Rites* 96–97, on analogies between rites of penitence and rites of mourning.

[24] John 9.22; cf. Doskocil, *Bann* 21.

community[25]—"but if he neglect to hear the church, let him be unto thee as a heathen man and a publican."[26] These famous words established both the procedures of ecclesiastical discipline and their sanction, social exclusion—though it must be remembered that since Christ himself associated with publicans, the exclusion was less radical than it later became.[27] The words attributed to Christ invest this discipline with the transcendent power to redeem sin, joining the rabbinical "power to bind and loose" and the charismatic power of the Holy Spirit.[28]

The New Testament describes several examples of social ostracism as a form of discipline. For medieval excommunication the most important is that of the Corinthian guilty of incestuous fornication. The Apostle's rebuke of the Corinthians for misguidedly tolerating such a sinner is imbued with the symbols of a rite of separation: "Know ye not that a little leaven leaveneth the whole lump? Purge out therefore the old leaven. . . . But now I have written unto you not to keep company, if any man that is called a brother be a fornicator . . . with such an one not to eat."[29] Paul is referring to the Passover feast: the communal meals that symbolized incorporation, including the Eucharist, were the most prominent boundaries of social life in the early Christian community.[30]

[25] Matt. 18, esp. 15–19. Doskocil (*Bann* 30–38), while acknowledging the importance of the passage in the evolution of excommunication, stresses that fraternal correction is the theme of Matt. 18. Hein (*Eucharist* 69–70) points out that the words cannot be Christ's own since they assume the existence of a Christian community that came only later. Cf. also Hein 91 and Watkins, *Penance* I 9–10.

[26] Matt. 18.17.

[27] The apostle Matthew was himself a publican (Matt. 9.9); cf. E. Badian, *Publicans and Sinners* (Ithaca, N.Y., 1972) 11. Certainly, however, even the earliest commentators, like Origen, interpreted the act as one of excommunication (cf. Poschmann, *Paenitentia* 441).

[28] Matt. 18.18–20, where the power is given to all the apostles, as later in John 20.22, whereas in Matt. 16.19 it is given to Peter alone. See Hein, *Eucharist* 69; Doskocil, *Bann* 35–40; and Watkins, *Penance*, esp. I 9 and II 568–71.

[29] 1 Cor. 5.6–11; see Doskocil, *Bann* 59–68, and Hein, *Eucharist* 92–103, the latter noting this as the first definite New Testament description of an excommunication (see also below at n. 45 and Chapter 2 at n. 7). 3 John describes an excommunication of orthodox Christians by the rebel Diotrephes (Doskocil 99–101).

[30] For other examples of disciplinary exclusion from meals see 2 Thess. 3.10 (perhaps not Pauline) and the explicit reference to the "altar" in Heb. 3.10 (not Pauline). See Hein, *Eucharist* passim, on the transformation of "cultic purity" (p. 194) into the "ethical purity" required of participants in the Eucharist. On communal meals as rites of incorporation see van Gennep, *Rites* passim, esp. 28–29, 103, 164–65, and 170.

But the boundaries between sinners and the faithful were not permanent, and those on the other side were not usually portrayed as enemies. Social exclusion was therapeutic: "Have no company with him that he may be ashamed. Yet count him not as an enemy, but admonish him as a brother."[31] Only sinners who virtually condemned themselves by turning obstinately against Christ were wholly shunned: Christ's own words implied that they had in fact consigned themselves to eternal damnation.[32] The real barrier to salvation was one that sinners themselves raised. Believers were given the tokens of incorporation, the greeting and the kiss.[33] But as for the stubborn sinner, "Let him be anathema."[34]

THE EARLY CHURCH

Little is known of early ecclesiastical institutions.[35] A hierarchical organization existed by the second century, and by the third century the bishop's supreme disciplinary authority was exercised in episcopal courts.[36] But the soteriological role of the community, expressed by members' confessing to each other and praying together, and by giving oblations and alms, was at least as important in penitence and for-

[31] 2 Thess. 3.14–15; cf. Doskocil, *Bann* 68–71, and Hein, *Eucharist* 90–91.

[32] E.g., Titus 3.10–11; Heb. 10.26. Hein emphasizes the biblical doctrine that all repented sins are forgivable; even in the rigoristic Book of Hebrews, it is the sinner's psychological state that renders salvation unlikely (*Eucharist*, esp. 111–12 and 144–45; cf. Watkins, *Penance* I passim).

[33] 1. Cor. 16.20–21. On greetings as rituals of incorporation, see van Gennep, *Rites* 32; on the kiss see ibid. 29, and N. J. Perella, *The Kiss Sacred and Profane* (Berkeley and Los Angeles 1969) 13–27. Cf. also 2 John 10, denying greetings and hospitality to heretics (cf. Doskocil, *Bann* 98–99); and Ps. 129(128).8, where greetings signify a blessing (cf. Hein, *Eucharist* 256 n. 26). See also Chapter 3 at n. 35.

[34] 1 Cor. 16.22; see Doskocil, *Bann* 55–56. The term "anathema" in the sense of a curse leading to social exclusion took root in the Pauline letters; cf. Doskocil 27–28 and 56–59, and Hein, *Eucharist* 104–5.

[35] Dauvillier, *Temps* 587–88; W. M. Plöchl, *Geschichte des Kirchenrechts*, 2d ed. (Vienna and Munich 1960) I 105–10.

[36] On episcopal court procedures see the early third-century *Didascalia Apostolorum. The Syriac Version Translated and Accompanied by the Verona Latin Fragments*, ed. R. Hugh Connolly (Oxford 1929), esp. c.11, p. 111. (For the date I have followed J. Quasten, "Didascalia Apostolorum," *New Catholic Encyclopedia* 4.860–61; cf. Plöchl, *Geschichte* I 108, and E. Tidner, ed., *Didascaliae Apostolorum, Canonum ecclesiasticorum, Traditionis Apostolicae, Versiones Latinae* [Berlin 1963] ix–x.) On the ecclesiastical hierarchy see also H. E. Feine, *Kirchliche Rechtsgeschichte*, 4th ed. (Cologne and Graz 1964) 39–46.

giveness.[37] Bishop and community shared both the rite and the responsibility for the sinner in one of the first detailed descriptions we have of penitence, the third-century Syrian *Didascalia*, which apocryphally claimed to be the apostles' own composition.[38] Here repentant sinners were ritually put out of the church while the congregation entreated the bishop to pardon them. Brought back into the church, sinners were assigned a penance of up to seven weeks of fasting.[39] During this term penitents, like catechumens, joined the congregation to hear the word of God but were barred from prayers and the Eucharist. After finishing their terms, penitents came weeping to seek reconciliation, which the bishop granted through the laying on of hands.

Liturgical exclusion was thus different from social exclusion. Penitents were excommunicated in that they could not participate in the Eucharist, but they remained a part of the community. A famous passage in the *Didascalia* obliges the faithful to watch over sinners: "therefore consort with those who have been convicted of sins and are sick, and attach them to you, and be careful of them, and speak to them and comfort them, and keep hold of them and convert them."[40] But an equally strong obligation bound the faithful to shun unrepentant wrongdoers. In fact, the *Didascalia* for the first time prescribed that anyone who associated with an excommunicate be similarly disciplined. Although complete ostracism was certainly customary from the time of the New Testament, other contemporary and later sources excommunicated only clerics for all contacts with excommunicates and laymen only for praying with an excommunicate in their homes.[41]

---

[37] Poschmann, *Paenitentia* esp. 464–67; Doskocil, *Bann* esp. 98–99, 106–8, 117–20, and 126; Hein, *Eucharist* esp. 439–44; Watkins, *Penance* I passim, esp. 23 and 74; E. F. Latko, *Origen's Concept of Penance* (Quebec 1949) 91–92; and H. C. Lea, *A History of Auricular Confession and Indulgences*, 3 vols. (Philadelphia 1896; repr. New York 1968) passim, esp. I 76–93.

[38] On penitence in the *Didascalia*, see Hein, *Eucharist* 353–60; Watkins, *Penance* I 248–54; J. N. D. Kelly, *Early Christian Doctrines*, rev. ed. (New York 1978) 219; and Hinschius, *Kirchenrecht* IV 704 n. 8 on 704–5.

[39] *Didascalia* c.6, ed. Connolly 52–53.

[40] *Didascalia* c.10, ed. Connolly 104, in Connolly's translation. Cf. c.6, p. 44, for a similar passage.

[41] *Didascalia* c.15, ed. Connolly 140. This seems to be the earliest text indicating that all laymen and clerics who have contact with excommunicates are excommunicated, although one should note that it is contradicted by the *Didascalia*'s doctrine that one person's sins do not affect another (c.6, *ed. cit.* 43–44) and, more generally,

Grave sins entailed many years of penance, which completely changed a penitent's way of life.[42] Rules for penitents, included in some of the first genuine papal decretals, resemble the "mourning" required of those under the synagogue ban.[43] Marriage and sexual re-

---

by the compassion that characterizes the work. The Council of Antioch of 341 still excommunicated only clerics for all contacts with excommunicates, while warning laymen to avoid such contacts: "Si quis cum excommunicato vel in domo simul oraverit, hic segregetur" (c.2; Mansi 2.1310). The late fourth-century *Apostolic Canons* excommunicated laymen only for praying with excommunicates (c.10, in F. X. Funk, ed., *Didascalia et Constitutiones Apostolorum* [Paderborn 1905; repr. Turin 1970] I 567. I have followed the date of J. Quasten, "Apostolic Constitutions," *New Catholic Encyclopedia* 1.689–90; cf. Plöchl, *Geschichte* I 110). In the early sixth-century Latin translation of Dionysius Exiguus, the sanction clause was omitted (c.11, in C. H. Turner, ed., *Ecclesiae Occidentalis monumenta iuris antiquissima* [Oxford 1899–1939] I 3). In a canon of the ca. 397–400 Council of Toledo it is not clear whether the sanction affects only clerics or extends to all who were warned to avoid the excommunicate, whether he is a layman or a cleric: "Quisquis laicus abstinetur, ad hunc vel ad domum eius clericorum vel religiosorum nullus accedat: similter et clericus, si abstinetur a clericis evitetur: si quis cum illo colloqui aut convivere fuerit deprehensus, etiam ipse abstineatur, sed hoc pertineat ad eos clericos qui eius sunt episcopi et ad omnes qui commoniti fuerint de eo qui abstinetur, sive laico quolibet sive clerico" (Mansi 3.1000–1001; the text of J. Vives, ed., *Concilios visigóticos* [Barcelona and Madrid 1963] 23, has "conmuniti" for "commoniti" in the last line, wrongly, I think). Hinschius (*Kirchenrecht* IV 704 n. 8) believed that laymen were legally obligated to avoid all contacts with excommunicates only from the mid-fifth century, the date of the canonical collection known as the Second Council of Arles, to which Hinschius assigned the conventional date, ca. 443–52. C. Munier, ed., *Concilia Galliae A. 314–A. 506*, *CCL* 148.111 has revised the date to 442–506; but in any event, the canon in question (c.49, ed. 123–24), though it certainly states that excommunicates must be avoided by both laymen and clerics, imposes no sanction. Since Hinschius acknowledged that customary avoidance of excommunicates by laymen as well as clerics was of long standing, and since he was attempting to date the actual legal obligation, it is unclear why he chose this canon and ignored the *Didascalia*. The earliest canon after the *Didascalia* that excommunicates laymen for all contacts with excommunicates seems to be c.40 of the *Statuta ecclesiae antiqua*, now shown to be probably the work of Gennadius of Marseille, and to date from ca. 476–85 (C. Munier, ed., *Les Statuta ecclesiae antiqua* [Paris 1960] 86; cf. 209–42 on provenance. Munier, *Concilia Galliae* 173, has a slightly different version of the canon). For further discussion see Munier's observations in *Statuta* 137–38 and Kober, *Kirchenbann* 380–83.

[42] One day's torment, qualitatively equivalent to a year, was the toll for one day's sin, according to the second-century Shepherd of Hermas (2.6.4–5, PG 2.967–70). On the varying prescriptions on length of penance see Poschmann, *Paenitentia* 446 and passim; Watkins, *Penance* I 62–63, 128, 239, 276; II 552–54 and passim; and Lea, *Confession* I 20–26, 33; II 76, 235–36 and passim.

[43] See van Gennep, *Rites* 93–97, for some comparisons between Christian penances and other rites of separation. Striking resemblances lie in the prescriptions on hair,

lations were forbidden even after reconciliation to the church, though Pope Leo I (440–61) conceded that young men who found continence too demanding and might be tempted to fornicate could marry after finishing penitence.[44] Commerce, litigation, military pursuits, and public baths, games, and feasts were also proscribed. These strictures, which left a definite though peculiar impress on medieval excommunication, underscored the penitents' passage into a state very different from their fellow Christians'. But the rites of penitence were not merely rites of separation; they also protected sinners in their fragility from the temptations and incursions of the profane world.

Strict rules governed excommunication from an early period. A pseudo-Augustinian sermon on penitence forbade prelates to excommunicate anyone who had not been found guilty in a secular or ecclesiastical court, on the basis of Paul's words in the first letter to the Corinthians, "Si quis frater nominatur aut fornicator . . . cum hujusmodi nec quidem cibum sumere."[45] In the biblical translation cited in the sermon, "nominare" was linked to the identification of the individual as a sinner, not as a Christian, though the latter interpretation was favored in the Vulgate ("Si is qui frater nominatur est fornicator . . .") and in the King James version quoted above.[46] "Nominatio," the sermon emphasized, meant conviction by due pro-

---

that it be disheveled (e.g., Jerome's famous description of the penitence of Fabiola in *Ep.* 77 to Oceanus, *PL* 22.692), shaved (e.g., the 506 Council of Agde, c.15: Munier, *Concilia Galliae* 201), or allowed to grow (e.g., Isidore of Seville, "De ecclesiasticis officiis" 2.17 § 3, *PL* 83.802). Here, as elsewhere, Roman *infamia* might have linked pagan and Christian rituals: one way to infame an adversary informally was to follow him about with disheveled hair, which signified mourning (Dig. 47.10.15.27; see D. Daube, "*Collatio* 2.6.5," in I. Epstein et al., eds., *Essays in Honour of the Very Rev. Dr. J. H. Hertz* [London (1943)] 111–29, esp. 121–25; and, by the same author, "'Ne quid infamandi causa fiat'. The Roman Law of Defamation," *Atti del Congresso internazionale di diritto romano e di storia del diritto . . . Verona . . . 1948*, ed. G. Moschetti [Milan 1951–53] III 413–50 esp. 413–15).

[44] The letter of Pope Siricius (384–98) to Bishop Himerius of Tarragona, among the first extant papal decretals, indicates that military service, public games, marriage, and sex were proscribed even after penitence was completed (c.5, *PL* 13.1137). Leo I's famous response to Rusticus of Narbonne added limitations on commerce and litigation but allowed sex after penitence for those unable to be continent (*Ep.* 167, *PL* 54.1199–1209). Cf. Watkins, *Penance* I 411–21.

[45] See the pseudo-Augustinian sermon 351 § 10, *PL* 39.1546–47. (E. Dekkers notes, in *Clavis Patrum Latinorum*, 2d ed. [Steenbrugge 1961] 75, that the attribution to Augustine is almost certainly not authentic.)

[46] On this passage see also above at n. 29 and Chapter 2 at n. 7.

cess; the faithful were warned not to censure sinners approaching the altar to receive the sacraments.[47] Good Christians were silent unless they had proof of others' sins; judges must decide on the basis of "certa indicia."[48] Early conciliar canons also secured excommunicates' rights of appeal.[49]

Since penance was therapeutic, however, excommunicates were warned not to be arrogant even if they were excommunicated unjustly. In a famous homily expounding the resurrection of Lazarus as a metaphor for absolution, Gregory I (590–604) argued that contempt for excommunication was itself a sin: "Whether the shepherd binds justly or unjustly, the flock fear his sentence, lest, bound unjustly, they earn the sentence by contemning it."[50] This principle of passive submission was crucial both in penitential theology and, later, in legal doctrine on excommunication.

The early church knew only public penitence. The prospect of lengthy subjection to the rigors of penance must have persuaded a good many sinners to choose alternative means of redemption, such as almsgiving, prayers, or masses. Increasingly, it seems, only those guilty of grave and notorious sins sought the public sacrament;[51] a letter (416) of Pope Innocent I requiring penitence for minor as well as serious sins probably only accelerated its obsolescence.[52] Over the next centuries it was replaced by the Celtic system of penitential tariffs, under which penance mainly entailed a certain number of years

[47] Pseudo–Augustine, Sermon 351 § 10, *PL* 39.1547.

[48] Ibid. 1546.

[49] One of the most famous was c.11 of the Council of Sardica of 343, allowing appeals to a synod (Turner, *Monumenta* I 480–82 = Gratian C.11 q.3 c.4, cited in X 5.39.40). See also c.66 of the *Statuta ecclesiae antiqua* (ed. Munier, *Concilia Galliae* 180 = C.11 q.3 c.30).

[50] Gregory I, *Hom. in Evang.* John 20.19–31, referring to John 11.43 (*PL* 76.1291). Of course this was only a more precise statement of the traditional distinction between ecclesiastical judgments and their ontological effects.

[51] Most famous were Origen's seven means of redeeming sins: baptism, martyrdom, almsgiving, forgiveness or correction of others, love, and penitence (*Homil. 2 in Lev.* c.4, *PG* 12.417–18; cf. Poschmann, *Paenitentia* 448–49). The Council of Agde of 506 acknowledged that penance, because it was so rigorous, could not easily be prescribed for young men (c.15, in Munier, *Concilia Galliae* 201). Cf. also Watkins, *Penance* II 536–80, and C. Vogel, "Composition légale et commutations dans le système de la pénitence tarifée" part 1, *RDC* 8 (1958) 289–318 at 293.

[52] For a new edition of Innocent I's letter, with commentary, see R. Cabié, ed., *La Lettre du pape Innocent Ier à Décentius de Gubio (19 Mars 416)* (Louvain 1973) 28, on this point. On the letter see also Watkins, *Penance* I 415–16.

of fasting, although other penalties sometimes accompanied the fast, including the prohibitions of sex and military service that were invariably features of ancient penitence.[53]

Precisely how excommunication and penitence were related remains obscure for the centuries preceding the Carolingian reform. In an analysis of conciliar canons down to the late seventh century, Vogel concluded that reparation for crime, rather than penance, was required of excommunicates seeking reconciliation.[54] Conversely, penitents were not normally "excommunicated" except by being excluded from the Eucharist.[55] Moreover, the penitential manuals make clear that restoration to the Eucharist was no longer reserved as a ritual of reconciliation, since penitents were sometimes readmitted partway through their terms of penance.[56] Perhaps for this period even more than for others it is best to speak of "excommunications": exclusion from all community life, from communal worship, or merely from the Eucharist are the categories proposed by Vogel.[57]

From the late seventh century, public penitence was prescribed only for notorious sins.[58] Secret offenses were confessed privately to priests, who administered penitence with the aid of the tariffs of the penitential manuals, while public sins—or, more accurately, crimes—were remitted through composition and penances administered by the secular or ecclesiastical courts. Lay and ecclesiastical authority were closely related. Bishop and count were the joint agents of Carolingian royal authority; excommunication was transformed into a fully public criminal sanction.[59] A pattern that began to be estab-

---

[53] See Watkins, *Penance* II 616; Vogel, "Composition" part 1, 295–96; and Lea, *Confession* II 119–20 on the equivalence of penance and fasting. On the enduring prohibition of sex see Vogel, "Composition" part 2, *RDC* 9 (1959) 1–38 and 341–59 at 28; and Lea, *Confession* II 121.

[54] C. Vogel, "Les Sanctions infligées aux laïcs et aux clercs par les conciles gallo-romains et mérovingiens," *RDC* 2 (1952) 5–29, 171–94, and 311–28 at 317–18 and 326–27.

[55] Vogel, "Composition" part 1, 289.

[56] F. W. H. Wasserschleben, ed., *Die Bussordnungen der abendländischen Kirche* (Halle 1851) passim, e.g., 105.

[57] Vogel, "Sanctions" 313–16.

[58] P. Brommer, "Die bischöfliche Gesetzgebung Theodulfs von Orléans," *ZRG Kan. Abt.* 60 (1975) 1–120 at 96–97, identifying Theodulf (d. 821) as one of the first Carolingian reformers to promote this distinction. See also Vogel, "Composition" part 1, 314–18; Lea, *Confession*, esp. I 20–22, 43–49, and II 73–79.

[59] E. Eichmann, *Acht und Bann im Reichsrecht des Mittelalters* (Paderborn 1909) 5–26; Lea, "Excommunication" 313–42; T. P. Oakley, "The Cooperation of Mediaeval

lished in the sixth century, when Childebert II in 596 banned from the royal palace all who had contracted incestuous marriages in defiance of ecclesiastical legislation and decreed that their possessions be confiscated, was gradually developed until a full panoply of royal punishments buttressed excommunication.[60] Payment of the royal *bannus* (sixty shillings), imprisonment, confiscation, and exile sanctioned the bishop's mandate to do penance.[61] The capitulary of Olonna (825) described the cooperation of episcopal and royal authority in detail.[62] A sinner, after being warned to reform, would be summoned to a court jointly administered by bishop and count and would be required to pay the royal ban. If this measure failed, the sinner would be excommunicated. Finally, the truly contumacious sinner would be imprisoned by the count to await the judgment of the king himself.

For the church, the price of royal enforcement was gradual surrender of control over excommunication. In 803 Charlemagne warned bishops not to use the sanction indiscriminately, advice that was to be repeated throughout the century.[63] Presaging the intervention in ecclesiastical affairs that would be resented in so many medieval kings, the royal court became virtually an appeal tribunal from excommunication when the secular sanctions were invoked.[64] But in the an-

---

Penance and Secular Law," *Speculum* 7 (1932) 515–24; idem, *English Penitential Discipline and Anglo-Saxon Law in Their Joint Influence* (New York 1923) 167–96.

[60] *MGH Capit.* I 15–17; cf. M. Morel, *L'Excommunication et le pouvoir civil en France* (Paris 1926) 8, and Eichmann, *Acht* 15.

[61] See Morel, *Pouvoir* 5–12; Eichmann, *Acht* 14–21; Lea, "Excommunication" 315–42; and *Confession* II 107–12 and passim.

[62] First capitulary of Olonna (ao. 825) c.1, *MGH Capit.* I 326. Cf., e.g., the 755 capitulary of Pippin in the Council of Verneuil (*MGH Capit.* I 33–37, esp. c.9 at p. 35); the "Capitula de rebus ecclesiasticis" of ca. 787–813 (*MGH Capit.* I 185–86); the second Council of Marsanne (ao. 851), c.4, *MGH Capit.* I 408; and the Capitulary of Verneuil of 884 (*MGH Capit.* II 371–75, esp. cc.4–5, pp. 372–73).

[63] "Capitulare missorum" (ao. 803) c.2, *MGH Capit.* I 115. See also, under Charles the Bald, the 846 Council of Epernay, c.56, declaring that no bishop should excommunicate without "certain and manifest" grounds (*MGH LL.* I 392), although it must be noted that since Archbishop Hincmar of Reims was involved in this legislation (*MGH Capit.* II 260–62; see below at n. 73) the chapter might be directed against Hincmar's suffragan Hincmar of Laon, who, the archbishop charged, had excommunicated his subjects without just cause ("Opusculum LV capitulorum" c.30, *PL* 126.407). See also the Capitulary of Pitres (ao. 869) c.10, *MGH Capit.* II 335–36, forbidding excommunication without proof of cause.

[64] Thus in 869 Charles the Bald stated that he would discipline contumacious excommunicates only if they had been excommunicated "de causis designatis et manifestis"; see the Capitulary of Pitres c.10, *MGH Capit.* II 335–36.

archy that resulted from the breakdown of Carolingian rule, the church had to seek secular protection of its property, at first from the imperial contenders, later, as authority was increasingly fragmented, from local feudal dynasts.

Several ninth-century attempts to make anathema a more severe penalty than excommunication might have been a response to the same need. Although there was little to substantiate such a distinction,[65] several ninth-century councils proclaimed that anathema meant eternal death;[66] a synod of Pavia (850) even denied the viaticum to those under anathema, though from the first Council of Nicea (325) ecclesiastical policy dictated that no one be refused this final sacrament.[67] Perhaps imitating pagan curse-inscriptions, this use of anathema might have been merely to protect property against plunderers not deterred by the more refined theological concepts of excommunication.[68] In the Council of Ravenna in 877 Pope John VIII threat-

---

[65] The Pauline letters (above, n. 34) do not treat "anathema" in enough detail to constitute a real theology. No consistent substantive distinction emerges in the sources of the early church, although "excommunication" and "anathema" are sometimes differentiated by implication—e.g., the Council of Carthage of 390, c.8, states that an excommunicated priest who celebrates mass is anathema (C. Munier, ed., *Concilia Africae A. 345–A. 525, CCL* 149.15–16). Cf. Hinschius, *Kirchenrecht* IV 800–801, noting that anathema in the Merovingian period was a solemn form of excommunication and implied greater certainty of eternal damnation. Vogel, "Sanctions" 7–8 and 311–12, also draws attention to the greater certainty of eternal damnation implied by anathema, but warns that one should not conclude that anathema always meant eternal death, since on occasion Merovingian councils prescribed it for slight offenses.

[66] E.g., the 846 Council of Epernay, c.56 (above, n. 63), declaring that "anathema aeternae mortis est damnatio. . . ."

[67] Synod of Pavia, ao. 850, c.12, *MGH Capit.* II 120. Since the first Council of Nicea of 325 (c.13, *COD* 12) the official policy of the church was never to withhold the viaticum. See also Hincmar of Reims's rebuke of Hincmar of Laon when the latter denied his subjects the viaticum, having interdicted them to avenge a personal injury ("Opusculum LV capitulorum" c.32, *PL* 126.413). On the development of the policy see Watkins, *Penance*, esp. I 221–39; for some variations see Lea, "Excommunication" 258–66.

[68] Cf. Little, "Morphologie" 47–48, proposing that curse sanctions protecting monastic property in this period might have been used to compensate for the instability of Germanic forms of possession. Supporting this link, perhaps, is the pagan meaning of "anathema"; cf. Gregory Thaumaturgus (d. 270), "Epistola canonica" c.3, *PG* 10.1031–32, noting that property stolen from the Christian community during times of violence will be anathema, i.e., devoted to the gods. As is clear in the text, however, my interpretation of canonical sources distinguishing anathema from excommunication differs from Little's (p. 50). Also, Vogel has shown that conciliar anathemas were used for other purposes besides protecting property ("Sanctions" 7–8).

ened despoilers of church property with the "penalty of Ananias and Sapphira, who fell dead at the feet of the apostles" and went on to a "fiery eternity with Judas, betrayer of our Lord."[69]

But in this age of Pseudoisidore merely polemical origins should not be ruled out. The most enduring testimony of the attempt to distinguish excommunication and anathema is a letter of Pope John VIII (872–82) regarding Engiltrude, fugitive wife of the great Count Boso.[70] Alluding to the repeated censures unleashed against her by Pope Nicholas I (858–67) and by a number of bishops, Pope John proclaimed that Engiltrude had been "struck repeatedly not only by excommunication, which separates from fraternal society, but also by anathema, which severs from the body of Christ, that is, the church."[71] Though the meaning of these words is obscure, and though they may be rhetorical, the motive might be easier to discern. Archbishop Hincmar of Reims was very much involved in the case,[72] and

[69] Council of Ravenna, ao. 877, c.16 (Mansi 17.340), directed against plunderers of the papal patrimony. C.5 of the same council merely excludes from "communion" those guilty of lesser sacrilege (Mansi 17.338). Ananias and Sapphira were prominent also in Pseudoisidore; see, for example, the proclamation that those who steal church property will die in soul if not, like Ananias and Sapphira, in body (P. Hinschius, ed., *Decretales Pseudo-Isidorianae et Capitula Angilramni* [Leipzig 1863; repr. Aalen 1963] 145.

[70] *MGH Epp.* VII 280. It is cited in Gratian, C.3 q.4 c.12, and its influence on Gratian will be discussed below.

[71] *MGH Epp.* VII 280: "noveris non solum excommunicatione, que a fraterna societate separat, sed etiam anathemate, quod ab ipso corpore Christi, quod est aecclesia, recidit, crebro percussam." For the excommunications by Nicholas I, etc., see *MGH Epp.* VI passim, e.g. 221 and 267–68. The phrasing "non solum . . . sed etiam" was very common in penalties, especially excommunication. But, as Vogel has shown, the usual progression was from the lesser exclusion, from religious contacts—and it was here that the phrase "ab ecclesia" was used, whereas "ecclesia" is linked with the greater exclusion in John VIII's phrase—to the greater exclusion, from all social contacts ("etiam a convivio," etc.; see Vogel, "Sanctions" 314–15). As Vogel points out, the terminology is so fluid that it is impossible to assign definite meanings to these phrases. In the 877 Council of Ravenna the combination of the two-step form of sanction and the desire for rhetorical variety makes the canons read like a repertorium of synonyms for "excommunication" (Mansi 17.337–40). Cf. also the phrasing in Hinschius, *Pseudo-Isidorianae* 53; and in Hincmar of Reims, "Opusculum LV capitulorum" c.30, *PL* 126.407; and c.33, ibid. 450.

[72] He was the addressee of a number of the papal letters on the subject; cf. the references cited above, and see also E. Perels, "Die Briefe Papst Nikolaus' I." part 1, *Neues Archiv der Gesellschaft für ältere deutsche Geschichtskunde* 37 (1911–12) 537–86 at 558. A lively account is P. R. McKeon, *Hincmar of Laon and Carolingian Politics* (Urbana, Ill., 1978), dealing not with the Engiltrude matter (about which almost nothing is known) but with the related conflict over the marriage of King Lothar II.

his exaltation of the authority of metropolitans over their suffragan bishops might well lie behind this attempt to separate excommunication and anathema.[73] A law of Charles the Bald based on one of Hincmar's synods forbade bishops to anathematize without their archbishop's or fellow bishops' consent.[74] In the contentious "*Opusculum in Fifty-Five Chapters*," written to deflate the pretensions of his nephew Bishop Hincmar of Laon, Archbishop Hincmar observed that anathema is portrayed as alienation from God in both the Old and New Testaments.[75] Bishop Hincmar himself stood in grave danger of anathema, the archbishop warned. It was, of course, a sanction against which his nephew and suffragan could not retaliate.

It would be wrong to read too much significance into such experiments in differentiating the two terms. Distinctions were perennially revived, especially when excommunication was undergoing important changes; but they invariably foundered on the very devotion to tradition that canon law so strongly fostered: there were no ancient sources to support a distinction, and had one been established it would have had the undesirable effect of diminishing the terrors of excommunication itself, which stood as sanction in so many ancient canons.[76]

Still, in the intellectual atmosphere that produced the Pseudo-isidorian forgeries, written tradition was malleable. Another ninth-century innovation would radically alter canon law, though not for several centuries. Laymen and clerics had been excommunicated for associating with excommunicates since at least the third century. Pope Gelasius I (492–96) returned to this theme so often that he might be said to have created an ideology on excommunicates' contagion. Especially in his many letters on the schism Patriarch Acacius of Constantinople (472–89) caused by too warmly supporting imperial efforts to reconcile opponents of the ecumenical Council of Chalcedon (451), Gelasius referred almost obsessively to the "con-

---

[73] On Hincmar's defense of metropolitan privileges, one of the central issues in Pseudoisidorian literature, see esp. H. Fuhrmann, *Einfluss und Verbreitung der pseudoisidorischen Fälschungen* (Stuttgart 1972–74) passim, esp. I 119–22 and 146.

[74] Council of Epernay, ao. 846, c.56 (above, n. 63).

[75] Hincmar of Reims, "Opusculum LV capitulorum" c.33 (*PL* 126.433).

[76] See esp. Ivo of Chartres, *Decretum* 14.49–52, *PL* 161.837–38), where Ivo's attempt to augment the gravity of anathema founders on a citation of Augustine that uses the term "excommunication" (c.50, cols. 837–38).

tagion of depravity" and "pollution of communion" with the schismatics.[77] Studied during all the later crises of the church, Gelasius's letters held that heretical doctrines alone could pollute their adherents. Not only those who associated with a contemporary condemned for heresy but also those who endorsed his ideas in the future were to be automatically excommunicated.[78]

In the ninth century, however, certain authors seem to have tried to limit the contagion by reducing the penalty for converse with excommunicates.[79] A forged decretal prescribed only forty days of penance for those who "voluntarily associate with an excommunicate in conversation, prayer, food, or drink";[80] and the Council of Ravenna of 877 prescribed only exclusion from the Eucharist, and a suitable penance, for those who "knowingly communicate with an excommunicate . . . and give him so much moral support that he is disinclined to seek absolution."[81] Since neither penance nor exclusion from the Eucharist were "contagious," these canons mitigated excommunication both by lessening the penalty for associating with excommunicates and by confining the contagion to those who had direct contact.

One can only guess why these authors wished to modify the traditional rules. Many of the prominent enemies of Archbishop Hincmar

[77] E.g., *Ep.* 3, *PL* 59.24 and 43–44; *Ep.* 11, *PL* 59.59 and 64.

[78] E.g., *Ep.* 13, *PL* 59.62C.

[79] Among the many genuine sources of this period that proclaim the traditional penalty of major excommunication for associating with excommunicates are c.9 of the Council of Verneuil of 755 (*MGH Capit.* I 35) and the "Admonitio generalis" of 789, no. 36 (*MGH Capit.* I 30).

[80] Burch., *Decr.* 11.40, *PL* 140.867, attributed to Pope Fabian. A Pseudoisidorian letter attributed to the same pope, by contrast, confirms the traditional rule that communication is punished by full excommunication (Hinschius, *Pseudo-Isidorianae* 159 c.6). Unfortunately, *Decr.* 11.40 is not among the pseudonymous letters of Fabian identified in P. Fournier, "Etudes critiques sur le Décret de Burchard de Worms," *RHDFE*, ser. 3, 34 (1910) 41–112, 213–21, 289–331, and 564–84 at 310–311. For citations of the letter besides Burchard's see L. Fowler-Magerl, *Französische und spanische vor-Gratianische Kanonessammlungen*, Universität Regensburg, Juristische Fakultät, MS Computer Indices, s.v. "Si quis sponte."

[81] Council of Ravenna of 877, c.9, Mansi 17.338: "Qui uero excommunicato scienter communicaverit, vel communicavit, et amodo saltem in domo simul oraverit, atque latebras defensionis ne cominus ad satisfactionem perducatur praebuerit, donec ab excommunicatore poenitentiam suscipiat, corporis et sanguinis Domini communione se privatum esse cognoscat." Notice how the author underscores the magnitude of the sin before prescribing the diminished sanction. Cf. Chapter 2 at n. 52.

of Reims had suffered excommunication at his instigation;[82] they, and all who associated with them, would have benefited from these mitigations. If, as has been convincingly argued,[83] Pseudoisidore was forged (ca. 847–52) by the archbishop's antagonists, this might be a partial explanation. But not only Pseudoisidore was involved. The canon of the Council of Ravenna is especially perplexing. It is based on one of the spurious fourth-century "Apostolic Canons" stating that anyone who prays with an excommunicate will incur excommunication.[84] (The canon dates from the period before laymen were excommunicated for all contacts with excommunicates.) By choosing this canon as his foundation, the author of the Ravenna canon may be deliberately recalling the milder sanctions of the early church; his own phrases are so smoothly grafted to the original that his changes are almost imperceptible. In fact, although further investigation might reveal that these canons governed local customs, they rested unnoticed by papal canon law for several centuries.

By the end of the ninth century the dissipation of royal power seems to have rendered ecclesiastical appeals for secular enforcement of excommunication vain. A canon of the Council of Tribur of 895 decreeing that contumacious excommunicates could be killed without secular or ecclesiastical penalty was perhaps promulgated in de-

---

[82] E.g., Rothad of Soissons (for details see McKeon, *Hincmar* 58), and of course, Hincmar of Laon himself (see n. 63 and text at n. 75).

[83] See Fuhrmann, *Einfluss* I 192–94 for a summary of the discussion and 191 for the dates quoted here.

[84] *Apostolic canon* no. 10 (11), in Funk, *Didascalia* I 567: "Si quis cum excommunicato uel in domo simul orauerit, hic segregetur." (As noted [n. 41], the Latin translation of Dionysius Exiguus deleted the sanction clause.) Of the many variations of this canon, the most important for the reduction of the sanction for communication with excommunicates to mere exclusion from the Eucharist, as in the Council of Ravenna canon (n. 81), is that in a few copies of a fragmentary, and possibly pseudonymous, Gelasian letter: "Qui uero excommunicato scientes [*sic*] communicaverit, et amodo saltem in domo simul oraverit, atque latebras defensionis, ne quo minus ad satisfactionem perducatur, praebuerit, donec ab excommunicatore poenitentiam accipiat, corporis et sanguinis Domini communione privatum se esse cognoscat, et secundum canones poeniteat" (A. Thiel, *Epistolae Romanorum pontificum* I [Braunsberg 1867–68; repr. Hildesheim and New York 1974; no more volumes published], frag. 37, pp. 502–3). This Gelasian fragment differs from the Ravenna canon only in insignificant changes of wording, and a number of canonical collections attributed the fragment to Gelasius rather than to the Ravenna Council (e.g. Burch., *Decr.* 11.48, *PL* 140.868; J. T. Gilchrist, ed., *Diuersorum patrum sententie siue Collectio in LXXIV titulos digesta*, *MIC* B-1 [Vatican City 1973] c.324, p. 184).

spair.[85] Sometime afterward, forgers tried to revive and even enhance the orderly measures of the Carolingian capitularies by circulating a canon decreeing that excommunicates would be deprived of their fiefs or allods; the latter, taken under royal ban, would be permanently confiscated after one year, and the excommunicate, if captured, would be exiled until he satisfied the church.[86] Observing that the royal capitularies had directed bishops to notify feudal lords if their subjects remained contumacious in excommunication, some have regarded this forged canon, which was attributed to the 895 Council of Tribur or alternatively to a council of Diedenhof, as little more than a restatement of Carolingian procedures.[87] Though such notification may imply confiscation, however, the reason given in the laws themselves is simply that the lord must be informed so that he will avoid his subject.[88] It would be surprising if so drastic a penalty as confiscation were not spelled out clearly in the capitularies. More likely, the forged canon looked to the future rather than the past. Bishops who were great feudal lords wielded both secular and ecclesiastical sanctions.[89] From the late tenth century, violations of the

[85] Council of Tribur, ao. 895 c.3, *MGH Capit.* II 214–15. Cf. C.23 q.5 c.47, a decretal of Urban II to the same effect, which Lea ("Excommunication" 379) implied was a veiled invitation to assassinate Henry IV. (Cf. H. Maisonneuve, *Etudes sur les origines de l'inquisition*, 2d ed. [Paris 1960] 77, on its relation to the evolution of the death penalty for heresy.) On the breakdown of royal authority and its effect on excommunication see J. Goebel, *Felony and Misdemeanor* (Philadelphia 1937; repr. 1976), 310–11, and Lea, "Excommunication" 342–44.

[86] *MGH LL.* II, pars altera, p. 6, "Capit. aeccles. ap. Theod. vill.," c.6.

[87] In particular, Eichmann (*Acht* 21–24), noting that the genuine Tribur canon implied that excommunicates were outlawed, since they could be killed without penalty; hence the forged canon actually mitigated the genuine one by providing one year's probation.

[88] Thus Eichmann (*Acht* 16–17 and 23–24) believed that Carolingian procedures already required a feudal lord to confiscate the fief of a vassal who remained contumacious in excommunication, noting the many capitularies that direct bishops to inform feudal lords of their vassals' excommunications. But the capitularies specify that the lord is to be informed so that he will avoid his vassal as an excommunicate (e.g., Capitulary of Quierzy of 882, c.5, *MGH Capit.* II 552; Capitulary of Verneuil of 884, c.5, *MGH Capit.* II 373). Interestingly, one manuscript of the Capitulary of Olonna of 825 has an addition, written over an erasure, calling for confiscation of the property of a contumacious excommunicate whom authorities cannot arrest (c.1, *MGH Capit.* I 326–27).

[89] Goebel, *Felony* 169, 216, 315–19 and passim; H. Hoffmann, *Gottesfriede und Treuga Dei* (Stuttgart 1964) 3, 16–17 and passim; Morel, *Pouvoir* 29–32. P. Fournier, "Le Décret de Burchard de Worms—ses caractères, son influence," *RHE* 12 (1911)

Truce of God, which protected the property of the church and of defenseless laymen by forbidding violence on several days each week, were punished by excommunication.[90] Bishops with temporal as well as spiritual power might in enforcing the truce have been forging the first link between excommunication and feudal law.

GREGORY VII: EXCOMMUNICATION AND FEUDALISM

Gregory VII (1073–85) inaugurated the ecclesiastical policy on excommunication's effects on feudal power, drawing on the model of the feudal bishop in justifying his innovations. As late as 1080, in his final excommunication and deposition of King Henry IV, the pope portrayed the act as that of a great feudal overlord: you have often deprived immoral spiritual prelates of their offices, he tells the Lenten synod; how much greater is your authority over secular rulers?[91] A few months later, in his famous second letter to Bishop Hermann of Metz, Gregory was even more explicit. In the single concrete example he could cite for depriving secular immoral rulers of the right to rule, Gregory pointed out that the church often absolved vassals from oaths of fidelity to deposed bishops.[92] The pope's vision of the sublimity of sacerdotal authority elevated the feudal model to a higher plane: if even an exorcist, the lowest grade of cleric, was superior to any earthly prince, could anyone doubt the pope's power to depose an unworthy king?[93]

Gregory VII's influence over the future lay in his rhetoric rather

---

451–73, is a sensitive analysis of the balance of secular and ecclesiastical authority in the eleventh century.

[90] On the origins of the Truce of God and the use of excommunication as its sanction, see Hoffmann, *Gottesfriede*, esp. 4–20; T. N. Bisson, "The Organized Peace in Southern France and Catalonia, ca. 1140–ca. 1233," *American Historical R.* 82 (1977) 290–311; Goebel, *Felony*, esp. 299–313; Y. Bongert, *Recherches sur les cours laïques du Xe au XIIIe siècle* (Paris 1949) 38; Morel, *Pouvoir* 89.

[91] *Das Register Gregors VII.*, ed. E. Caspar, 2 vols., *MGH Epp. Sel.* 10 (Berlin 1920–23; repr. 1967) VII 14(a), vol. 2, p. 487. C. Mirbt, *Die Publizistik im Zeitalter Gregors VII.* (Leipzig 1894), remains indispensable; on excommunication see esp. 131–213. For a recent survey of the events see U.-R. Blumenthal, *Der Investiturstreit* (Stuttgart 1982).

[92] Greg., *Reg.* VIII 21, ed. Caspar II 554.

[93] Ibid. p. 555.

than in his acts. But the impact of his policies cannot be understood without an analysis of the events themselves. The Gregorian revolution in fact proceeded by degrees over many decades, as recent scholars have emphasized.[94] The pope's most radical ideas had to be modified by his successors and even by his partisans to be practicable.[95] The papal policy on excommunication well illustrates this process. Indeed, Gregory himself at first approached the excommunication of King Henry very tentatively. He did not so much excommunicate the king as show that the king had excommunicated himself by associating with excommunicates, the royal counselors punished for simony in the Lenten synod of 1075.[96] In the king's excommunication, pronounced in the Lenten synod of 1076, and in justificatory letters to Bishop Hermann and to the German faithful, Gregory returned to the theme again and again: the king was responsible for his own condemnation.[97] Canon law surely supported his excommunication, Gregory declared—but even if, God forbid, the excommunication were found unjust, the king was bound according to the patristic doctrine of obedience to submit humbly to it.[98]

Deposition and the release of the king's subjects from their oaths of fidelity were carefully separated from excommunication in this first papal action of 1076.[99] The deposition has been rightly described as

[94] Most recently, J. Gilchrist, "The Reception of Pope Gregory VII into the Canon Law (1073–1141)" part 1, *ZRG Kan. Abt.* 59 (1973) 35–82; and part 2, ibid. 66 (1980) 192–229, concluding that, quantitatively, Gregory VII contributed far less to canon law than his successors; and Schieffer, *Entstehung* 204–5, showing that implementation of the papal policy on lay investitures was delayed until after about 1110.

[95] See esp. F. Kempf, "Ein zweiter Dictatus Papae?" *Archivum historiae pontificiae* 13 (1975) 119–39, esp. 134–35.

[96] Mansi 20.443. Cf. the warning Gregory addressed to the king in December 1075 to cease associating with excommunicates (*Reg.* III 10, ed. Caspar I 263).

[97] For the excommunication itself, see Greg., *Reg.* III 10a, ed. Caspar I 270–71; for the letters to the German faithful see *Gregorii VII epistolae collectae*, ed. P. Jaffé (Berlin 1865) *Ep.* 14, pp. 535–40; and *Reg.* IV 3, ed. I 298 and 300; for the letter to Bishop Hermann, see *Reg.* IV 2, ed. Caspar I 293.

[98] From one of the letters to the German faithful, in Jaffé, *Epp. coll.*, *Ep.* 14, p. 539.

[99] Greg., *Reg.* III 10, ed. Caspar I 270. Release of the king's subjects from their fealty oaths is linked to deposition; excommunication is a separate act, based on the king's association with excommunicates. Note also that in the trenchant measures Gregory took against King Philip I in 1074, release of the king's subjects was not linked with excommunication—nor indeed was it even mentioned—though the pope announced his intention to depose the king in the future if these measures failed; see Greg., *Reg.* II 5 and 18, ed. Caspar I 130–33 and 150–51.

provisional.[100] Unless Henry's own subjects rose in rebellion, papal deposition would be meaningless. But when, at the Diet of Tribur in October 1076, the German princes agreed to withdraw allegiance unless Henry obtained absolution by February 1077, the papal threat became more pressing.[101] The settlement attained with the king's absolution at Canossa in January 1077 was destroyed by the election of the anti-king Rudolph of Swabia at the Diet of Forchheim in March.[102] Whatever Gregory's own wishes might have been, events in Germany determined the outcome.[103] After the defeat and death of Rudolph, Gregory's final (1080) deposition of King Henry was futile.[104]

But something that happened in the interim, in 1078, was to survive this chaos. In the Lenten synod of that year Gregory published a canon that later became the charter of the papal policy on excommunication and feudalism: "By the statutes of our holy predecessors and by apostolic authority we absolve those bound by fealty or oath to excommunicates and forbid them to observe their obligations in any way."[105] In both 1076 and 1080, release of the king's subjects from

---

[100] Kempf, "Dictatus" 128; cf. J. Gilchrist, "Gregory VII and the Juristic Sources," *St. Gratiana* 12 (1967) 3–37 at 32. Gregory himself in 1080 said that absolution from excommunication had not reversed the deposition or restored the fealty of Henry's subjects (*Reg.* VII 14, ed. Caspar II 484).

[101] Blumenthal, *Investiturstreit* 134. In the account of the Diet in the *Annales* of Lampert of Hersfeld (ao. 1077, *MGH Scriptores* V 258) the German princes cited "leges palatinae" that released from their oaths of fealty the vassals of a prince who remained excommunicated for a year. Eichmann (*Acht* 104–8) proposed that this was a reference to the forged capitulary of Tribur/Diedenhof.

[102] Blumenthal, *Investiturstreit* 136–37.

[103] In 1080 the pope emphasized that he had not advised the election of Rudolf (*Reg.* VII 14, ed. Caspar II 484).

[104] Cf. Kempf, "Dictatus" 130–31, showing that Gregory's partisans spent little time on the question of the papal right of deposition, realizing it rested on very weak grounds.

[105] Greg., *Reg.* V 14, c.15, ed. Caspar II 372: "predecessorum nostrorum statuta eos, qui excommunicatis fidelitate aut sacramento constricti sunt, apostolica auctoritate a sacramento absolvimus et, ne sibi fidelitatem observent, omnibus modis prohibemus" (in Gratian, C.15 q.6 c.4, *Nos, sanctorum*). Cf. Gilchrist, "Reception" part 1, 71, noting that this canon (paired with *Quoniam multos*, discussed in my next section) was second only to the investiture canons of November 1078 in frequency of citation in the canonical collections up to Gratian's. Nonetheless, the Lenten synod of 1078 remains cloaked in obscurity (see, most recently, Schieffer, *Entstehung* 168–72). Mirbt (*Publizistik* 222) noted that Gregory never modified or indeed even referred to *Quoniam*, even though he described it as a merely temporary measure.

their fealty oaths was linked to deposition. But excommunication effected this release in the 1078 canon.

The canon is *prima facie* less radical than the papal depositions that preceded and followed it. Whereas they were a complete break from the past, the 1078 canon seems concerned with traditional matters of the ecclesiastical jurisdiction, namely, excommunication and dissolution of immoral oaths.[106] In fact, the canon's very appearance of normality makes it the more extreme: depriving any excommunicated feudal lord of his authority, it calls for an act tantamount to deposition but uses the phrases of customary canonical procedures.

Even Gregory's supporters saw that such a policy meant anarchy.[107] Soon after the canon was promulgated, revisers rendered the "absolution" from feudal obligations a merely temporary suspension by interpolating the phrase "until they have made amends."[108] Urban II (1088–99), moreover, confirmed the milder policy in a decretal forbidding the vassals of an excommunicated lord to observe their oaths "while he is excommunicated."[109] Standing side by side in the canonical collections, the two canons presented an acceptable compromise for the ecclesiastical policy on excommunication and feudalism. By the middle of the twelfth century, the policy had been adopted in the *Consuetudines feudorum*, which stated that vassals were released from their oaths of fealty for the duration of their lords' excommunication.[110]

---

[106] In particular, see Bernold of Constance, "De solutione iuramentorum," *MGH Libelli de lite* II 146–49, on the history of papal power to dissolve oaths, including those to excommunicated or deposed bishops (149 lines 3–8).

[107] Cf. Kempf, "Dictatus" 130–39, tracing the steps by which the papal claims of deposition were toned down by the author(s) of the revised version.

[108] The interpolation already appears in the version in the collection (ca. 1087) of Cardinal Deusdedit (*Die Kanonessammlung des Kardinals Deusdedit*, ed. V. W. von Glanvell [Paderborn 1905; repr. Aalen 1967] 4.185, *ed.* 491), where, after the word "absolvimus" of the original canon (quoted in n. 105) there is the interpolation "quousque ipsi ad satisfactionem veniant." Since, as Kempf ("Dictatus," esp. 138–39) has shown, Deusdedit was involved in revision of Gregory's policies, he himself might be the interpolator. In any event it would not be difficult to identify the first appearance of the interpolation—if this is not its first appearance—with the aid of Gilchrist's invaluable lists ("Reception"), but I have not done so.

[109] Ivo, *Panormia* 5.111, *PL* 161.1236 = Gratian C.15 q.6 c.5.

[110] *Consuetudines feudorum*, ed. K. Lehmann, rev. K. A. Eckhardt (Aalen 1971) 2.28, p. 158: "quod, quemadmodum dominum excommunicatum vel a rege bannitum non est obligatus vassallus ad adjuvandum vel servitium ei praestandum, immo solutus est interim sacramento fidelitatis, nisi ab ecclesia vel a rege fuerit restitutus. . . ." For the date see Lehmann's introduction, pp. 27–28.

QUONIAM MULTOS

As the Acacian schism had inspired Gelasius's writings, so the crisis in Germany and the empire prompted Gregory VII to issue the first papal law on the contagion of excommunication, the canon *Quoniam multos*.[111] Promulgated in 1078 in the same synod as the canon on dissolution of feudal oaths, *Quoniam multos* offered real reforms, declaring that the wife and children of an excommunicated lord could associate with him without incurring excommunication; so, too, could his other dependents and servants (*servi, ancillae, mancipia, rustici, servientes*) and his courtiers (*curiales*) unless their advice had contributed to the crime. People who associated with an excommunicate in ignorance of his status were also to be spared according to *Quoniam multos*; since earlier canons had explicitly excommunicated only those who knowingly or voluntarily associated with excommunicates, this mitigation was less novel than the others.[112] Finally, and most controversially, *Quoniam* decreed that excommunication was contagious only at first hand: contact with these *communicatores* would not be penalized. Thus, unlike the ninth-century canons that required forty days' penance or exclusion from the Eucharist for any association with excommunicates, *Quoniam multos* retained the full penalty, ordinary excommunication, limiting only its contagion.

Why did Gregory initiate these changes? It would not be the last time that drastic measures against potentates would be combined with relief for their subjects; Innocent III in the Fourth Lateran Council of 1215 and Innocent IV in the first Council of Lyon of 1245 acted likewise.[113] But there may have been a more urgent reason also, a feeling that matters had gone too far. Many were being "lost to sin,"

---

[111] *Quoniam multos*: Greg., *Reg.* V 14 c.6, ed. Caspar II 372–73 = C.11 q.3 c.103.

[112] For example, see nn. 81 and 84. In emphasizing that *Quoniam* conforms to canonical tradition in this respect, Gilchrist ("Sources" 13–14 and 28) might be overlooking those aspects of the canon that are radically new.

[113] Thus Lateran IV provided sanctions against unjust excommunications (c.47, *COD* 255–56) while confirming that princes who neglected to pursue heretics would be deposed and disinherited (c.3, *COD* 234), penalties then being unleashed against the count of Toulouse (below, Chapter 7 at n. 27). The first Council of Lyon provided further relief from unjust excommunication by forbidding judges to impose full major excommunication for converse with excommunicates except after a warning (cc.19–21, *COD* 291–92) but deposed Frederick II (*COD* 278–83; cf. Chapter 3 at n. 124).

Quoniam said, because of the epidemic of excommunications generated by the papal reforms. A few years later, in 1080, Gregory wrote that physical as well as spiritual deaths were being ascribed to the excommunications in Germany; the resulting panic had devastated the Germans.[114] The bishop of Utrecht had died soon after excommunicating Gregory on King Henry's behalf in 1076.[115] Sensitive to the cosmological repercussions of his every act, Gregory in his 1080 deposition and excommunication invited the apostles to send a quick judgment against Henry "that his spirit may be saved in the day of the Lord," as an example from which all men might learn.[116]

Gregory VII described *Quoniam's* concessions as temporary. Its fate during the first decades after publication is obscure.[117] In 1089 Urban II issued a decretal purporting to confirm *Quoniam multos* (which, he said, was divinely inspired) but in fact tacitly changing its meaning.[118] Those who associated with *communicatores* would not be excommunicated, Urban declared; rather, "they condemn themselves by these contacts, and we do not associate with them until they have done penance and received absolution. For the sacred canons make it clear that whoever communicates with an excommunicate is excommunicated." In effect, then, Urban II negated *Quoniam multos's* permission to associate with *communicatores*. The circumstances in which the decretal was issued, however, may explain why Urban II hesitated to pronounce definitively whether *Quoniam multos* should govern contacts with excommunicates in the future. Guibert of Ravenna, in Rome until 1089 as the antipope Clement III, was named in Urban's

---

[114]Greg., *Reg.* VII 14, ed. Caspar II 486: "magnamque multitudinem christianorum morti tradi et ecclesias fecit dissipari et totum poene Teutonicorum regnum desolationi dedit." See Lea, "Excommunication" 364–65, on the stories that aroused hysteria in Germany.

[115]Greg., *Reg.* IV 6, ed. Caspar I 303–4.

[116]Greg., *Reg.* VII 14, ed. Caspar II 487.

[117]See n. 105.

[118]JL 5393 (*PL* 151.297–99), addressed to Bishop Gebhard of Constance; a shorter version (JL 5394 [*PL* 151.299]) was simultaneously sent to the German bishops. See C.11 q.3 c.110. Gregory did not claim to be acting by divine inspiration but rather by apostolic authority when he issued *Quoniam*, and he explicitly referred to the limitations of his authority ("prout possumus"). In a wholly different context, the 1080 deposition of King Henry, Gregory did describe his own earlier action in calling for a synod to determine Henry's fate as divinely inspired (*Reg.* VII 14, ed. Caspar II 485). Presumably the phrase came to be associated with *Quoniam's* innovations because they were such a radical break with tradition, as Gregory's opponents charged.

decretal as an excommunicate of the first grade; his schismatic followers were noted as excommunicates of the second grade. Any associate of the latter was to be avoided until he or she, though not directly excommunicated, had obtained absolution.[119]

Urban II might also have been responding to pressures from Gregorian partisans. The decretal was addressed to Bishop Gebhard of Constance, who, as papal legate, was trying to recover the schismatic German bishops for the church.[120] The monk Bernold of Constance was among the most radical of the Gregorians;[121] even when others had accepted the compromise calling for mere suspension of excommunicates' feudal rights, Bernold continued to speak of "the deposition of kings," and he forged materials based on Gregory VII's register to prove his point.[122] He did research on the Acacian schism, noting in the margin of a manuscript of the Constance cathedral school that the Council of Chalcedon was to be defended "usque ad sanguinem."[123] And like others deeply involved in ecclesiastical polemics, Bernold had something of an obsession with the topic of converse with excommunicates.[124] Within a decade of the promulgation of *Quoniam multos* he wrote a tract insisting that all who had contact with excommunicates were excommunicated.[125] Shortly after Urban II sent

[119] Cf. JL 5363 (*PL* 151.357), C.24 q.2 c.3, where Urban observed that in the present emergency the faithful could afford to close ranks only against schismatics.

[120] On Gebhard's activities and association with Bernold of Constance, see J. Autenrieth, *Die Domschule von Konstanz zur Zeit des Investiturstreits* (Stuttgart 1956) 16.

[121] Bernold left Constance for Schaffhausen ca. 1077; see Autenrieth, *Domschule* 133–34.

[122] In particular, Bernold almost certainly wrote the "Swabian Appendix" of the *Collection in Seventy-Four Titles* (J. Autenrieth, "Bernold von Konstanz und die erweiterte 74-Titelsammlung," *Deutsches Archiv für Erforschung des Mittelalters* 14 (1958) 375–94 at 388–90. For the appendix, see Gilchrist, *Coll. in LXXIV tit.*, tit. 75–89, pp. 180–96; cf. ibid. lxxviii on author and date (ca. 1086–1100).

[123] Autenrieth, *Domschule* 46. For Bernold's specialized knowledge of the Acacian schism (Autenrieth, "Bernold" 388–90) see esp. Gilchrist, *Coll. in LXXIV tit.*, tit. 85–86, pp. 185–95.

[124] Besides the tracts discussed in the text, the "Swabian Appendix" (see n. 122) is wholly on excommunication. One member of the Constance cathedral chapter, evidently not Bernold himself, wrote "Unus porcus scabiosus totum gregem contaminat" next to a chapter on this subject in a Constance manuscript (Autenrieth, *Domschule* 54).

[125] Bernold, "De lege excommunicationis," *MGH Libelli de lite* II 101–6, esp. 104 lines 12–37 and 106 lines 4–11. For the date of the tract, 1084–89, see Mirbt, *Publizistik* 37. The tract contradicted *Quoniam* both by failing to mention those specially allowed to communicate and by implying (as Urban II's decretal did) that contacts with *communicatores* were punished by excommunication.

his ambiguous confirmation of *Quoniam multos* to Bishop Gebhard, Bernold returned to the theme in another tract, showing that the pope rightly penalized *all* association with excommunicates.[126]

Urban's decretal, then, seems to have been an attempt to placate the extremist wing of the papalist party without yielding anything concrete.[127] For the moment, however, Bernold's position triumphed: as late as 1139 the Second Lateran Council decreed that those associating with excommunicates were "held by an equal penalty."[128] By the time *Quoniam multos's* concessions really penetrated canon law, a half-century later, the sanction of excommunication had been wholly transformed.

[126] Bernold, "De excommunicatis vitandis, de reconciliatione lapsorum et de fontibus iuris ecclesiastici," *MGH Libelli de lite* II 112–42 (on avoidance of excommunicates, only 112–14). See esp. 113 lines 2–3 and 30–36. For the date—after 1084, and probably in the 1090s—see Mirbt, *Publizistik* 47. The "Swabian Appendix" of the *Collection in Seventy-Four Titles* contained neither *Quoniam multos* nor either of Urban II's two decretals on this subject; it did contain (c.324, p. 184) the 877 Council of Ravenna canon (above, n. 81; here the canon is attributed to Gelasius) prescribing mere exclusion from the Eucharist, rather than full excommunication, for contact with excommunicates, and it does indeed seem that Bernold would have accepted this lesser sanction as a compromise for not (as in *Quoniam*) surrendering all penalties for communication with *communicatores*. Cf. Bernold, "De leg. excom.," *MGH Libelli de lite* II 106 lines 4–7. As will be seen below, this was the compromise eventually reached.

[127] Not only Gregorians objected to *Quoniam's* concessions; anti-Gregorians also described *Quoniam* as "erring in faith and doctrine" (Gilchrist, "Reception" part 1, 72 n. 44).

[128] Lateran II c.3 *COD* 197. Interestingly, the Pisan canon on which this was based had no sanction clause; see R. Somerville, "The Council of Pisa, 1135: A Re-Examination of the Evidence for the Canons," *Speculum* 45 (1970) 98–114 at 105–6.

II

Forms of Excommunication in the High Middle Ages

The monarchical papacy began to flex its legal arm in a canon of the Second Lateran Council (1139), *Si quis suadente*, excommunicating those who laid violent hands on clerics or monks and requiring them to get a papal mandate of absolution at the Apostolic See.[1] Besides enlarging papal jurisdiction at the expense of the bishops, *Si quis suadente* widened the social division between laymen and clerics. To heretical laymen trying to overstep that division by translating and discussing the Scriptures and the works of the Church Fathers, Innocent III would write a few decades later that the simplest parish priest, because of his sacerdotal office, should be treated as a "god" in his community.[2]

Si quis also created a new form of excommunication, excommunication *latae sententiae*, a sentence that took effect immediately as

---

[1] Lateran II c.15 = C.17 q.4 c.29; see P. Huizing, "The Earliest Development of Excommunication *Latae Sententiae*," *St. Gratiana* 2 (1955) 279–320; J. Zeliauskas, *De excommunicatione vitiata apud Glossatores (1140–1350)* 64–72. Already in the early eleventh century the French bishops resented papal penances requiring pilgrimages to Rome without diocesan consultation; see Fulbert of Chartres, *Ep.* 84, ao. 1024, *PL* 141.241–42.

[2] X 5.7.12, Friedberg col. 786. On the origins of the concept see G. Tellenbach, *Church, State and Christian Society at the Time of the Investiture Contest*, trans. R. F. Bennett (New York 1970) 48. On Innocent III's actions on lay preaching see R. I. Moore, *The Origins of European Dissent* (London 1977) 227–30.

the crime was committed. Earlier canon law had punished certain crimes, especially heresy, with automatic excommunication,[3] and of course the sanction of excommunication for those associating with excommunicates was immediate. But the implications of such a sentence were realized only as canon law began to be studied in the universities as a branch of jurisprudence.

Several of the most prominent early canonists challenged or even rejected entirely the concept of excommunication *latae sententiae*. Most important was Gratian, whose Decretum, published within a few years of the Second Lateran Council, contained *Si quis suadente*.[4] Exploiting the rhetorical distinction between anathema and excommunication in earlier canons, Gratian used "anathema" to designate the full social and religious exclusion traditionally associated with excommunication, and "excommunication" to mean mere exclusion from the Eucharist and the other sacraments.[5] Only named ("nominatim") excommunicates, those convicted by judicial procedures, could be anathematized.[6] Thus Gratian resisted the new excommunication *latae sententiae*, with its requirement that sinners be ostracized without trial. The apostle Paul, he stressed, did not instruct the faithful to avoid those who *were* sinners but those who were *named*

[3] Huizing, "Development" 279–80, noting that persistent doubts surrounded such sentences because of the belief that sinners should be given three warnings.

[4] At C.17 q.4 c.29. See Huizing, "Development" 292–93, and Zeliauskas, *De excommunicatione* 62 and 70–72, on decretist opposition to excommunication *latae sententiae*. Both argue that Gratian reduced the penalty of *Si quis suadente* from full social exclusion (the canon itself used the term "anathema") to mere exclusion from the Eucharist by referring in his discussion of *Si quis* in C.11 q.3 d. p. c.24 § 2 to a canon of John VIII (C.17 q.4 c.21) that prescribed mere exclusion from the Eucharist as the initial penalty for sacrilege, full excommunication coming into effect only after three warnings. Though I certainly believe Gratian opposed excommunication *latae sententiae* in principle, I think that C.11 q.3 d. p. c.24 is more ambiguous—and the ambiguous terminology for the various forms of excommunication in the letters of John VIII, of which Gratian was well aware, adds yet more layers of meaning to the discussion. To choose but one example: in § 1, Gratian declares that excommunication excludes one from the Eucharist, anathema from all social contacts. But in § 3, he says that the sanction of *Si quis*—anathema—must be interpreted "iuxta ethimologiam vocabuli anathemati, id est separationi, subiaceat qui in edictum illud inciderit quia a corpore et sanguine Christi et ab ingressu ecclesiae se alienum facit. . . ."

[5] C.11 q.3 d. p. c.24 § 1. Elsewhere Gratian abandoned this special use of "anathema," and C.3 q.4. d. a. c.12–d. p. c.12 (cf. C.4 q.1 c.2), rehearsing the ninth-century distinctions discussed here in Chapter 1 at n. 65, offer nothing of substance.

[6] C.11 q.3 d. p. c.24, esp. pr.; ibid. d. a. and p. c.21, and d. p. c.26, in both latter discussions referring to the decretal of Urban II cited (Chapter 1 n. 119), C.24 q.2 c.3.

sinners by judicial sentence.[7] The early church had actually punished bishops for shunning sinners who had not been legally convicted.[8] Excommunication, exclusion from the sacraments, was for sins of conscience, which concerned only God. Sinners might even inflict this censure on themselves.[9]

Gratian's sense of justice greatly influenced ordinary legal procedures. But even while he worked on the Decretum, the church was experiencing the first signs of a heresy crisis that would necessitate extraordinary legal measures.[10] Excommunication *latae sententiae* took its real impetus from the reaction of the church to the dangerously popular heretical movements of the second half of the twelfth century. Whereas Gratian could still debate whether a heretic incurred excommunication for subscribing to a heretical opinion not yet condemned by the church,[11] the Third Lateran Council (1179) excommunicated all who joined heretical sects or defended or concealed heretics. A few years later the Council of Verona (1184) by a joint decree of emperor and pope excommunicated all who "believed or taught" sacramental doctrines different from those of the Roman church.[12]

In the 1170s, Johannes Faventinus (Faenza) briefly but notoriously reconnoitered Gratian's rule that the faithful ostracize only named excommunicates as an obstacle to excommunication *latae sententiae*. While conceding that even before any denunciation contacts were gravely sinful, Johannes maintained that only after church authorities had intervened to denounce such criminals as excommunicates did the penalty of excommunication come into effect for those who associated with them.[13] But by the 1180s the canonists had overcome re-

---

[7] C.11 q.3 d. p. c.21. Gratian, like the author of the pseudo–Augustinian sermon on penitence cited in Chapter 1 at n. 45, used a version of 1 Cor. 5.11 that read "Si quis frater nominatur fornicator. . . ."

[8] E.g., C.6 q.2 cc.2–3, cited in C.11 q.3 d. p. c.24 § 4.

[9] C.11 q.3 d. p. c.24 § 1.

[10] Most recently, Moore, *Origins* (esp. 168–75), has marshaled the evidence indicating that the first Bogomil-influenced dualist heresy appeared in the West ca. 1143, though only in the mid-1160s did it spread to Italy (ibid. 204–6).

[11] C.24 q.1, esp. d. p. c.4.

[12] For Lateran III c.27, X 5.7.8, see *COD* 224–25; for the Council of Verona see X 5.7.9, quoting, evidently, the Pseudoisidorian C.24 q.1 c.15.

[13] This opinion of Johannes Faventinus is cited by Laurentius Hispanus in his *Glossa Palatina* (ca. 1210) C.11 q.3 d. p. c.24, v. *Subiaceat*, Vat. MSS Reg. 977, fol. 134ra, and Pal. 658, fol. 47va: "Ego eum puto non nominatim sed ipso iure anathemati-

sistance to excommunication *latae sententiae*.[14] Acceptance of the new form of excommunication was sealed by the immense doctrinal authority of Huguccio (d. 1210), the most famous of the twelfth-century commentators on Gratian's Decretum (decretists) and a friend—if not, as was once thought, the teacher—of Pope Innocent III.[15] Refuting objections that the new institution omitted the required warning, Huguccio wrote that the canon embodying excommunication *latae sententiae* was a warning in itself.[16] Moreover, anyone

---

zatum. Ideoque si publicus est, grauiter peccat qui ei communicat. Non est tamen excommunicatus, ut infra xxiv. q. ii. Sane quod [3]. Et hoc ante denunciationem, qua quidem in talibus opus est, ut infra xxiv. q. i. Acatius [3]. Post denunciationem nominatim excommunicatus est. Nec mirum, quia in primo casu fit iniuria iuri soli, in secundo tam iuri quam ministro eius. Io." (Cf. P. Huizing, *Doctrina Decretistarum de excommunicatione usque ad Glossam ordinariam Joannis Teutonici* [Rome 1952] 50; and Zeliauskas, *De excommunicatione* p. *179 in appendix.) Johannes did not express this opinion in his *Summa* (ca. 1171) but in glosses written later (see A. Stickler, "Jean de Faenza," *DDC* 6.99–102 on chronology); citations by his contemporaries (see n. 16, and cf. Huizing, *Doctrina* 51–55, and Zeliauskas 62–63 and 62 n. 274) make the attribution certain.

[14] Huizing, "Development" 280–83 and 301–9; Zeliauskas, *De excommunicatione* 69–72.

[15] K. Pennington recently questioned whether Huguccio really taught Innocent III; see "The Legal Education of Pope Innocent III," *BMCL* 4 (1974) 70–77.

[16] Hug., *Sum.* C.11 q.3 c.41, v. *Non poterint*, Admont 7, fol. 230rb, and Vat. 2280, fol. 176vb: "Ergo ante admonitionem non debet quis excommunicari. . . . Quid ergo de illo qui percutit clericum? Dico illum excommunicari pro contumacia et post admonitionem. Permissa est admonitio ab Innocentio ⟨II⟩ et aliis sanctis patribus iamdiu et sepe, et adhuc perseuerat illa admonitio. Qui ergo percutit clericum contumax est cum sciat esse prohibitum uel debeat scire." See also D.93 c.1, v. *Commonitione*, Admont 7, fol. 116vb–117ra, and Vat. 2280, fol. 82vb: "Speciali idest. Et si non interueniat commonitio ipse tamen commonere debet, ar. xi. q. iii. Cure. Debent [20 and 106]. Sed qui uerberat clericum excommunicatus est a papa, ut xvii. q. iiii. Si quis suadente [29]. Ergo absque omni commonitione et denuntiatione episcopi uitanda est eius communio, sicut hic dicitur aperte. Utile est tamen ut ad cautelam ignorantium et ut remoueatur excusatio denuntietur excommunicatus, ut xi. q. iii. Cure. Debent. Ubi est ergo illa pessima opinio qua asseritur denuntiatio episcopi esse expectanda, nunquid in talibus plus facit denuntiatio episcopi quam canon apostolici, aut plus episcopi cartula quam apostolici sententia? Non est ergo uerum quod ille qui communicat illi qui uerberat clericum ante denuntiationem non sit excommunicatus sicut uti communicat post denuntiationem, sicut dixit magister Jo. infra xi. q. iii § Euidenter [d. p. c.24], in illa glossa 'Ego autem [*leg.* eum] puto sufficit.' Igitur sola apostolica sententia sine alia denuntiatione ad uitandam eius communionem si publicum est eum uerberasse clericum uel alias excommunicatum esse. Si uero est occultum et probare non possum in secreto uitabo eius communionem sed non in publico nisi latenter." Cf. Cambridge, Gonv. and Caius Coll. 676, C.11 q.3 c. 29, v. *Fuerint*, fol. 112va: "Secundum Jo. Fa. incidens in canonem

assaulting a cleric should know it was a crime! (Johannes Faventinus's imperialist sympathies may partly account for a trace of rancor in Huguccio's rejection of the doctrine; but as we shall see, the issue remained sensitive into the fifteenth century, when it became the focus of the most important attempt to reform excommunication before the Council of Trent.)

For the most part the canonists scrupulously differentiated excommunication for heresy from other excommunications.[17] For heretics who refused to recant, excommunication was only a prelude to the penalties that quickly followed transfer to lay officials—often imprisonment, even death, and confiscation of property.[18] For suspected heretics, those whose fidelity was in doubt for their associating with or helping heretics, excommunication was a test: after one year they could be convicted as heretics.[19] Since the sacramental doctrines were emerging as the touchstones of orthodoxy both in the decretals on heresy and in the creed of the Fourth Lateran Council (1215), a willingness to forgo the sacraments for a year or more, quite apart from implying contumacy toward ecclesiastical authorities, per se gave rise to a legal presumption of contempt for the sacraments and therefore of heresy.[20] But no medieval pope or general council ever declared that

---

excommunicatus est, licet non nominatim [i.e., not "to be avoided"; see C.11 q.3 d. a. c.22] ante denunciationem. Quod falsum est, quia eodem modo excommunicatus est statim nominatim et is qui incidens in heresim dampnatam scienter. . . ."

[17] The inclusion of "omnis excommunicatus" in lists of persons to be classified as heretics (e.g., Glos. ord. C.4 q.1 c.2, v. Ab ecclesia) had mainly polemical significance—"non . . . vere sed interpretive," as Johannes Andreae put it (Comm. VI 1.3.1). Cf. the careful analysis of the penalties affecting heretics and other excommunicates in Guido de Baysio, Comm. VI 1.3.1, no. 3.

[18] In particular see Maisonneuve, Etudes 152–231; J. Havet, L'Hérésie et le bras séculier au moyen âge (Paris 1896) II 154–60; H. C. Lea, A History of the Inquisition of the Middle Ages, rev. ed. (London and New York 1906; repr. New York 1958) I 405–509; and Hinschius, Kirchenrecht V 449–92.

[19] Lateran IV c.3, COD 233–35 = X 5.7.13.

[20] Lateran IV c.1, COD 230–31, is the profession of faith, which seems to have evolved from the one elicited from abjuring heretics; cf. Maisonneuve, Etudes 176 and 183. See also Franciscus Zabarella, Lectura super tertio (–quinto) Decretalium (Lyon 1517–18) X 5.7.3 § 5, describing as heretics "qui male sentiunt de articulis fidei vel de sacramentis, et generaliter de omnibus qui sunt obligati Catholicae unitati per baptismum et ab ea pertinaciter recedunt dogmatizando vel imitando aliquid contra unitatem predictam. . . . Ex hoc infero quod non est hereticus nisi qui esse vult."

a contumacious excommunicate should be regarded as a heresy suspect,[21] and a 1260 decretal of Alexander IV stated that contumacy in excommunication gave rise to a presumption of heresy principally if the original sentence was for suspected heresy.[22]

Still, the legal procedures that late twelfth-century decretals set in motion against heretics certainly influenced ecclesiastical legal procedures. In the 1180s, as the heresy crisis approached its peak, canon law initiated the criminal procedure *inquisitio*, activated by public

---

[21] Only in 1563, at the twenty-fifth session of the Council of Trent, did canon law universally proclaim that any excommunicate could be treated as a heresy suspect after one year ("Decr. de reform. gen." c.3, *COD* 786). Local councils in areas troubled by heresy had enacted canons to this effect much earlier (e.g., Tarragona 1234, c.18 [Mansi 23.331–32]; Béziers 1310 c.17 [Mansi 25.364]). For application of the doctrine in individual cases, see J. Petit, ed., *Registre des causes civiles de l'officialité épiscopale de Paris 1384–1387, CDI* V.6.a. (Paris 1919) 443; R. M. Haines, *The Administration of the Diocese of Worcester in the First Half of the Thirteenth Century* (London 1965) 190 n. 4; P. Adam, *La Vie paroissiale en France au XIVe siècle* (Paris 1964) 194; R. E. Lerner, "An 'Angel of Philadelphia' in the Reign of Philip the Fair: The Case of Guiard of Cressonessart," in W. C. Jordan et al., eds., *Order and Innovation in the Middle Ages. Essays in Honor of Joseph R. Strayer* (Princeton 1976) 343–64 at 359–60 (it is a pleasure to thank Professor Mario Ascheri for drawing my attention to this document); and G. Mollat, *The Popes at Avignon*, 9th ed., trans. J. Love (London 1963) 89.

[22] VI 5.2.7. A decretal of Honorius III (X 5.37.13; below, Chapter 3 n. 128) had pronounced that contumacy in excommunication—here more than two years—gave rise to suspicion of heresy. But the excommunicate in question, the count of Rethel, was not, in fact, punished as a heretic. On the other hand, the pope said he was deferring to the count's noble status. Hence definite principles could not be drawn from the decretal, and the canonists' recommendations varied. Bernard of Parma declared that mere excommunicates should never be treated as heresy suspects (*Glos. ord.* X 5.37.13, v. *Haereticae pravitatis*). But most believed that after a year in excommunication, an individual could be treated as a heresy suspect because of his contempt for church authorities. Hostiensis wrote that after one year excommunicates could be compelled to purge themselves of the suspicion of heresy. If they failed, they should be judged heretics; if they neglected to try, they should be reexcommunicated, and after another year judged heretics (*Lect.* X 5.7.13, v. *Extunc*; see also *Sum.* 5.14 [*De haeret.*].4). Innocent IV was more restrained, though he acknowledged that a "probable" presumption (i.e., one requiring purgation) of heresy arose after a year in excommunication (*App.* X 5.37.13, v. *Haereticae*). Later canonists tended toward his views rather than Hostiensis's; see Jo. An., *Nov.* X 5.37.13, v. *Scrupulo*; Franciscus Zabarella, *Lect.* X 5.37.13, v. *Qui autem*, no. 1, and ibid. qu. 3, noting that most Florentine attorneys insisted upon exploring all other defenses excommunicates submitted (e.g., that they could not pay their debts to obtain absolution) before regarding them as heresy suspects; and Panormitanus, *Commentaria in quinque libros Decretalium* (Lyon 1534 [I–V, except II.1], 1522 [II.1] X 5.37.13, nos. 3 and 7.

rumor (*fama*).[23] Bishops were held to inquire into reputed crimes in their dioceses rather than rely exclusively on charges brought by the informers or accusers needed in the existing criminal procedures of the church courts, *denunciatio* and *accusatio*.[24] Certainly the new method was most conspicuously applied against heretics, and it was thereby gradually institutionalized as the Inquisition.[25] But *inquisitio* could be used in any criminal case. Inevitably, *inquisitio* and excommunication *latae sententiae* influenced each other; both were designed to enlist community pressures to identify criminals and repress crime. Since the effects of excommunication *latae sententiae* were immediate, ostracism by those who knew of an excommunicate's crime was like the *fama* that triggered *inquisitio*. Clement III (1187–91) decreed that unless or until they purged themselves in the bishop's court, people rumored to be excommunicated must be avoided even if they had not been publicly identified and denounced.[26]

Excommunication *latae sententiae* shielded the spiritual and material estate of the medieval church by punishing crimes against the clergy and the faith and, from the late twelfth century, by deterring unauthorized taxation and other incursions on ecclesiastical liberties, forgery of papal documents, aid to the Saracen enemy, and other acts that jeopardized the security of the monarchical papacy.[27] But for all

[23] On the origins of *inquisitio* see P. Fournier, *Les Officialités au moyen âge* (Paris 1880) 233 and 267–75; see also Bongert, *Cours* 273–75, on the influence of these ecclesiastical procedures on secular courts. Cf. Chapter 4 n. 30.

[24] See, e.g., X 5.3.31, X 5.1.16–19 and 21, and the summary in Lateran IV c.8 (*COD* 237–39); see also Innocent IV's decretals *Romana. Licet* (VI 5.9.1) and *Romana. Statuimus* (VI 3.20.1), ed. P.-J. Kessler, "Untersuchungen über die Novellen-Gesetzgebung Papst Innocenz' IV" part 1, *ZRG Kan. Abt.* 32 (1942) 142–320 at 174 and 179–81. On *Romana* see also Chapter 3 n. 83 and passim.

[25] See esp. X 5.7.9, the 1184 Council of Verona, for a clear description of procedures binding both lay and church officials by oath and on pain of severe penalties and suspicion of heresy to seek out heretics in their communities under episcopal supervision. On the evolution of these procedures into the Inquisition see Maisonneuve, *Etudes* 151–56 and passim; and Lea, *Inquisition* I 310–13 and passim.

[26] X 5.39.14–15; cf. also 22. On canonical purgation see Fournier, *Officialités* 250 and 262–66; J. P. Lévy, *La Hiérarchie des preuves dans le droit savant du moyen-âge* (Paris 1939) 114–22; and L. C. Gabel, *Benefit of Clergy in England in the Later Middle Ages* (New York 1928; repr. 1969) 94–99.

[27] For the standard lists of excommunications *latae sententiae* around the mid-thirteenth century see Inn. IV, *App.* X 5.39.1, v. *Super eo*, and Host., *Sum.* 5.59 (*De sen. exc.*).3, cols. 1880–84. One of the earliest lists, that of the *Glossa Palatina*, is

its ideological significance, excommunication *latae sententiae* was a very specialized application of excommunication. Its ordinary function now was to enforce procedures in the church courts.

EXCOMMUNICATION AND ADVERSARY RELATIONSHIPS

By the second half of the twelfth century the Gregorian ideological strife had subsided. Violent polemics were replaced by tense exchanges of bureaucratic memoranda, ecclesiastical gravamina periodically submitted to royal officials. The outcome of Becket's martyrdom, a temporary jurisdictional settlement couched in a series of terse legal phrases, signaled the way of the future.[28] Rhetoric exalting the superiority of spiritual over secular authority was now compressed into cryptic glosses on the minutiae of legal procedure.

In another way, too, canon law had become more concerned with law and legal practice than with the theological doctrines that had once belonged to its sphere. While university training in jurisprudence, and especially study of the *Corpus iuris civilis*, had intensified the canonists' focus on purely juristic themes, academic study of theology had also produced changes that affected canon law. The twelfth-century sacramental theologians had established a theoretical foundation for the progressive separation of the church's judicial and

---

printed in Zeliauskas, *De excommunicatione* 70; another early (pre-1234) list was written in the margins of a Decretum manuscript, Vat., Pal. 624, fol. 178v. During the later thirteenth century these excommunications multiplied rapidly, and compilations of them became a minor literary form; see, e.g., *Le "Liber de excommunicatione" du Cardinal Bérenger Frédol*, ed. E. Vernay (Paris 1912), listing one hundred papal excommunications *latae sententiae*. Bishops likewise promulgated general sentences of excommunication in their dioceses, though subject to restrictions (see *Romana. Ceterum*, VI 5.11.5, ed. Kessler, "Untersuchungen" part 1, 175–76). On the episcopal sentences see Lea, "Excommunication" 457–59 and *Confession*, I 312–20; Haines, *Worcester* 186–87; Adam, *Vie* 180–81; and J. Toussaert, *Le Sentiment religieux en Flandre à la fin du moyen-âge* (Paris 1963) 435–36.

[28] For the general lines of the jurisdictional settlement in England see Maitland, *History*, esp. I 124–31, 158–59; and II 195–203. For France, see Fournier, *Officialités* 1–126; and Bongert, *Cours* 92–94, and 142–46. On the role of the Becket controversy in particular, see C. Duggan, "The Significance of the Becket Dispute in the History of the English Church," *Ampleforth J.* 75 (1970) 365–75; and M. Cheney, "The Compromise of Avranches of 1172 and the Spread of Canon Law in England," *English Historical R.* 56 (1941) 177–97.

penitential forums, a split resulting from academic specialization.[29] The sacrament of penitence, comprising the private confession and sacramental absolution administered by priests, was now the main venue of relations between the sinner and God. Ecclesiastical court procedures, independent from sacramental penitence, were divorced from their theological origins. By the turn of the twelfth and thirteenth centuries excommunication had been divided into two essentially different sanctions. The penitential forum, though it ministered to mortal sin (which had to be confessed and expiated on pain of eternal damnation), retained only the penalty of exclusion from the Eucharist and the other sacraments, soon to be called "minor excommunication."[30] Major excommunication, entailing the full social exclusion of the biblical tradition, belonged to the ecclesiastical courts. The judges who imposed it needed not priestly ordination (which many of them lacked) but the power of jurisdiction, the authority—"virile," as one commentator praised it[31]—to discipline subjects.

Major excommunication, inflicted by the ecclesiastical courts, had only a rather artificial link to sin. From the theological tradition permitting excommunication only of incorrigible sinners, the decretists distilled a juristic maxim that excommunication could be used only against contumacy: failure to appear in court when summoned, or failure to obey a judicial mandate.[32] Crime or sin might have been

---

[29] F. Russo, "Pénitence et excommunication. Etude historique sur les rapports entre la théologie et le droit canonique dans le domaine pénitentiel du IXe au XIIIe siècle," *Recherches de science religieuse* 33 (1946) 257–79 and 431–61, esp. 437–51; L. Hödl, *Die Geschichte der scholastischen Literatur und der Theologie der Schlüsselgewalt*, part 1 (Münster in Westfalen 1960) esp. 181–94 and 350–88; A. Landgraf, "Grundlagen für ein Verständnis der Busslehre der Früh- und Hochscholastik," *Z. für katholische Theologie* 51 (1927) 161–93; idem, "Sunde und Trennung von der Kirche in der Frühscholastik," *Scholastik* 5 (1930) 210–47, esp. 246; Lea, *Confession*, esp. I 56–59 and 274–92.

[30] X 5.38.12; see Host., *Sum.* 5.59(*De sen. exc.*).5b, col. 1889 med., and ibid. 11, col. 1908 med., for a very lucid analysis.

[31] Rudolfus de Liebegg, *Pastorale novellum*, ed. A. P. Orbán, *CCLM* 55, 5.9, p. 326.

[32] Gratian summarized the sources in C.11 q.3 d. a. c.41–d. p. c.64. Among the decretists see, e.g., Rufinus, *Summa Decretorum*, ed. H. Singer (Paderborn 1902; repr. Aalen 1963) C.11 q.3 c.2, p. 315; and Hug., *Sum.* C.11 q.3 c.8, v. *Minimis causis*, Vat. 2280, fol. 173rb: "Sed quot sunt cause excommunicationis? Dico quod una sola, scilicet, contumacia. . . ." On theological aspects see A. Gommenginger, "Bedeutet die Exkommunikation Verlust der Kirchengliedschaft?" *Z. für katholische*

committed or not;[33] excommunication resulted from contumacy alone and was used as an alternative to *missio in possessionem* (award of the disputed article to a plaintiff) in civil suits and to confiscation and other penalties in criminal suits.[34] Excommunication was fully integrated into adversary procedures; in civil suits a litigant petitioned and paid for the excommunication of his opponent and if necessary blocked the latter's absolution in court.[35] When the ecclesiastical court itself acted against a defendant in a criminal suit, the judge became the excommunicate's adversary in an absolution suit.[36] Even the public denunciation of an excommunicate could be obtained by his adversary through court procedures.[37] Absolution from excommunication, now contingent on an oath and guarantees to obey the court,[38]

Theologie 73 (1951) 1–71 at 42–45. A late twelfth-century canonist tried to restore the old theological proportions: "Sed non excommunicatur quis nisi ob contumaciam, infra eodem Nemo [31]. Ergo contumacia maximum peccatum est." (Cambridge, Gonv. and Caius Coll. 676, C.11 q.3 c.33, v. *Separari*, fol. 12vb. On the glosses in this manuscript see esp. C. Duggan, "The Reception of Canon Law in England in the Later-Twelfth Century," *MIC* C-1 [Vatican City 1965] 359–90 at 371–77.)

[33] Cf. Thomas Aquinas, *Summa theologiae*, in *Opera omnia*, Leonine edition (Rome 1882–) 3-supp., q.21, a.3, resp., emphasizing that excommunication was not inflicted for mortal sin unless the sinner was contumacious. (The supplement was compiled by Reginald of Piperno; see T. L. Miethe and V. J. Bourke, *Thomistic Bibliography 1940–1978* [Westport, Conn., and London 1980] xx.)

[34] X 2.6.3 and X 5.40.23; cf. Bernard of Pavia, *Summa Decretalium*, ed. E. A. T. Laspeyres (Regensburg 1860; repr. Graz 1956) 2.10.4, p. 41; Tancred, *Ordo*, in F. C. Bergmann, ed., *Pillius, Tancredus, Gratia, Libri de iudiciorum ordine* (Göttingen 1842; repr. Aalen 1965) 4.1, p. 136; and Host., *Sum.* 5.55(*De poen.*).3, col. 1735. On actual practice see Fournier, *Officialités* 153–56 and B. L. Woodcock, *Medieval Ecclesiastical Courts in the Diocese of Canterbury* (Oxford 1952) 93–94.

[35] On the payments see Woodcock, *Canterbury* 99; on the plaintiff's right to oppose his opponent's absolution see VI 5.11.2, and for an example see Petit, *Registre* 60. This adversarial nature of the procedures of excommunication probably explains the form ("excommunicated *pro*," followed by a name) of the entries in the register of excommunicates described by Toussaert, *Flandre* 438–39.

[36] VI 5.11.2; cf. Woodcock, *Canterbury* 99.

[37] Petit, *Registre* 446 and 450–51 for examples; cf. X 5.39.46.

[38] X 5.39.10, 12, and 51; VI 5.5.2; cf. Petit, *Registre* 60 for an example. I briefly discussed the nature of the guarantees in "Legal Precision in the Decretist Period," *BMCL* 6 (1976) 55–63. Johannes Andreae gives a useful historical survey of *absolutio ad cautelam* in *Comm.* VI 5.11.2. On absolution in general see the excellent discussion in F. D. Logan, *Excommunication and the Secular Arm in Medieval England* (Toronto 1968) 136–55; and in relation to heresy, see A. C. Shannon, *The Popes and Heresy in the Thirteenth Century* (Villanova, Pa., 1949) 101.

was so closely identified with legal reparation that Clement III found it necessary to forbid association with excommunicates who had taken the oath or had reached a private agreement with their adversaries but had not yet been absolved.[39]

EXCOMMUNICATION AND LITIGATION

Debt cases were among the commonest suits in which excommunication was used, since here, of course, there was no disputed article to be put into the possession of the defendant in the event of the plaintiff's contumacy. Lay debt cases came to the church courts by custom or concession of the secular jurisdiction and, above all, in the guise of perjury cases, because contracts were habitually sealed with an oath.[40] In the early thirteenth century, moreover, excommunication was transformed into an even more efficient legal sanction by a decretal of Innocent III, *A nobis*, which declared that the heirs of an excommunicate who died contrite but unabsolved would be compelled to satisfy the court so that he could be absolved *post mortem*.[41] A good many grim records "in negotio exhumationis"—the bodies of excommuni-

---

[39] X 5.39.15.

[40] Arrangements for jurisdiction were worked out locally, but in general it can be said that in France, laymen could take debt cases to the church courts by prior agreement between the parties or because an oath was used to seal the contract (Fournier, *Officialités* 81, 86 and 95; Bongert, *Cours* 43). As late as the 1280s, Beaumanoir allowed laymen to bring contract litigation to the ecclesiastical courts if both parties agreed (Philippe de Beaumanoir, *Coutumes de Clermont en Beauvaisis*, ed. A. Salmon [Paris 1899–1900] c.11 § 342, vol. 1 p. 165). In England, as early as 1164 the Constitutions of Clarendon forbade the church courts to take lay litigation on contracts merely because an oath had sealed the contract (c.15, in W. Stubbs, *Select Charters*, 9th ed., rev. H. W. C. Davis [Oxford 1913] 167). But although such cases were removed from the church courts if challenged (G. B. Flahiff, "The Writ of Prohibition to Court Christian in the Thirteenth Century" part 2, *Medieval St.* 7 [1945] 229–90 at 260; cf. Maitland, *History* I 128–29), they continued to be tried by the church courts in great numbers, and an early sixteenth-century experiment in the consistory court at Canterbury to treat them as real perjury cases, imposing penance rather than excommunication, was abandoned after only a decade (Woodcock, *Canterbury* 100–101).

[41] X 5.39.28; cf. X 3.28.14. As early as the fifth century the episcopal courts denied burial to debtors as a means of enforcing judgments, though Roman law forbade this (A. Esmein, "Débiteurs privés de sépulture," in *Mélanges d'histoire du droit. Droit romain* [Paris 1886] 245–68 at 257).

cates could not be buried in consecrated ground—testify that the sanction was frequently used in this way,[42] and not surprisingly, since it bypassed the delays and uncertainties of probate and circumvented the secular jurisdictions' competence over immovables. Court records show many excommunicates and their heirs ceding all their possessions to the court and promising to pay the remaining deficit to obtain absolution when they become more prosperous.[43] Thus in 1386 Jacob de Wousel, cleric and scholar of Paris, approached the bishop's court to obtain absolution for his late brother, ceding his own property "in manu ecclesie" and offering his promise, guaranteed by several fideiussors, that the outstanding debts of the deceased would be paid.[44]

Resentment for the excommunication of debtors was sometimes caused by unscrupulous officials who exploited the sanction's social humiliation. In late sixteenth-century Besançon, a *Lumpenproletariat* of diocesan agents demanded bribes to refrain from publicizing the excommunications of debtors, who willingly compounded their debts to conceal their status.[45] Long before this, church authorities had recognized that even legitimate ecclesiastical punishment of debtors estranged many of the faithful: an internal recommendation of the Council of Vienne (1311–12) proposed that excommunication not be used for small debts, though the council acknowledged that such restriction would be detrimental to the ecclesiastical courts.[46] Again, a

[42] Here quoting *Registrum Roberti Winchelsey* in London, Lambeth Palace MS 244, fol. 96v: "In negotio exhumationis ab ecclesiastica sepultura corporis Nicholai Daleroni notorie excommunicati. . . ." (Mrs. D. M. Owen kindly drew my attention to this case and loaned me a rotograph of the manuscript.) For further examples see D. M. Owen, ed., *John Lydford's Book* (London 1974) 133–34; R. Graham, ed., *Registrum Roberti Winchelsey, Cantuariensis archiepiscopi, A.D. 1294–1313* (Oxford 1952–56) I 402–3; C. Jourdain, "Les Excommunications pour dettes," *R. des Sociétés savantes*, ser. 6, vol. 6, part 2 (1877) 75–82; L. Febvre, "L'Application du Concile de Trente et l'excommunication pour dettes en Franche-Comté" part 2, *R. Historique* 104 (1910) 1–39 at 31; and Esmein, "Débiteurs" 257.

[43] Petit, *Registre* 49 and 91 for cases in which absolution was granted on the basis of a promise of future repayment; ibid. 60, 109, 136, 175, 177, and 197 for cases in which defendants ceded their possessions to obtain absolution. See Morel, *Pouvoir* 51, 87, 165–66, and 170–72 for further details on excommunication for debt in France.

[44] Petit, *Registre* 295.

[45] Febvre, "Franche-Comté" part 2, 8 n. 2, 18 n. 1, 17, and 31.

[46] F. Ehrle, "Ein Bruchstück der Acten des Concils von Vienne," *Archiv für Literatur und Kirchengeschichte des Mittelalters* 4 (1888) 361–470 at 416. On resentment against

century later, the agenda for the Council of Constance (1414–18) offered for debate a suggestion that ecclesiastical court judges not impose excommunication lightly, especially in debt cases.[47] In the event, however, it was not until the Council of Trent (in 1563) that reformers succeeded in limiting excommunication's use as a judicial sanction.[48] Febvre's study of the courts at Besançon shows why it took so long: the Trent decree caused the rapid eclipse of the ecclesiastical court at Besançon and with it the decline of the town itself, since the court's business had been the mainstay of the economy.[49]

As a consequence of the split between the penitential and the judicial forums, legal solutions sometimes contradicted moral solutions: excommunication, as a judicial sanction, was used on occasion to enforce law against moral conscience. In marriage litigation, perhaps the preeminent concern of the church courts, papal decretals explicitly acknowledged this: thus one woman, who refuses her husband sexual intercourse because she knows but cannot legally prove the marriage is illicit, is advised by a decretal of Innocent III to endure the court's excommunication rather than incur mortal sin by having intercourse.[50] Adultery or excommunication were the alternatives sometimes faced by couples who had contracted a valid but legally unprovable marriage.[51]

Legal decisions, of course, often turn on paradoxical cases, but undoubtedly the division between sacramental penitence and the ecclesiastical courts heightened the tension that always exists between conscience and law. Was it appropriate to subject persons who might be innocent of any offense except disobedience to court orders to the severities of traditional excommunication? During the second half of the twelfth century, as the power of binding and solving was being

---

this use of excommunication see also Lea, "Excommunication" 439–48, and E. Le Roy Ladurie, *Montaillou. The Promised Land of Error*, trans. B. Bray (New York 1978) 335.

[47] "Capitula agendorum" no. 18, in H. Finke et al., eds., *Acta Concilii Constanciensis* (Münster in Westfalen 1896–1928) IV 572. A 1302 decretal forbade the use of interdicts for enforcing payment of debts, but it was not promulgated with an official collection (Extrav. comm. 5.10.2).

[48] Council of Trent, sess. 25, *COD* 785–86.

[49] Febvre, "Franche-Comté" part 2, esp. pp. 21–22 and 38.

[50] X 5.39.44.

[51] R. M. Helmholz, *Marriage Litigation in Medieval England* (Cambridge 1974) 62–63.

partitioned between confessional and court, rules on avoiding excommunicates became uncertain. Initially some canonists proposed that only those excommunicated by judicial sentence be avoided. But the doctrine eventually endorsed by the canonists, and the law itself, retained the mandate that all excommunicates be avoided but reduced the sanction for communication to exclusion from the Eucharist and the other sacraments. The canon of the Council of Ravenna of 877, which had (uniquely, and, it seems, unsuccessfully) introduced this lesser sanction, was included in Gratian's Decretum as a *palea*, a later addition to the text.[52] Even so, the many Decretum texts embodying the traditional sanction of excommunication could be interpreted to mean mere exclusion from the sacraments because of Gratian's terminological distinction between anathema and excommunication (employed not for this purpose but for opposing excommunication *latae sententiae*).[53] By the end of the century, papal decretals confirmed the decretist doctrine that contact with excommunicates was punished by exclusion from the sacraments rather than by full social exclusion.[54] Given the name "minor excommunication," the new sanction

[52] C.11 q.3 c.38; see Chapter 1 at n. 81.

[53] See, e.g., the complex scheme outlined in Rufinus, *Sum.* C.11 q.3 c.2, ed. Singer 315–16; on Gratian's use of "anathema" and "excommunication" see above at n. 5.

[54] The decretists elaborated doctrines along the lines of *Quoniam multos* (C.11 q.3 c.103), i.e., to contain the contagion of excommunication with the first communicator rather than to reduce the sanction itself. See, e.g., Hug., *Sum.*, C.11 q.3 c.25, v. *Rogo*, Admont 7, fol. 228ra, and Vat. 2280, fol. 175va: "Et est argutum quod excommunicatio transit in tertiam personam, ar. infra c. Excellentissimus [102]. et di. xviiii. Anastasius [9]. Quod tamen non est uerum. Nunquam enim excommunicatio transit in tertiam personam. Dicunt ergo quidam quod hoc capitulum loquitur de consilio, ut dum illis presbyteris denegaretur communio rubore confusi cessarent a communione Maximi. Sed hoc stare non potest propter id quod sequitur, 'contra animam suam.' Facere enim contra ea que sunt consilii non est facere contra salutem anime, quia qui facit contra consilium aut non peccat aut tantum uenialiter. . . . Magister Io. dicit quod hoc speciale est in presbytero communicante excommunicato, uel quod iste Maximus nominatim erat excommunicatus cum omnibus suis communicatoribus, et ita omnes eius communicatores et fautores erant nominatim excommunicati, quod Gratianus uult in sequenti paragrapho [d. a. c.27]. Alii dicunt, et melius, quod omnes presbyteris communicantibus illi communicabant fauendo eis et consentiendo et approbando factum illorum, et hoc prohibet. Non prohibet quin aliter possint talibus communicare. . . . Ego autem intelligo hoc capitulum de alia communione, scilicet de illa de qua dicitur di. xxxii. Nullus [5]. . . . Precipit enim ne communicet talibus presbyteris audiendo missam eorum uel recipiendo sacramenta ab eis. Ipsi enim presbyteri communicando Maximo ipso iure auctoritate canonis erant excommunicati id est ab introitu ecclesie et officio et participatione sac-

was made a function of the penitential forum: communication with excommunicates was a sin, to be confessed to the parish priest and absolved by him.[55] The full contagion of excommunication now affected only those whose contact with the excommunicate was criminal—they conspired or participated in the crime—or those who associated with someone excommunicated "with all his *communicatores*" because of the gravity of his crime.[56] Excommunicates who remained contumacious might eventually be subjected to this harsher ostracism as an "aggravation" (strengthening) of the original sentence: all contacts would after judicial warning be punished by full major excommunication.[57] But on the whole, rather than reducing the category of excommunicates to be ostracized by eliminating those not yet publicly identified as such, as Johannes Faventinus proposed, canon law at the turn of the twelfth and thirteenth centuries chose instead to reduce the contagion of excommunication.

Perhaps the most momentous change of all was the one that according to Luther went largely unnoticed by the faithful. Innocent IV and the first Council of Lyon (1245) declared that excommunication did not jeopardize salvation unless it was ignored or condemned.[58]

---

ramentorum. Nullus debebat eis communicare audiendo missam uel orationes uel percipiendo ab eis sacramenta, et hoc prohibet Gregorius." (Further texts can be found in Huizing, *Doctrina* 9–33 passim; Zeliauskas, *De excommunicatione* 28–38; and in my "The Status of the Individual within the Community according to Ecclesiastical Doctrine in the High Middle Ages," Ph.D. diss., Cambridge Univ., 1975, II 65–67.) An undated decretal of Clement III (1187–91) retains full excommunication as the sanction for communication (X 5.39.15; JL 16555), while an 1196 decretal of Celestine III ambiguously requires the faithful to avoid all contact with minor excommunicates—the term is here used in papal legislation for the first time (Huizing, *Doctrina* 20 n. 19)—though acknowledging that they are excluded only from the Eucharist (Mansi 22.617). Finally, an undated decretal of Innocent III (1198–1216) implied that minor excommunication, not entailing social exclusion, was the sanction for associating with major excommunicates (X 2.25.2). Cf. also X 5.39.59, and see nn. 55 and 57.

[55] X 5.39.29. The term "suspensio" was often used for minor excommunication; Woodcock (*Canterbury* 93 n. 1) notes that he found no instances of the use of the terms "major" and "minor" excommunication. On terminology see also Hinschius, *Kirchenrecht* V 6 n. 3.

[56] X 5.39.29, 30, and 55. These concepts were especially important in excommunication for heresy; see X 5.7.9–11 and 13.

[57] VI 5.11.3; cf. X 5.39.30, sentence beginning "Illi autem," but with variant "innodati" that contradicts reduction of the sanction.

[58] VI 5.11.1.

This formal pronouncement of a theological doctrine originating in the Bible finalized the division between the sacraments and the courts. The sanction was at least conceptually divested of immediate soteriological consequences: excommunication does not directly affect one's state of grace but only withdraws the suffrage of the church, which prepares a person to receive grace or preserves that already existing in him, as Aquinas enunciated the teaching.[59]

[59] Thomas Aquinas, *Sum. theo.* 3-supp., q.22, a.2, resp.: "Sed excommunicatio non directe respicit gratiam, sed ex consequenti, inquantum homo suffragiis Ecclesiae privatur, quae ad gratiam disponunt vel in gratia conservant." Cf. *Scriptum super libros Sententiarum*, ed. P. F. Mandonnet and M. F. Moos (Paris 1929–47) IV, D.18, q.2, a.2, *quaestiuncula* 2, sol.

III

Excommunicates in the Community

Can the pope extract a soul from purgatory? "Yes" was the outcome of a debate held in the Visconti palace between Cardinal Simon de Borsano and the archbishop of Milan in the 1370s.[1] True, papal jurisdiction extended only to this world, but purgatory, many maintained, was located in the center of the earth.[2] More abstractly, papal jurisdiction applied to those in a state of grace and thus to souls in purgatory, though not to those in hell. Reporting the debate in his tract on indulgences, however, Antonius de Rosellis (d. 1466) disagreed, arguing that the pope had no jurisdiction whatever over the dead.[3] Like any other Christian, the pope could help souls in purgatory through prayer, alms, and other charitable works; but by way of jurisdiction he could accomplish nothing.[4]

Such baroque debates, though they contributed nothing to substantive theology, are valuable for contrasting so clearly the vertical

---

[1] Antonius de Rosellis, "De indulgentiis," *TUI* 14, fol. 150rb, no. 30. Simon was a cardinal 1371–81.

[2] Ibid. no. 29.

[3] Ibid. nos. 31–35.

[4] Antonius was denied a cardinalate because he had been married twice (R. Naz, "Roselli [Antoine de]," *DDC* 7.731–32); C. G. Jöcher, *Allgemeines Gelehrten-Lexicon* (Leipzig 1750–51) 3.2225, suggests that bitterness over this setback lay behind his teaching on the limits of papal jurisdiction.

channels of grace characteristic of the high middle ages and the horizontal channels—the prayers, alms, oblations, and other charitable works of suffrage—characteristic of earlier centuries.[5] Only after the scholastic theologians had confined the sacrament to the penitential forum was it possible to say that the excommunication of the church courts did not affect an individual's state of grace. It was evident by the early thirteenth century that major excommunication concerned only the punishment (*poena*) that detained a soul in purgatory, not the guilt (*culpa*) that consigned it to hell.[6] Hence Innocent III's decretal *A nobis* logically permitted *post mortem* absolution from the *poena* of excommunication for those whose contrition guaranteed them divine absolution from the *culpa* of their sins.[7]

Anathema, the solemn ritual of excommunication, was used in the high middle ages to strengthen the sentence of an excommunicate who neglected to seek absolution.[8] Innocent IV's doctrine that the "medicine" of excommunication became a fatal potion for contumacious excommunicates was thus symbolized in the rituals of anathema.[9] Excommunicates who would have remained in a state of grace had they submitted to their sentences were now transformed into sinners who had earned the sentences through their guilt; the rites of anathema dramatized their passage from one state to the other. In sol-

---

[5] Thomas Aquinas, *Sum. theo.* 3-supp., q.21, a.1, obj. 1: "Excommunicatio est separatio a communione Ecclesiae quoad fructum et suffragia generalia."

[6] Cf. Inn. IV, *App.* X 2.20.54, v. *Per exceptionem*: "Excommunicatio non est culpa, sed est medicina, uel poenitentia. . . ."

[7] I.e., X 5.39.28, discussed in Chapter 2 at n. 41. Cf. X 3.42.3, on baptism, which I discussed in "*Fides et Culpa*: The Use of Roman Law in Ecclesiastical Ideology," in B. Tierney and P. Linehan, eds., *Authority and Power. Studies in Medieval Law and Government Presented to Walter Ullmann on His Seventieth Birthday* (Cambridge 1980) 83–97 at 95–96. On the *culpa/poena* distinction see esp. E. Göller, *Die päpstliche Pönitentiarie* (Rome 1907–11) I.1 pp. 213–27, and Lea, *Confession* III 39–49.

[8] Host., *Sum.* 5.59(*De sen. exc.*).2, col. 1880; cf. the anonymous French *summa* on legal procedures known as "Curialis" (1251–70), in L. Wahrmund, ed., *Quellen zur Geschichte des römisch-kanonischen Processes im Mittelalter* (Innsbruck/Heidelberg 1905–28/1931) I.3, c.15, p. 8, and c.90, p. 28; and the *Summa minorum* (second half of the thirteenth century) of Magister Arnulphus, in Wahrmund, *Quellen* I.2, cc.8–9, pp. 9–10. From the later middle ages see Panormitanus, *Comm.* X 2.2.4, no. 20; and Johannes Franciscus de Pavinis, "De visitationibus" 2.3.20, *TUI* 14, fol. 195vb. Excommunication itself was imposed with the simple judicial formula "Excommunico te" (X 5.39.59).

[9] VI 5.11.1; see Chapter 2 at n. 58.

emn, elegant cadences ("damnatum cum diabolo et angelis ejus . . . in igne aeterno judicamus") or in the brutal litany of a curse ("Maledicti sint a planta pedis usque ad verticem capitis") the message was transmitted to the congregation, which ratified the act with its "Fiat" or "Amen."[10] Candles thrown to the floor, foot stamping, door closing, and spitting—common rites of separation—were used in anathema liturgies, to signify, as Cardinal Johannes de Turrecremata (d. 1468) put it, the excommunicate's delivery to Satan.[11]

Excommunication was burdened with great ambivalence. It put the sinner "into the hands of the devil, who could do with him as he wished."[12] By withdrawing its protection, the community gave the devil power to rage inside an excommunicate and disintegrate his personality;[13] "Renew in him, most holy Father, whatever has been violated by the devil's fraud," the bishop prayed in an early medieval absolution formula.[14] As urbane a scholar as the canonist Johannes Andreae (d. 1348) wrote that excommunication hastened sickness and death.[15] Hostile fear colored medieval images of excommunicates. Turrecremata compared them to lepers, dogs, and pigs; centuries earlier a partisan of Gregory VII had written in reference to the

[10]Burch., *Decr.* 11.3, *PL* 140.858.

[11]See C.11 q.3 c.106 (= Burch. 11.3; see n. 10) for the dashing of candles to the floor and stamping of feet. Spitting was described in Myrc's *Instructions* (above, Chapter 1 n. 9). For the ritual of closing the door against excommunicates—and of opening it when absolving them—see the Council of Limoges of 1031 (Mansi 19.540). For Johannes de Turrecremata's observation see *In Gratiani Decretorum primam (–tertiam) partem commentarii. Repertorium* (Venice 1578) C.11 q.3 c.106, v. *Lucernas.*

[12]See, e.g., the anonymous twelfth-century *Commentarius Cantabrigiensis in Epistolas Pauli e Schola Petri Abaelardi*, ed. A. Landgraf (Notre Dame, Ind., 1937–45) 1 Cor. 5, vol. 2, p. 232: "Cum enim aliquis iuste sit excommunicatus, ita satane traditus est, ut, cum voluerit, in eum manum ponat et, quocumque modo placuerit, eum tractet. Sed quamdiu quis quantumque pessimus est in unitate ecclesie . . . non habet diabolus in eum potestatem. . . . Cf. *Glos. ord.* C.11 q.3 c.21, v. *Sathanae.*

[13]Peter Lombard, *Sententiae in IV libris distinctae*, ed. Collegium S. Bonaventurae, 3d ed. (Quaracchi 1971–81) IV, D.18, c.6: "quia gratia Dei et protectio illis amplius subtrahitur, ac sibi ipsis relinquuntur, ut sit eis liberum ruere in interitum peccati. In quos etiam diabolo maior saeviendi datur potestas. Orationes quoque Ecclesiae et benedictionum ac meritorum suffragia eis nequaquam suffragari putantur."

[14]Burch., *Decr.* 11.8, *PL* 140.861.

[15]*Glos. ord.* VI 5.11.2, v. *Opponat*. Cf. Lateran IV c.22 (X 5.38.13): physicians must warn patients to consult a priest before beginning treatment, "cum infirmitas corporalis nonnunquam ex peccato proueniat. . . ." See Kuttner's introduction to Jo. An.'s *Nov.* for the details of Andreae's career.

contagion of excommunication that "one scabrous pig contaminates the whole herd."[16] Anyone who rebelled against the law was a lunatic, said the great canonist Hostiensis (d. 1271).[17] Earlier in the same century, the cardinal legate in Germany called the archbishop of Magdeburg a madman just before excommunicating him.[18]

By the high middle ages there was no question of real exclusion. The enduring impress of the baptismal "character"—an Augustinian concept given new emphasis in twelfth-century sacramental theology and in decretals of Innocent III—indissolubly joined Christians to the church.[19] Indeed, it was the marginal status of excommunicates that made them dangerous: they were relegated to the borders but remained a part of the whole.[20] A fourth-century imperial constitution on apostasy ordered expulsion of apostates unless it would be even harsher punishment for them "to live among people and yet lack all human solaces."[21]

Medieval canonists and theologians devised elaborate rules for the

[16]Johannes de Turrecremata, *Repertorium* C.11 q.3 c.26; cf. *Glos. ord.* C.11 q.3 c.23. For the marginalia of the Gregorian partisan see Chapter 1 at n. 124.

[17]Host., *Sum.* 5.59(*De sen. exc.*).7: "Nam et qui venit contra ius, contumax potest dici et etiam furiosus, supra, de temp. ord. Vel non est compos. [X 1.2.14]."

[18]G. A. von Mülverstedt, ed., *Regesta Archiepiscopatus Magdeburgensis* (Magdeburg 1876–99) II 79–80, no. 182. The classic study on these themes—though in a later period—is M. Foucault, *Madness and Civilization: A History of Insanity in the Age of Reason*, trans R. Howard (London 1967).

[19]I have discussed the theologians' treatment of baptism more fully in "Individual" I 47–67. Among the important Innocentian decretals on the character of baptism were X 3.42.3 (on baptism) and X 4.19.7 (on marriage). An interesting contradiction is Hostiensis's inclusion of excommunicates, with pagans, Saracens, and schismatics, among the extrinsic enemies and persecutors of the church (*Lect.* X 1.9.10 no. 22, v. *Deserere*).

[20]Excommunicates were held to avoid other excommunicates and to keep themselves from contact with the faithful (Panormitanus, *Comm.* X 5.39.8, no. 3), but the faithful were not required to shun pagans and Jews in the same way as excommunicates, not only because the former "did not care much" when they were ostracized (*Glos. ord.* C.11 q.3 c.24, v. *Ad mensam*, with modifications ibid., v. *Permittimus*; and C.27 q.1 c.27) but also because the church had no responsibility or authority to discipline non-Christians (Thomas Aquinas, *Script. sup. lib. Sent.* IV, D.18 q.2 a.4 *ad* 1). For anthropological analysis of the dangers associated with marginal status, see M. Douglas, *Purity and Danger: An Analysis of the Concepts of Pollution and Taboo* (London 1966) esp. 96. Cf. V. W. Turner, *The Ritual Process: Structure and Anti-Structure* (London 1969) esp. 95–97 and 102–13.

[21]Cod. 1.7.3, quoted, e.g., by Tancred, *App.* 1 Comp. 5.6.10, v. *Ut solatio*, London, B. L. Royal 11.C.VII, fol. 68vb; Host., *App.*, *Pia* (VI 2.12.1), v. *Excluduntur*.

tabus surrounding excommunicates. To investigate them as closely as medieval authors did would be tedious and indeed fruitless, since the rules quickly degenerated into the anarchy of casuistry. But a survey will illumine both the status of excommunicates and, by showing the activities from which they were expressly excluded, normal medieval social life.

FRIENDSHIPS

"One needn't desert an excommunicated friend immediately," wrote the famous canonist Johannes Teutonicus early in the thirteenth century—"at least not if it would be terribly inconvenient"![22] Secret excommunicates should be avoided only privately, or "secretly in public," Huguccio believed, especially if one had no proof of their guilt.[23] Robert Courçon (d. 1219), papal legate in France, wrote in his theological *Summa* that one should publicly give only vague explanations for avoiding those not yet officially denounced as excommunicates.[24]

---

[22] Jo. Teut., *App.* 3 Comp. 5.21.7, v. *Excommunicatorum*, in K. Pennington, *A Study of Johannes Teutonicus' Theories of Church Government* (Ann Arbor, Mich., Xerox Microfilms 1975) II.1, p. 749: "Arg. est hic quod si socius meus incidit in canonem, non statim teneor deserere ipsum, arg. xi. q. iii. Antecessor [104]. xxiii. q. iii. c. i. . . . quod intellige si magna ex hoc habetur incommoditas, ut hic. Arg. contra supra de maior. et obed. Illud [X 1.33.5]. . . ." (The first two books of the *Apparatus* are now available in an excellent edition by the same author, *Johannis Teutonici Apparatus glossarum in Compilationem tertiam* I, *MIC* A-3 [Vatican City 1981].) The same gloss appears in Tancred's *Glos. ord.* in 3 Comp. 5.21.7, v. *Excommunicatorum* (Vat., Borgh. 264, fol. 226ra); in Goff. Tr., *App.* X 5.39.34, v. *Continget* (Vienna 2197, fol. 156va); and in Vinc. Hisp.'s *App.* X 5.39.34, v. *Excommunicatorum* (Paris, B.N. 3967, fol. 206rb). As the Vatican manuscripts of Vinc.'s *App.* have a version ending at X 5.37.9 (cf. J. Ochoa Sanz, *Vincentius Hispanus* [Rome and Madrid 1960] 145–46) I have also used this one here and elsewhere. I have found a new copy of the *Apparatus* in Vat., Ottob. 2524, fol. 82ra–97vb and 99ra, excerpts extending from the middle of the preface through the end of Book 2.

[23] Quoted in Chapter 2 n. 16. Cf. C.11 q.3 c.18, v. *Palam*, Vat. 2280, fol. 174rb, and Admont 7, fol. 227vb: "Mentiuntur ergo illi qui dicunt quod non tenemur uitare excommunicatum in publico. Et est argutum quod qui occulte percutit clericum incidit tamen in canonem et uitandus est a scientibus."

[24] Robert Courçon, *Sum.*, Cambridge, Gonville and Caius Coll. 331, fol. 12va: "si tu scis quis sit ille qui commisit furtum contra sententiam illam et communicas ei excommunicatus es. Et immo non debes ei communicare aut in secreto aut in publico. Et in secreto debes ei exprimere causam quare non communicas ei, sed in publico non nisi indefinite. Non pocius sis prodicor fratris quam corrector."

Friends knowing of the excommunication would incur the like penalty for socializing either privately or publicly, but "you should correct your friend, not betray him."

When these counsels were written, excommunication *latae sententiae* was still undeveloped, punishing only such very serious crimes as
heresy and violence to clerics. As sentences of excommunication *latae
sententiae* proliferated, it became ever less appropriate to set in motion
the pressures of public ostracism immediately. Rules for avoidance,
especially in the confessional manuals for priests "in the field," became less stringent. Even in the early thirteenth century, Robert of
Flamborough insisted that one should not avoid an excommunicated
acquaintance if no one else was aware of his status.[25] Raymond of
Peñafort, writing in the 1220s, held that one should associate in public even with judicially excommunicated friends if others were unaware of the sentence; and frivolous rumors, Raymond remarked,
should never lead to ostracism.[26] Whereas Clement III had decreed
that people reputed to be excommunicated must be avoided until
they had purged themselves in court, the Franciscan author Monaldus in the 1270s urged his readers not to avoid such people unless
they had failed to purge themselves or had refused to try.[27]

Ecclesiastical officials designed procedures to expedite public identification of secret excommunicates. When the perpetrators of a crime
punished by excommunication were still unknown, the bishop directed local officials to have the sentence read out in church without
naming anyone.[28] Information from parishioners was funneled to diocesan officials through the parish priest, who could not take testimony on his own authority, nor, of course, act on information learned
in the confessional.[29] Once an excommunicate was identified, his
name was registered and announced "on the first Sunday of every

---

[25] Robert of Flamborough, *Liber poenitentialis*, ed. J. J. F. Firth (Toronto 1971)
3.3.155, p. 155.

[26] Raym. Peñaf., *Sum.* 3.33(*De sen. praec.*).42, pp. 421–22.

[27] Monaldus, *Summa de iure canonico* (Lyon 1516), rubr. "In quib. cau. quis pot.
excom. partic.," fol. 69rb.

[28] Cf. Haines, *Worcester* 187–88; and Fournier, *Officialités* 21.

[29] See in particular Peter Sampson's statutes of Nîmes, ao. 1252, Mansi 24.556–57.
Cf. O. Pontal, "Quelques remarques sur l'oeuvre canonique de Pierre de Sampzon,"
Annuarium historiae conciliorum 8 (1976) 126–42 at 127–32, announcing a forth-
coming edition.

month at Vespers or during the mass," to quote a typical statute.[30] This cannot have been a welcome duty. Bishop Simon of Worcester (1125–50) is reported to have wept as he read out a sentence of excommunication against his friend William de Beauchamp.[31] Episcopal statutes forbade curates to accept bribes to refrain from denouncing excommunicates.[32]

Although the community was bound to avoid excommunicates even before their names had been publicized in this way, at least one canonist, Johannes Andreae, argued that to be with excommunicates after they had been denounced was a mortal sin, whereas beforehand it was only venial sin.[33] Moreover, by the early fourteenth century denunciation created a legal presumption of excommunication; Boniface VIII's decretal *Licet*, in the Liber Sextus, required public denunciation and avoidance of excommunicates who had not appealed within a year, even from an invalid sentence of excommunication.[34]

"Neither manners, familiarity, nor fear of scandal" excused association with excommunicates.[35] They could not be greeted in the street, though the popular Paris theologian Peter the Chanter (d. 1197) allowed acquaintances to respond, "Deus emendat vos" if an excom-

---

[30] From a 1297 synod of Metz, c.23, in Vat. 9868, fol. 229r: "quando mandaverimus in suis ecclesiis excommunicatos nuntiandos, nec non et causam et tempus latae sententiae excommunicationis penes se registratas retineant; et eos quolibet mense prima die dominicali in vesperis aut in missa palam et publice nuntient, donec ipsorum absolutio per nostras litteras eisdem presbyteris fuerit intimata. . . ." (This eighteenth-century manuscript contains copies of many otherwise-lost medieval synods; cf. A. Artonne et al., *Répertoire des statuts synodaux des diocèses de l'ancienne France du XIIIe à la fin du XVIII siècle*, 2d ed. [Paris 1969] passim. For the procedures see also Adam, *Vie* 186 and 196, and Toussaert, *Flandre* 438–42).

[31] See M. Brett, *The English Church under Henry I* (Oxford 1975) 137, on Bishop Simon.

[32] See the collection issued ca. 1300 by Archbishop Peter of Carcassonne, in Vat. 9868, fol. 277r: "Cum aliqui sacerdotes curati nostrae diocesis, prout intelleximus, a denuntiatione excommunicatorum pro pecunia uel muneribus eis datis uel promissis desistant diebus quibus iuxta mandatum eis factum denuntiare tenentur ut citius redeant ad ecclesiae unitatem, idcirco. . . ."

[33] Jo. An., *Comm.* VI 5.11.3, v. *Censura*.

[34] VI 5.11.14, further discussed below, especially Chapter 4 at n. 138 and Chapter 6 at n. 112.

[35] Quoting Antoninus of Florence, *Summa theologica* (Verona 1740) 3.25.2, vol. 3, col. 1411. Titles 24 and 25 of part 3 of the *Summa*, on major and minor excommunication, respectively, comprise Antoninus's earlier tract "De excommunicatione," in *TUI* 14, fols. 366rb–387ra.

municate spoke first.[36] (Possibly in this Bible-reading age salutation still implied a blessing: "Neither do they which go by say, The blessing of the Lord be upon you . . . ," Ps. 129.8.)[37] All normal conversation was forbidden, but in talking to an excommunicated friend about the welfare of his soul one could introduce other topics "ut apud eum magis proficiat."[38]

By an ancient tradition (the gods signified apotheosis by dining with a new immortal)[39] a superior's greeting betokened absolution. A canon of the Council of Toledo of 681 held that an excommunicate who dined with the king was absolved.[40] Several canonists argued that if the pope or a bishop knowingly conversed with someone he himself had excommunicated, that person was absolved.[41] The pope, in particular, could excommunicate according to his will, which *de iure naturae* had the force of law, and absolve excommunicates "de eius conscientia."[42] Several papal decretals were necessary to dispel

---

[36] Peter the Chanter, *Summa de sacramentis et animae consiliis*, ed. J.-A. Dugauquier, Analecta medievalia Namurcensia 4, 7, 11, 16 and 21 (Louvain 1954–67), part 2 (vol. 7, 1957) c.4 § 153, p. 373; and Appendix 2 § 13, p. 458. Vincentius Hispanus even believed one would incur excommunication for calling out "May God convert you" to a heretical acquaintance: see his *Apparatus*, 3 Comp. 1.2.2, v. *(Propter) hoc*, Vat. 1378, fol. 2ra, and Bamberg, Can. 20, fol. 100vb: "Set quid si dixi heretico cum transirem per plateam, "Conuertat te deus," uel 'Deus te saluet'—sum excommunicatus? Solutio: excommunicatus sum quia est uerbum otiosum, nec debeo ei loqui nisi de salute anime, nisi in casu ubi conuenitur et uult me constituere procuratorem, ar. de iudic. Intelleximus, l. iii [1 Comp. 2.1.19 = X 2.1.7]." From the fifteenth century, see Antoninus of Florence, *Sum. theo.* 3.25.2, vol. 3, col. 1411.

[37] The ritual significance of greetings was discussed in Chapter 1 at n. 33.

[38] X 5.39.54.

[39] Thus the great seventeenth-century scholar Innocentius Cironius traced the origins of the tradition on this form of absolution in his *Paratitla in quinque libros Decretalium*, ed. J. A. de Riegger (Vienna 1761) 5 *De sen. exc.*, p. 544. Besides the poetical fiction about the gods, Cironius noted the Roman precedent of a master's giving his slave the right to recline at his meal as a sign of emancipation. Cf. Gaius, *Institutiones*, ed. F. de Zulueta (Oxford 1946–53) 1 § 44, vol. 1, p. 14.

[40] Council of Toledo, ao. 681, c.3, Mansi 11.1030; cf. Lea, "Excommunication" 339. The canon was taken up by Ivo of Chartres (d. 1115) (*Decr.* 16.344, *PL* 161.965, and *Ep.* 62.171, *PL* 162.177) but omitted by Gratian, perhaps because it implied that excommunication lay within royal control.

[41] E.g., Robert of Flamborough, *Lib. poen.* 3.3.151, p. 153; *Glos. ord.* D.93 c.1, v. *Exspectare*; and C.11 q.3 c.29, v. *Pari*.

[42] Hostiensis wrote that not only the pope but any ecclesiastical judge could excommunicate according to his will—but the latter would be punished if the excommunication was groundless (*Sum.* 5.59 [*De sen. exc.*].8, col. 1898). In general, canon law held judges to decide on the basis of evidence, not conscience (Lévy, *Preuves* 8).

the notion that the recipient of a papal rescript was automatically absolved by virtue of the papal greeting.[43] The papal kiss, too, was scrutinized for shades of meaning. Gerald of Wales, in Rome in 1201 to pursue his claim to the see of St. David's, intervened when Innocent III refused to kiss his excommunicated companion, the bishop-elect of Bangor, reminding the pope that he should not prejudge the pending case in which the bishop-elect had been excommunicated by his adversaries.[44] The same pope asked the abbot and convent of St. Peter's at Gubbio why, if they were really exempt from episcopal jurisdiction, Celestine III had refused to kiss them when they lay under the bishop's excommunication.[45]

The kiss, often specified as an act forbidden to excommunicates, was an important medieval symbol of incorporation.[46] Members of social confraternities and guilds exchanged a ceremonial kiss; some guilds in any event excluded excommunicates by charter.[47] Synodal

---

For a lucid discussion of the issue see W. Ullmann, *The Medieval Idea of Law as Represented by Lucas de Penna* (London 1946) 126–30. For the view that the pope could absolve excommunicates "de eius conscientia" see Antonius de Rosellis's "De consiliis," *TUI* 2, fol. 61ra (his less papalist views have been cited above at n. 1); cf. Franciscus Zabarella, *Lect.* X 5.39.41 nos. 1–2, noting, as a precedent, the Roman principle that emperors could free slaves "by will alone."

[43] X 5.39.41; Clem. 5.10.4. Cf. the protestations of Gregory VII in *Reg.* VII 2, ed. Caspar II 460. In the high middle ages the papal chancery had special formulas for letters to excommunicates; see P. Herde, *Audientia litterarum contradictarum* (Tübingen 1970) II 38–39.

[44] Giraldus Cambrensis, *De iure et statu Menuensis ecclesiae distinctiones VII*, ed. J. S. Brewer, RS V.21.3, D.4, p. 241. This case will be discussed in greater detail in Chapter 5 at n. 47.

[45] X 5.33.12.

[46] The ritual significance of the kiss in the Bible was discussed in Chapter 1 at n. 33. For a later period, see, for example, the Council of Verneuil of 755, c.9, *MGH Capit.* I 35: "in ecclesia non debet intrare, nec cum nullo christiano cybum uel potum sumere; nec eius munera accipere debet, vel osculum porregere, nec in oratione iungere, nec salutare. . . ." Cf. the many canons, above all Pseudoisidorian, quoted by Gratian in C.11 q.3. In the popular verse of the high middle ages—"Si pro delictis anathema quis efficiatur / Os, orare, vale, communio, mensa negatur" (quoted, e.g., in Raym. Peñaf., *Sum.* 3.33[*De sen. praec.*].28)—might "os" stand for "osculum" as well as "conversation"?

[47] A gild charter from Kingston-upon-Hull (ao. 1357) explicitly excluded excommunicates; see J. T. Smith, ed., *English Gilds* (London 1870) 158. Adam, *Vie* 16 and 20, points out that some French confraternities required members to take an oath to avoid excommunicates.

statutes of Nogara forbade excommunicates to kiss a prelate's hand.[48] The kiss might also have stood for feudal relationships, since it accompanied the ceremony of homage that sealed the bond between vassal and lord.[49]

Excommunicates are often portrayed freezing onlookers at public events or gatherings. Robert Courçon describes the uncertain reaction of the one person who knows, when a knight secretly excommunicated for fighting in a tournament makes his way into a gathering at a noble's hall.[50] According to a story retold in one of the canons of the Decretum, when the heretic Cerinth entered the baths at Ephesus the apostle John departed immediately.[51] This, however, showed a "superabundance of justice" in the opinion of Guido de Baysio (d. 1313), canonist and papal chaplain, a member of a noble Bolognese family.[52] It was enough to withdraw luxuries and ornaments when an excommunicate was present!

Anxiety about pollution by excommunicates is betrayed in many tabus about food and drink. In an anecdote told by Peter the Chanter, Bishop Gilbert Foliot destroyed his own utensils after eating while he lay under Becket's excommunication.[53] Scholars could share lodgings

---

[48] Council of Nogara (ao. 1290) c.10, Vat. 9868, fol. 222v: "Quia jus ecclesiasticae disciplinae contemnitur, eo quod excommunicati arctius non vitantur, et quod agitur a praelatis facile trahitur a subditis in exemplum . . . , statuimus quod praelati excommunicatos publice ad manus osculum non admittant, et etiam quod ab ipsis praelatis vitentur comedendo et bibendo. . . ."

[49] See, for example, Salatiele (Salathiel Bononiensis), *Ars notarie*, ed. G. Orlandelli (Milan 1961) 2.4, p. 260.

[50] Robert Courçon, *Sum.*, Cambridge, Gonv. and Caius Coll. 331, fol. 12va: "oritur questio de illa sententia generaliter lata a legato auctoritate domini pape in Gallicana ecclesia contra exercentes torneamenta. Puta tu es in aula principis uel in ecclesia uel in conuiuio multorum. Miles qui interfuit torneamentis se ingerit ubi tu es cum aliis. Constans est quod si taces et communicas ei in predictis excommunicatus es. Si autem exis, generas scandalum." The solution, after several lines: "Preterea dicimus quod sententia lata contra exercentes torneamenta siue conferatur a domino papa siue ab eius legato ligat omnes qui contra illam uenire presumant. Et tu omnes tales teneris uitare si sciuisti pro certo eos esse transgressores." On the prohibition of tournaments see N. Denholm-Young, "The Tournament in the Thirteenth Century," in R. W. Hunt et al., eds., *Studies in Medieval History Presented to Frederick Maurice Powicke* (Oxford 1948) 240–68.

[51] C.24 q.1 c.24; cf. Hein, *Eucharist* 256–57.

[52] Guido de Baysio, *Rosarium* (Venice 1577) C.11 q.3 c.17, v. *Aliis prohibitis*.

[53] Peter the Chanter, *Sum.* 2.4.153, AMN 7, p. 372. In another version a wayward monk is reformed by seeing his dishes smashed after dinner (part 2, appendix 2 § 13,

with an excommunicate, Huguccio believed, as long as they did not eat, drink, or converse with him.[54] Though necessity excused contacts with excommunicates, Peter the Chanter suggested that a penurious excommunicated relative be sent outside to take his meals as an object of neighborly derision.[55] In glosses on Raymond of Peñafort's *Summa*, the Dominican William of Rennes wrote that a man offering a meal to a destitute excommunicate should see that his wife took her meal in a different room.[56]

Naturally, letters and gifts, with their burdens of reciprocity, could not be exchanged with excommunicates; the contagion of minor excommunication was transmitted through them.[57]

RELIGIOUS LIFE

Peter the Chanter wondered what one was to do if praying or meditating alone in some corner of the church when an excommunicate came in.[58] Sacral surroundings increase tabus, and so those of excommunication, though by the mid-thirteenth century the famous canonist Peter Sampson, who wrote an influential compilation of synodal statutes for the bishop of Nîmes, was prepared to allow excommunicates inside a church to pray without fear of sin, "especially

---

p. 459); perhaps Peter Damian's report of the excommunication of Robert the Pious was the model (*Opusc.* 34, *De var. mirac. narr.* c.6, *PL* 145.580; cf. Lea, "Excommunication" 349–54).

[54] Hug., *Sum.* C.11 q.3 c.17, v. *Aliis prohibitis*, Admont 7, fol. 226vb, and Vat. 2280, fol. 174rb: "Sed quid de scolari qui habet in hospitio socium excommunicatum? Non potest eum expellere. Nunquid dimittet hospitium? Sic si uult, et potest sine incommodo. Alias credo quod possit remanere ibi dummodo non communicet ei in cibo uel potu uel loquela et huiusmodi."

[55] Peter the Chanter, *Sum.* 2.4.153, AMN 7, pp. 371–72.

[56] Printed as apparatus in the Rome 1603 edition of Raymond of Peñafort's *Summa* with misattribution to John of Freiburg. See 3.33(*De sen. praec.*).29, v. *Uxores*.

[57] Hug., *Sum.* C.11 q.3 c.103, v. *Subtrahimus*, Admont 7, fol. 234vb: "Sed nunquid debemus recipere litteras excommunicati uel ei nostras mittere? Credo quod non. Idem dico de nuntiis et exeniis"; Cambridge, Gonv. and Caius Coll. 676, C.11 q.3 c.16, v. *Sicut apostoli*, fol. 111vb: "Immo et si excommunicatus mittat munus alias non debita? Non accipiuntur." Cf. William of Rennes, *App.*, in Raym. of Peñaf., *Sum.* 3.33(*De sen. praec.*).37, v. *Bona est*; Guido de Baysio, *Rosarium* C.11 q.3 c.18, v. *Cum excommunicato*; and Antoninus of Florence, *Sum. theo.* 3.25.2, vol. 3, col. 1411.

[58] Peter the Chanter, *Sum.* 2.4.153, AMN 7, p. 373. Peter noted that it would be "medicinal" to leave only if the excommunicate would witness the departure.

if the church is not consecrated."[59] During mass, however, excommunicates could not even stand outside the church "to hear the divine word or see the *corpus Christi*," as a Carcassonne statute (1342) phrased it.[60] A priest who voluntarily served mass to an excommunicate incurred an excommunication that could be removed only by the pope.[61]

Innumerable laws on the subject testify to how frequently excommunicates tried to insinuate themselves into their congregations during mass by stealth or force. Unless the mass had begun, priest and congregation must leave at once, the former to prepare a sealed account of the affair for diocesan officials.[62] If the mass had begun, the priest must remain with one or two assistants to proceed through the reception of the body and blood, eyes constantly averted from the excommunicate.[63] This compromise was resorted to only when warnings and even violent coercion had failed.[64] Hostiensis wrote that a

[59] Pet. Samp., *Statutes*, Mansi 24.555–56.

[60] Vat. 9868, fol. 433r: "ut non patiantur excommunicatos audire divina vel videre corpus Christi infra ecclesiam vel extra portam earum etiam existentes." Cf. *Glos. ord.* X 5.38.11, v. *Audiri*, and Johannes de Selva, "De beneficio" 3.4.37, *TUI* 15.1, fol. 54vb. See also R. C. Trexler, *The Spiritual Power. Republican Florence under Interdict* (Leiden 1974) 117 and 119, on prohibition of exhibition of the host during the 1376–78 interdict; and on pollution by seeing in another culture see Evans-Pritchard, *Nuer Religion* 187.

[61] X 5.39.18. In VI 5.11.18, however, Boniface VIII limited the penalty to priests celebrating during interdict.

[62] Synod of Metz, ao. 1297, c.5, Vat. 9868, fol. 226v: "Item praecipimus vobis sub poena suspensionis . . . ne aliquis presbyter . . . in presentia publice excommunicatorum divina officia scienter celebrare praesumat. Sed ante introitum missae, postquam sacerdos suum Confiteor dixerit, avertat se ad populum, ac moneat excommunicatos qui fuerint in ecclesia ut exeant ne divinum officium perturbetur. Quod si aliquis excommunicatus . . . noluerit, sacerdos in divino officio ulterius non procedat. Testimonium astantium invocans, nobis qualitatem facti sub sigillo suo indilate rescribat." See also Morel, *Pouvoir* 106, on difficulties entailed by excommunicates' presence in church.

[63] *Glos. ord.* C.11 q.3 c.16, v. *Oraverit*; Nicolaus de Plowe, "De excommunicatione" rubr. "De partic. cum excom.," *TUI* 14, fol. 365ra (for aversion of eyes and retirement to sacristy). Cf. Johannes de Turrecremata, *Repertorium* C.11 q.3 c.16, v. *Sicut apostoli* (on rules for rural priests).

[64] E.g., Pet. Samp., *Statutes*, Mansi 24.555–56; cf. the 1234 statutes of Archbishop Gerald of Bordeaux, c.46, Vat. 9868, fol. 74v: "De laicis autem excommunicatis qui induto sacerdote intrant ecclesiam et divinum perturbant officium, statuimus quod talium bona per saecularem dominum confiscentur. Qui si noluerit occupare, excommunicationis sententia innodetur." Beaumanoir (*Coutumes* c.1 § 50, ed. Salmon I 39) held bailiffs to remove excommunicates from churches if informed of their presence "par gens creables."

priest faced with having to celebrate mass in an excommunicate's presence might prefer martyrdom.[65]

These rules give the lie to any superficial correlation of excommunication and irreverence. Moreover, for the regular clergy the threat of Mendicant competition arose partly from the Mendicants' willingness to admit excommunicates and people under interdict to religious services—through secret holes in doors and windows, on occasion—and give them the sacraments, though in the early fourteenth century the peasants of Montaillou, excommunicated for not paying tithes, were furious at the irony of being excluded from the Mendicants' church there.[66] But of course it was not only the solace of the sacraments that was sought in church. "If you're forced to be alone when everyone else is in church, all your friends and relatives know you're unworthy of taking communion," a peasant of Besançon ruefully told ecclesiastical investigators after the Council of Trent.[67] The great were not spared this embarrassment. Emperor Frederick II, under papal excommunication in March 1229, was chagrined to find no priest in the Church of the Holy Sepulcher at Jerusalem.[68] In 1209, King Otto of Germany wrongly calculated that his own prestige would persuade the archbishop of Magdeburg to celebrate mass when he went to Whitsun services with his friend the excommunicated margrave of Meissen.[69] Spurned, the king "left the church with the margrave to lessen his shame."

Minor excommunicates were excluded from the sacraments and could not receive them without mortal sin.[70] In the case of the sacrament of penitence the reasons for exclusion were practical as well as spiritual: a secret excommunicate who revealed his crime in the confessional could block testimony from his confessor and so hinder

---

[65] Host., *Sum.* 5.59(*De sen. exc.*).17, col. 1938, admitting, however, that priests could be excused for celebrating the mass under such duress.

[66] See Clem. 5.10.1, and cf. Adam, *Vie* 190 and 201, on Mendicants giving the sacraments to excommunicates and those under interdict. Woodcock, *Canterbury* 101, noted that rectors were also cited for admitting excommunicates to communion. On the excommunications at Montaillou (ca. 1313) see Le Roy Ladurie, *Montaillou* 22.

[67] Febvre, "Franche-Comté" part 2, 18 n. 1.

[68] S. Runciman, *A History of the Crusades* (Cambridge 1951–54) III 188–89.

[69] von Mülverstedt, *Regesta* II 141–42, no. 337. Cf. Clem. 5.10.2, excommunicating magnates who forced priests to celebrate during interdict.

[70] Pet. Samp., *Statutes*, Mansi 24.553. Sampson recommended that even minor excommunicates voluntarily stay out of church except for private prayer (ibid. 555).

prosecution.[71] Even when Boniface VIII mitigated ecclesiastical interdicts by permitting limited dispensation of the sacraments, excommunicates were explicitly excluded from penitence.[72] But the plenary indulgences offered by the papal chancery from the fourteenth century onward seem to have offered a way to circumvent this: recipients of these indulgences could choose a confessor empowered to absolve them from all excommunications *latae sententiae*, in some cases even those reserved to the pope.[73]

In theory excommunicates were also excluded from all forms of ecclesiastical suffrage,[74] but many concessions seem to have been allowed. Gregory IX permitted preachers to support themselves on alms given by excommunicates if necessary.[75] Innocent IV wrote in an academic gloss that alms were allowed because they were given privately, whereas oblations from excommunicates were forbidden because they were given publicly and might thus be of consolation.[76]

Priests suffered especially from the religious consequences of excommunication: a major excommunicate who celebrated mass was liable to deposition, and even for a minor excommunicate to do so was a serious sin.[77] With the exception of penitence, however, the sac-

---

[71] X 1.31.2; cf. Host., *Lect.* X 5.39.14, v. *In quo casu*. See Lea, *Confession* I 417–27 and 510 and II 220–22, on conflicts between confessional and court. A canonical *quaestio* of the 1170s has a priest who tries to make secret restitution on behalf of a criminous parishioner sued after the parishioner's death; see G. Fransen, "Les 'Questiones' des canonistes (II)," *Traditio* 13 (1957) 481–501 at 484, no. 15.

[72] VI 5.11.24.

[73] Göller, *Pönitentiarie* I.1 218 and 224–25. Nicolaus de Gangio, O.M., "Tractatus de indulgentiis" (ao. 1450) seems to deny excommunicates the use of indulgences (Vat. 2644, fol. 33rb): "Ideo nec hereticis, excommunicatis, sismaticis sic existentibus prosunt orationes nec ieiunia nec eleemosyne nec remissiones quo ad effectum spiritualem. . . ." Antonius de Rosellis conceded that after the death of an excommunicate who had obtained an indulgence and fulfilled its requirements, the benefits of the indulgence would take effect ("De indulgentiis" no. 137, *TUI* 14, fol. 151vb).

[74] See Thomas Aquinas's statement quoted in Chapter 2 n. 59. Burch., *Decr.* 11.51, *PL* 140.869, allows *post mortem* oblations from relatives of a deceased excommunicate; see also C.24 q.2 c.3, the decretal of Urban II discussed above, Chapter 1 n. 119.

[75] X 5.39.54.

[76] Inn. IV, *App.* X 5.39.34, v. *Eleemosynas*, no. 1. Hostiensis, however, believed that alms could not be received from excommunicates (*App.*, *Pia* [VI 2.12.1], v. *Actibus*, no. 10).

[77] X 5.27.3–5 for the first; X 5.27.10 for the second. See Hinschius, *Kirchenrecht* V 75–77 and 616–22 on penalties affecting excommunicated clerics, and for practical details and examples see Adam, *Vie* 203–4; Mollat, *Avignon* 208, 327, and 333–34; and C. R. Cheney, "The Diocese of Grenoble in the Fourteenth Century," *Speculum* 10 (1935) 162–77 at 173.

•

raments were valid when performed by excommunicates unless received in a spirit of contempt for the church.[78] Closer to the bone, the income from an ecclesiastical benefice was cut off for the duration, though by the end of the fourteenth century judges at the Roman Rota were allowing excommunicates to acquire legal title to benefices.[79] Excommunicates could not be elected to ecclesiastical office or even participate in elections.[80] Socially, an excommunicated prelate was humbled by the rule that he be avoided by inferiors in the ecclesiastical hierarchy, though within the monastic "family" an excommunicated abbot did not have to be avoided by his monks.[81]

[78] X 5.27.10; Inn. IV, *App.* X 5.7.4, v. *Damnantur*, no. 2. Because of the dangers of schism, ordination had historically been fraught with special perils (see, e.g., C.9 q.1 c.4). On the inability of excommunicated priests to perform valid absolutions see Host., *Sum.* 5.59(*De sen. exc.*).11, cols. 1907–8; similar problems, including whether confession to an excommunicated priest was valid, are discussed by Lea in *Confession* I 280, 287, and 361.

[79] On withdrawal of income see X 2.28.53; cf. *Glos. ord.* C.11 q.3 c.103, v. *Dare*, and *Glos. ord.* X 5.27.7, v. *Retinere*; on disposal of the money see *Glos. ord.* D.91 c.3, v. *Stipendio privatio*, and *Glos. ord.* X 2.28.53, v. *Assignes.* In X 5.27.7, Innocent III invalidated excommunicates' acquisitions of benefices; but for the late fourteenth-century Rota decision see Guilhelmus Horborch, *Decisiones novae* (Rome 1472, *sine fol.*) rubr. "De sen. exc.," no. 126: "Nota quod excommunicatus potest beneficium acceptare. Quia licet excommunicato non potest prouideri nec ius sibi acquiri in beneficio tamen illa que sunt preparatoria iuris uidetur quod possit facere. . . ."

[80] X 1.6.39; X 1.4.8. See Inn. IV, *App.* X 1.6.39, v. *Canonicam*; Host., *Sum.* 1.41(*De synd.*).8; and *Lect.* X 1.38.15, v. *Auctoritate*, and X 1.6.39, v. *De plenitudine*; Jo. An., *Nov.* X 1.6.58, qu.16; Dur., *Spec.* 2.1.13(*De exc. et replic.*).2. Cf. Baldus de Ubaldis, *Super Decretalium volumen commentaria* (Lyon 1551) X 1.6.40, no. 2, arguing that participation of secret excommunicates should not invalidate an election if the other electors were unaware, and Johannes de Selva, "De beneficio" 3 q.4, no. 34, *TUI* 15.1, fol. 54rb, rebutting this opinion. Excommunicated cardinals could, however, participate in the election of a pope (Clem. 1.3.2). On expulsion of excommunicates from canonical elections, see L. Moulin, "Sanior et maior pars," *RHDFE*, ser. 4, 36 (1958) 491–521 at 502.

[81] On secular clergy see Hug., *Sum.* C.11 q.3 c.103, v. *Servientes*, Admont 7, fol. 234va–vb, and Vat. 2280, fol. 181ra: "et di. xciii. Miratus [2] contra. Sed ibi loquitur de clericis qui non sunt ita astricti episcopis et prelatis suis sicut uxores et filii et serui et rustici et seruientes dominis suis uel maritis uel patribus. Et ideo clerici tenentur uitare prelatum excommunicatum ut ibi dicitur, non autem isti dominos, ut hic dicitur. Si tamen seruiens est clericus alicuius et subest ei non ratione officii uel ordinis clericalis sed ratione temporalis seruitii non tenetur uitare eum excommunicatum." On monastic relations see Robert Courçon, *Sum.*, Cambridge, Gonv. and Caius Coll. 331, fol. 13ra: "Immo capitulum licite communicat abbati excommunicato et subditi episcopo suo excommunicato. . . ." (An argument *contra* follows, then:) "Solutio. Si claustrales uideant abbatem suum excommunicatum et contumacem non debent ut credimus ei obedientiam nec ei communicare. Ita dicimus de subditis

FAMILY RELATIONSHIPS

Benefits of the Eucharist, from which all excommunicates were excluded, comprised pardon of sins, spiritual union with Christ, and liberation from the devil.[82] Paradoxically, ecclesiastical interdicts tacitly denied these spiritual gains. Canonists and theologians rightly applauded Innocent IV's famous decretal *Romana* (1246), in which the pope prohibited indiscriminate excommunication of corporate groups (*universitates*) on the grounds that innocent people should not be subjected to the spiritual dangers of excommunication.[83] But ecclesiastical interdicts continued to jeopardize innocent souls by depriving them of the grace imparted through the Eucharist and of the benefits of other forms of worship and suffrage.[84]

---

episcopo." Cf. Host., *Sum.* 5.59(*De sen. exc.*).15, col. 1932. For a contrary view see Cambridge, Gonv. and Caius Coll. 676, C.11 q.3 c.103, v. *Quoniam*, fol. 116ra: "Queritur nunquid monachus communicans abbati excommunicato excusatur. R. non, supra 8. q.4. Nonne directa [*unic.*] ar." Since an abbot was authorized to absolve his own monks from excommunication (X 5.39.32), Raymond of Peñafort argued, abbots could admit excommunicates and accept their professions, though an oath not to return to secular life should be required to avoid fraud (*Sum.* 3.33[*De sen. praec.*].16).

[82] Alexander of Hales, *Glossa in quatuor libros Sententiarum Petri Lombardi*, ed. Collegium S. Bonaventurae (Quaracchi 1951–57) IV, D.8, q.1, vol. 15, pp. 132–33. Cf. Thomas Aquinas, *Sum. theo.* 3, q.65, a.3, *ad* 1: "bonum commune spirituale totius ecclesiae continetur substantialiter in ipso eucharistiae sacramento."

[83] *Romana. Ceterum* VI 5.11.5. Divided into ten sections, *Romana* formed the second official collection of Innocent IV's *Novellae*, published 21 April 1246. Kessler ("Untersuchungen" part 1, 156–82) edited the original decretal; for *Ceterum* see § 5a and § 5c (pp. 174–75) and § 9b (pp. 178–79). I. T. Eschmann, "Studies on the Notion of Society in St. Thomas Aquinas. I: St. Thomas and the Decretal of Innocent IV *Romana Ecclesia: Ceterum*," *Medieval St.* 8 (1946) 1–42, is best on background and doctrine. On punishment of the innocent see also V. Piergiovanni, *La Punibilità degli innocenti nel diritto canonico dell'età classica* (Milan 1971–74). In the article "Interdict" in a forthcoming volume of J. Strayer, ed., *Dictionary of the Middle Ages*, I propose that Innocent IV might have been laying the foundation for a future abolition of ecclesiastical interdicts with the decretal *Romana*. In particular, it should be noted that *Romana* did not inhibit the Apostolic See itself from excommunicating an entire *universitas*: in 1277 Nicholas III excommunicated the Commune of Novara for admitting Spanish soldiers (A. Ceruti, ed., *Statuta communitatis Novariae anno 1277 lata* [Novara 1879] 393), though the practice of excommunicating cities or communes, illustrated by several earlier decretals (e.g., X 5.39.43 and 53), naturally seemed to be prohibited by *Romana* (see, e.g., Inn. IV, *App.* X 5.39.43, v. *Cives*; Host., *Lect.* X 5.39.43, v. *Civitas*).

[84] Aquinas tried to justify interdicts: though they deprived innocent people of the sacraments, they did not exclude people from the community of the faithful, as ex-

Punishment of the innocent was especially sensitive in family relations. While it was admitted that temporal penalties could be inflicted on the children of criminals, St. Augustine in a famous letter rebuked a colleague who excommunicated a whole family for the sins of its head: the death of one innocent soul was unimaginably worse than the corporeal death of many.[85]

Innocence, however, was not quite freedom from the pollution of sin. All who came into contact with excommunicates were touched by their pollution; Augustine himself, in excommunicating a man for the particularly vile crime of stealing church property, rejected oblations from his whole family.[86] Gregory VII's canon *Quoniam multos*, by decreeing that the wife and family of an excommunicated *dominus* would not incur excommunication in associating with him, seemed to break with this tradition of shared guilt.[87] Only in the second half of the twelfth century, however, did the canonists begin to discuss this aspect of *Quoniam*. Although Gratian vehemently argued against any notion that excommunication should affect the family members of an excommunicate,[88] other canonists took a cooler look at the question. Paucapalea, one of the first decretists, rightly noted that Augustine had not forbidden his colleague to excommunicate an entire family but had only warned him to weigh the matter carefully.[89] Paucapalea and others believed that if family members had somehow fostered the crime they could be excommunicated together with the criminal.[90] Huguccio went even farther, claiming that the gravity

---

communication did (see Eschmann, "*Romana*" 11); Innocent IV merely characterized the interdict as a "special penalty" (ibid. 31 line 95). Though Eschmann (p. 23) regrets this as an evasion, I see it as intellectual candor—i.e., the refusal to try to justify what is basically unsound.

[85] Augustine, *Ep.* 250 (75) to Auxilius, *PL* 33.1066–68 = C.24 q.3 c.1; cf. Eschmann, "*Romana*" 20–21.

[86] C.17 q.4 c.8.

[87] C.11 q.3 c.103; see Chapter 1 "*Quoniam multos.*"

[88] Esp. C.24 q.3 d. a. c.1 § 4 and d. a. c.2.

[89] Paucapalea, *Summa über das Decretum Gratiani*, ed. J. F. von Schulte (Giessen 1890; repr. Aalen 1965) C.24 q.3, p. 105. J. T. Noonan, "The True Paucapalea," *MIC* C-6 (Vatican City 1980) 157–86, has convincingly argued that this is not the work of Paucapalea, but until irrefutable textual evidence is found (and another author!) it remains convenient to refer to it as such.

[90] E.g., *The Summa Parisiensis on the Decretum Gratiani*, ed. T. P. McLaughlin (Toronto 1952) C.24 q.3 c.1, p. 228; *Glos. ord.* C.11 q.3 c.103, v. *Quoniam.*

of the crime itself might warrant the excommunication of a whole family.[91]

The issue was put to Rome. In a decretal of 1198, responding to questions submitted by the archbishop of Gran, Innocent III declared that no one was held to associate with an excommunicate except those whose communication was excused by *Quoniam multos*. Did the pope really mean to say "held"?[92] the canonists of Bologna asked. A decretal addressed to them in 1200 affirmed that he did: those already bound by familial obligations when the excommunication was incurred must continue to fulfill their necessary duties.[93] Whether this obligation might be abrogated for very grave crimes, the pope said in the latter decretal, he had not determined, since the question had not been put to him![94]

Reasons for the pope's apparent circumspection are not hard to find. In France, and perhaps elsewhere, some form of excommunication was frequently imposed on entire households. In 1200, the very year of Innocent's decretal, the archbishop of Reims excommunicated a man for damaging ecclesiastical property and simultaneously forbade his family to enter the church and laid his lands under interdict.[95] Long after this the mitigations of *Quoniam multos* continued

[91] Hug., *Sum.* C.11 q.3 c.103, v. *Subtrahimus*, Admont 7, fol. 234rb: "Hinc aperte habetur quod aliquis potest excommunicari pro alio. Sed potest hoc esse de iure? Forte sic, propter magnitudinem sceleris, ar. xxiiii. q. iii. Si habes [1]. Ibi enim dicit Augustinus quod non auderet aliquem excommunicare pro alio nisi grauissime commoueretur. Ubi innuitur a contrario quod hoc auderet facere si grauissime commoueretur, nisi quis dicat quod ibi non dicitur quid fieri debeat sed quid fiat quandoque aggrauitur commoto."

[92] X 5.39.30.

[93] X 5.39.31, one of the two decretals Innocent III addressed to the canonists at Bologna; see K. W. Nörr, "Päpstliche Dekretalen und römisch-kanonischer Zivilprozess," in W. Wilhelm, ed., *St. zur europäischen Rechtsgeschichte* (Frankfurt am Main 1972) 53–65 at 64.

[94] X 5.39.31 *in fine*. Because the problem was raised early in Innocent III's pontificate, before the noncontagious penalty of minor excommunication had definitely replaced full major excommunication as the sanction for contact with excommunicates (in the undated decretal X 2.25.2; see Chapter 2 n. 54), the question took the form "Can a whole family be excommunicated because of a very grave crime committed by one member of the family?"—i.e., the excommunication incurred by other family members, if their communication was not excused under the terms of *Quoniam multos* (C.11 q.3 c.103), would be full major excommunication. Cf. *Glos. ord.* C.11 q.3 c.103, v. *Ex necessitate*.

[95] P. Varin, ed., *Archives législatives de la ville de Reims CDI* II.14 (Paris 1840–52) vol. 1, pp. 737–38. See also a 1234 statute of Archbishop Gerald of Bordeaux, c.73, Vat. 9868, fol. 76v–77r: "De baronibus excommunicandis statuimus observandum,

to be ignored. A 1329 ordinance of the Reims court curtailed the abusive denial of the sacraments and even of ecclesiastical burial to excommunicates' wives and children who had continued their contacts in order to sustain familial duties.[96] The papal court offered relief to families injured in this way, but only if the sanctions against the family had begun with the original excommunication rather than with a separate sentence aggravating the excommunication because of contumacy.[97] While acknowledging that this form of aggravation was not strictly legal (*de iure*), the papal penitentiary of the fifteenth century declined to intervene; since the penalty rested on a separate judicial sentence, it observed, a family that felt it had been punished unjustly could appeal to the judge's superior.[98] Nor was minor excommunication, exclusion from the sacraments and the church, the harshest sanction against families of contumacious excommunicates.[99] In some places families were subjected to full major excommunication and along with "all who knowingly associate[d] with them in meals, shelter, fire, or water, or at furnace or mill" were publicly denounced on Sundays and holidays.[100]

---

ut cum eos excommunicari necesse fuerit, personae eorum excommunicentur, et eorum uxores et familiae interdicantur, et ipsorum excommunicatio publice tribus diebus dominicis et festivis nuntietur"; and cf. Adam, *Vie* 184.

[96] P. Varin, ed., *Archives administratives de la ville de Reims CDI* II.13 (Paris 1839–48) vol. II.1, p. 594, "Ordinatio de curiis remensibus" c.26, forbidding penalizing family members "occasione participacionis cum excommunicatis."

[97] See, e.g., the model in a fourteenth-century papal formulary for instructing a judge to see that the rector of a church ceases ostracizing and denying the sacraments to an excommunicate's wife and family merely because they continued associating with him, in Herde, *Audientia* II 263.

[98] Göller, *Pönitentiarie* I.2, p. 51, nos. 19–20; for the date see I.1, p. 70.

[99] Since families were allowed and indeed under Innocent III's decretals obligated to associate with an excommunicated head of house, family relations were in theory not affected by reduction of the sanction for contacts to minor excommunication (see Chapter 2 at n. 54) nor therefore by the provision that the traditional sanction of full major excommunication could be imposed by judicial sentence and after a warning as an aggravation against contumacy (ibid. at n. 57). Nonetheless this provision must be the implicit legal basis for excommunication (whether minor or major) of a contumacious excommunicate's family.

[100] E.g., the *summa* "Curialis," c.91, ed. Wahrmund, *Quellen* I.3 pp. 28–29; c.92, p. 29; and c.16, pp. 8–9; and Arnulphus, *Sum.* c.10, in Wahrmund, *Quellen* I.2 p. 11. For an actual case see the thirteenth-century Breton document calling for public denunciation "on Sundays and holidays, with lighted candles," of the wife and children of one Gaufridus Gaiglip, who had been involved in a conflict with the monks of Villevieille, in G. A. Lobineau, *Histoire de Bretagne* (Paris 1707) II 342. In late

The pathogeny of family excommunication may have lain in the very canons intended to cure it, *Quoniam multos* and the confirmations of Innocent III. By permitting and later requiring the wife and family of an excommunicated *dominus* to continue associating with him they reinforced the hierarchical structure of the family. Ecclesiastical interdicts were used to put pressure on potentates by punishing their innocent subjects; family excommunication applied the same principles to households.

The conventional structure of the family did not suggest that the same principles of shared guilt obtained when other members were excommunicated. Canon law said nothing on the subject, and the commentators were divided. Some believed that the concession of communication was reciprocal, at least between husband and wife, between whom, as Huguccio phrased it, God did not wish contacts to be severed.[101] Very few, however, believed that excommunicated children should benefit from this reciprocity; the only argument was whether parents better served the spirit of the law by avoiding excommunicated children or by having the contacts necessary to discipline them.[102] Those who believed that "the law regards women as the

---

sixteenth-century Besançon it was still customary to subject an entire family to major excommunication and penalize all contacts with them by major excommunication if the father remained excommunicated fifteen days or more; see Febvre, "Franche-Comté" part 2, notes on pp. 9–10.

[101] Hug., *Sum.* C.11 q.3 c.103, v. *Uxores*, Admont 7, fol. 234va, and Vat. 2280, fol. 181rb: "Hic est reciprocatio, quia idem est et de uiris, quia dominus noluit communionem debiti denegari uiro ab uxore uel econtra. Et ideo uxor licite communicat uiro excommunicato et uir uxori excommunicate. Et credo quod sicut in reddendo debitum ita in exigendo et in aliis omnibus." Cf. Cambridge, Gonv. and Caius Coll. 676, C.11 q.3 c.103, v. *Quoniam*, fol. 116ra: "Nunquid idem dicendum de uiro communicante uxori excommunicate? Videtur quod non, quia uir caput uxoris est, ut infra 33. q. ult. Cum caput [15] et q. 2. Placuit [10]. Contra: ad paria iudicantur uir et uxor, infra, 32. q. i. Si quis uxorem, id est in fine [4]. Solutio: Quidam dicunt uirum in tali casu excommunicari. Sed d. G[andulphus] et Jo. Ti. [John of Tynemouth] dicunt in debita reddendo tantum ad paria iudicari, ita quod sicut uxor reddens debitum uiro petenti excommunicato excusatur, ita uir uxori excommunicate. In aliis uero secus." John of Tynemouth's glosses are discussed in S. Kuttner and E. Rathbone, "Anglo-Norman Canonists of the Twelfth Century," *Traditio* 7 (1949–51) 279–358 at 317–21. See also Chapter 5 at n. 47. On the same theme, see Robert of Flamborough, *Lib. poen.* 3.3.156, p. 155; and Johannes de Turrecremata, *Repertorium* C.11 q.3 c.103, v. *Uxores*.

[102] For the first line of reasoning see Hug., *Sum.* C.11 q.3 c.103, v. *Uxores*, Admont 7, fol. 234va, and Vat. 2280, fol. 181rb: "Sed hec reciprocatio non habetur in sequentibus, scilicet de patre et filio, de domino et de seruo et ancilla et rustico et seruiente.

subjects, almost servants, of their husbands," as did the papal chaplain Goffredus de Trano (d. 1245), assimilated excommunicated wives to the same discipline.[103] Siblings were to avoid an excommunicated brother, Huguccio wrote, unless they were under his *patriapotestas*.[104]

Sexual intercourse was an important consideration in these debates. In an inversion of the old rules for penitents, sexual relations were regarded as obligatory for husband and wife, regardless of which was excommunicated: "licite communicat uxor in hoc, quod pertinet ad regimen uite, solum vir in hiis, huic coniugio que debita sunt . . . ," in the verses of a fourteenth-century German pastoral handbook.[105] As guardians of family and marriage, the church courts were unlikely to enforce any policy that jeopardized marriage.[106]

Dominus enim uel pater quia non subest eis debet uitare eos excommunicatos, ar. xxvii. q. i. De filia [26]. Ipsi uero ratione et necessitate subiectionis non tenentur uitare patrem uel dominum excommunicatum." Likewise Cambridge, Gonv. and Caius Coll. 676, ibid., v. *Filios*, fol. 116ra: "Solutio. Ita et pater impune non possit communicare proli sue excommunicate, potest tamen proles patri excommunicato ratione patrie potestatis"; and Pet. Samp., *Statutes*, Mansi 24.554. For the second viewpoint see, e.g., *Glos. ord.* C.27 q.1 c.26, v. *Reciperent*; Goff. Tr., *Sum.* 5.39.31; Host., *Sum.* 5.59(*De sen. exc.*).15, col. 1932.

[103]Goff. Tr., *Sum.* 5.39.21. Cf. Pet. Samp., *Statutes*, Mansi 24.554. Hostiensis permitted contacts only if excommunication resulted from a legal defect in the marriage (*Sum.* 5.59[*De sen. exc.*].15, col. 1931).

[104]Hug., *Sum.* C.11 q.3 c.103, v. *Servientes*, Admont 7, fol. 234vb, and Vat. 2280, fol. 181rb: "Sed quid de sociis? Quid de fratribus? Credo quod socius debeat uitare socium excommunicatum et quod frater fratrem excommunicatum nisi sit in potestate eius." But cf. Cambridge, Gonv. and Caius Coll. 676, fol. 116ra: "Queritur nunquid frater excommunicato fratri communicans excusatur. Quidam dicunt sic, ratione sanguinis. Alii non nisi cohabitent." Many canonists added that an emancipated son should avoid an excommunicated father, and, conversely, that parents should not avoid an excommunicated son on whom they were dependent. Thus Hug., *Sum.* ibid., v. *Uxores*, Admont 7, fol. 234va, and Vat. 2280, fol. 181rb: "Intelligo tamen de filio qui est in potestate patris. Nam si est emancipatus credo quod debeat uitare patrem excommunicatum nisi cohabitet illi et habeat ab eo necessaria. Similiter dico quod pater teneatur uitare filium excommunicatum nisi alimenta ab eo recipiat uel ei tribuat, cum de facili iste uel ille non possit habere aliunde." For this opinion see also Goff. Tr., *Sum.* 5.39.30; Thomas Aquinas, *Script. sup. lib. Sent.* IV, D.18, q.2, a.4, *quaestiuncula* 3, sol.; and Nicolaus de Plowe, "De excom.," rubr. "De partic. cum excom.," *TUI* 14, fol. 365rb.

[105]Rudolfus de Liebegg, *Pastorale* 5.20, p. 379. See also nn. 101–4, and cf. *Glos. ord.* C.11 q.3 c.103, v. *Uxores*, with the opinion that a wife was obligated to continue having sex with her excommunicated husband even though he could not demand it as his right.

[106]On enforcement of the conjugal debt, see A. Esmein, *Le Mariage en droit canonique* (Paris 1898) II 8–13.

Roffredus Beneventanus, judge at the court of Frederick II and expert in civil and canon law, proposed that a wife suing for divorce and the return of her dowry on the grounds that her husband had long been excommunicated be told that she herself was excommunicated, since man and wife are one flesh.[107] Moreover, while cohabitation with an excommunicated spouse was bad, desertion was worse! For these and other reasons, Roffredus concluded, divorce would be denied under canon law, though perhaps allowed under civil law, which would treat the spouse as it would a criminal subjected to deportation.[108]

Whether an excommunicate could marry was a question that theologians and canonists debated at length: since excommunicates were excluded from the sacraments, it invited exploration of the sacramental and contractual status of marriage.[109] In practice, however, forbidding excommunicates to marry in churches would only have multiplied clandestine marriages, which, naturally, the ecclesiastical courts were bound to do what they could to prevent.[110] Moreover, if early canons protected penitents from sexual sins, the church of the high middle ages had to guard against the worse threat of abstinence, the

---

[107] Roffredus Beneventanus, *Quaestiones Sabbatinae* (Avignon 1500; repr. Turin 1968) p. 448a.

[108] Ibid. col. b: "quia matrimonium soluitur excommunicatione sicut et deportatione."

[109] See, e.g., a disputed question from late twelfth-century Barcelona, in Barcelona, Arch. Corona de Aragón, S. Cugat 55 [no. 14], fol. 55va: "Item, queritur utrum excommunicatus possit matrimonium contrahere cum ea que non est excommunicata. Et uidetur quod non. Cum enim excommunicatis cetera sacramenta denegentur, et illud sit sacramentum magnum in Christo et ecclesia. . . . Item, si est prohibitum ne cum excommunicatis debeamus inire temporales contractus, ut in decretali In partibus Tolose [1 Comp. 5.6.10], multo fortius est prohibitum ne cum eis spirituales debeamus inire. Sed econtra uidetur quod quis possit cum excommunicata contrahere. Ipsa enim per caracterem dominicum adhuc ouis ecclesie iudicatur, ut xxiii. q. iiii. Displicet [38]." (Although the author changed the hypothetical excommunicate's sex as he began the *contra* arguments, the question remained the same, whether any excommunicate, male or female, could marry. On these *quaestiones* see also Appendix lc.)

[110] For examples of synodal statutes forbidding clandestine marriages, see O. Pontal, *Les Statuts synodaux français du XIIIe siècle, CDI, sér. in 8,* vol. 9 (Paris 1971) p. 66, nos. 41–42, and p. 88, no. 98. For some fourteenth-century examples of irregular solemnizations, see *Registrum Hamonis Hethe,* ed. C. Johnson (Oxford 1948) I 252 and 459–60. On canonical policy see Helmholz, *Marriage* 26–31 and passim; and C. Donahue, "The Policy of Alexander the Third's Consent Theory of Marriage," *MIC* C-5 (Vatican City 1975) 251–81, esp. 258, 266–67, and 274–76.

celibacy endorsed by puritanical heretics:[111] the Fourth Lateran Council was obliged to proclaim that not only virgins and the continent but also married couples could achieve beatitude.[112] It is unlikely that excommunication often prevented marriage or that separations or divorces were often granted on account of excommunication.[113]

Still, the academic debates air some interesting social topics. In the late twelfth century an anonymous disputed question analyzed a hypothetical marriage in which husband and wife are discovered to be related within prohibited degrees and are summoned to court.[114] Failing to appear, they are excommunicated, and while in that state they have three children. Then they are reconciled to the church, and divorce is celebrated—an odd but of course not unique antinomy. Are the children legitimate? Can they inherit the parental estate? Yes, the author concludes; for if the couple's sexual relations were permitted under the Gregorian canon *Quoniam multos*, how can the offspring of such relations be judged illegitimate?

---

[111] See Moore, *Origins* 165, 169–71, 180–81 and passim; and C. Thouzellier, *Catharisme et Valdéisme en Languedoc*, 2d ed. (Louvain and Paris 1969) 91–92.

[112] X 1.1.1 § 5.

[113] Hostiensis said some congregations openly permitted excommunicates to marry (*Sum.* 4.2[*De matr.*].2, cols. 1245–46). *Li Livres de jostice et de plet*, from mid-thirteenth-century Orléans, also allowed excommunicates to marry (ed. G. Rapetti [Paris 1850] 10.7 § 6, p. 196). But a ca. 1300 Carcassonne synodal statute excommunicated those who "cum excommunicatis uel interdictis . . . contrahere matrimonialiter non verentur. . . ." (Vat. 9868, fol. 273r). By the fifteenth century, Zabarella could say that the church simply preferred excommunicates to obtain absolution before marrying (*Lect.* X 4.7.6, nos. 2 and 4). Where political factors were involved, of course, excommunication might still be an impediment, as in the marriage of King Alfonso I of Aragon; see S. Runciman, *The Sicilian Vespers* (Cambridge 1952) 268. In the case of heresy, papal policy sometimes allowed separation; see Maisonneuve, *Études* 148, 302, and 355.

[114] Bamberg, Can. 45, fol. 50vb, and Fulda D.7, fol. 68r–v: "Fateor utrumque esse excommunicatum. Neuter tamen alteri propter hoc communicationem subtrahere debuit, ut xi. q. iii. Quoniam [103]. Si ergo approbante canone uterque alteri copiam sui corporis exhibuit quis illius commixtionis prolem illegitimam iudicare debuit uel potuit, ut ext. qui fi. si. le. Cum inter [X 4.17.2]. Sepe enim accidit ut nec sit nec possit esse matrimonium ubi tamen proles est legitima, ut xxxiiii. q. ii.. In lectum [6]." In the solution, it was determined that the children were legitimate, since the church had not forced the couple to separate before they had children: "Pronuntio filios legitimos natos uel conceptos ante sententiam. . . . Nam quamuis ecclesia probationes non haberet tamen post annum excommunicationis potuit diuortium celebrari, ut xi. q. iii. Rursus [36]. Ergo si toleravit factum pari ratione et prolem toleret." For the date see G. Fransen, "Les 'Questiones' des canonistes (III)," *Traditio* 19 (1963) 516–31 at 519 and 523.

Few of the canonists and theologians debating these issues had any experience of marriage. One who did was Johannes Andreae, whose discussion of excommunication and family relationships includes a stilted but genuine allusion to familial affection. Can an excommunicate ask his wife to tell his children how much he loves his family or ask his children to say the same things to his wife? Andreae decided that he could—and that these incidental topics would not mar the conversation they licitly exchanged on the subject of absolution and salvation, just as superfluous words did not invalidate the verbal contract *stipulatio!*[115]

FEUDAL RELATIONSHIPS

Peter Sampson wrote in his synodal statutes that shepherds, plowmen, porters, footmen, male and female slaves (including baptized Saracens), and all who served for wages were obligated by *Quoniam multos* to communicate with an excommunicated master.[116] But feudal relations were not governed by the canon. In the late twelfth century, Huguccio summarized the effects of excommunication on feudal ties: vassals should not fight for an excommunicated lord or aid or defend him; they must not form a court for him, visit him, travel with him, or eat or drink with him.[117]

Thus canon law—and an important source on feudal law itself, the *Consuetudines feudorum*—called for the suspension of feudal ties during excommunication.[118] "Yet in practice we see the contrary done every day," the Dominican canonist William of Rennes exclaimed in a gloss in the 1240s.[119] Although Gratian's Decretum included the

---

[115] Jo. An., *Nov.* X 5.39.54, v. *Incidenter.*

[116] Pet. Samp., *Statutes*, Mansi 24.554. When these dependents were excommunicated, they should be avoided, Sampson wrote (ibid.); but Aquinas held masters to support excommunicated dependents with the necessities of life; see *Script. sup. lib. Sent.* IV, D.18, q.2, a.4, *quaestiuncula* 3, sol.

[117] Appendix 3a lines 12–17.

[118] On the *Consuetudines feudorum* see Chapter 1 at n. 110.

[119] William of Rennes, *App.*, in Raym. Peñaf., *Sum.* 3.33(*De sen. praec.*).37, v. *Fidelitatis.* It should be noted that the bishop of Rennes, William's native city, was a principal coordinator of ecclesiastical efforts to suppress the anticlerical campaigns of Pierre de Dreux, further discussed below, especially Chapter 4 at n. 86 and Chapter 7 at n. 11.

canons of Gregory VII and Urban II decreeing that vassals withhold allegiance from an excommunicated lord, implementation of the papal policy was a matter of politics and diplomacy.[120] Moreover, the exigencies of the heresy crisis dictated the course that implementation would take. The Third Lateran Council demanded that the vassals of heretics be released from fidelity, but, as Maisonneuve has demonstrated in careful detail, papal actions even against such notorious heretics as Count Raymond VI of Toulouse were always contingent on cooperation from feudal overlords: Innocent III's invitation to faithful Catholics to occupy the count's lands was limited by the caution "salvo jure domini principalis."[121] The earliest papal decretals calling for confiscation of heretics' property—in the context of feudal law this resulted from dissolution of fealty oaths—were sent to lands within the papal patrimony.[122] Although, as Maisonneuve has shown, the "faithful" subjects of the patrimony were soon subsumed into the "faithful" subjects of the universal church, it is noteworthy that even in deposing Frederick II in the Council of Lyon, Innocent IV belabored the emperor's injuries to subjects in the "kingdom of Sicily, a special patrimony of B. Peter that the same prince holds as a fief from the Holy See. . . ."[123] One is never very far from the feudal model.[124]

Thus in abstract law excommunication immediately suspended feudal obligations, and innumerable witnesses to that law can be found among civil lawyers (including feudal specialists) and canonists alike down to the sixteenth century.[125] But more realistic canonists, among

[120] C.15 q.6 cc.4–5. By introducing these texts in a debate on whether popes could annul oaths extracted by force, Gratian diluted their impact; as Kempf has recently argued ("Dictatus" 136–37), this was intentional. Still, as so often, Gratian leaves a loophole through which the extremist viewpoints might gain admission: he speaks (d. a. c.3) of "deposition," whereas the texts, as pointed out above, have been toned down so that they speak only of temporary suspension of feudal ties. Rufinus (*Sum.* C.15 q.6 c.3, p. 350) and Huguccio (quoted by A. Stickler, "Der Schwerterbegriff bei Huguccio," *Ephemerides juris canonici* 3 [1947] 201–42 at 211–12 n. 1) carefully pointed out that deposition was a wholly different matter.

[121] Lateran III c.27 (*COD* 225). Maisonneuve, *Etudes* 195–233, esp. 202–3.

[122] Maisonneuve, *Etudes* 155 on the point that for a vassal confiscation meant loss of fief; ibid. 171 on expansion of the confiscation policy outside papal lands in 1207.

[123] *COD* 283.

[124] Cf. X 5.39.53, Innocent III threatening to confiscate ecclesiastical fiefs of Pisan authors of statutes violating ecclesiastical liberties.

[125] Among civilians see especially Accursius (*Glos. ord., Libr. feud.* 2.28.1, v. *Solutus est*), who even asserted that if a vassal sold his fief while his lord was excommunicated, the lord could not retract the sale after absolution; Baldus de Ubaldis, *In Usus*

them Innocent IV himself in his academic glosses, argued that the suspension of feudal oaths required a separate judicial act.[126] In practice, it was reserved as an aggravation for contumacy.[127] Only after two years did Honorius III (1216–27) threaten to absolve the vassals of the excommunicated count of Rethel from their oaths of fidelity on the grounds that the count's contumacy in excommunication was beginning to resemble heresy.[128] Included in the Liber Extra of 1234, Honorius's decretal tacitly admitted that feudal ties were not abrogated by excommunication alone. But even the hardened Count Pierre de Dreux, excommunicated repeatedly after initiating his anticlerical conspiracy in Brittany in 1225 and confronted in 1228 with Gregory IX's threat to release his vassals, took the precaution of seeking absolution in 1230 lest his vassals desert him before an impending royal invasion.[129]

---

feudorum commentaria (Lyon 1585) 2.28.1 (doubting, however, that such sales would be irrevocable); Martinus Sillimanus, "Tractatus super usibus feudorum" § 17, *TUI* 11.1, fol. 9ra; and, from the sixteenth century, Ulricus Zasius, "De feudis" 7.37, *TUI* 11.1, fol. 311ra. Among canonists see *Glos. ord.* C.15 q.6 c.4, v. *Constricti sunt*, and C.11 q.3 c.94, v. *Obediebant*; Goff. Tr., *Sum.* 5.7.11; Host., *Sum.* 2.27(*De iureiur.*).3; Jo. An., *Nov.* X 2.14.8, v. *Excommunicationem* (wrongly including Inn. IV among those sharing this opinion; see below at n. 126); Franciscus Zabarella, *Lect.* X 5.37.13, no. 1; Johannes de Turrecremata, *Repertorium* C.15 q.6 c.4, qu.; Antoninus of Florence, *Sum. theo.* 3.24.76, vol. 3, col. 1400. On excommunication and loss of feudal rights see Eichmann, *Acht*, esp. 79–87; and Morel, *Pouvoir* 46–47, 110, and 116–29.

[126] Inn. IV, *App.* X 2.14.8, no. 4; cf. Guido de Baysio, *Rosarium* C.15 q.6 c.4, v. *Absolvimus*. Among earlier canonists, see in particular Laurentius Hispanus, quoted in O. Hageneder, "Exkommunikation und Thronfolgverlust bei Innozenz III," *Römische historische Mitteilungen* 11 (1957–58) 9–50 at 28. The theologian Richard of Middleton (d. 1300) argued that the church often released vassals from their oaths by special sentence, which would be superfluous if excommunication itself dissolved the oaths (*Super quatuor libros Sententiarum Petri Lombardi questiones* [Brescia 1591] IV, D.18, a.11, q.1).

[127] See the analysis of a number of thirteenth-century cases in Hageneder, "Exkommunikation" esp. 9–14 and 29–35 (but, as will have been clear in Chapter 1 at n. 65 and Chapter 2 at n. 4, I do not agree that loss of feudal rights and other civil incapacities were linked to anathema rather than excommunication [p. 35]). Cf. also Morel, *Pouvoir* 46–47.

[128] X 5.37.13: important for excommunication and feudal rights, and also the only medieval statement of a pope or general council from which it could be inferred that mere contumacy in excommunication was grounds for suspicion of heresy (cf. Chapter 2 at n. 22).

[129] S. Painter, *The Scourge of the Clergy. Peter of Dreux, Duke of Brittany* (Baltimore 1937) 73; cf. n. 119. Thus also Lord John of Beirut in 1232 refused his own son a command because the latter was excommunicated (Runciman, *History of the Crusades* III 200).

IV

Excommunication and the Loss of Legal Rights

The feudal penalties of excommunication were peculiarly medieval, and its social and religious consequences, conditioned by medieval society, have left no conscious trace. But excommunication's legal effects were the medieval expression of a much broader historical phenomenon, derived from ancient law and passed on to modern societies, the hierarchical organizing of social groups by differing degrees of legal status. Though sometimes punitive, the reduction or withdrawal of legal rights was principally intended to order society according to social and moral values.

Courts and legal procedures institutionalized the hierarchical ranking. Excommunicates could not sue in civil litigation or accuse in criminal trials; the present chapter surveys this deprivation of legal remedies from its foundations in Roman law through its embodiment as the main sanction of the ecclesiastical courts at their height, in the late twelfth and thirteenth centuries. The courts also barred excommunicates as judges, proctors, advocates, and witnesses and curtailed their rights as defendants; Chapter 5 concerns these topics. Outside the courts, as Chapter 6 shows, excommunicates suffered legal disabilities, such as the inability to enforce contracts, that reflected their social isolation as well as their judicial handicaps. As will be clear in Chapter 6, attempts to reform excommunication in the high middle ages centered on these extrajudicial legal consequences; the most palpable form of ostracism, they doubtless seemed most susceptible to control. Chapter 7, finally, takes up once again the withdrawal of legal rights. Secular courts were held by canon law and in some instances by secular law to enforce the withdrawal; the success of this aim in France and England is tested by an examination of secular law books and court records, which survive in far greater numbers for the lay courts than for those of the church.

Excommunication's social and religious penalties originated in the Bible; its legal consequences were derived from the Roman diminution of legal status known as *infamia*.[1] During the early republic, from about the mid-fifth century B.C., *infamia* disgraced an individual and disqualified him from voting; it was a stigma (*nota*) inflicted on immoral persons by the censor, who controlled the voting lists.[2] Censorian *infamia*, attenuated by the drastic social policies of the late republic, ended, of course, with the demise of democratic government; but *infamia* had since (from about the end of the second century B.C., with the institution of flexible legal actions) been adopted by civil law in the praetor's edicts on capacity to sue.[3] The edicts created two categories of *infames*: those allowed to sue (*postulare*) only for themselves (e.g., capital criminals, calumniators, gladiators, and those who engaged in passive homosexual acts) and those allowed to sue as well for close relatives and others to whom they had obligatory ties, such as patrons (e.g., persons convicted of such serious delicts as theft or injury, actors, usurers, and violators of the mourning laws).[4] Roman criminal law created separate restrictions on the capacity to

[1] A. H. J. Greenidge, *Infamia. Its Place in Roman Public and Private Law* (Oxford 1894) remains the best survey of *infamia*, though now corrected in many places by M. Kaser, "Infamia und Ignominia in den römischen Rechtsquellen," *ZRG Kan. Abt.* 73 (1956) 220–78, and by Daube, "'Ne Quid.'" Although "ignominia" rather than "infamia" was the usual term until the late principate (Kaser 234–35) I have used "infamia" throughout to prevent confusion.

[2] On censorian *infamia* see Greenidge, *Infamia* 7–14 and Kaser, "Ignominia" 224–29.

[3] On decline of the censor's office in the late republic see L. R. Taylor, *Party Politics in the Age of Caesar* (Berkeley and Los Angeles 1949) 70; and H. H. Scullard, *From the Gracchi to Nero*, 5th ed. (London and New York 1982) 81 and passim. On praetorian *infamia* see Greenidge, *Infamia* 14–16 and passim, and Kaser, "Ignominia" 245–54; for the date of the new (formulary) system see B. Nicholas, *An Introduction to Roman Law* (Oxford 1962) 21.

[4] See Dig. 3.1.1.5–6 for the first category and Dig. 3.1.1.7–3.1.6 for the second. Dig. 3.1–2 passim, and 48.2 passim, and Cod. 2.11 and 9.1 passim, have inclusive lists of *infames*; for analysis see Greenidge, *Infamia* 34 and 121–53, and Kaser, "Ignominia" 242–43 and 260–63. Dig. 3.1.1.6, imposing *infamia* on anyone "qui corpore

accuse (except in trials for a few very grave crimes, e.g., treason); here, too, *infames* were excluded, together with women, minors, and soldiers, among others.[5] But in criminal law a general mitigation allowed all to accuse in cases of crimes against themselves or relatives and others to whom they were bound by obligatory ties ("si suas suorumque iniurias exsequantur").[6] The civil and criminal restrictions were distinct in context and vocabulary, though they resembled each other and similarly affected some of the same classes of persons; *infames* of the less dishonorable class, for example, could represent themselves and those within their circle of obligation in the civil courts and could, like anyone else, accuse in the criminal courts to avenge crimes against themselves and those to whom they were obligated.

In the early centuries of the church, when Roman law was beginning to influence canon law, the concept of *infamia* was being simplified and generalized; imperial laws exploited its emotive value while reproducing its detailed juristic applications.[7] Both aspects of *infamia* were strikingly well suited to the needs of early canon law. As early as the New Testament, in second Thessalonians, the moral disgrace of censorian *infamia* ("hunc notate") was rhetorically linked to excommunication ("ne commisceamini").[8] More technically, *infamia*

---

suo muliebra passus est," may, even if an interpolation, show that Roman dislike of homosexual passivity was given legal coloring before the third century, when laws began to be passed banning specific homosexual acts, as recently shown by J. Boswell, *Christianity, Social Tolerance, and Homosexuality* (Chicago and London 1980) 70–71; on passivity, cf. 74–76, 122–24, and 157 n. 88. However, the phrase might refer not to homosexual acts in general but to ritual pederasty; cf. T. Reik, *Masochism in Modern Man*, trans. M. H. Beigel and G. M. Kurth (New York 1941) 127–28; and van Gennep, *Rites* 172.

[5]Dig. 48.2 and Cod. 9.1. On adoption of *infamia* by criminal law see Greenidge, *Infamia* 28–30, and Kaser "Ignominia" 235–45. On the excepted crimes see below at n. 33.

[6]Cod. 9.1.8 is quoted; cf. Dig. 48.2.4 and 11; Cod. 9.1.5, 8–10, and 12.

[7]Kaser, "Ignominia" 220–21 and 230–35.

[8]2 Thess. 3.14. Use of "infamia" in ecclesiastical rhetoric might indeed have influenced the trends toward simplification and emotiveness in secular usage. See, for example, Origen speaking of the "infamia" of separation from God and the church (*In Ezechielem homilia* 10.1, referring to Ezech. 16.52 [*PG* 13.740]; cf. Latko, *Penance* 70) and Augustine referring to excommunicates as "noti famosique" ("De fide et operibus" 2.3, *Corpus scriptorum ecclesiasticorum Latinorum* 41.38). Though much of this chapter discusses the influence of Roman on canon law, I now think, especially in relation to *infamia*, that the possibility of mutual influence would repay investigation.

was to be pressed into the service of immunizing bishops and other clerics from wanton lawsuits. But the elaborations of Roman law had to be reduced to brief, simple phrases appropriate for the rudimentary church courts and their mainly untrained administrators. So began a process of textual abstraction and modification that would eventually pose considerable problems of interpretation for Gratian and the decretists, the first canonists who had to confront all the original Roman texts as well as their diverse canonical incarnations.

EARLY CANONS ON LEGAL PROCEDURES

To shield clerics from immoral or subversive accusers, councils of the fourth and fifth centuries transformed the Roman restrictions on legal capacity to accommodate ecclesiastical procedures. The emperors of these centuries not only acquiesced but often led the way; many of them were zealous Christians, and as Oost has observed, the concessions kept the church from withdrawing from the increasingly dangerous secular world.[9] Politically motivated litigation, in the Roman tradition, should not be allowed to damage the still-fragile structures of ecclesiastical authority. In 381 the first Council of Constantinople under Theodosius I, establishing diocesan synods as the courts for trying bishops, declared that excommunicates, heretics, and anyone facing criminal charges could not accuse bishops except to redress personal injuries ("propria querela").[10] Though the canon superficially resembles the Roman law provision permitting *infames* and others prohibited from accusing to submit charges in trials for crimes against themselves or their families, its intent actually seems to be to shelter bishops in their official capacity: "ecclesiastical crimes" (such as heresy) and "in ecclesiastical matters" are the terms characterizing trials in which a bishop's accuser must be scrutinized for moral and spiritual worthiness, and the stated aim is to prevent sycophantic charges against bishops as administrators of church property.[11] The canon seems concerned mainly, if not wholly, with

[9] S. I. Oost, *Galla Placidia Augusta* (Chicago and London 1968) 186.
[10] Council of Constantinople, ao. 381, c.6, *COD* 33–34.
[11] Ibid. p. 33: "nec omnibus eorum, qui ecclesias administrant, accusationes permittere, nec omnes excludere; sed si quis propriam quidem querelam, id est pri-

criminal trials.[12] Complete immunity against any class of accusers is not envisaged: the canon notes that bishops must have free consciences and does not bar anyone from charging them with non-ecclesiastical crimes.[13]

Twelve years later, in 393, a Council of Carthage forbade immoral ("culpabiles") plaintiffs to sue or accuse in the episcopal courts except in personal and non-ecclesiastical cases: "si fuerit accusatoris persona culpabilis, ad accusandum uel agendum non admittatur, nisi proprias causas, non tamen si ecclesiasticas, dicere uoluerit."[14] Here "propriae causae" embodies both the civil and the criminal Roman law restrictions on legal capacity; even in trials for non-ecclesiastical crimes immoral accusers are allowed to sue or accuse only for themselves or their families.[15] An imperial rescript of 412 further increased clerical immunity by barring from all future accusations anyone who failed to prove charges against clerics.[16]

Finally, the Council of Carthage of 419 enacted a group of canons that became the backbone of canon law on court procedures.[17] The council introduced the term *infamia* into canon law.[18] Except in personal cases ("in causis propriis"), the council declared in its second session, excommunicates, *infames*, heretics, pagans, Jews, and "all

---

vatam, intendat episcopo, ut detrimento aliquo, vel iniuria aliqua ab ipso affectus, in eiusmodi accusationibus nec accusatoris personam, nec religionem examinari. . . . Si autem sit crimen ecclesiasticum . . . tunc examinari personas accusatorum; ut primum quidem haereticis non liceat orthodoxos episcopos pro rebus ecclesiasticis accusare. . . ."

[12] Ibid. "Accusator," etc., are used throughout.

[13] See n. 11; "propriae querelae" are evidently being opposed to those for "crimen ecclesiasticum."

[14] From the *Breviarium Hipponense*, ao. 397, based on the Council of Carthage of 393, c.7c, in Munier, *Concilia Africae* 35.

[15] Ibid. Despite the phrase "accusatoris persona," civil as well as criminal trials are specified. "Non tamen . . ." apparently restricts "nisi proprias causas."

[16] CT 16.2.41: "intellegat se iacturae famae propriae subiacere, ut . . . discat sibi alienae verecundiae inpune insidiari saltem de cetero non licere."

[17] Council of Carthage, ao. 419, cc. 128–31, in Munier, *Concilia Africae* 230–31. See G. May, "Anklage- und Zeugnisfähigkeit nach der zweiten Sitzung des Konzils zu Karthago vom Jahre 419," *Theologische Quartalschrift* 140 (1960) 163–205; on the council see also F. L. Cross, "History and Fiction in the African Canons," *J. of Theological St.* 12 (1961) 227–47; and C. Munier, "La Tradition littéraire des canons africains (345–525)," *Recherches augustiniennes* 10 (1975) 3–22 with bibliography.

[18] Council of Carthage, ao. 419, c.129b (Munier, *Concilia Africae* 231) = C.4 q.1 c.1 § 1. See G. May, "Die Anfänge der Infamie im kanonischen Recht," *ZRG Kan. Abt.* 47 (1961) 77–94 at 82.

others whom the public criminal laws prohibit from accusing" were forbidden to accuse clerics.[19] The one concession resembles the Roman legal reservation allowing persons normally excluded to accuse in trials for crimes against themselves or their families; but a canon from the first session of this council reproduced the 393 canon on immoral accusers with textual changes that seemingly opposed personal ("propriae") causes to ecclesiastical ones, as had the canon of the Council of Constantinople.[20] The council of 419 further immunized clerics by decreeing that all forbidden to accuse should also be forbidden to testify, a link Roman law never made.[21] Another Carthage canon modified the 412 imperial rescript: a plaintiff unable to prove the first of several charges against a cleric should be denied an attempt to prove the others ("ad cetera iam non admittatur"); the rescript had banned such plaintiffs from all future accusation.[22]

These measures were intended to protect bishops and other clerics from subversive or frivolous criminal charges, though not, of course, from all imputations of guilt. In the next centuries, however, other motives superseded the original ones. The church came to use restriction of legal rights as a means of expressing its claims of clerical superiority. By the early seventh century, the important canonical collection *Vetus Gallica* held that any layman wishing to accuse a cleric must obtain his bishop's permission.[23] In the ninth century, protecting clerics from unworthy accusers was the central issue in the branch of Pseudoisidorian polemics concerned with the conflict be-

---

[19] Council of Carthage, ao. 419, c.128 (Munier, *Concilia Africae* 230) = C.4 q.1 c.1 pr.; c.129a–b (Munier 231; on 129b see above, n. 18); and c.129c (Munier 231) = C.4 q.6 c.2: "sed tamen omnibus, quibus accusatio denegatur, in causis propriis accusandi licentiam non negandam."

[20] Council of Carthage, ao. 419, c.19 (Munier, *Concilia Africae* 107): "si fuerit accusatoris persona culpabilis, ad arguendum non admittatur, nisi proprias causas, non tamen ecclesiasticas, adserere uoluerit." Compare c.7c of the 393 council, quoted in the text at n. 14. For the Constantinople canon see n. 11 and the text there. Of course as these changes are in words whose paleographic abbreviations are susceptible to scribal error, definitive conclusions about the changes and their import should be reserved.

[21] Council of Carthage, ao. 419, c.131 (Munier, *Concilia Africae* 231) = C.4 q.2 and 3 c.1, discussed further in Chapter 5 "Witnesses."

[22] Council of Carthage, ao. 419, c.130 (Munier, *Concilia Africae* 231) = C.3 q.10 c.1; for the rescript see n. 16.

[23] H. Mordek, *Kirchenrecht und Reform im Frankenreich: Die Collectio Vetus Gallica . . . Studien und Edition* (Berlin and New York 1975) 28–29. (For the date, ca. 600, and probable author, Etherius of Lyon, see ibid. 82.) On the future influence of *Vetus Gallica* on this issue see esp. ibid. 155–57.

tween Archbishop Hincmar of Reims and his nephew Hincmar, bishop of Laon.[24] Forged decretals introduced the notion that all excommunicates were *infames*, thus fully integrating the secular penalty into canon law—although the innovation was fully appreciated only in the twelfth century, when the papacy had the authority to invoke a wholly public *infamia*.[25]

Another Pseudoisidorian novelty resulted from the conflation, in several variations, of the Carthage canons barring criminal accusations of clerics by *culpabiles* or by those who had been unable to prove earlier allegations.[26] In the resulting patchwork the word "criminal" was interpolated to produce the principle that such accusers would thenceforth be excluded from criminal or ecclesiastical trials but allowed to sue in the civil courts.[27]

Gratian and the early decretists saw the Roman law on legal capacity through the prism of these earlier texts.[28] Roman criminal law al-

---

[24] Fuhrmann, *Einfluss* passim, esp. I 145 n. 11 and 146–47, on Pseudoisidore. On the importance of the Hincmars' conflict for procedures see ibid. III 625–728 and I 219–24, and L. Fowler-Magerl, *Ordo Iudiciorum vel Ordo iudiciarius. Begriff und Literaturgattung* (Frankfurt am Main 1984) esp. 13–24. I was fortunate in being able to read Dr. Fowler-Magerl's work in typescript; it greatly enhanced my understanding of sources discussed in the present chapter.

[25] C.6 q.1 c.17 and C.2 q.7 c.23 (Hinschius, *Pseudo-Isidorianae* 182 and 196). Many other Pseudoisidorian passages fuse material on *infamia* and excommunication; see esp. Hinschius 164 and cf., e.g., 140, 158, 196, 247, and 563. On Pseudoisidorian *infamia* see also G. May, "Die Bedeutung der pseudoisidorischen Sammlung für die Infamie im kanonischen Recht," *Österreichisches Archiv für Kirchenrecht* 12 (1961) 87–113 and 191–207, and idem, "Anfänge" 89–94. Papal authority to invoke a fully public *infamia* took root in the 1184 Council of Verona (X 5.7.9), when Emperor Frederick I was present to endorse the sanction.

[26] In Gratian, C.3 q.10 c.3 and C.4 q.6 cc.3 and 4; see Friedberg's apparatus for references in Hinschius, *Pseudo-Isidorianae*.

[27] E.g., c.19 of the 419 Council of Carthage (Munier, *Concilia Africae* 107) states that a culpable accuser "ad arguendum non admittatur, nisi proprias causas, non tamen ecclesiasticas, adserere uoluerit." The Pseudoisidorian version (Hinschius, *Pseudo-Isidorianae* 202, c.13) states that such accusers "ad arguendum non admittantur, nisi proprias causas asserere, non tamen criminales uel ecclesiasticas, uoluerint." On the forgers' methods see the illuminating article by J. Richter, "Stufen pseudoisidorischer Verfälschung," *ZRG Kan. Abt.* 64 (1978) 1–72.

[28] E. Jacobi, "Der Prozess im Decretum Gratiani und bei den ältesten Dekretisten," *ZRG Kan. Abt.* 3 (1913) 223–43, remains best on procedural law in the Decretum. On Gratian's treatment of *infamia* see P. Landau, *Die Entstehung des kanonischen Infamiebegriffs von Gratian bis zur Glossa ordinaria* (Cologne 1966) and G. May, "Die Infamie im Decretum Gratiani," *Archiv für katholisches Kirchenrecht* 129 (1959–60) 389–408.

lowed all to accuse in personal cases. Early canon law adopted this principle, using the phrase "in propriis causis" to express the mitigation but sometimes giving it special meaning by opposing personal and ecclesiastical cases. Pseudoisidore transformed "propriae causae" into civil cases, by implication if not in so many words.

Gratian and the other canonists who shaped the Decretum into its final form made the Pseudoisidorian implications explicit with rubrics and interpolations. Excommunicates, *infames*, and all others who were excluded from criminal accusation could nonetheless sue in civil trials.[29] (They might also have been allowed to redress crimes by *denunciatio*, in which a judge acted *ex officio* on the basis of information from an informer, as distinguished from the strictly criminal procedure of *accusatio*.)[30] But the Roman texts on *infamia* were also incorporated into the Decretum, though not by Gratian himself, and analysis soon revealed how far interpretation had strayed from its source.[31]

Gratian's interest in litigation was mainly the moral one of imputing sin in a world in which no one is free from guilt. Rather than establish absolute rules on legal capacity, Gratian preferred to balance the moral worth of all the participants in a trial, judge, litigants, and wit-

[29] In particular see the rubric of C.3 q.10 c.3. Moreover, whereas "ad cetera" in c.130 of the 419 Carthage Council (quoted in the text at n. 22) referred to the "other" charges that an accuser who was unable to prove the first of several charges would be forbidden to try to prove, in C.3 q.10 c.3 "de cetero" refers to any other noncivil litigation (cf. C.4 q.6 c.1). But see Landau, *Entstehung* 113 for a different interpretation.

[30] This might explain Huguccio's emphasis in Appendix 1d lines 7–10 and 15–17. In Gratian's time *denunciatio* was the only civil procedure for trying crimes; *inquisitio* was added later (see Chapter 2 at n. 23). See X 3.12.*unic.*, X 5.34.10, X 5.1.15, and X 5.3.30 on these procedures; and cf. Fournier, *Officialités* 256–62 on technical aspects, and Woodcock, *Canterbury* 30, 49, and 69–82, and F. S. Hockaday, "The Consistory Court of the Diocese of Gloucester," *Transactions of the Bristol and Gloucestershire Archaeological Society* 46 (1924) 195–287 at 198–200, for practice.

[31] The Roman law on praetorian *infamia*, i.e., a pastiche of the praetor's edicts, is at C.3 q.7 c.2. The most important Digest text on criminal accusation is excerpted at C.2 q.1 c.14. On the addition of the Roman law texts to the Decretum, see, most recently, B. Basdevant-Gaudemet, "Les Sources de droit romain en matière de procédure dans le Décret de Gratien," *RDC* 27 (1977) 193–242; and on their modifications of the Decretum's procedural law, see W. Litewski, "Les Textes procéduraux du droit de Justinien dans le Décret de Gratien," *St. Gratiana* 9 (1966) 65–109, esp. 74–77 on these texts.

nesses.[32] Two broad principles did, however, emerge: that a plaintiff must be morally at least equal to the defendant he opposed and that some crimes were so grave that all restrictions on accusation should be waived.[33] The second principle, of excepted crimes, was adopted from Roman criminal law's dispensation for *infames* and other unworthy accusers to submit charges in trials for treason and for fraud connected with the grain supply and, in the late empire, in trials for simony.[34] Gratian also made heresy and sacrilege excepted crimes.[35]

DECRETIST INTERPRETATION

Until the pontificate of Alexander III (1159–81)—that is, for about three decades—the Decretum governed the legal status of excom-

[32] See Jacobi, "Prozess" 248. To my knowledge, the Decretum has not been investigated as a source for the medieval principle of judgment by peers; B. C. Keeney, *Judgment by Peers* (Cambridge, Mass., 1949), did not consider canonical sources.

[33] For the first see esp. C.2 q.7 d. p. c. 25. On these grounds Gratian rejected the Pseudoisidorian principle that prelates should be shielded from all accusation by their lay or clerical inferiors (C.2 q.7 passim, esp. cc.1–9 on laymen), arguing that the rule applied only to criminous or infamed inferiors (ibid. d. a. c.14). But X 5.1.10 and X 2.20.14 forbade laymen to accuse clerics except to prosecute "suam suorumque iniuriam"; even then, laymen could not testify against clerics.

[34] Treason: Dig. 48.4.7–8 (the latter = C.15 q.3 c.3 § 3) and Cod. 9.1.20 (not in Gratian). Fraud in relation to the grain supply: Dig. 48.2.13 = C.2 q.1 c.14 § 2; simony: Cod. 1.3.30 (ao. 469).

[35] Nov. 45 c.1, ao. 537, had gone partway toward making heresy an excepted crime by permitting heretics to accuse and testify against other heretics, whereas they could not accuse or testify against orthodox Christians (Cod. 1.3.30, ao. 469). In the Decretum, fraud concerning the grain supply played a role only in developing the theory of excepted crimes. Treason was important both theoretically (e.g., in C.1 q.7 d. a. c.5, where by ideological analogy to treason heresy was elevated to an excepted crime) and practically, since until the end of the thirteenth century treason trials involving clerics were heard in the church courts (Maitland, *History* II 446; Gabel, *Benefit* 58–59). The Roman law making simony an excepted crime, Cod. 1.3.30, was cited, though not quoted, in C.6 q.1 d. a. c.23. Several papal decretals also dealt with its status as an excepted crime (e.g., X 2.20.45, X 5.3.31), and a decree of the Council of Constance made simony punishable by excommunication *latae sententiae* (*COD* 448). On heresy as an excepted crime, see esp. C.2 q.7 d. p. c.22 and d. a. c.23; as discussed in Chapter 2 at n. 10, heresy was governed by excommunication *latae sententiae* from the late twelfth century on. VI 5.2.5 and 8 made heresy an excepted crime in relation to testimony. Sacrilege was a public crime—one for which anyone capable of accusing could submit accusations—in Roman law (Cod. 1.3.10). Gratian seems to regard "public crime" as equivalent to treason (C.17

municates. The decretists did not find it easy to draw general conclusions from its conflicting texts. In view of Gratian's requirement that litigants be equal, Master Rolandus (no longer identified as the later Alexander III) concluded that excommunicates could accuse other excommunicates.[36] Rolandus's interpretation of the Roman law in the Decretum mirrors the confusion in the text itself. He concluded that apart from the excepted crimes *infames* were excluded from criminal accusation but could "avenge injuries to themselves or their families."[37] This concession, though expressed in the Digest's phrases for criminal law, seems to have meant that *infames* could be plaintiffs only in civil trials.[38]

Rufinus, writing in the 1150s, was the first decretist who understood the Roman texts on this subject. He noted that the Pseudoisidorian canons forbidding calumniators to accuse must be subordinated to the Roman legal rule that *infames* could bring criminal accusations for private injuries.[39] But Rufinus (later successively bishop of Assisi and archbishop of Sorrento) drew the line at accusing bishops.[40]

---

q.4 d. a. c.30) and elevates sacrilege to an excepted crime by means of this analogy, a step for which Gregory I had already prepared the way (C.2 q.1 c.7 § 6–7, citing Cod. 1.3.10). No papal excommunication *latae sententiae* punished sacrilegious property damage, though synodal statutes sometimes imposed automatic excommunication for this crime (Göller, *Pönitentiarie* I.2, p. 51; see also Haines, *Worcester* 187 n. 3).

[36] See *Die Summa Magistri Rolandi*, ed. F. Thaner (Innsbruck 1874; repr. Aalen 1962) C.4 q.1, pp. 19–20. Gratian himself had never drawn this conclusion; he cited the *novella* allowing heretics to accuse and testify against other heretics (C.2 q.7 c.26 and d. p. c.26) but limited its application to the excepted crime of heresy. (Several recent studies have shown that this canonist named Rolandus should not be identified with the future pope: see J. Noonan, "Who Was Rolandus?" in K. Pennington and R. Somerville, eds., *Law, Church and Society. Essays in Honor of Stephan Kuttner* [Philadelphia 1977] 21–48; and R. Weigand, "Magister Rolandus und Papst Alexander III," *Archiv für katholisches Kirchenrecht* 149 [1980] 3–44.) The other famous *summa* of the 1140s, that attributed to Paucapalea, simply stated that excommunicates could not accuse, without attempting to interpret the Roman law texts; see C.4 q.1, p. 68. See C.3 q.4, pp. 64–65 for Paucapalea's failure to clarify the exclusion from accusation.

[37] Rolandus, *Sum.* C.3 q.4 (Qu. VI *ed.*), p. 18.

[38] Ibid.: "repudiandos . . . in civili quoque, nisi suam suorumque exsequantur iniuriam." This resembled the phrase used, e.g., in Dig. 48.2.11.pr.

[39] Rufinus, *Sum.* C.3 q.10 c.3, p. 272, v. *Arguendum*: "i.e., accusandum"; and v. *Non tamen criminales*: "quod in propria et criminali causa accusare non poterit . . . ; ex legibus autem habetur infames accusare posse, cum suas suorumque iniurias persecuntur. . . ."

[40] Rufinus, *Sum.* C.3 q.10 c.3, v. *Non tamen criminales*, p. 272; and C.2 q.1 c.7, v. *Si vero de crimine maiestatis*, p. 239; cf. C.6 q.1 pr., p. 281.

Rufinus also distinguished between persons excommunicated for crime and contumacy and those excommunicated for contumacy alone. Legal rights should be restored to the latter as soon as they had been absolved; but excommunicates guilty of crime, who might be absolved *ad cautelam* upon guaranteeing satisfaction, should be excluded until they had amended their crimes.[41]

Rufinus's policy accommodated the decretists' reservation of judicial excommunication to punish contumacy. But too much tampering to protect the barely guilty might seriously vitiate the sanction. Rufinus's student Stephen of Tournai broadened the distinction to reflect the decretists' uncertainty about excommunication *latae sententiae*: only excommunicates convicted of crime by judicial process should suffer withdrawal of their legal rights until they had given satisfaction.[42] Stephen wrote his *Summa* in Orléans in the 1160s; in the next decades it was an important source for procedural law in the north.[43] Another northern work with ties to Rufinus, the Franco-Rhenish *Summa Coloniensis* (ca. 1169), went even farther, arguing that legal rights should be withdrawn only from excommunicates convicted by judicial process, not from those who incurred excommunication *latae sententiae*.[44] Though only a temporary sidestream of universal canon law, the doctrine left an important alluvium in the procedures of the English royal courts, which refused to consider excommunication *latae sententiae* a bar to lawsuits.

Stephen of Tournai doubted that excommunicates should be al-

---

[41] Rufinus, *Sum.* C.4 q.1, v. *De prima questione*, pp. 273–74. Cf. Landau, *Entstehung* 65–66 and 78–81.

[42] Stephan von Doornick (Stephanus Tornacensis), *Die Summa über das Decretum Gratiani*, ed. J. F. von Schulte (Giessen 1891; repr. Aalen 1965) C.4 q.1, p. 200. Faventinus held the same opinion in his slightly later (ca. 1171) *Summa*, C.4 q.1 d. a. c.1, v. *De prima questione*, Vat., Borgh. 71, fol. 89vb, and Arras 271, fol. 61ra: "Sed queritur cum excommunicatione fuerit absolutus si mox admissibilis sit ad accusationem. Ad quod dicimus referre satis utrum sit excommunicatus pro crimine uel pro alicuius rei faciende contumaci inobedientia. Si enim pro crimine pro quo iam ordine iudiciario dampnatus fuerit excommunicatus post absolutionem non statim accusare poterit nisi in statum pristinum usquequam restitutus. Si autem solummodo pro contumaci inobedientia excommunicatus fuerit continuo post absolutionem poterit accusare."

[43] G. Fransen, "Colligite fragmenta: La Summa Elnonensis," *St. Gratiana* 13 (1967) 85–108 at 97–100; Fowler-Magerl, *Ordo* 26–27 and passim.

[44] *Summa "Elegantius in iure divino" seu Coloniensis,* ed. G. Fransen adlaborante S. Kuttner, *MIC* A-1 (New York 1969 and Vatican City 1978) 6.37, vol. 2, p. 121. Cf. Chapter 6 at n. 101.

lowed to bring charges for the excepted crimes—certainly not when the defendants were people of good reputation.[45] Like Rolandus, he believed that one excommunicate could sue another, though only if the defendant's excommunication had been for a crime more grave than the plaintiff's.[46] In his *Summa* (ca. 1171) Johannes Faventinus passed over this notion and restricted excommunicates' accusations to trials for the excepted crimes; even then, they could bring charges only against defendants already tainted by public suspicion.[47]

Gratian and the decretists, though failing to create a consistent or uniform doctrine, at least agreed that excommunicates' legal rights should not be absolutely withdrawn. The Decretum itself allowed excommunicates to sue in civil trials, and the decretists considered a number of other interpretations of the existing texts. Excommunication was undergoing important changes in the decades after the publication of the Decretum, and caution was appropriate in discussing its legal effects. Moreover, the scientific textual analysis stimulated by the recovery of Roman legal sources encouraged careful scrutiny of texts almost impenetrable in the form they took in Gratian's Decretum.

But perhaps most important, the canonists' interest in excommunicates' legal capacity cannot be separated from a larger trend in both secular and canon law, a concern with legal procedures that focused on the rights of defendants.[48] Tracts on legal defenses proliferated during the last decades of the twelfth century, as Fowler-Magerl has recently shown.[49] Prohibiting lawsuits by excommunicated plaintiffs was part of this elaboration of defendants' rights, a central feature of canon law for about a century after the publication of the Decretum.

---

[45] Stephanus, *Sum.* C.4 q.1 c.1, p. 200.

[46] Ibid.

[47] Johannes Faventinus, *Sum.* C.4 q.1 c.1, v. *Diffinimus*, Vat., Borgh. 71, fol. 89vb, and Arras 271, fol. 61ra: "Sunt tamen casus in quibus excommunicatus accusare potest, ut in crimine lese maiestatis, simonie, hereseos, si eum in aliquo predictorum accusat quando fama publica uexat. Aliter non. Potest secundum quosdam etiam excommunicatus pro minori crimine excommunicatum pro maiori accusare." For the date see Chapter 2 n. 13.

[48] On the secular side, see in particular the paean to the late twelfth-century development of legal exceptions that closes Maitland's *History of English Law*, in vol. 2, pp. 611–22. On France, see Bongert, *Cours* 183–86, 193–94, and 209; and for canon law, see Fournier, *Officialités* 161–69.

[49] Fowler-Magerl, *Ordo* passim.

NEW DECRETALS

Decretist debate received a new focal point with the publication of Alexander III's *Quaesitum* (1171–79).[50] Since "excommunicates are not admitted to court until they have been absolved," *Quaesitum* declared, excommunicates wishing to appeal their sentences should be absolved upon promising to satisfy the court if the sentence was pronounced just.

Although it explicitly treated only appellant excommunicates, *Quaesitum* implied contrarily to the Decretum and to the principles discussed by the early decretists that excommunicates were deprived of all legal remedies.[51] Certainly this was the canonists' interpretation. Writing in the 1180s, Bazianus declared that *Quaesitum* negated even the narrow concessions of Roman law.[52] Much less could the proposals of Gratian and the early decretists stand. Even if one excommunicate did have the right to litigate against another, what judge would be willing to hear the case and risk pollution?[53] In about the same period, the anonymous author of the famous apparatus *Ordinaturus magister*, while offering the first lucid explication of the Roman texts, wrote that *Quaesitum* foreclosed all civil or criminal actions by excommunicates.[54] Not even in cases of the excepted crimes, heresy, simony, and treason, could excommunicates submit charges, the author of *Ordinaturus* wrote, though he acknowledged that some jurists believed that excommunicates could be forced to obtain absolution in order to be fit accusers in such cases.[55] An anonymous Catalan author reviewed earlier decretist debate in arguing, like *Ordinaturus*'s

---

[50] 1 Comp. 1.23.2. *Quaesitum* was left out of the Liber Extra (1234), and its importance was limited to this early period. Its literal statement that excommunicates could not prosecute appeals was overturned by decretals of Innocent III, while the other legal deprivations of excommunication were better articulated by later decretals.

[51] Cf. X 1.29.21 § 2, which, giving judges delegate the authority to grant absolution *ad cautelam* to excommunicated plaintiffs, indirectly confirmed that excommunicates could never sue.

[52] Appendix 1a.

[53] Appendix 1a lines 6–9 and 1d lines 11–15.

[54] Appendix 1b. The author's expertise and clarity are evident, for example, in his careful distinction between civil ("conuenire") and criminal ("accussare") actions, used in lines 7–10 to show that the concession to prosecute "suas uel suorum iniurias" was from Roman criminal law.

[55] Appendix 1b lines 16–23.

author, for a complete bar on lawsuits.[56] Plaintiffs had to swear an oath against calumny, but allowing excommunicates to swear on sacred objects was like throwing pearls before swine.

By this time the struggle against heresy was undoubtedly exerting an influence on canonical doctrines: the Catalan author rhetorically proclaimed that all excommunicates were heretics.[57] Huguccio, probably reacting to the pressures of the heresy crisis, brought the rigor against excommunicates' legal rights to its utmost. Heretics who followed a sect that had already been condemned and so were automatically excommunicated could not sue or accuse even to prosecute private injuries or the excepted crimes, although others normally forbidden to accuse, pagans and Jews, still enjoyed these concessions.[58] Huguccio even made the unprecedented proposal that excommunicates who had remained contumacious for a year or more—and perhaps, indeed, all excommunicates—be permanently excluded from judicial accusation and testimony.[59] Although he defended this novel principle with arguments based on the decretists' doctrine that excommunication be imposed only for contumacy—which, he observed, was punishable by death in the Old Testament[60]—Huguccio

---

[56] Appendix 1c, esp. lines 5–11 and 21–25 for the conclusion.

[57] Ibid. lines 2–3.

[58] Hug., *Sum.* C.2 q.7 c.25, v. *Accusare*, Admont 7, fol. 167vb, and Vat. 2280, fol. 124ra: "Nisi suam uel suorum iniuriam prosequantur. Tunc enim credo eos esse admittendos, scilicet paganos et Iudeos. Sed heretici in nulla causa si uelint agere debent audiri si heresim dampnatam secuntur, et iam omnes tales sunt excommunicati. Ergo nullum possunt uocare in causam, et in nulla causa possunt agere contra aliquem ciuiliter uel criminaliter. Nec etiam in propria iniuria uel criminibus exceptis." In stating that only heretics who follow a sect already condemned are automatically excommunicated, Huguccio is expressing the doctrine of Gratian rather than the newer doctrine proclaimed at the 1184 Council of Verona (X 5.7.9). See Chapter 2 at n. 12.

[59] Appendix 1e. Cf. C.3 q.4 c.2, v. *Ante reversionem*, Admont 7, fol. 177va–vb, and Vat. 2280, fol. 130vb: "Videtur quod post reuersionem sit recipiendus ad accusationem uel testimonium. Sed vi. q. i. Qui crimen [6] contra, ubi dicitur qui crimen intendit inquirendum est an antea fuerit criminosus. Sed dicunt subintelligendum est, et non penituerit. Sed dico generaliter quod nullus apostata ante uel post reuersionem est admittendus ad accusationem uel testimonium. Similiter nullus excommunicatus iuste"; and C.6 q.1 c.4, v. *Suscipiendi*, Admont 7, fol. 194ra, and Vat. 2280, fol. 145rb: "Ad communionem sacramentorum. . . . Vel si dicatur "suscipiendi" ad accusationem uel testimonium, et est argutum quod excommunicati post satisfactionem ecclesie possunt admitti ad testimonium et ad accusationem. Quod credo non uerum esse. Sed subintelligitur hic maxime, hoc tamen optime. Inuenies distinctum supra, iiii. q. i [Appendix 1e]."

[60] Appendix 1e lines 17–23.

was probably treating excommunicates as if they were in the same category as heretics. His proposal that excommunicates be permanently barred from accusation and testimony foreshadowed the irrevocable *infamia* that Innocent III was soon to inflict on all who aided or defended heretics.[61] Perhaps there was also an element of sheer idiosyncrasy, however; for Huguccio even suggested that minor excommunicates too should be deprived of their legal rights. The concessions that the other decretists extended to major excommunicates (i.e., accusation in personal cases or for the excepted crimes) were in Huguccio's view to be granted to minor excommunicates.[62]

In any event, the dangers of merging heretics and other excommunicates soon called forth a series of papal decretals that precisely defined excommunicates' legal status. Lucius III's *Intelleximus* affirmed that excommunicates could be present in court only as defendants; other decretals of Innocent III and Honorius III forbade excommunicates to prosecute crimes in the civil procedures of *denunciatio* or the more recently introduced *inquisitio*, thus abolishing the Decretum's implied concessions.[63] Rolandus's suggestion that one excommunicate be allowed to litigate against another was repressed by a decretal of Honorius III.[64] But a decretal of Innocent III checked Huguccio's

---

[61] X 5.7.9 and 11.

[62] Appendix 1d lines 52–57. In using "anathematizatus" for "major excommunicate" and "excommunicatus" for "minor excommunicate," Huguccio is adopting Gratian's usage in C.11 q.3 d. p. c.24, discussed in Chapter 2 nn. 4–9.

[63] *Intelleximus*, X 2.1.7, will be discussed further in Chapter 5 at n. 2. It is usually ascribed to Alexander III, but the reference to the murder of Bishop John of Vicenza (1184) dates it to Lucius III's pontificate. See P. F. Kehr, *Italia pontificia* (Berlin 1906; repr. 1961–65) VII.1, p. 164, no. 34 (information from file among papers of W. Holtzmann at the Institute of Medieval Canon Law, School of Law, University of California, Berkeley, no. 580. I am indebted to Professor Charles Duggan for this information). X 5.1.20 denied excommunicates the right to submit criminal charges by *denunciatio*. It was rarely cited; for an instance, see Appendix 2f, lines 56–57, equating the canonical *denunciatio* with the Roman *popularis actio*, in which *infames* could not be actors (Dig. 47.23.4; cf. Greenidge, *Infamia* 159). X 2.1.19 likewise prohibited excommunicates from bringing criminal charges through *inquisitio*. It, too, was rarely cited; for examples, see Appendix 2f, line 56, and Jo. An., *Nov.* X 2.25.8, v. *Opponunt*.

[64] X 2.25.8. The canonists rightly found the decretal impossible to understand literally. It prevents proctors representing their churches (whether as actors or defendants) from being removed because they are excommunicates or otherwise unfit. But the decretal was also applied to a more urgent need. In X 2.25.2 (see n. 65) Innocent III implicitly (and probably inadvertently) raised the possibility that an excommunicated plaintiff could successfully block attempts to remove him by proving that

excesses, proclaiming that minor excommunication had no legal consequences. Other papal legislation made it clear that the legal deprivations of major excommunication ceased with absolution.[65]

By the early thirteenth century, then, canon law prescribed an absolute ban on criminal or civil actions by excommunicates. Only one small mitigation was considered: Laurentius Hispanus's *Glossa Palatina* (ca. 1210) suggested that an excommunicated husband deserted by his wife of many years should be allowed to sue for restitution of matrimonial rights.[66] Though the ecclesiastical courts' concern with marriage might have seemed to justify this waiver, Johannes Teutonicus did not adopt it when he revised the *Palatina* for his *Glossa ordinaria* (ca. 1217) on the Decretum.[67] In such a case the judge should order restitution *ex officio*, Johannes believed.[68]

The long trend of reducing excommunicates' legal rights reached its extreme in the pontificate of Gregory IX. Gratian's Decretum had not described the means for removing excommunicates from the

---

his adversary, the defendant, was a major excommunicate; for judgment turned on the fact that the defendant was only a minor excommunicate. Thus X 2.25.8 was interpreted in its broadest sense to mean that an excommunicated plaintiff could not avert the exception against himself (and so proceed with his litigation) by showing that his adversary was also excommunicated. See, e.g., Goff. Tr., *Sum.* 2.25, no. 7, fol. 114vb: "Sed queritur an exceptio excommunicationis tollatur per replicationem excommunicationis si de maiori excipiatur et replicetur. Et licet olim diceretur quod sic, per decreta. i. eodem A nobis [X 2.25.2] sumpto argumen. a contrario sensu. Hodie tamen dicendum quod no. per aliam i. eodem titu. Dilecti [X 2.25.8]."

[65] X 2.25.2 (see also n. 64) for the rule that minor excommunication had no legal effects. The many decretals already mentioned in the text affirmed that the legal disabilities ended with absolution; see also X 2.25.12, discussed below at n. 73.

[66] Laurentius Hispanus, *Glossa Palatina* C.4 q.6 c.2, v. *Omnibus*, Vat. MSS Pal. 658, fol. 38va, and Reg. 977, fol. 111vb: "Nisi excommunicatis, qui non habent personas idoneas standi in iudicio. Qui nec etiam in propriis causis audiuntur, ut supra eodem q. i. c. i. et ii. Et nisi in matrimonio quando quis cum uxore diu mansit. Et si qua inuenies similia, dic esse speciale in ciuili etiam qui prohibetur a procuratore suorum causas non tractabit, C. de procur. Militem [Cod. 2.12.7]. In criminali qualiter suorum causas possit agere, distingue per l. supra iii. q. vii. Alii [c.2 § 2 *infra*]." On the *Palatina* see A. M. Stickler, "Il Decretista Laurentius Hispanus," *St. Gratiana* 9 (1966) 461–550; and S. Kuttner, "Johannes Teutonicus," *Neue deutsche Biographie* 10 (1974) 571a–573a at 571b.

[67] On the *Palatina* as prototype for the *Ordinaria*, see Kuttner, ibid.

[68] *Glos. ord.* C.11 q.3 c.103, v. *Uxores*: "Sed si petat uir mulierem in iudicio et ipsa obiicit ei excommunicationem, iudex tenetur ex suo officio restituere ei mulierem, cum in hoc casu possit ei communicare"; also adopted by Host., *Sum.* 2.15(*De rest. spol.*).2, col. 549b; Dur., *Spec.* 2.1.17(*De pet. et pos. et spol.*) § "Quoniam in superioribus," vol. 2, fol. 156ra, no. 3; and Jo. An., *Nov.* X 5.39.31, v. *Solute.*

courts. Perhaps the clumsy machinery of counteraccusation—by which a defendant could accuse his adversary of crimes more serious than those alleged against himself—was used for this purpose, as might be inferred from several decretists' proposals that one excommunicate be allowed to sue another.[69] But the legal *exceptio*, just coming into its own in this era of defendants' rights, soon became the means for excluding excommunicated plaintiffs.[70] Exceptions enabled defendants to elude lawsuits on grounds that might be irrelevant to the substantive issues by proving lack of legal capacity, as in the case of excommunicates, or some other bar.

The exception of excommunication was only dilatory; without destroying the grounds for legal action as peremptory exceptions did, it postponed a lawsuit until the plaintiff obtained absolution.[71] Because they were tantamount to substantive defenses, peremptory exceptions could be introduced during a trial itself, whereas dilatory exceptions had to be submitted and adjudicated before a trial began.[72] Gregory IX's *Exceptionem* gave the exception of excommunication the best of both worlds.[73] Since, as the decretal observed, "no one should be forced to endanger his soul through contact with an excommunicate," the exception of excommunication could be submitted at any time during a trial. Moreover, if the defendant did not submit the exception, the judge was obliged to remove a publicly ex-

---

[69] On counteraccusation see esp. C.3 q.11, esp. d. p. c.3, and C.6 q.2; cf. Jacobi, "Prozess" 288–93, and Fournier, *Officialités* 246. The Decretum had little material on exceptions; see C.3 q.6 d. p. c.2, C.2 q.2, and C.3 q.1; cf. Jacobi, "Prozess" 261–62, and Fournier, *Officialités* 162–67. Stephen of Tournai's proposal that one excommunicate could sue another if the alleged crimes of the defendant were graver than those for which the plaintiff was excommunicated is especially suggestive of counteraccusation.

[70] Among the decretists, the earliest mention of exceptions might be that of Paucapalea, who noted that persons incapable of submitting real accusations could nonetheless "accuse by exceptions" (*Sum.* C.3 q.11 c.1, p. 67). The implication that a defendant could thus remove his accuser was explicit in Rufinus, *Sum.* C.3 q.11, p. 273; see also the *Summa "Elegantius" (Coloniensis)*, ed. Fransen, 6.37, vol. 2, p. 121. Huguccio was one of the first canonists to use the terminology of exceptions in describing procedures for removing excommunicates (see Appendix 1d lines 62–63). Renewed study of Roman law was probably the impetus for adapting the procedures of legal exceptions for this purpose; until it was abolished by Justinian, an exception had been the means for removing *infames* from the courts (Inst. 4.13.11).

[71] On the forms of exceptions see Fournier, *Officialités* 161–66.

[72] C.3 q.6 d. p. c.2.

communicated plaintiff *ex officio*. If defendants deliberately delayed submitting their exceptions in order to harass their opponents by forcing them to waste time and money on cases that would be terminated once the exceptions were proved, they were assessed the expenses incurred by their exceptions. This was *Exceptionem*'s sole, slight safeguard against chicanery. It might well have been a small price to pay for the psychological advantage of wearing down an adversary.

Exceptionem was taken up in the Liber Extra of 1234 and so became common law. Another severe decretal of Gregory IX on excommunicates' legal rights obtained this status only at the end of the century, a delay that led to curious results: *Ipso iure* declared that papal rescripts obtained by excommunicates for legal processes under judges delegate and all transactions based on such rescripts were automatically invalid.[74] *Ipso iure* remained an *extravagans*, circulating in some unofficial canonical collections with decretals of Innocent IV and other popes, until it was officially promulgated in the Liber Sextus of 1298.[75] Most canonists knew of it, if only in a vague way, and occasionally sprang it from its obscurity to challenge reforms introduced by Innocent IV in mid-century.[76]

---

[73] *Exceptionem*: X 2.25.12 (undated).

[74] *Ipso iure*: VI 1.3.1. That rescripts impetrated by excommunicates were null was certainly implied by *Exceptionem* with its nullification of everything transacted by an excommunicated plaintiff once the exception was brought. But in *Prudentiam* (X 1.29.21) Celestine III directed judges delegate to absolve an excommunicated plaintiff so that he could sue, the implication being that his original rescript was still valid. Vincentius Hispanus concluded that the plaintiff must have been excommunicated after beginning litigation; otherwise anything accomplished would be null: *App.* 3 Comp. 1.2.2 (X 5.39.41), v. *Non propter hoc*, Vat. 1378, fol. 2ra: "Hic habes quod ⟨si?⟩ mittantur littere excommunicato non ualent. Ita de ⟨cler.⟩ excom., Postulastis [X 5.27.7], S. de etate et qua. Bone, l. ii [X 1.14.8]. Contra, S. de officio dele. Prudenciam, l. ii [X 1.29.21]. Sed excommunicatio ibi subsecuta est impetrationem litterarum. . . ." And, by the same author, *App.* X 1.3.26, v. *Carere*, Vat. MSS Vat. 6769, fol. 10ra, and Barb. 1626, fol. 39r: "Et dico quod retractanda est sententia per in integrum restitutionem. Vel si uis dicere quod ⟨per?⟩ litteras illas nulla fuit data iurisdictio, tunc non est necessaria restitutio, quia ipso iure nulla est sententia."

[75] See Kessler, "Untersuchungen" part 1, 283–84 and 284 n. 366, on *Ipso iure* in *extravagantes* collections.

[76] See below at n. 106. Duranti referred to *Ipso iure* once as a decretal of Innocent IV (*Spec.* 2.1 [*De rescr. pres.*] § "Ratione ne forma," vol. 2, fol. 46ra, no. 36) and once as a decretal of Gregory IX (ibid. § "Ratione autem," fol. 48vb, no. 14d). Cf. Jo. An., *Comm.* VI 1.3.1 pr.

INNOCENT IV AND *PIA*

In Pope Innocent IV's glosses one has a rare opportunity to study a legislator's comments on his own laws. Though preoccupied by constant conflict with Frederick II, the pope continued work on his *Apparatus* until his death in 1254, updating his glosses on decretals in the Liber Extra to reflect changes wrought by his own *novellae* and incorporating commentaries on those *novellae* into his *Apparatus*.[77] According to Hostiensis, Innocent IV often said that his academic glosses were not to be taken as law.[78] Naturally not—but Innocent's prestige as a legal scholar ensured that they would be very influential. Since as pope he could try to enact some of his doctrines into law, his glosses are especially interesting for historians.

Innocent IV is a mysterious personality. His skillful diplomacy and ruthless centralization of ecclesiastical power seem like the work of an archconservative papal monarch.[79] But his private writings and his legislation reveal a quite different figure. In glosses he wrote before becoming pope in 1243, Innocent IV recorded his disapproval of how far legal procedures had been tailored to favor defendants against excommunicated plaintiffs.[80] At the very least, he wrote regarding *Exceptionem*, a defendant should be allowed to overrule a judge's *ex officio* expulsion of his opponent.[81] Only defendants who believed they

---

[77] See S. Kuttner, "Die Konstitutionen des ersten allgemeinen Konzils von Lyon," *St. et documenta historiae et iuris* 1 (1940) 70–131 at 114, noting that Innocent IV worked on the *Apparatus* throughout his pontificate. On Innocent's work see also Kuttner, "Decretalistica," *ZRG Kan. Abt.* 26 (1937) 436–70, esp. 462–63; Kessler, "Untersuchungen," esp. part 2, 354–69; and most recently M. Bertram, "Angebliche Originale des Dekretalenapparats Innocenz' IV," *MIC* C-7 (Vatican City 1985) 41–47. On Innocent IV's doctrines see esp. C. Lefebvre, "Sinibalde dei Fieschi," *DDC* 7.1029–62.

[78] Host., *App.*, *Solet* (VI 5.11.2), v. *Non negetur*: "Nonne dominus noster hanc constitutionem fecit, et nonne exprimit hic intentionem suam? Quid ergo ultra quaeris? Resp., non exprimit tanquam papa sed tanquam magister. Et saepe ab eo audivimus quod non intendebat quod ius facerent glossae suae."

[79] For references see my article "Innocent IV," forthcoming in J. Strayer, ed., *Dictionary of the Middle Ages*.

[80] Any Innocentian gloss that does not account for changes wrought by Innocent IV's own legislation will be called "early." As will be clear, these glosses stand side by side with "later" glosses that either refer to *novellae* or reflect their innovations or both.

[81] Inn. IV, *App.* X 2.25.12, v. *Repellendus*, p. 356 no. 3. For at least a partial example see the case between Alicia Clement and Hamo de Bidun discussed below.

could make a strong case would wish to overrule such an order; but why, Innocent exclaimed, should excommunicated plaintiffs benefit from a law intended to punish them? Moreover, judges should have discretionary power to overrule an exception of excommunication (presumably in cases in which evidence favored the defendant), and canon law should not punish a defendant who obeyed a judicial order to litigate with an excommunicate.[82] Still more forcefully, Innocent IV rehearsed the suggestion made by some canonists that *Exceptionem* be disregarded in the case of secret excommunicates, so that whatever they had managed to transact before the revelation of their status removed them from court would stand as valid.[83] Innocent remarked impersonally that this was perhaps not a bad proposal; his own legislation soon showed his strong agreement.

But more than Innocent IV's private opinions pointed toward change. In England, because the exception of excommunication had been abused to block the writs of prohibition that enforced the royal courts' authority in jurisdictional disputes, those courts were already by the 1220s allowing plaintiffs to replicate (respond in defense) that they had been excommunicated for obtaining writs of prohibition impeding their ecclesiastical court trials.[84] By mid-century, such abuses probably jeopardized even legitimate exceptions of excommunication in the English royal courts. Still more serious was the contempt for excommunication expressed by anticlerical heretical sects like the Stedingers in Germany.[85]

---

[82] Inn. IV, *App.* X 2.25.12, v. *Prohibetur*, no. 2, p. 356. Appendix 5 case 18 probably contains an example: the defendant in a writ of prohibition suit submitted an exception of excommunication but agreed to carry on if the judge so directed. He must have, since the trial was not interrupted even though no replication is mentioned. The defendant won, and the plaintiff was fined. (Flahiff proposed a different explanation, namely, that the plaintiff submitted proof of absolution ["Writ" part 2, 265 n. 5], though this was not recorded.)

[83] Inn. IV, *App.* X 2.25.12, v. *Prohibetur*, no. 1: "Imo plus dicant quidem, et forte non male, quia omnia quae fiunt cum excommunicato occulte siue in iudicio siue extra non retractantur etiam ante sententiam." This sentence must antedate *Pia*, which declared that excommunicated plaintiffs' transactions were no longer invalid. But other glosses even on this very lemma do refer to *Pia*.

[84] See the discussion of English cases in Chapter 7 at n. 114 for details.

[85] See Maisonneuve, *Etudes* 264, on contempt for ecclesiastical censures among the Stedingers, who were crushed by Gregory IX in the 1230s. Cf. E. Berger, *Saint Louis et Innocent IV*, in *Les Registres d'Innocent IV* (Paris 1884–1920) I.2, pp. xlvi–xlvii, noting that in 1243 Innocent stopped the use of interdicts against heretics in the Midi, saying the censures merely increased the heretics' disdain for church authority.

In Brittany, by the mid-1220s Count Pierre de Dreux's extortionate fiscal policies had expanded into a notorious anticlerical campaign.[86] Pierre's papal excommunications in 1217 and 1219 had been provisionally relaxed when he joined Prince Louis's crusade against the Albigensians in 1219; in 1221 Pierre agreed to compensate the church of Nantes, the chief object of his plunders.[87] But he soon rebounded with fresh hostilities that culminated in a conspiracy with his Breton vassals in 1225 at the monastery of Redon.[88] Full legal rights for excommunicates were a central plank in the count's program; presumably it was a practical measure—intended to vitiate ecclesiastical retaliation—as well as an ideological one.[89] With widespread support from clerics as well as from laymen, the count's campaign throve for several decades. Though Gregory IX threatened in 1228 to release Pierre's vassals from their oaths of fidelity, the count did not respond until 1230, when his traitorous alliance with King Henry III provoked a royal invasion, against which he needed his vassals' support.[90] In 1234 the papal censure was once again allowed to abate so that Pierre could participate in an upcoming crusade, but the respite was brief.

[86] For details of Pierre's career see Painter, *Peter* passim; B.-A. Pocquet du Haut-Jussé, *Les Papes et les ducs de Bretagne* (Paris 1928) I 45–129; and Morel, *Pouvoir* 103–4. For consistency I have referred to Pierre and his son, Jean le Roux, as "count." As Professor Joseph Strayer has kindly informed me, the title "duke" for the lord of Brittany was not fixed until the end of the thirteenth century. St. Louis and popes Honorius III, Gregory IX, and Innocent IV in the various documents discussed here always refer to Pierre as "count." In 1247 Innocent also referred to Jean as "count," but in 1252 the Official of Paris and in 1256 Alexander IV call him "duke." (For the 1252 document see H. Morice, *Mémoires pour servir de preuves à l'histoire ecclésiastique et civile de Bretagne* [Paris 1742–47] I 951; for the others see Lobineau, *Bretagne* II 374–402 passim.)

[87] For details see Painter, *Peter* 24–25 and Pocquet du Haut-Jussé, *Papes* I 62–71. The papal documents are in Lobineau, *Bretagne* II 374–77.

[88] See J. B. A. T. Teulet, *Layettes du trésor des chartes* (Paris 1863–66) II, no. 1734, for the document in which the conferees asked for royal help in ameliorating the alleged abuses by the clergy so that the conspiracy could be avoided. For details of the conspiracy see Painter, *Peter* 48–49, and Pocquet du Haut-Jussé, *Papes* I 79–80.

[89] See the 1228 letter of Gregory IX in Lobineau, *Bretagne* II 379–81, which charged that the count not only associated with excommunicates himself but forced others to do so by refusing to accept the exception of excommunication in his court, and which threatened to absolve his vassals from their oaths after four months. On the conspirators' program see also Painter, *Peter* 48–49.

[90] See preceding note, and on the events of 1230 see Painter, *Peter* 73 and 97–99. Details of Pierre's 1230 absolution are contained in a 1230 letter of Gregory IX that is incorporated in a 1239 letter of the same pope (Lobineau, *Bretagne* II 381–82).

When Pierre's son Count Jean le Roux came of age, in 1237, he carried on his father's anticlerical activities.[91]

Innocent IV, conscious of problems in the canonical policy depriving excommunicates of their legal rights, was familiar with the situation in Brittany. In May of 1245, one month before the first Council of Lyon, he wrote instructing the Breton bishops to see that excommunicates were excluded from all judicial acts as plaintiffs or witnesses and from all other legal or public offices.[92] Yet only a year before, in May of 1244, Innocent had dramatically changed the canon law on excommunicates' rights. *Pia*, circulated first in a small group of Innocentian *novellae* that were formally repromulgated with other constitutions at the council, declared that the exception of excommunication would no longer retroactively invalidate legal transactions.[93] Though proceedings would continue to be halted by the exception and judges would still be obliged to expel public excommunicates not challenged by the exception, anything excommunicates had already accomplished in court before the exception was submitted would stand. Moreover, defendants would be given only eight days (rather than the usual fifteen) to prove an exception of excommunication, would be required to do so by "very lucid proofs," and would have to pay expenses for the delay if they failed. A second try would be given to defendants if they believed they could prove their opponents bound by an excommunication different from the one originally alleged or if they fell upon "evident and prompt" proofs of the sentence first alleged.

Clearly Innocent IV did not wish to abolish the exception of excommunication; his instructions to the Breton bishops in 1245 show

[91] Painter, *Peter* 98–99 on the crusade of 1234. Pierre became count only through marriage and so lost the title when his son came of age.

[92] Lobineau, *Bretagne* II 393–94: "excommunicati vitentur, et in judiciis ab agendo, testificando, et aliis actibus legitimis, necnon publicis officiis, quamdiu in excommunicatione permanserint, repellantur. . . ."

[93] *Pia* (VI 2.12.1). *Pia* itself can be dated before 31 May 1244 because of a reference to the vice-chancellor Jacopo Buoncambio, who died then, as having been present when it was drafted (below, n. 112). The group of eight constitutions originally issued before the council and repromulgated at it includes two others important for excommunication, *Solet* (VI 5.11.2; see below, Chapter 6 at n. 35) and *Cum medicinalis* (VI 5.11.1; see Chapter 6 at n. 48). All eight can be dated before April 1245, since Goffredus de Trano, who died then, wrote an apparatus on them. See Kuttner, "Konstitutionen" 79–80 and 105–6, and Kessler, "Untersuchungen" part 1, 214–35, 307–8, and 312.

that in principle he endorsed its use. But as the pope stated in what one canonist rightly called a good *arenga*, what had been created as a remedy to obviate the dangers of communication with excommunicates and to elicit respect from the faithful had now through chicanery become a vice.[94] The elaboration of defense strategies begun in the last decades of the twelfth century had now choked the courts with protracted litigation.[95] The trend favoring defendants was beginning to be reversed, and with it those patterns of litigation "in detestation of excommunicates" developed by canonists of the late twelfth century.[96]

REACTION TO *PIA*

An anonymous gloss—interpolated, ironically, into Innocent IV's own *Apparatus!*—wondered in alarm whether the pope intended to destroy all laws with one word.[97] In his celebrated *Distinctiones*, written soon after the publication in April 1246 of Innocent IV's second collection of *Novellae*, Peter Sampson wrote that *Pia*'s concessions should be applied only to extrajudicial legal transactions.[98] In court, excommunicates were still prohibited from suing, and their transactions were invalid.

But other canonists saw the merits of *Pia* at once. Excommunicates might well be suing to obtain what was rightly theirs. Moreover, according to the papal chaplain Goffredus de Trano, even if a defendant successfully excluded his adversary by an exception of excommunication, he did not thereby free himself entirely from obligation, but only from the court's observation.[99] This was the sort of cool reason-

---

[94] Abb. Ant., *Lect.*, *Pia* (VI 2.12.1), v. *Pia*, Vat., Borgh. 231, fol. 141va: "Hec decretalis bonam habet arengam siue prefationem."

[95] Another Lyon constitution (VI 2.5.1) restricted use of the *exceptio spolii* for the same reason.

[96] For the phrase see, e.g., Appendix 1b lines 15–16.

[97] Appendix 2c, lines 23–26. The addition is in the six manuscripts of Innocent's *Apparatus* I have checked: Vat. MSS Ross. 596 (fol. 138va), 597 (135va); Vat. 1439 (120vb), 1440 (148rb), 1441 (160ra), 1442 (135va).

[98] Appendix 2d esp. lines 1–24.

[99] Appendix 2a lines 14–16; cf. Bernard of Compostella in Appendix 2b, lines 43–46.

ing Innocent IV encouraged, and embellishing Goffredus's gloss in his own commentary on *Pia* the pope pointed out that by settling disputes judicial sentences benefited even the losing party.[100] More pragmatically, Innocent IV noted that it behooved the courts to uphold their own transactions—no idle observation, since clerical grievances often charged the secular courts with ignoring the *res iudicatae* of the church courts.[101] By the time he wrote a set of lectures on the Liber Extra in the 1250s, Peter Sampson acknowledged the changes *Pia* wrought.[102] Gregory IX's *Exceptionem* was now applicable only to an exception submitted against an excommunicated judge; for a defendant who delayed submitting the exception against his opponent was no longer forcing him to "labour in vain" and should not be penalized by expenses.[103] Sampson did, however, preserve a trace of the old vigor of the exception, arguing that defendants could appeal if judges rejected their exceptions.[104] His argument contradicted Innocent IV's dictum that judges should have discretionary powers to overrule ex-

---

[100] Appendix 2c lines 14–17.

[101] Appendix 2c line 15. See, e.g., the text excised from the decretal *Quia nonnulli* (VI 3.23.1) in Friedberg's appendix.

[102] Appendix 2e. On Sampson's lectures on the Liber Extra see also Appendix 6.

[103] Appendix 2e lines 4–20, with the caveat that defendants should still be charged expenses (as decreed by *Exceptionem*) if they deliberately delayed until the end of the period assigned for dilatory exceptions. Since the plaintiff would have endured the delay of the pretrial procedures, this was clearly harassment without the compensation of some substantive accomplishment. Rules governing the civil court at Reims (1481, revised 1507) required plaintiffs to pay all expenses if exceptions of excommunication were submitted against them before trial was joined and expenses entailed by the exceptions themselves if they were submitted after trial was joined (Varin, *Arch. lég.* I 816, no. [vii]). In a 1385 case in the ecclesiastical court at Paris, the plaintiff paid expenses when the defendant proved he was excommunicated before trial was joined. The defendant claimed this payment had been promised beforehand and insisted it be made at once (Petit, *Registre* 204).

[104] Pet. Samp., *Lect.* X 2.25.12, v. *Officio*, Vienna 2083, fol. 27vb, and Vienna 2113, fol. 48rb: "Sed quid si iudex non repellebat actorem ex officio suo—nunquid poterit appellari? Dico quod non, quia licet iudex malefaciat tamen non ualebit huius appellatio. Tunc enim ualet appellatio cum propter exceptionem non admissam extiterit[?] appellatio, infra de appe. Dilecto [X 2.28.63]. Unde ad hoc quod posset appellari necesse esset exceptionem huius proponere, qua non admissa posset appellari." The emendation "extiterit" is from *Dilecto*. MS 2083 has a corrupt version of *Dilecto*'s "constiterit," MS 2113 a corrupt version of its "exstiterit." On the latter manuscript see also Appendix 6.

ceptions of excommunication; nonetheless several canonists concurred with Sampson, among them Duranti.[105]

Pia's full implications were felt only gradually. In the earliest known gloss, Goffredus de Trano noted that it was odd to validate transactions accomplished by an excommunicate in court and yet to prohibit excommunicates from obtaining rescripts to initiate litigation.[106] Writing soon after the decretal's conciliar promulgation in August 1245, the papal judge Bernard of Compostella found *Pia*'s concessions "astonishing" in view of the old rule that excommunicates could not impetrate rescripts.[107] But a few years later (1253–54) in the second recension of his *Apparatus*, which became an unofficial *Glossa ordinaria* on Innocent IV's *Novellae*, Bernard's astonishment had given way to enthusiasm.[108] It no longer mattered if plaintiffs had been excommunicated before procuring their rescripts, Bernard now maintained, provided they had since obtained absolution: "Thus a rescript impetrated by an excommunicate is not *ipso iure* null, and anything

---

[105] Innocent IV's opinion was discussed above at n. 82. For support of Sampson's views see, e.g., the anonymous lecturer, very dependent on Sampson, recorded in Vat., Borgh. 228, X 2.25.12, fol. 107rb: "Pone quod iudex actorem excommunicatum publice non repellat ex officio suo—nunquid reus poterit appellare a iudice? Dic quod non, ex quo nihil obiicit. Quia tunc potest appellari a iudice cum grauat uel exceptionem non admisit, i. de ap. Dilecto [X 2.28.63] et c. Cum cessante [X 2.28.60]." (On these lectures see also Appendix 6 n. 6.) Cf. Dur., *Spec.* 1.1(*De off. om. iudi.*) § "Impedit quoque," vol. 1, fol. 109rb. The 1269 case of Gaufridus de Plessaico, discussed in Chapter 7 at n. 40, offers an example of a defendant appealing because his exception of excommunication was overruled by the judge, but as the case was in a secular court, and indeed that of the count of Brittany, one cannot infer anything about normal practice. Nonetheless, it might have been the special difficulties in France that prompted Sampson and Duranti, who were French, to take this view.

[106] Appendix 2a lines 1–3. For the date of Goffredus's *Apparatus* see above, n. 93; cf. Kessler, "Untersuchungen" part 2, 307, 315 n. 21, and 357 n. 113. In his *Apparatus* on the Liber Extra a few years earlier (ca. 1241), Goffredus wrote that excommunicates could impetrate rescripts if they mentioned their excommunication (cf. X 1.3.26) or if they were appealing a judgment as defendants (*Sum.* 2.25, no. 6, fol. 114vb).

[107] Appendix 2b lines 1–2 and 7–9. This gloss was probably written before 1246: although Bernard published the first recension of his *Apparatus* only after the promulgation of Innocent IV's second collection of *Novellae* in April 1246 (Kuttner, "Decretalistica" 455), the version of the *Apparatus* in Vat. 1365 shows that the glosses for *Collectio 1* were already written when *Collectio 2* was published (Kessler, "Untersuchungen" part 2, 329–30).

[108] See Kessler, "Untersuchungen" part 2, 344–46 for the dates.

you find to the contrary should be modified by what is said here"—in *Pia*.[109] But his pointed allusion to Gregory IX's *Ipso iure*, which stated that excommunicates' rescripts were null, was unnoticed even by some of Bernard's more distinguished contemporaries. Marinus of Eboli included in a tract he composed as papal vice-chancellor (1244–52) a model for exceptions against plaintiffs on the grounds that they were already excommunicated when obtaining their rescripts.[110] Even at the highest court, evidently, confusion still reigned on this subject. A few years later, in the 1260s, Egidius de Fuscarariis wrote that such exceptions were no longer valid.[111] Not only was Egidius's *Ordo* one of the most important legal manuals of its time, but at least some of his information on the interpretation of *Pia* came straight from the vice-chancellor in office when *Pia* was first issued.[112]

Only one prominent canonist, Hostiensis, felt no compulsion to change his views in light of *Pia*. On the specific issue of rescripts impetrated by excommunicates, he observed that judges need not hesitate to invalidate them under *Ipso iure*; for even though it was only an *extravagans*, the decretal conformed to common law (*ius commune*).[113] This rather disingenuous observation was only one part of Hostiensis's attack on *Pia*. In his *Summa* and his *Apparatus* on Innocent's *Novellae*, both written during Innocent's pontificate, Hostiensis obscured his most radical views on *Pia* in glosses replete with respectful allusions to the "intentions" and opinions of "dominus noster."[114] But twenty

---

[109] Appendix 2b lines 15–22 and 50–67.

[110] P. Herde, ed., *Marinus von Eboli, "Super revocatoriis" und "De confirmationibus"* (Rome 1964) § 16, p. 217. See also *Glos. ord.* X 1.38.15, v. *Iurati*.

[111] Egidius de Fuscarariis, *Ordo* c.34, Wahrmund, *Quellen* III.1, pp. 62–63. A reference to "Urbanus papa [1261–65], predecessor uester" in an imperfect and aberrant copy of Egidius's *Ordo* in Vat. 2647 (fol. 67vb) enables us to date the work more closely than before.

[112] In c.34 of his *Ordo* Egidius quoted the vice-chancellor's remarks on interpretation of the term "species" (cause) in *Pia* (VI 2.12.1), reporting the vice-chancellor's claims that he had been present when *Pia* was drafted and that this interpretation conveyed the "mens et intentio" of Innocent IV (ed. Wahrmund, *Quellen* III.1, p. 65). Cf. Kuttner, "Konstitutionen" 105, and above, n. 93.

[113] Host., *Lect.* X 2.28.8, v. *Merito dubitet*. Cf. K. Pennington, "The French Recension of Compilatio tertia," *BMCL* 5 (1975) 53–72 at 70–71.

[114] E.g., Host., *Sum.* 2.30(*De excep.*).3, col. 696. The *Summa* and *Novellae* apparatus probably date before September 1253, the latter slightly later than the former (Kuttner, "Decretalistica" 461; Kessler, "Untersuchungen" part 3, 69–70). The lectures on the Liber Extra took their final form between June 1270 and April 1271

years later in his massive lectures on the Liber Extra, Hostiensis frankly admitted his distaste for Innocent IV's "subtleties."[115]

In Hostiensis's view, Gregory IX's *Exceptionem* was still valid law.[116] *Pia*'s mitigations did not benefit public excommunicates, he believed; and though in his earlier writings he was willing to restrict the category of public excommunicates to those who had been excommunicated by judicial sentences or who had publicly perpetrated a crime punishable by excommunication *latae sententiae*, in the later *Lectura* he counted as secret excommunicates only those privately excommunicated in judicial chambers to avoid scandal.[117] Any other excommunicate was to be excluded from court by the judge if the defendant failed to submit the exception of excommunication.[118] To underscore this judicial obligation, Hostiensis invoked a principle of Roman law requiring the praetor to exclude unworthy litigants even if their opponents did not object—a well-chosen citation, since the praetorian edict on *infamia* was aimed at upholding the dignity of the courts, just as the object of the rule excluding excommunicated plaintiffs was to protect litigants from excommunicates.[119] Innocent IV's opinion that a judge could overrule an exception of excommunication was "either incomprehensible or just plain wrong. For I find that a public excommunicate is incapable of legal action under any circumstances."[120] Nor should a defendant be charged legal expenses for delaying to submit an exception; on this score Hostiensis was unwilling to comply even with *Exceptionem*'s precautions. Any fraud perpetrated by delaying was easily outweighed by the plaintiff's deceptive insin-

---

(S. Kuttner, "Wer war der Dekretalist 'Abbas antiquus'?" *ZRG Kan. Abt.* 26 [1937] 471–89 at 486 n. 3); I have, however, cited evidence suggesting an earlier recension, in an article "Hostiensis," in J. Strayer, ed., *Dictionary of the Middle Ages* (forthcoming).

[115] Host., *Lect.* X 1.38.15, v. *Sententia*, vol. 1, p. 190A: "Haec et quasdam alias subtilitates notavit [Innocentius IV] hic, quas non prosequor, quia non multum placent."

[116] Host., *Lect.* X 2.25.12, v. *In dilatoriis*, vol. 1, p. 146A; v. *Opponere*, ibid.; and v. *Legitimus*, p. 147.

[117] For the earlier opinion see Host., *Sum.* 2.30(*De excep.*).3, col. 696; Host., *App.*, *Pia* (VI 2.12.1), v. *Excluduntur*, p. 16A no. 13; v. *Non minus*, p. 17 no. 32; v. *Obtinebat*; and v. *Eo tamen salvo*. For the later opinion see Host., *Lect.* X 2.25.12, v. *Publice*, vol. 1, p. 147; Host., *Lect.* X 1.38.15, v. *Sententia*, vol. 1, p. 190A.

[118] Host., *Lect.* X 2.25.12, v. *Minime*, no. 3. See Kuttner, "Konstitutionen" 114 n. 1 on additions by Hostiensis in manuscripts of Innocent IV's *Apparatus*.

[119] Host., *Lect.* X 2.25.12, v. *Officio*.

[120] Host., *Lect.* X 2.25.12, v. *Minime*, no. 3.

uation into community life despite excommunication.[121] Plaintiffs should be charged expenses for the exception.[122]

Pia, Hostiensis thought, was wrongheaded in principle and practice. Concessions for those already "slumbering" in excommunication were foolish, he believed; every possible means should be used to elicit their respect for the censure.[123] Why should legislation benefit people who were "hateful, and whose delict and contumacy the laws should punish"?[124] Ironically, it was Hostiensis's views that were expressed in the anonymous gloss interpolated into Innocent IV's *Apparatus*: "it should not be presumed that the pope wishes to destroy all laws with a single word. Therefore, any law not explicitly revoked should stand."[125]

THE EXCEPTION OF EXCOMMUNICATION IN PRACTICE

Like a play within a play, a legal exception expanded a trial into new dimensions. Yet besides throwing fresh light on the principals, the exception of excommunication might end the original drama. "By submitting an exception the defendant becomes plaintiff";[126] the often-quoted maxim of Roman law was borne out by the procedural literature exploring defense strategies. An exception could even result in judicial punishment if it proved a crime related to the matter being tried.[127] At the very least, an exception of excommunication stopped a trial, even after *Pia*.

The exception was thus an ingenious legal device, giving responsibility for revealing the status of an excommunicate to the one who would profit most from the revelation. A defendant with a good deal at stake might find it a worthy investment, especially if he could not construct an effective substantive defense. Thus on Monday, 8 Oc-

---

[121] Host., *Lect.* X 2.25.12, v. *Legitimus*.

[122] Ibid.; only if the plaintiffs had unbeknownst to themselves been publicly excommunicated "in remotis partibus" and the defendants knew of the excommunications even when their trials began should the defendants be charged expenses for malicious delay in submitting their exceptions.

[123] Host., *App.*, *Pia* (VI 2.12.1), v. *Publice* and v. *Non postponat*.

[124] Host., *App.*, *Pia*, v. *Publice*; "quia odiosus est, et in poenam delicti sui et contumaciae hoc dicimus tenendum esse. . . ."

[125] Appendix 2c lines 23–26 (see above at n. 97).

[126] Dig. 44.1.1; cf. Dig. 22.3.19.pr.

[127] Cf. X 2.25.1.

tober 1386, Peter d'Avalleur, priest and "bachelor in decretals"—a degree he would need very much in the ensuing days—sued Jordan Singuarelli in the episcopal court of Paris over an ecclesiastical benefice.[128] With all his documents at hand, Peter requested that Jordan produce his. Jordan absented himself from the next hearing, a month later; but on 4 December his proctor submitted an exception of excommunication against Peter.[129] Within the eight days allotted for proof he produced two witnesses who recognized the small seal of the court of Poitiers and the appended seal of judge delegate Aymelius de Brolio (5 Dec.); two curates who recognized both these seals and the great seal of Poitiers (10 Dec.); a public notary from the diocese of Bordeaux, who proved the notary's sign and the seal of Lord Aymelius (11 Dec.); and finally (on the same day) Lord Aymelius himself, who, having been summoned the day before, "deposed and recognized his seal."[130] Not surprisingly, Peter "contumaciously" absented himself from the last two hearings after protesting injuries to himself.

In spite of these beautifully orchestrated proofs, however, the case went on, and by early spring it was Jordan who regularly absented himself.[131] Peter must have done whatever was necessary to obtain absolution; not even a bachelor in canon law could defend himself against such a volley! Jordan had surely provided the "very lucid evidence" of excommunication *Pia* required.[132] But few defendants can have assembled a case like this. Innocent IV himself wrote in a private gloss that testimony from the excommunicating judge and one independent witness was sufficient proof.[133]

---

[128] Petit, *Registre* 373.

[129] Petit, *Registre* 387, 389, and 398.

[130] Petit, *Registre* 399, 401, and 402–3.

[131] Arguments by the plaintiff were to be heard on 2 January 1387 (Petit, *Registre* 404). The record does not show whether these were replications or substantive arguments allowed despite the exception, or whether Peter's absolution was anticipated in the interim. See Petit, *Registre* 409–10, 419, 429, 439, and 449.

[132] VI 2.12.1.

[133] Inn. IV, *App.* X 5.39.48, v. *Praesentibus*. Cf. Pet. Samp. (cf. Appendix 6), *Lect.* X 5.39.48, v. *Personis ydoneis*, Vienna 2113, fol. 73va: "Sed quot personas dices sufficere? Dicit Inno. quod una sufficit, cum per unam possit probari monitio, supra de testibus. In omni [X 2.20.4]. Sed illa loquitur de monitione que fit in denunciatione. Unde oportet esse duas personas ad minus. . . ." See also Abb. Ant., *Lect.*, *Pia* (VI 2.12.1), v. *Apertissimis*, Vat. MSS Borgh. 231, fol. 141vb, and Vat. 2542, fol. 86ra: "Non ergo sufficit unus testis, nec iuramentum deferri debet" (cf. Appendix 6 n. 3); and Host., *App.*, *Pia*, v. *Documentis*: "Idest testibus vel instrumentis."

Normally, excommunication *latae sententiae* would be harder to prove than judicial excommunication, which was registered in court records. Hostiensis pointed out, however, that any attempt to distinguish between the two forms of excommunication in proving the exception must be resisted, since it might lead to the conclusion that excommunication *latae sententiae* was somehow less authentic.[134] Evidence was subject to judicial discretion, and if an important matter was involved the period of eight days could be extended.[135]

The burden of proving excommunication *latae sententiae* was lightened by Clement III's ruling that people reputed to be excommunicated were to be avoided until they had undergone purgation.[136] As a result, proof of *fama* was sufficient to support an exception of excommunication, at least until the mid-thirteenth century, when Peter Sampson advised his readers to take care in framing their exceptions and to allege only that the plaintiff was rumored to be an excommunicate if that was all they could prove.[137] By the fourteenth century, however, plaintiffs were probably not being excluded on these grounds. Boniface VIII's *Licet* implied that denunciation created a legal presumption of excommunication; the decretal stated that people denounced as excommunicates because they had not appealed the sentence within the allotted year must be avoided in court and extra-judicially, albeit the sentence was invalid, until they had successfully completed their appeals.[138] He thus implied that denunciation created

---

[134] Host., *App.*, *Pia* (VI 2.12.1) v. *Infra octo*, no. 19.

[135] Cf. Inn. IV, *App.*, *Pia* (VI 2.12.1) v. *Octo*, noting that the term for proof could be extended if, for example, the validity of an election or a contract or other document was involved.

[136] X 5.39.15, discussed in Chapter 2 at n. 26.

[137] Pet. Samp., *Dist.* X 5.39.15, v. *Secundae quaestioni*, Vat., Pal. 656, fol. 157ra: "Caue quomodo excipies contra actorem. Nam si forte dices: 'Ego dabo ipsum esse excommunicatum et propter hoc nullatenus est audiendus,' et probares quod erat publica fama ipsum esse excommunicatum, nihilominus non obstante probatione tua audietur, quia non probasti id ad quod probandum te astrixisti, scilicet quod erat excommunicatus, supra, de probac. Licet [X 2.19.9]. Unde excipias sicut: 'Ego dico quod fama publica est ipsum esse excommunicatum et propter hoc nullatenus est audiendus.' Et hoc probato quod sic fama ipsum esse excommunicatum postmodum nullatenus audietur. Et sic loquitur P. S." The advice was adopted by the anonymous lecturer of Vat., Borgh. 228, *Pia* (VI 2.12.1), fol. 108ra: "Pone quod ponatur sic: 'Propono quod fama est quod actor est excommunicatus et immo peto ipsum re-moueri donec super hoc se purget.' Nunquid talis modus excipiendi est admitten-dus? Dic quod sic, de sen. exco. Cum desideres [X 5.39.15] § 2."

[138] VI 5.11.14.

a legal presumption of excommunication. But Johannes Andreae noted that proof of denunciation hardly constituted the manifest evidence of excommunication required by *Pia*.[139] In a 1302 case in the English royal court, an exception of excommunication was successfully overturned when plaintiffs' counsel replicated that the defense's letters proved only that the plaintiffs had been denounced as excommunicates, not that they were in fact excommunicated.[140] At the end of the century the issue was still debated by judges of the Roman Rota, which—as one judge admitted—because of the very high standards of proof *Pia* called for only rarely accepted the exception of excommunication.[141]

Plaintiffs confronted with an exception of excommunication had the burden of proving themselves absolved.[142] Egidius de Fuscarariis

---

[139] *Glos. ord.* VI 5.11.14, v. *Nuntiari.*

[140] Appendix 5 case 29.

[141] Recorded by Bernhardus de Bisgneto (ca. 1370), who believed that denunciation was not sufficient proof: "Et uidebatur aliquibus dominis quod non, per no. in c. Pia de excep. li. vi [VI 2.12.1] per Io. an., ubi expresse tenet quod per denunciationem non probatur sufficienter excommunicatio. Quod fateor de plano in casu ipso quando excommunicatio opponitur per partem adversario [*sic*] in uim peremptoriam uel dilatoriam ad repellendum eum, cum ibi [i.e., in *Pia*, VI 2.12.1] tex. dicat 'apertissimis docuit.' Et eius opinio seruatur in curia, ubi rarissime exceptio excommunicationis admittitur" (*Conclusiones sive decisiones . . . causarum auditorum* [Rome 1475, *sine fol.*] vol. 2, rubr. "De sen. excom." [third page from last]; on this work see G. Dolezalek, "Die handschriftliche Verbreitung von Rechtsprechungssammlungen der Rota," *ZRG Kan. Abt.* 58 [1972] 1–106 at 8). A more famous compiler of Rota decisions, Guilhelmus Horborch, wrote in 1381 that denunciation was felt by some to be sufficient proof when the exception was being used only to delay litigation; all now agreed it was not sufficient to invalidate a rescript (*Decisiones novae*, rubr. "De excep. et de sen. ex.," no. 256: "Licet sit concertatio inter doctores in capitulo Pia, de excep., et in c. Licet, de sen. ex. li. VI [VI 5.11.14], utrum per denuntiationem probatur quis excommunicatus quando in uim dilatorie excommunicatio proponitur, tamen domini habuerunt et uoluerunt habere pro indubitato quod denuntiatio non probat exceptionem excommunicationis oppositam in uim peremptorie contra impetrantem rescriptum, quia non sequitur, talis est denuntiatus, ergo est excommunicatus").

[142] Then, of course, the validity of the absolution might be challenged on a number of grounds, outlined, e.g., in the tract "De exceptionibus," *TUI* 3.2, fol. 105ra, tit. 4 § 1. Innocent IV's authorship has been questioned by Fowler-Magerl (*Ordo* 216–18), who proposes an Anglo-Norman provenance and dates the tract before 1234. In Appendix 5 cases 1 and 6 plaintiffs' failures to prove they were absolved (not merely that they deserved to be, and had taken the necessary steps) stymied their lawsuits.

advised excommunicates to have instruments drawn up testifying to absolution in case they were needed in the future; for absolution was not performed publicly, and once excommunicated a person was presumed to remain so until proven otherwise.[143] Duranti, a judge at the papal court from the early 1260s, required an oath denying malice from a defendant wishing to submit an exception of excommunication a third time against the same opponent.[144]

Defenses against the exception were very limited. Already in the decretist period the canonists rejected the replication that an excommunication was unjust, since even unjust excommunications were usually valid.[145] Absolution was not hard to obtain, and the law greatly favored absolution over appeal. Technically, a plaintiff could replicate that the excommunicating judge lacked jurisdiction, grounds also for appeal from excommunication.[146] This replication was successfully used in 1234 in the Norman exchequer's court by a plaintiff who claimed that he had been excommunicated by the bishop of Seéz but that his own ordinary, the bishop of Evreux, did not "hold him as an excommunicate."[147] The claim that excommunication had been imposed after and for the purpose of blocking an appeal was also grounds for appeal from excommunication, but the canonists disputed whether it could be used in replication against an exception of excommunication.[148] Innocent IV declared in *Solet* (1244) that excommunicates appealing on the grounds that they had been excommunicated after appeal must continue to be avoided in judicial

---

[143] Egidius de Fuscarariis, *Ordo*, c.102, Wahrmund, *Quellen* III.1, pp. 176–77; cf. X 5.39.39. Johannes Andreae, writing ca. 1338–42, supplied an interesting example of the problem: at the time (i.e., 1317) of the Ferrara rebellion against papal rule, many were excommunicated for trading with citizens of Ferrara. The absolutions were performed *en masse* by "religiosi"; hence individuals had no proof of absolution (*Comm.* VI 5.11.8, v. *Ut dicunt*).

[144] Dur., *Spec.* 2.1.13(*De excep. et replic.*), vol. 2, fol. 120ra, no. 9, and fol. 120vb, no. 19.

[145] Appendix 1d lines 61–70.

[146] Appendix 1d lines 69–70.

[147] A.-J. Marnier, ed., *Etablissements et coutumes, assises et arrêts de l'échiquier de Normandie au treizième siècle (1207 à 1245)* (Paris 1839) 163. Cf. the 1314 English case (Appendix 5 case 36) in which the court contemplated a replication of failure to prove jurisdiction, though it was on different grounds that the exception was ultimately rejected.

[148] Huguccio seems to endorse this replication; see Appendix 1d lines 69–70.

matters, though not extrajudicially, until their appeals had been successfully completed.[149] Goffredus de Trano believed that a plaintiff
facing an exception could force the judge to try his replication that
the excommunication had been imposed after appeal, but Innocent
IV himself was unsure whether the matter could be entrusted to anyone other than the appellate judge.[150] The question must have come
up often; for later canonists were vexed that Innocent had not settled
it once and for all.[151]

TWO CASES

On 14 November 1207, King John addressed a writ to his judges at
Westminster, demanding within one month minutes of a hearing that
was to take place on 18 November between Alicia Clement, plaintiff,
and Jordan of Newton, defendant.[152] The dispute had begun in the

[149] VI 5.11.2, discussed further below, Chapter 6 at n. 35.

[150] Goff. Tr., *App.*, *Solet* (VI 5.11.2), v. *In iudiciis*, Fulda D.10, fol. 7rb: "Necessitas
iuris cogit iudicem ⟨in⟩ iudiciis uitare excommunicatum post appellationem. Quod
sic probo. Contra excommunicatum agentem excipitur quod sit excommunicatus,
et ipse actor confitetur se excommunicatum, sed dicit excommunicationem non
ualere propter appellationem que precessit. Necesse est ergo quod supersedeatur
principali questioni excommunicati qui confitetur de exceptione excommunicationis
quo usque probet replicaturam, scilicet, appellationem semper precessisse." Innocent IV considered the problem in two glosses, one written, or revised, during
his pontificate. In the earlier gloss he wrote that there could be no replication that the
exception was "post legitimam appellationem"; even an excommunicate who claimed
this must be avoided until he proved his claim (Inn. IV, *App.* X 2.28.44, v. *Peremptorie*). In the later gloss he vacillated, first accepting the validity of the replication,
then acknowledging that the contrary opinion might be better (Inn. IV, *App.* X
5.39.40, v. *Constiterit*).

[151] See Johannes Monachus, *Glosa aurea super Sexto Decretalium* (Paris 1535; repr.
Aalen 1968) VI 5.11.14, v. *Convalescat*: "Hoc no. s. de appella. Sepe, licet ibi Inno.
vacilet." And see the addition of Philippus Probus, ibid., v. *Vacillet*: "Ibi est una
tristissima maxima in rota et in auribus meis. XVI annis rotaui. Probus." But there
was no vacillation in the English courts, where both "Bracton" (*Bracton*, fol. 426b,
vol. 4, pp. 326–27) and *Fleta* (6.44.2, p. 438) accepted the replication.

[152] M 9J, *CRR* V 79; the actual writ is on the roll, followed by a summary of the
1204 proceedings, i.e., H 5J (pp. 79–80), for which no roll survives (79 n. 1). There
are two main repositories of information about the pre–1207 events: the 1207 summary, and a series of documents enrolled under E 9–10J (*CRR* V 183–86), for reasons that will be clear below. The latter seem to correspond partly to the evidence
Avenell and Jordan are said in the 1207 summary to have submitted in 1204; see
also n. 163.

mid-1180s with an ecclesiastical court's prosecution of Alicia for apostasy and had come into the royal court in January or February 1204 as a suit over lands and a house in Oxfordshire.[153] More than twelve years were still to pass before an agreement would be reached in mid-February 1220.[154]

In the late winter of 1204 Alicia had sued her brother-in-law Avenell and, as warrantor, his son Jordan, claiming they had disinherited her of the legacy of her father, William.[155] Avenell (a knight of the diocese of Lincoln) and his son Jordan had refused to respond on the grounds that Alicia had been excommunicated as an apostate nun, having abandoned the habit after living as a nun for fifteen years.[156] They had produced a document from a panel of judges delegate headed by the abbot of Reading, in Berkshire, who had convicted and excommunicated Alicia; other documents of popes Clement III (1187–91) and Celestine III (1191–98) confirming the conviction; and testimony from the convent of Ankerwyke, in Buckinghamshire, where she had been a nun.[157]

Alicia objected that the evidence Avenell and Jordan had submitted should not prejudice the court against her and gave her version of the story.[158] When she was five years old, she said, Avenell and his wife, her sister Christiana, had put her in the convent. After she had been

---

[153] At the instigation of her former convent, Ankerwyke, the Lincoln diocesan court prosecuted Alicia and convicted her, certainly before 1187, since the trial is discussed in a letter that refers to actions taken afterward by "G.," late bishop of London, i.e., Gilbert Foliot, d. 1187 (E 9–10J; *CRR* V 185). The first royal court litigation was evidently that of the Hilary (January–February) term of 1204 (see n. 152). Many of the dates in the present account are approximate, because the rolls are arranged by legal terms, which lasted from several weeks to two months. Evidence for more precise dates is given in the appropriate notes. With further research identifying more of the officials named in the documents a more exact chronology could be established.

[154] For the last date see below, n. 194.

[155] M 9J, *CRR* V 79.

[156] Ibid. 79–80; see E 9–10J, *CRR* V 183–84, for Avenell's identification as a knight.

[157] M 9J, *CRR* V 80. The panel's account of its actions, enrolled under E 9–10J (*CRR* V 183–84), incorporates the mandate of appointment by Celestine III, dated 2 March 1196. This mandate might be one of the two papal confirmations Avenell referred to; no document of Clement III survives. The mandate is listed in W. Holtzmann, *Papsturkunden in England* (Berlin 1931–35, Göttingen 1952; repr. vols. 1–2 Göttingen 1970) III 588–89, no. 498, from the CR rolls.

[158] M 9J, *CRR* V 80. None of Alicia's evidence is enrolled.

there three years (at age eight, therefore), she had asked to become a nun, as she had been instructed to; she did not say by whom.[159] But "at the age of discretion" she had left the habit. Alicia produced documents from a different panel of judges delegate, headed by an abbot "H." of Buildwas, Shropshire, absolving her by authority of Innocent III (1198–1216) from a suit by the nuns of Ankerwyke, and confirmation of her marriage to Alan of Wodecot from the same pope.[160] A day had been appointed for judgment seven weeks after Easter 1204; but postponements had delayed the case until 14 November 1207, when Alicia obtained the writ ordering a hearing before the royal justiciars, to be reviewed by the king himself on 9 December.[161] Jordan was now the sole defendant; Avenell must have died in the interim.

Alicia evidently failed to quash the exception.[162] For in the next hearing, in the first week of May 1208, Jordan repeated that Alicia had been excommunicated for apostasy.[163] Alicia had not sufficiently

---

[159] Ibid.: "ibi fuit in custodia per iii. annos; et tunc, sicut edocta fuit, peciit se monialem fieri; et postea, cum haberet annos discrecionis, reliquit habitum. . . ."

[160] Ibid. For reasons that will be clear below, it is doubtless significant that Alicia repeatedly stated that the judges absolved her not from excommunication but from the convent's suit. But that suit resulted in her conviction, and it occurred before 1187, more than a decade before Innocent's pontificate. Unfortunately, the panel's actions cannot be precisely dated from the offices held by its members, "H." abbot of Buildwas (D. Knowles et al., *Heads of Religious Houses, England and Wales, 940–1216* [Cambridge 1972] 129), "H." abbot of Haughmond (ibid. 165) and "R." prior of Wombridge (ibid. 190); either their tenures were too long to aid dating, or they are still uncertain. Another problem in Alicia's evidence: Celestine III's 1196 mandate (see n. 157) invalidated an impetration by Alicia for a panel of judges delegate to be headed by an abbot of Buildwas—no name or initial given. In this interrupted suit, discussed further below, Alicia must be plaintiff and Avenell defendant; the convent was evidently not a party. Both of Innocent III's documents are listed in C. R. Cheney and Mary G. Cheney, *The Letters of Pope Innocent III (1198–1216) concerning England and Wales* (Oxford 1967) nos. 525–26, from the CR rolls.

[161] M 9J, *CRR* V 79–80. The writ ordered the justiciars to conduct the hearing on 18 November, the octave of St. Martin's day (11 Nov.), and to present the record a month after St. Martin's day, hence 9 December. This was confirmed 18 November (*CRR* V 123), but no record of the December hearing survives.

[162] In 1204 Alicia defended herself with the claim that she had never really been a nun and so could not have been validly excommunicated for apostasy. But at the 18 November 1207 hearing she must also have tried to prove absolution from excommunication; see n. 164.

[163] E 9–10J, *CRR* V 171, one month after Easter, which was April 6. The evidence Jordan cited at this hearing corresponds partly to that he cited in 1204 (it was not

proved that she had been absolved, the court recorded, and Jordan was allowed to go "sine die."[164] And a few months later, on 1 July, a specific reference to proof at the 18 November hearing that Alicia was excommunicated was enough to bar her participation in another case.[165] Since the pope who had supposedly exculpated her was still alive and could have been asked to send new documents if necessary, one must suspect that Alicia's evidence was less than sound. Nonetheless, through the dark glass of the incomplete and partly mutilated evidence that survives she emerges as a heroine of sorts, probably, it is true, an apostate nun in the literal record, but also the confused victim of childhood trauma. She must have been about twenty-three when she left the convent in the mid-1180s.[166] The prioress and nuns of her former convent testified that she had spent her fifteen years sometimes at Ankerwyke, sometimes abroad on the convent's business (she had been *precentrix*); though they firmly stated that she had taken vows after the age of discretion, their testimony suggests that there was room for ambiguity in her mode of life.[167] At some point she mentally shed her childhood commitment; possibly she was hon-

---

listed exhaustively in the summary of the 1204 hearing or in the present [May 1208] hearing); this seems to be the evidence enrolled under E 9–10J, *CRR* V 183–86.

[164] E 9–10J, *CRR* V 171. In the 18 November 1207 hearing Alicia must have added the defense that she had been absolved from excommunication to the substantive (and contradictory) defense that she had never truly been a nun; for after Jordan's charges the record states that the suit was dismissed *sine die* because Alicia "non ostendit sufficienter quod absoluta esset."

[165] T 10J, *CRR* V 293 (see text at n. 187). When the defendant, Hamo de Bidun, summoned Alicia to warrant himself, the plaintiff, the abbot of Pipewell, objected that she had been proved excommunicated in the court of "lord G.," i.e., the justiciar Geoffrey FitzPeter (see F. West, *The Justiciarship in England 1066–1232* [Cambridge 1966] 156 and 167, briefly mentioning this case) and "coram episcopis et justiciariis." It is unclear whether the latter phrase refers to earlier trials or simply to other judges at the 18 November hearing.

[166] Both the convent (deposition enrolled under E 9–10J, *CRR* V 185) and Avenell and Jordan (testimony, M 9J, *CRR* V 79–80) stated that Alicia had been in the convent fifteen years after professing. She herself said that she had asked to become a nun after three years in the convent, where she had been placed at age five (see n. 159). Hence she must have been around twenty–three when she left. Reasons for dating her departure to the mid-1180s are given in n. 153.

[167] See the convent's deposition, under E 9–10J (*CRR* V 185): "quandoque claustralis, quandoque precentrix, in domo nostra et extra domum militans in negociis nostris, conservavit et inconcusse et religiose habuit." Alicia herself testified ca. 1193–98 (see n. 170) "se nunquam monia[lem] fuisse neque regulariter vixisse . . ." (E 9–10J, *CRR* V 186; emendations are in the edition).

est when she said she "left the convent" at the age of discretion, though she clearly did not take the appropriate legal steps.[168] She believed the profession had been forced on her anyway; in her mind, as in the litigation that ensued, the convent and her brother-in-law may have blurred into a single enemy.

Soon after Alicia left, the prioress and convent obtained her conviction in the Lincoln diocesan court.[169] At least two other ecclesiastical courts—the panel of judges delegate headed by the abbot of Reading (before 1196) and a tribunal headed by the archdeacon of Derby (ca. 1193–98)—had renewed her excommunication after again ordering her to return to the convent.[170] Throughout the diocese of Lincoln she had been repeatedly denounced as an excommunicate to be avoided by all.[171] By the mid-1190s, however, she had gained the loyal friendship of a knight named W. de Bidun, whom the archdeacon of Derby and others excommunicated and denounced as her main supporter.[172] (Indeed, the fragmentary remains of the archdeacon's letter seem to show that he eventually invoked the secular arm against Alicia and de Bidun, presumably to have them imprisoned as contumacious excommunicates.)[173] Alicia, now with W. de Bidun, at first cooperated with the archdeacon's summons but scorned his offer of absolution in exchange for a promise to obey court orders, insisting she had never been a nun.[174] Perhaps it was after this, and on de Bidun's advice, that Alicia herself took the ini-

---

[168] In the prosecution in the Lincoln diocesan court the prioress testified that Alicia "irregulariter evagetur" (E 9–10J, *CRR* V 185). Similar phrases were used ca. 1193–98 in the court of the archdeacon of Derby (see n. 170).

[169] See n. 153.

[170] See n. 157 for the first. The evidence for the second is a badly mutilated letter from I[vo of Cornwall], archdeacon of Derby until 1198 (C. R. Cheney, *English Bishops' Chanceries, 1100–1250* [Manchester 1950] 16), and a co-judge, to H[ubert Walter], archbishop of Canterbury 1193–1205, enrolled under E 9–10J (*CRR* V 185–86).

[171] See the dean of Lincoln's account of actions taken after the initial conviction, and the archdeacon of Derby's letter (see n. 170), both enrolled under E 9–10J, *CRR* V 185–86.

[172] See the archdeacon of Derby's letter, E 9–10J, *CRR* V 185–86.

[173] Ibid. 186: "gladio . . . a nobis cuiquam justiciario domini regis quatenus ad reprimendam maliciam predicte ipsius A. et W. militis. . . ." (The ellipsis marks represent illegible passages in the letter itself.)

[174] See the archdeacon of Derby's letter, E 9–10J, *CRR* V 186.

tiative and impetrated papal letters to sue her brother-in-law under the abbot of Buildwas, whose sympathies she must have had reason to trust.[175] Avenell obtained a mandate from Celestine III, dated 2 March 1196, to curtail this trial on the grounds that the judges were "suspect and very remote"; the abbot of Reading was instructed to try the case notwithstanding the previous impetration.[176] Though Avenell apparently intended to reverse the balance of the dispute in his own favor, Alicia sent a proctor to represent her at the first hearing.[177] Thereafter, though summoned many times, she absented herself; the judges, after hearing Avenell's witnesses, convicted her and ordered her to return to the convent on pain of anathema.[178]

So much can be said of the events before Alicia sued Avenell in the royal court in 1204. The abbot of Reading's conviction must have occurred soon after March 1196, the date of Celestine's mandate. Perhaps Alicia's claim to have been vindicated by an abbot of Buildwas on authority of Innocent III indicates that she tried to reinstate her earlier suit.[179] Or maybe she simply escaped from the turmoil into marriage: in 1214 she had a son old enough to act as her attorney.[180] When in 1204 she resumed the role of plaintiff it was in the royal court, which, she might have hoped, would confine its interest to the legacy. That hope was stymied in 1204 with the exception of excommunication and must have seemed defeated by the royal hearing of 1207. But circumstances were changing. By the spring of 1208 Alicia's suit against Jordan in Oxfordshire was surrounded by a small constellation of other lawsuits, suggesting new alliances from which she might entertain hopes. In Warwickshire another case had begun around Easter 1207, about seven months before Alicia obtained her royal writ: the abbot of Pipewell sued Hamo de Bidun for advowson

[175] E 9–10J, *CRR* V 183; see also n. 160.
[176] Ibid. 184.
[177] Ibid.
[178] Ibid.
[179] See n. 160. The abbot of Reading seems to have been apprehensive about proceeding in Alicia's absence; he referred many times to the repeated summonses he gave and declared that he was acting "virorum prudentum consilio" (E 9–10J, *CRR* V 184). But apart from Alicia's references to Innocent III's absolution—which, according to her, freed her from prosecution by the convent, not by Avenell—there is no reason to doubt the validity of the conviction.
[180] H 15J, *CRR* VII 108–9.

of the church of Dunchirch.[181] Presumably Hamo was a relation, perhaps the son, of Alicia's friend W. de Bidun. Since at a hearing in November 1207 he was excused by royal warrant for his absence from the hearing of the previous spring, Hamo might have been a friend sufficiently highly placed to encourage her persistence even after the rebuff of December 1207.[182] But their first court encounter was as adversaries: in the spring of 1208 in Warwickshire, Alicia herself sued Hamo in a plea involving land.[183] Were they colluding? No mention was made of the December judgment that Alicia was indeed an excommunicate; Hamo could easily, it seems, have had her barred from court. Instead, by late April they reached an agreement: Alicia conceded the land for her lifetime in return for an annual rent.[184]

A few weeks later, however, came the dismissal of Alicia's suit against Jordan in Oxford.[185] Meanwhile, Jordan had added his claim to the advowson for which the abbot of Pipewell was suing Hamo de Bidun.[186] Sure enough, the advowson was part of Alicia's inheritance; perhaps she had entrusted it to Hamo in gratitude or for safekeeping. The abbot of Pipewell's suit against him resumed in June; on 1 July Hamo summoned Alicia, as his landlady, to warrant himself.[187] The abbot objected at once: Alicia could not stand as warrantor; for she had been proven to be an excommunicate "in the court of Lord G[eoffrey FitzPeter, justiciar]"—that is, in the hearing the previous December.[188] Alicia, present in court, made a last, passionate plea that she was not excommunicated and even promised to summon the judges who had absolved her (the abbot of Buildwas and co-judges?) at the next hearing.[189] Should she lose her inheritance because of the allegations of this abbot of Pipewell? she asked the court.

---

[181] Our first notice of this case comes from the same term in which Alicia was granted her royal hearing, i.e., Michaelmas 1207 (*CRR* V 83); but since Hamo was then excused by royal warrant for absence from a hearing in Easter term, the case must have begun by spring 1207 at the latest.

[182] See previous note.

[183] H 9J, *CRR* V 133; undated, but 21 April was fixed for the next hearing.

[184] E 9–10J, *CRR* V 162 (presumably 21 April; see previous note).

[185] See above at n. 164.

[186] E 9–10J, *CRR* V 188. Since this is among the roll's first cases it might date from early in Easter term, which in 1208 began 23 April.

[187] T 10J, *CRR* V 293; see n. 165.

[188] T 10J, *CRR* V 293.

[189] Ibid.: "Econtra Alicia defendit quod non est excommunicata; et inde vocat judices suos qui eam absolverunt ad warantizandum, quorum warantiam habebit ad

And now, in July 1208, a curtain once again drops over the whole scene, to lift only in the summer of 1214, when Alicia reopened her case against Jordan, again at Oxford.[190] Alicia must have been about fifty by then; her son, Robert, served as her attorney, and the court did not refer to her excommunication or to the earlier litigation. Alicia's claim stated simply that the disputed land was part of her inheritance. Perhaps she reentered the fray for her son's sake, or perhaps because her adversary was vulnerable: Jordan was excused twice in 1214 because of illness.[191] Once again there were long delays. Civil war had, of course, interfered with the courts' business, but perhaps also the parties were weary and ambivalent. In the autumn of 1219 Jordan was once again excused because of illness, and a panel of knights appointed to certify his excuse appeared in the late winter of 1220 to request another postponement.[192]

Finally, in November of the same year, this remarkable case began to find an amicable conclusion.[193] The court duly recorded the essential details: Alicia claimed the lands as her free tenement, inherited from her father, who was seised of them in the time of Henry, grandfather of the present king; her sister's son Jordan now held all the lands; Alicia had sued to reclaim her portion. Not surprisingly, no further litigation but a license to compromise settled the dispute. The seventeenth of February 1221 was appointed for the litigants to receive their chirograph, and we hear no more.[194]

The one thing Alicia could not have done if she wished to triumph in this dispute, which lasted most of her adult life, was accept absolution from excommunication—she would thereby have implied her apostasy and thus her profession as a nun. Only had she conceded that she had voluntarily surrendered her inheritance, therefore, could

---

diem alium competentem; et preterea dicit quod ipsa tradidit terram quandam cum advocatione illa ad firmam sine calumpnia aliqua, et inde adhuc est in saisina; et petit considerationem curie utrum debeat perdere hereditatem suam pro dicto abbatis."

[190] H 15J, *CRR* VII 108–9.

[191] T 16J, *CRR* VII 180; T 16J, *CRR* VII 246.

[192] M 3–4HIII, *CRR* VIII 173; H 4HIII, *CRR* VIII 184, requesting postponement until the day after St. Edmund's day (which is 16 November) the following year.

[193] M 4–5HIII, *CRR* IX 381–82; see previous note.

[194] M 4–5HIII, *CRR* IX 385. (The appointed day, five weeks from St. Hilary [which is 13 January], is not recorded on the roll, which extends only to the octave of St. Hilary [*CRR* X 19].)

Alicia free herself from the excommunication that prevented her from claiming it.

A second case illustrating the exception of excommunication comes from the registers of the bishop's court of Paris. On 5 February 1385, Huetus Ringart, a cleric giving his address as the house bearing the sign of the *gros de Tours* in the Dominican street of the parish of St. Eustace, sued Stephaneta, daughter of Girard Bersaut, claiming that they had exchanged vows to marry.[195] Stephaneta agreed that Huetus had asked her to be his betrothed but claimed she had told him she could do nothing without her parents' consent. Stephaneta's parents swore that they did not and could not approve the engagement. Stephaneta protested that any of her words that might have had the force of a betrothal should be revoked since she was a minor. The case was continued.

Arguments were to begin on 17 February.[196] The register relates that Stephaneta through her advocate asked to have Huetus excluded from the court as an excommunicate under the synodal statutes forbidding clandestine marriages.[197] The judge began to make a declaration, presumably an interlocutory judgment on Stephaneta's exception of excommunication, but stopped in mid-sentence.[198]

On the same day, the registrar of fines made the following entry: "We declare that Huetus Ringart, excommunicated because of a clandestine marriage contracted with [Stephaneta Bersaut], is absolved by fine."[199] Huetus evidently did not protest the exception. He just paid the fine so that he could get on with the suit.

The simplicity of this solution contrasts sharply with the vicissitudes of Alicia Clement's case. Alicia could obtain absolution only at the expense of losing her inheritance. But Huetus's admission of excommunication actually improved his prospects: if Stephaneta's exception was valid, then he had, as he claimed, contracted marriage with her. One is not surprised to see Huetus hurrying to the registrar of fines.

Three days later he was back in court, this time with Stephaneta's

---

[195] Petit, *Registre* 47; cf. ibid. 130 for Huetus's identification as a cleric.
[196] Ibid. 53–54 and 56.
[197] See Pontal, *Statuts* 66 and 88 for Parisian statutes forbidding clandestine marriage.
[198] Petit, *Registre* 56.
[199] Ibid. The register reverses the two entries, presumably accidentally.

father (who took charge of her defense since she was a minor), and another day was appointed for Huetus's responses.[200] Stephaneta herself was required to appear under penalty of contumacy. On 27 February, with Stephaneta present, Huetus produced seven witnesses, one of them sharing his surname and another identified as the "pediseca Scuti Francie in porta Parisius."[201] On 20 March, Huetus produced another witness, Marion la Boutarde.[202] A day was appointed for publication of all the testimony except that of two witnesses who were "in remote parts," namely, Agnestota la Charboniere and Johanneta, "once maidservant of the defendant's father." Huetus seems to have been making a good case for himself with witnesses who must have known Stephaneta intimately. But the exception of excommunication once again delayed him. On 18 April the testimony was published "save for that of the two excommunicated women."[203] One of them may have been Agnestota la Charboniere, whose testimony was not published until 13 June.[204] Between June and October, the parties appeared in court nine times, mostly through proctors.[205] No witnesses for Stephaneta are mentioned; she submitted arguments and objected to Huetus's witnesses.[206] Finally on 6 October a date was set for an interlocutory judgment.[207] There is no further mention of the case in the records, but the court ominously ordered a celebration of the sacrament on the Sunday before the next hearing. Stephaneta's exception of excommunication seems to have ricocheted against her.

---

[200] Petit, *Registre* 59.

[201] Ibid. 64–65.

[202] Ibid. 81–82.

[203] Ibid. 98.

[204] Ibid. 135; for the other hearings see ibid. 109, 115, 120, 125, 129, 130, and 135.

[205] Ibid. 140, 144, 149, 155, 159, 167, 173, 183, and 191.

[206] Ibid. 115 (10 May): "hodie rea reclamavit . . . ," which, since the case goes on, must mean "objected," not "confessed," unless Stephaneta confessed to allegations that did not demolish her case; ibid. 129 (6 June): "super rationibus ex parte ree traditis. . . ."

[207] Ibid. 197: "et fiat collatio dominica ante."

V

Excommunicates in the Courtroom

DEFENDANT

Late twelfth-century canonists regarded litigation against excommunicates as a salutary harassment, analogous to a measure Gregory I endorsed in a famous letter, the use of heavy taxes to coerce a recalcitrant pagan to join the church.[1] Lucius III (1181–85) decreed that excommunicates should be admitted to court as defendants—that is, they could be sued—lest their status as excommunicates be an advantage.[2] But whereas Roman law forbade *infames* to defend themselves through legal representatives, presumably in the hope that the ignominious presence of the infamed defendant would benefit his adversary, Lucius III proposed that excommunicated defendants respond through proctors.[3] The facts of the case envisaged in Lucius III's decretal obviously encouraged such a rule; for the defendant, being sued by his betrothed, had been excommunicated for murdering the bishop of Vicenza. Although Tancred suggested that an excommunicated defendant unwilling to appoint a proctor should be treated as contumaciously absent, it was generally agreed that no one could be

[1] E.g., Appendix 1b lines 2–5.
[2] X 2.1.7; see Chapter 4 n. 63.
[3] Greenidge, *Infamia* 159–60.

forced to appoint a proctor and that excommunicates might be unable to find anyone to defend them faithfully.[4] A decretal of Innocent III ensured that proctors for excommunicated defendants would not incur the usual penalty of minor excommunication.[5]

The twelfth-century decretists wrote about excommunicated defendants in negative terms: even though excommunicates were normally forbidden all contact with sacred objects, one canonist wrote in the 1180s, excommunicated defendants giving the oath against calumny could touch the Gospels since procedures were arrayed against them.[6] This is a rather naive (or perhaps disingenuous) view of litigation. The defendant's position is very often the advantageous one, especially in property disputes, and the procedural literature of the late twelfth century inevitably enhanced defendants' rights.[7] But the decretists strictly limited the defenses available to excommunicates, allowing them only factual defenses related to the issue under dispute.[8] Opprobrious themselves, excommunicated defendants could not use personal exceptions against plaintiffs or witnesses.[9]

By the early thirteenth century, several decretals shored the rights of excommunicated defendants.[10] As Innocent III stipulated, judicial equity required that they be allowed to challenge a suspect judge and to appeal.[11] But excommunicated defendants had to be prevented from transforming defense into aggression; in particular, they could not bring countersuits.[12] In the commentaries of the thirteenth-century canonists the balance of litigation had clearly gone far to favor defendants. The danger was that excommunicated defendants might accomplish what they were forbidden to do as plaintiffs. Thus Johannes Teutonicus protested that excommunicates must not be allowed to

---

[4]Tancred, *App.* 1 Comp. 2.1.9, v. *Respondere*, Vat. 1377, fol. 20rb: "procedetur in negotio tanquam abesset contumaciter, uel captis pignoribus satisdare compellatur, uel ipse in propria persona respondebit. Nec in hoc actor uel iudex uel testis ei communicans incidit in minorem excommunicationem." See *Glos. ord.* X 2.1.7, v. *Conveniri potest* for arguments against requiring excommunicates to appoint proctors.

[5]X 2.25.2.

[6]Appendix 1b lines 15–16; cf. *Glos. ord.* X 2.25.5, v. *Defensio.*

[7]Maitland, *History* II 47 and 147; see also VI 5.12.65.

[8]Appendix 1d lines 26–30.

[9]*Sum. "Elegantius" (Coloniensis)*, ed. Fransen, 6.37, vol. 2, p. 121.

[10]X 2.25.5, 11, and 14.

[11]X 2.25.5.

[12]Ibid.; cf. Huguccio in Appendix 1d lines 30–32.

have themselves sued by fraudulent means in order to win their aims through clever use of exceptions.[13] *Compensatio*, by which a judge subtracted debts owed a defendant from a judgment favoring the plaintiff (as in the modern "set-off"), must certainly not be made available to excommunicated defendants.[14] The Bohemian canonist Damasus (ca. 1216) ruled that litigants who allowed an excommunicated defendant to profit from court transactions would incur minor excommunication. Vincentius Hispanus wondered whether scribes could with impunity draw up a plaintiff's responses to exceptions submitted by an excommunicated defendant.[15]

[13]Jo. Teut., *App.* 4 Comp. 2.1.2 (= X 2.25.5), v. *Defensio*, Vat. MSS Vat. 1377, fol. 290vb, Vat. 2509, fol. 284rb, Borgh. 264, fol. 239vb, and Chig. E.VII.207, fol. 265vb: "Hic habes quod excommunicatus potest excipere. Quod intelligo cum agens non est passus uiolentiam ab excommunicato, ut per fraudem talem cogeret ipsum agere, et sic posset excipere. Simile extra. iii. de symonia. Sicut [3 Comp. 5.2.5 = X 5.3.33], extra. ii. eod. t. A nobis [3 Comp. 2.16.1 = X 2.25.2]. . . . Et ita consuluitur alicui per exceptionem cui non consuluitur per actionem. . . . Eadem enim defensio debet competere excommunicato que non excommunicato sicut eadem seruo que libero, ut ff. de accusat. Seruos [Dig. 48.2.5]. . . . Sed nunquid potest excipere de pacto de non petendo? Videtur quod non, quia sola uidetur illi permitti que ad defensionem cause spectant, ut hic uidetur. Item cum excipiendo fiat actor. . . . Item, qualiter prestabit sacramentum calumpnie? Cum enim non liceat ei ingredi sacra, multo magis non licet ei tangere sacra, supra, di. v. Ad eius [4]. Item, si excipere potest ergo etiam compensare. Sed per exceptionem repelletur si ageret. Ergo non potest compensare, ff. de compens. Quecumque [Dig. 16.2.14]. . . . Dico quod sole exceptiones competunt excommunicato que faciunt ad defensionem cause, unde exceptionem pacti de non petendo potest proponere uel exceptionem rei iudicate uel iurisiurandi. Sed compensationem non. Sed quid si excommunicatus conuenitur super eo pro quo fuit excommunicatus—nunquid potest excipere quod non teneatur respondere nisi restituatur ei communio hominum qua iniuste est spoliatus? Dico quod sic, ut iii. q. ii. c. ii. et ii. q. v. Super causas [11] in fi. Io."

[14]Ibid. Curiously, Bartholomaeus Brixiensis recorded that Johannes Teutonicus, as well as his own master, Tancred, had ruled that excommunicates could benefit from *compensatio* (*Quaestiones dominicales et veneriales* qu. 33, in *Tractatus ex variis iuris interpretibus collecti* [Lyon 1549], vol. 17, fol. 54rb).

[15]For the first point see Damasus, *Quaestiones de iure canonico*, Vat. MSS Pal. 656, fol. 209ra–rb, and Borgh. 261, fol. 26vb: "et interdum reo admittitur facultas defendendi se quod non posset opponere exceptionem. . . . Sed contra. Permittitur soluendo id quod debetur perimere obligationem, extra de sententia excommu. Si uere [X 5.39.34]. Et inter solutionem et compensationem nichil interest. . . . Ergo si permissum est ei soluere permissum ei etiam compensare. Item, eadem ratione quare non admittitur compensatio, quia in fauorem conuenti inducta est. Et ita si communicaremus excommunicato in eo quod pertinet ad eius utilitatem, incideremus in excommunicationem, xi. q. iii. Cum excommunicato [18]." For the second point, see Vinc. Hisp., *App.* X 5.7.11, v. *Instrumenta*, Vat. MSS Vat. 6769, fol. 125rb, and Barb. 1626, fol. 544v: "Nonne ipsis postulantibus isti scriniarii scribent confessiones

Even Innocent IV, who as a private jurist and as pope was so concerned to protect excommunicated plaintiffs against the worst legal
disabilities, sharply restricted the rights of excommunicated defendants. Innocent III's rule that excommunicated defendants not be permitted aggressive litigation meant prohibiting all forms of voluntary
defense—so Innocent IV wrote in his *Apparatus*.[16] Thus excommunicates could not appear as interested parties in response to judicial
summonses for settling estates or submit exceptions that would invalidate elections.

Hostiensis, who wrote so vigorously against excommunicates
as plaintiffs, uncharacteristically celebrated excommunicates' legal
rights based on the judicial equity extolled and protected by one of
Innocent IV's own constitutions.[17] Hatred should not be allowed
to attenuate the rights of an excommunicate—or even, Hostiensis
wrote with irritable irony, those of the devil himself. Innocent IV's
distinction between necessary and voluntary defenses came not from
law but "from the top of his head."[18] For example, proclaimed Hostiensis—who had been excommunicated by William Ralegh in January 1244 for continued resistance to Ralegh's election as bishop of
Winchester, confirmed by Innocent IV in 1243—no defendant was
more necessary than one who submitted an exception against an unworthy candidate elected to office.[19] Against the virtually unanimous

---

actoris? Respondeo utique, si faciant ad exceptionem peremptoriam. Secus si dilatoriam. Mulieri etiam heretice Velleianum auxilium denegaretur, quod habetur C. ad
uelle. l. i. [Cod. 4.29.1]. . . . Sed hoc non est uerum, quia in talibus magis attenditur
equitas iudicantis quam fauor excommunicati, supra de excep. Cum inter [X 2.25.5].
Vincen." On the use of the Velleian exception in ecclesiastical courts see Fournier,
Officialités 168; and for a late example (1499), see Jourdain, "Dettes" 79.

[16] Inn. IV, *App.* X 2.25.5, v. *Vinculo excommunicationis* and v. *Reconvenire*.

[17] Host., *Lect.* X 2.25.5, v. *Sed equitas*, referring to VI 2.14.1.

[18] Host., *Lect.* X 2.25.5, v. *Excommunicationis*.

[19] Ibid., referring to a case in which Clement IV (1265–68) overruled such an exception. A note in Jo. An., *Nov.* X 2.25.8, v. *Opponunt*, enables us to identify
the bishop as Matthew of Viseu, in Lusitania, who was translated to Coimbra by
Clement IV in 1268 but was returned to Viseu in 1279 by Nicholas III, having passed
his Coimbra tenure in Rome; cf. C. Eubel, *Hierarchia Catholica medii aevi* (Regensburg 1913) I 196 n. 3 and I 531. For details of Hostiensis's involvement in the Ralegh
dispute see N. Didier, "Henri de Suse, prieur d'Antibes, prévôt de Grasse (1235?–
1245)," *St. Gratiana* 2 (1954) 597–617 at 605–9; and "Henri de Suse en Angleterre
(1236?–1244)," *Studi in onore di Vicenzo Arangio-Ruiz* (Naples 1952) II 333–51 at
335–46 and *Bracton*, vol. 3, pp. xli–xlii.

opinion of earlier canonists, Hostiensis further decided that excommunicated defendants could apply for *compensatio*: if their opponents did not object, a judge's prohibition would be "monstrous."[20]

Chicanery resulting from excessively permissive defense strategies had led Innocent IV to prune other rights of defendants; that, of course, was what lay behind *Pia*. Hostiensis's vehement reaction might have been prompted partly by personal hostility to the pope; at one point he scoffed that Innocent IV's logic must have been inspired by a "demonium meridianum"—heretic.[21] By the end of the thirteenth century, some proportion had been restored to litigation, partly through Innocent's own *Novellae*, and Guido de Baysio wrote that excommunicates could also use favorable defenses.[22] Anything in the laws that seemed to indicate the contrary should be applied only to accused heretics: "in other crimes justice is not denied," Guido declared, with perhaps unconscious candor.

JUDGE

Because the powers of an ecclesiastical judge were both legal and sacramental the canon law on judicial office was very complex.[23] Gratian's account of the subject, written in exactly the period when the penitential and juridical forums were being differentiated, is

---

[20] Host., *Lect.* X 2.25.5, v. *Materiam.*

[21] Host., *Lect.* X 2.25.5, v. *Excommunicationis.* Cf. R. Arbesmann, "The 'Daemonium Meridianum' and Greek and Latin Patristic Exegesis," *Traditio* 14 (1958) 17–31, on the demon (Ps. 90.6) as heretic. Hostiensis's antipathy to Innocent IV might have resulted partly from the reaction against Innocent IV that Alexander IV (1254–61) initiated; see C. Lefebvre, "Hostiensis," *DDC* 5.1211–27 at 1213–14.

[22] Guido de Baysio, *Rosarium* C.4 q.1 d. a. c.1, in gl. v. *Excipere*, fol. 168va. Guido (*Comm.* VI 2.12.1, v. *Agentes*) and Johannes Andreae (*Nov.* X 2.25.8, v. *Opponunt*) both argued against Innocent IV's rule that excommunicates could not submit exceptions against candidates elected to office, but Guido defended Innocent's general distinction between necessary and voluntary defenses and observed that if the pope had taken it "from the top of his head," as Hostiensis charged, that was his prerogative "tanquam pater et organum ueritatis"!

[23] Two *novellae* of Innocent IV show this duality clearly in the penalties they impose on delinquent judges. *Cum aeterni* (VI 2.14.1) requires unjust judges to pay damages to an injured party, suspends them for a year, and excludes them from divine services; *Cum medicinalis* (VI 5.11.1) has similar though lesser penalties for judges who neglect to put an excommunication in writing and state its cause.

nonetheless one of the most lucid discussions in the Decretum. Legal and ethical qualifications for judges were well served by Gratian's requirement that the participants in litigation be morally equal, which was not confined to the adversaries. A judge must be morally superior to the defendant in a case: under this maxim Gratian summarized the Roman provisions prohibiting *infames* to be judges.[24] Qualifying this, however, was another Roman principle upholding judgments rendered by a slave appointed as an imperial delegate under the misapprehension that he was free.[25] Thus certain persons were disqualified from the office of judge, but judicial acts performed by them were not retroactively invalidated.

From Roman law Gratian turned to theological sources.[26] Persuasive as he found the many patristic statements urging that "a priest . . . must purge his own sins before he can cleanse and heal others',"[27] Gratian could not set aside the many biblical passages in which the rulings of wicked judges prevailed. Though they could not serve as examples for their litigants, Gratian concluded, immoral judges could benefit them by coercion and correction.[28] Thus the theological route led to a conclusion similar to that of Roman law: as long as immoral judges were tolerated and retained in office their judgments could not be overturned.[29]

But on the sacramental side matters were rather different. Writing just as the heresy crisis was beginning—when tolerating heretical prelates was still conceivable—Gratian debated whether a heretical bishop could validly excommunicate; he concluded that orthodox Christians must respect an excommunication imposed by a heretic to discipline a criminal.[30] But this was true only if the bishop had not yet been excommunicated: when Gratian wrote, only those who subscribed to doctrines already condemned as heresy were *ipso facto* excommunicated.[31] At least in regard to excommunication, then,

---

[24] C.3 q.7 d. a. c.1–c.2. On *cognitor* as "judge" (C.3 q.7 c.1; cf. C.2 q.1 c.20) see May, "Infamie im Decretum" 404 n. 99.

[25] Dig. 1.14.3, *Barbarius*; Gratian is surely paraphrasing this in the last sentence of C.3 q.7 d. p. c.1; cf. Jacobi, "Prozess" 245 n. 6.

[26] C.3 q.7 d. a. c.3–end.

[27] C.3 q.7 c.7.

[28] C.3. q.7. d. p. c.7.

[29] See, e.g., *Sum. "Elegantius"* (*Coloniensis*), ed. Fransen, 7.13, vol. 2, p. 159.

[30] C.24 q.1 d. p. c.39; cf. d. p. c.37 § 2.

[31] C.24 q.1 d. a. c.1 and d. p. c.3.

that sanction itself distinguished judges tolerated in office from those no longer possessing jurisdiction: excommunicates could not excommunicate.[32]

By the end of the twelfth century the canonists had concluded, inevitably, that excommunicates could not be judges,[33] and a decretal of Innocent III proclaimed that a judicial sentence brought by a publicly excommunicated judge was null.[34] Noting that the decretal contradicted Gratian's principle of upholding legal judgments *de facto*, the canonists nonetheless agreed that such sentences should be retracted.[35] *Pia*'s mitigation of the exception of excommunication did not extend to the exception against excommunicated judges, whose transactions were invalid no matter when the exception was submitted.[36]

The problem was administrative, for politically the rule was dynamite. It could be brandished by subjects against an unwanted ruler, as in 1294, when, resisting their bishop's order to repeal statutes against his spiritual and temporal jurisdiction on pain of excommunication, the citizens of Speyer informed the Apostolic See that he was incapable of "publishing any penalties against them, since he himself [was] bound by the chain of . . . major excommunication for person-

---

[32] C.24 q.1 d. p. c.3, c.4, and c.37.

[33] Appendix 1a lines 7–9 and Appendix 1d lines 11–12. See also Bernard of Pavia, *Sum.* 5.34.9, p. 276.

[34] X 2.27.24, undated. Contemporary heresy decretals (X 5.7.10 and 13) also made it clear that excommunication *latae sententiae* for heresy disqualified judges excommunicated *latae sententiae*.

[35] E.g., Jo. Teut., *App.* 4 Comp. 2.11.2, v. *Innodatus*, Vat. 1377, fol. 295vb: "Et ita retractatur sententia si detegatur impedimentum post sententiam. Sic supra di. viii. Veritate [4]. xxix. q. ii. Si quis ingenuus [4]. Est contra id generale quod est iii. q. vii § Tria [d. p. c.1] in prin. . . . Et ita per rationem huius decretalis uidetur quod etiam retractanda sit sententia iudicis qui communicauit excommunicato. Et facit ad id s. de elec. Illa, l. iiii. [X 1.6.39]." See also Vinc. Hisp., *App.* 3 Comp. 5.4.1, v. *Firmitatem*, Vat. 1378, fol. 95rb: "Quid si ab ignorantibus ipsum esse talem eligatur et sententiam dicat? Respondeo tanquam a non suo iudice dicta non ualet, xi. q. i. c. penult. [49]. s. de consue. Ad nostram [X 1.4.3] . . . ff. de officio pretoris. Barbarius [Dig. 1.14.3] arg. contra."

[36] In early glosses Innocent IV wrote that a sentence by a secretly excommunicated judge should not be retracted unless he had been publicly denounced (*App.* X 2.25.12, v. *Prohibetur*, and X 2.27.24, v. *Infirmandum*). But Goffredus de Trano and Bernard of Compostella immediately made it clear that *Pia*'s mitigations did not extend to excommunicated judges (Appendix 2a lines 5–6 and 9–10, and Appendix 2b lines 5–6 and 24–34); and in his own gloss on *Pia*, Innocent IV retreated (Appendix 2c lines 5–6, 9–10, and 60–63).

ally laying violent hands on Gernod, a monk of Sinsheim. . . ."[37]
The measure was even more commonly invoked in the internal politics of the ecclesiastical hierarchy than in temporal matters: thus in
the late thirteenth century during a dispute over metropolitan prerogatives between John Romeyn, archbishop of York, and Antony
Bek, bishop of Durham, Romeyn's official excommunicated Bek's for
impeding appeals to York and wrote to Bek reminding him that any
legal transactions over which his official presided were null.[38] Naturally Bek ignored the mandate; for an exception of excommunication brought against his official would be tried in the archbishop's
court! This, at least, was the policy the canonists worked out on the
grounds that in the matter of the exception, a bishop against whom it
was brought was defendant; hence litigation, following the defendant's forum, went to his metropolitan.[39] The abrasions marring these
jurisdictional channels were manifest in Innocent IV's ruling that the
caseload of an excommunicated suffragan should not go to his metropolitan, even if the suffragan had been excommunicated "for his
own sins," not in the line of official duties: some other *poena* should
be found for the suffragan.[40] Exceptions of excommunication against
judges delegate had always been tried by arbiters, and by the four-

[37] A. Hilgard, ed., *Urkundenbuch zur Geschichte der Stadt Speyer* (Strasbourg 1885)
137–40, no. 183 (23 Sept. 1294). For details of the long conflict see L. G. Duggan,
Bishop and Chapter. The Governance of the Bishopric of Speyer to 1552 (New Brunswick,
N.J., 1978) esp. 51–69. I gratefully acknowledge the help of my late colleague
Charles McCurry in drawing my attention to this work.

[38] R. Brentano, *York Metropolitan Jurisdiction* (Berkeley and Los Angeles 1959) 166.

[39] So argued Host., *App.*, *Pia* (VI 2.12.1), v. *Iudex*, vol. 2, p. 17a, no. 25; Dur.,
Spec. 2.1(*De excep.*), vol. 2, fol. 120vb, no. 20; and the anonymous lectures in Vat.,
Borgh. 228, *Pia*, fol. 108ra: "Dic quod si opponatur contra ordinarium superior
proximus. Si autem contra delegatum tunc arbiter et non ipsemet iudex, quia nunquam pronunciaret se esse excommunicatum. . . ."

[40] *Romana. Edictum* (VI 1.8.1), ed. Kessler, "Untersuchungen" part 1, 177. A letter
of Gregory VII indicates that a judge who substituted for an excommunicated
bishop was himself liable to excommunication (*Reg.* III 10a, ed. Caspar I 268), but
Innocent IV forbade this (*Romana. Cum Remensis*, VI 1.13.1, ed. Kessler, "Untersuchungen," part 1, 177–78). In practice, many excommunicated judges must just
have delegated their jurisdictions (for a late thirteenth-century example from Durham, see Brentano, *York* 90–91), but Bernard of Compostella ruled it impermissible
(*App.*, *Romana. Cum Remensis*, v. *Astringit*, Vat. MSS Borgh. 268, fol. 129va, and
Vat. 1365, fol. 590rb–va: "Et ita mandatum inefficax est per excommunicationem
mandatoris quantum ad iurisdictionem. . . . Item excommunicatus non potest com-
mittere causam alii dum est excommunicatus. . . ."

teenth century Johannes Andreae recommended arbitration for exceptions against ordinary judges as well.[41] The complexities of litigation had made arbitration the most common recourse in both the secular and the ecclesiastical courts—in the latter it has been described by Brentano as "the almost universal end of observable provincial cases between two respectable parties at law. . . ."[42] (By the second half of the thirteenth century the canonists had agreed that excommunicates could not arbitrate, even though the qualifications required of arbiters were less stringent than those for judges.)[43]

Excommunication was also a bar to judges in the lay courts. *Decernimus* (1257), in which Alexander IV ordered secular enforcement of excommunicates' legal incapacities,[44] did not disqualify excommunicated judges, presumably because the decretal was addressed to the lay judges being ordered to enforce the other legal disabilities of excommunication. But another decretal of the same pope implied their disqualification by permitting the Inquisitors to enlist the aid of excommunicated secular judges in executing penalties against heretics, although as excommunicates these judges possessed no jurisdiction *de iure* and could not be asked to cooperate in other cases.[45] Several secular law books, moreover, confirmed the validity of the exception of excommunication against judges, among them the famous *Coutumes de Beauvaisis* of Philippe de Beaumanoir.[46]

---

[41] Jo. An., *Comm.* VI 2.12.1, v. *Iudex*. For a 1313 case from Worcester see Haines, *Worcester* 305–7.

[42] R. Brentano, "Three Thirteenth-Century Italian Cases in Ecclesiastical Courts," *MIC* C-1 (Vatican City 1965) 311–19 at 319. Cf. C. Donahue, "Roman Canon Law in the Medieval English Church: Stubbs vs. Maitland Reexamined," *Michigan Law R.* 72 (1974) 647–716 at 674, noting the high percentage of fourteenth-century York cases that ended in abandonment or compromise but pointing out (p. 705) that most modern cases do also. On the French secular courts see Bongert, *Cours* 71, estimating that about eight or nine of every ten cases ended up before arbitrators.

[43] See, e.g., Appendix 2d lines 1–11; Dur., *Spec.* 1.1(*De arbitr.*) § "Potest esse," no. 5, vol. 1, fol. 79rb; Guido de Baysio, *Comm.* VI 2.12.1, v. *Excludantur;* Vat., Borgh. 228, X 2.27.24, fol. 111rb: "Queritur an dictum arbitri publice excommunicati ualeat. . . . Item, excommunicatus est in peccato cum excommunicatio non debet fieri nisi pro peccato mortali. . . . Set qui est in peccato est seruus peccati. . . . Set seruus non potest esse arbiter." In Roman law, *infames* could be arbiters (Dig. 4.8.7.pr. = C.3. q.7 c.2 § 17).

[44] *Decernimus*: VI 5.11.8.

[45] VI 5.2.6.

[46] Beaumanoir, *Coutumes* c.5 § 191, vol. 1, p. 95 (restricting the prohibition to judges under aggravated excommunications). See also A. Tardif, *La Procédure civile et criminelle aux XIIIe et XIVe siècles* (Paris 1885) 17.

WITNESSES

In the bittersweet memoir of his sojourn at the Roman court in 1202, Gerald of Wales recalled the exception of excommunication against witnesses as the legal device that almost vindicated his claim to the episcopal see of St. David's.[47] Gerald had already been to the Curia twice, in 1199 and 1201, to pursue his claim despite the opposition of the archbishop of Canterbury. In March 1201, while the case was still pending, Gerald as archdeacon excommunicated two of the canons of St. David's for transgressing their oaths of fealty to St. David's by taking the archbishop's side. The papal judges delegate appointed to settle the case summoned Gerald because it was illegal to excommunicate litigants while a case was still pending. Gerald appealed to Rome and set off once again, late in 1201, to put his case before the pope. In the Consistory debate that ensued the famous canonist John of Tynemouth represented the archbishop of Canterbury. Believing that he could prove Gerald an unworthy administrator, Tynemouth described Gerald's "cruel and unjust" excommunication of the rebellious canons, who were among Tynemouth's witnesses. According to Gerald, Innocent III at once recognized the legal implications of Tynemouth's remarks: the proctor had admitted that two of his own witnesses were excommunicates. In a low voice, Innocent told the cardinals and papal chaplains sitting at his feet that Gerald could not have a better plea against his adversary. When the hearing ended for the day, one of the chaplains took the jubilant archdeacon aside and told him what the pope had said.

Unfortunately for Gerald, Tynemouth, imagining his master's wrath, bribed the cardinals during the recess. With the summer heat coming on, Innocent had no taste for protracted litigation and persuaded the opponents to renounce their right to trial and agree to compromise—to Gerald's later regret. Innocent pronounced both elections invalid, and Gerald was left with only the memory of that great day when the papal court buzzed at his adversary's unwittingly handing him the means to "blow the canons out of court."[48]

Inability to testify is not a deprivation comparable to inability to sue or accuse. In the middle ages, as now, testifying was as often as

---

[47] Giraldus Cambrensis, *De jure* D. 4, esp. pp. 241–68.
[48] Ibid. 264: "excommunicationis exceptione canonicos omnes exsufflante." On Tynemouth see also Chapter 3 n. 101.

not annoying and perhaps dangerous; excommunication itself was sometimes used to force witnesses to testify.[49] Nor did Roman *infamia* merge the two disabilities.[50] Nonetheless they were joined by a canon of the Council of Carthage of 419 and by the Pseudoisidorian collections in their program of protecting clerics from accusation.[51]

In the medieval ecclesiastical courts, exceptions against witnesses could be submitted at any point in the trial, even after the testimony was published;[52] and as it was peremptory, the exception of excommunication against witnesses was not governed by *Pia*'s allotment of eight days for proof.[53] In the early thirteenth century Vincentius Hispanus wrote that a judicial sentence based on testimony by excommunicates should be retracted.[54] But evaluation of testimony lay within a judge's discretion.[55] A decretal of Innocent III directed that certain canons involved in an election dispute be absolved *ad cautelam* in order to testify since their testimony was essential to the case.[56] By a custom of the lay court at Reims, a litigant needing the testimony of an excommunicate could have his witness absolved "quoad actum

---

[49] X 2.21.2; cf., e.g., Bernard of Pavia, *Sum.* 2.14.2, p. 49. For an example of excommunication (and a fine) to coerce witnesses in a secular court see P. Rogé, *Les Anciens Fors de Béarn* (Toulouse 1907). I have not been able to see the customs on which Rogé based this study; they were published by A. Mazure and J. Hatoulet, *Fors de Béarn* (Pau [1841–43]).

[50] Greenidge, *Infamia* 167.

[51] Council of Carthage, ao. 419, c.131, ed. Munier, *Concilia Africae* 231; in Gratian, C.4 q.2 and 3 c.1. On the Pseudoisidorian link between the prohibitions of accusation and testimony, see May, "Anklage-" 181–82 and "Anfänge" 92; on the same link in Gratian, see Jacobi, "Prozess" 248, 255, and 300–301.

[52] X 2.25.1. Cf. Egidius de Fuscarariis, *Ordo* c.61, ed. Wahrmund, *Quellen* III.1, p. 115, advising litigants to see if testimony would support a conviction before spending time and money on an exception of excommunication. The case of Stephaneta Bersaut, described in Chapter 4 "Two Cases," seems to illustrate this.

[53] Guido de Baysio, *Comm.* VI 2.12.1, v. *Opponit.*

[54] Vinc. Hisp., *App.* 3 Comp. 1.2.2, v. *Per ignorantiam*, Vat. 1378, fol. 2ra–rb: "Quid si excommunicatus fuit aduocatus in causa, nunquid retractanda est sententia? Quid si fuit hereticus? Ar. quod retractari debeat. d. p. di. i. Nemo [*de poen.* D.1 c.7] contrarium. Credo idem dicerem in procuratore. Secus in iudice uel in teste, i. de hereticis. Vergentis [X 5.7.10]. Vin."

[55] Dig. 22.5.3 in C.4 q.2 and 3 c.3 § 2. See also C.2 q.1 c.7 § 3, where Gregory I must be basing his opinion indirectly on the Digest.

[56] X 2.20.38. Johannes Andreae noted that one reason *absolutio ad cautelam* had been established was to enable the courts to obtain testimony from excommunicated witnesses (*Comm.* VI 5.11.2, in gl. v. *Bene admissum*, no. 12).

deponendum"; the absolution would be filed with the deposition to waylay the exception of excommunication.[57]

Decernimus ordered that the exception of excommunication against witnesses be accepted in the secular courts, and this seems to have been widely done in France.[58] Procedural rules enacted in 1268 deemed the exception valid in the royal court, and about a decade later Beaumanoir wrote that excommunicates could not testify, though in some manuscripts the prohibition was limited to excommunicates whose sentences had been aggravated.[59] In Verdun and in Reims, fourteenth-century customs required not only witnesses but also the compurgators who by local procedures supported a plaintiff's claim to be "free from excommunication."[60] But by the fourteenth century the French courts were beginning to abolish personal exceptions based on moral grounds. Around the turn of the fourteenth and fifteenth centuries, the Parisian custumal compiled by Jacques d'Ablieges stated that the exception of excommunication was no longer accepted in *parlement*.[61] In Poitou, customs drawn up in the late fourteenth century still allowed the exception, but the *Vieux coustumier* of 1417 did not.[62] Still, the exception against witnesses was hardier in France than most of the other legal penalties of excommunication. In the Pyrenees viscounty of Béarn, lay justice was jointly administered by viscount and bishop, and although in the late fourteenth century

[57] Varin, *Arch. légis.* I 816, no. [VI]. Cf. Jo. An., *Comm.* VI 5.11.2, v. *Aliis*, noting that an absolution might expire after testimony was given.

[58] VI 5.11.8; excommunicates could, however, testify in heresy trials (VI 5.2.5).

[59] *Olim* I 738, no. 32 (for the parliamentary rule); Beaumanoir, *Coutumes* c.39 § 1206, vol. 2, p. 121. (The *apparatus criticus*, note f, lists five manuscripts that omit "et renforcié.") However, a royal ordinance of 23 April 1299 confirming other points of the canonical policy on deprivation of excommunicates' legal rights did not mention the exception against witnesses (F. A. Isambert, ed., *Recueil général des anciennes lois françaises* [Paris 1822–23], vol. 2, no. 337, art. 4, pp. 720–21).

[60] For the Verdun rules, dating 1308–13, see *Le Livre des droits de Verdun*, ed. E. M. Meijers and S. de Grave (Haarlem 1940) c.[CIII], p. 76. Cf. introd. p. v for the date (this chapter is part of c¹) and p. xxi on the survival of Frankish elements in Verdun procedures. For the Reims rules see Varin, *Arch. légis.* I 634–35, no. [77]. VII.

[61] Jacques d'Ablieges, *Le Grand Coutumier de France*, ed. E. Laboulaye and R. Dareste (Paris 1868; repr. Aalen 1969) 3.18, p. 476. This subject will be discussed in more detail in Chapter 7 at n. 57.

[62] For the late fourteenth-century customs see C. J. Beautemps-Beaupré, *Le Livre des droiz et des commandemens d'office de justice* (Paris 1865) § 72, vol. 1, p. 352; for those promulgated in 1417 see R. Filhol, *Le Vieux Coustumier de Poictou* (Bourges 1956) tit. 35, art. 278, p. 116.

Viscount Mathieu de Castelbon was already struggling against eccle-siastical influence on secular law, the exception of excommunication against witnesses was still held valid in the *Fors et costumas*, published in 1551.[63]

PROCTORS AND ADVOCATES

"Proctors expound the facts, advocates expound the law."[64] But the duties of either blended with those of the other, and some courts made no distinction; in general, the office of advocate on its upper bound merged with that of judge and with that of proctor on its lower.[65] More definitely differentiated were their salaries: a maximum of twenty pounds for advocates and of twelve for proctors according to a canon on licensing procedures from the second Council of Lyon (1274).[66]

Legal representatives were the direct target of Roman *infamia*, which prohibited or restricted lawsuits conducted on behalf of others.[67] In Gratian's Decretum excerpts from the praetorian edicts on *infamia* were oddly introduced in the context of qualifications for judges.[68] True, the passages taken from Justinian had been added to an already "finished" text of the Decretum;[69] moreover, the position of these ex-

---

[63] On the fourteenth-century conflict see Rogé, *Fors* 420–21. For the rule of 1551, see *Les Fors et costumas de Bearn* (Pau 1715) rubr. "De test.," art. 3.

[64] William of Drogheda, *Sum.* c.119, Wahrmund, *Quellen* II.2, p. 128.

[65] See Fournier, *Officialités* 55, and M. A. von Bethmann-Hollweg, *Der Civilprozess des gemeinen Rechts* (Bonn 1868–74; repr. Aalen 1959) V 332, on interchangeability of court officials. Woodcock, *Canterbury* 42, notes that in Canterbury's diocesan courts proctors were not distinguished from advocates, though they were in the provincial courts.

[66] *COD* 324. Johannes de Turrecremata said *infamia* barred advocates but not proctors from court because an advocate's duties were an honor, a proctor's a burden (*Repertorium* C.3 q.7 c.1, *qu. incid.*).

[67] See Dig. 3.1.1.pr., the praetorian edicts on *infamia* and on other derogations of legal capacity. These edicts aimed at protecting the dignity of the civil courts.

[68] C.3 q.7 c.2, falling between two groups of texts (discussed above at n. 24) on the qualifications for judges but clearly identified in its opening statement (*pars* 1, pr.) as material on legal representation.

[69] Most recently, Basdevant-Gaudemet, "Sources" 212–13. Litewski, "Textes" 77–78, notes that most categories in C.3 q.7 c.2 were listed elsewhere in relation to capacity to sue. Thus the new Roman texts must have been directed specifically at representation.

cerpts is partly justified by the ambidextrous role of advocates as both advisers to the judge and representatives of the parties. Yet the Roman texts on *infamia*, though highly important, might not have seemed at the time altogether relevant to medieval litigation. Even in civil trials proctors were only gradually coming to be used in the twelfth century, and they were almost never allowed in criminal trials.[70] The Roman texts did not commend themselves to the Decretum's emphasis on criminal procedures.[71]

All this changed during the latter half of the twelfth century. Legal representation became more common as medieval society grew increasingly litigious; furthermore the "civil" criminal procedures of *denunciatio* and, by the end of the twelfth century, *inquisitio* did permit the use of proctors.[72] The difficult texts of the Decretum did not establish practicable guidelines on qualifications for these representatives, and to that end Innocent III enacted several decretals in the early thirteenth century. One granted *absolutio ad cautelam* to an abbot and a canon sent to Rome as defendants in an election dispute, the plaintiff having objected that they, and indeed all other inmates of the abbey, had been excommunicated in the course of the dispute.[73] Less lucky was a canon elected as proctor by the chapter of St. Martin of Troyes but removed from office by the pope when his opponents showed that he stood under sentence of excommunication for beating the late abbot of St. Martins's "ad effusionem sanguinis" and roughing up a priest of the same church so badly that his friends despaired of his life.[74] Evidently such an instinctive reaction to the exigencies of adversary relationships was not what was wanted in an attorney—at least not by his adversaries.

---

[70] In Italian civil procedures, proctors were used only from the twelfth century (von Bethmann-Hollweg, *Civilprozess* V 399); likewise in England (Maitland, *History* I 211; E. Rathbone, "Roman Law in the Anglo-Norman Realm," *St. Gratiana* 11 [1967] 253–69 at 264). Where customary law prevailed in France plaintiffs could appoint proctors only by royal grace even in the fourteenth century, according to Guillaume du Breuil, *Style du parlement de Paris*, ed. H. E. Lot (Paris 1877) 20–21.

[71] For Roman law: Dig. 3.3.42; Cod. 2.12.21, 9.2.3 and 5. For canon law: C.2 q.6 d. p. c.39 § 1 and c.40, C.3 q.9 c.18 and d. a. c.19, and C.5 q.3 d. a. c.2 (cf. Jacobi, "Prozess" 259) and X 5.1.15.

[72] Fournier, *Officialités* 270.

[73] X 2.20.38.

[74] X 2.19.7.

Certainly, then, excommunicates could not be proctors, but it is unlikely that the prohibition was commonly enforced except at an opponent's behest. Vincentius Hispanus and, later, Duranti agreed that a judicial sentence could not be revoked by an exception of excommunication belatedly submitted against a proctor.[75] Probably the church courts' concern with suits in which ecclesiastical institutions were parties contributed to this mildness; canon law favored a litigant defending his church and looked more tolerantly on any disabilities he might be laboring under than on others'.[76]

Because they operated in the realm of ideas and rhetoric, however, advocates were more closely monitored, particularly in heresy trials. The heresy decretals of the late twelfth century inflicted after one year a permanent bar on advocates excommunicated for "offering any aid, advice, or favor to these heretics . . . or giving them patronage in . . . litigation or creating public instruments or other documents for them."[77] (Documents drawn up by an excommunicated notary were invalid.)[78] Defending the Visconti family in the papal court of Benedict XII (1334–42), Albericus de Rosciate received a chilling warning from one of the cardinals "ne inciderem in fautoriam haereticorum."[79] On Albericus's behalf the cardinal protested to the court that the lawyer had never intended to say or do anything to benefit heretics; he was only defending true Catholics from unjust condemnation.

Decernimus extended the ban against excommunicated advocates to the lay courts.[80] In France, it was affirmed by Beaumanoir (though restricted to excommunicates whose sentences had been aggravated)

---

[75] For Vincentius see above n. 54; for Duranti, see *Spec.* 1.4(*De advoc.*) § "Objicitur," vol. 1, fol. 193ra. In relation to rescripts, see also Appendix 2a lines 1–3 and 7–8; Appendix 2f lines 49–55; Host., *Lect.* X 2.19.7, v. *Non duximus*; and Dur., *Spec.* 1.3(*De proc.*) § "Ratione," no. 1, vol. 1, fol. 152rb.

[76] X 2.25.8.

[77] X 5.7.11. More generally, anyone excommunicated for associating with heretics was subjected to *infamia* after one year and so was disqualified from being an advocate (X 5.7.9–10 and 13). See also Lea, *Inquisition* I 445.

[78] E.g., Appendix 2f lines 45–48. Baldus debated whether an excommunicated notary could compose valid public documents and, with earlier jurists, decided no; see V. Valentini, ed., "Il 'Tractatus de tabellionibus' di Baldo degli Ubaldi," *St. Urbinati* 18 (1965–66) qu. 17, pp. 134–35.

[79] Albericus de Rosciate, *Commentariorum de statutis libri IV* q. 32, *TUI* 2, fol. 71rb. This must be the case against the Visconti (though Alberico does not name them) described in Mollat, *Avignon* 111.

[80] VI 5.11.8.

and by a royal ordinance of 1299.[81] Breton customs of the early fourteenth century and late fourteenth-century customs of Poitou incorporated the prohibition against excommunicates serving as proctors.[82]

The canonists did not come down very hard on this prohibition, perhaps not surprisingly, since many of them had been advocates at some point in their careers. Hostiensis and Duranti on this issue abandoned their habitually stern attitudes toward excommunicates' legal rights, Hostiensis suggesting nothing more harsh than that the salary of an excommunicated advocate who dared to practice be withheld and Duranti proposing that only advocates excommunicated for suspicion of heresy be barred from practice.[83]

---

[81] Beaumanoir, *Coutumes* c.5 § 191, vol. 1, p. 95; Philip IV, Mandate of 23 April 1299, art. 4, Isambert, *Recueil* II 720–21.

[82] M. Planiol, ed., *La Très Ancienne Coutume de Bretagne* (Rennes 1896) c.[87], p. 136; for Poitou, Beautemps-Beaupré, *Livre* § 320, vol. 2, p. 9.

[83] Host., *App.*, *Pia* (VI 2.12.1), v. *Excluduntur*, p. 16b, no. 9. See also Duranti, *Spec.* 1.4(*De advoc.*) § "Objicitur," vol. 1, fol. 193ra; and Jo. An., *Comm.* VI 5.11.8, v. *Patrocinando*.

VI

Excommunicates Outside the Courts

NATURAL LAW

Extrajudicial legal transactions were harder to control than those in court. Roman *infamia*, the foundation of canon law on the excommunicate's status in judicial proceedings, did not extend to legal matters outside the courts, and indeed Roman law gave little guidance. Imperial constitutions of the early fifth century forbade Manicheans and Donatists to make contracts, sales, or gifts, but these were extreme measures against persons being treated like traitors.[1] Innocent III's decretal *Vergentis* (1198) renewed this analogy between heresy and treason, and councils of the late twelfth century prohibited contracts and commerce with heretics.[2] But the canonists were appropriately reluctant to apply such constitutions to ordinary excommunicates.

---

[1] See esp. CT 16.5.40.4 (= Cod. 1.5.4.3), 16.5.54.pr., 16.6.4.3; Cod. 1.5.19; and Nov. Val. III 18.3. Cf. Maisonneuve, *Etudes* 30–36; and C. Luibhéid, "Theodosius II and Heresy," *J. of Ecclesiastical History* 16 (1965) 13–38, esp. 13–14, 27–29, and 36–38.

[2] X 5.7.10; see W. Ullmann, "The Significance of Innocent III's Decretal 'Vergentis,'" in *Etudes d'histoire du droit canonique dédiées à Gabriel Le Bras* (Paris 1965) I 729–42. Quite apart from their ideology, Manicheans in particular were a threat because of their Persian connections (cf. Maisonneuve, *Etudes* 30 and 35).

Roman law emphasized that contractual obligations were governed by natural law.[3] Even capital penalties entailing loss of citizenship and freedom did not necessarily abrogate the rights conferred by natural law. Referring to a constitution of Antoninus Pius (138–61) that seems to have preserved inheritance rights for criminals condemned to labor in the mines, the jurist Marcianus observed that "persons who lose their citizenship . . . surrender the things conferred by civil law but keep the things given by natural law."[4] In the second century the jurist Africanus argued that contracts contained an implicit condition that creditors would retain their present legal status; hence debts should not be repaid to those punished by exile or loss of freedom.[5] But in the third century Tryphoninus saw a conflict between natural law, which called for fulfillment of contractual obligations, and civil law, which required that money owed to a criminal condemned to deportation and confiscation be turned over to the public treasury since the specter of indigence was an effective deterrent to crime.[6]

The canonists regarded natural law as the life force of their own written law;[7] accordingly the tension between natural and positive (written) law was a central theme in their discussion of excommunicates' legal rights in extrajudicial transactions. As Panormitanus phrased it, "Contracts are a function of natural law, whereas excommunication is a function of positive law."[8]

There were also compelling pragmatic reasons to uphold contracts, especially if, as commonly happened, they were sealed with an oath.[9] In the earliest decretist debates the canons of Gregory VII and Urban II suspending feudal oaths during excommunication were cited: they

[3] Inst. 1.2.2.

[4] Dig. 48.19.17.1; see P. Garnsey, *Social Status and Legal Privilege in the Roman Empire* (Oxford 1970) 165. Labor in the mines was a capital penalty for the lower classes, equivalent to deportation.

[5] Dig. 46.3.38.pr.

[6] Dig. 16.3.31.

[7] See R. Weigand, *Die Naturrechtslehre der Legisten und Dekretisten* (Munich 1967) esp. 100–106; on natural law as the integrative theme of Hostiensis's work in particular, see Lefebvre, "Hostiensis," 1219–24. Among the theologians, see in particular Thomas Aquinas, *Sum. theo.* 2-1, q.95, a.4, resp.

[8] Panormitanus, *Comm.* X 5.39.34, no. 8.

[9] X 2.24 passim.

seemed to indicate that debts to excommunicates should not be repaid.[10] But this argument was quickly overcome. As the anonymous
author of the famous Decretum apparatus *Ordinaturus magister* argued
around 1180, out of reverence for oaths one could make the repayment through an agent, thereby avoiding direct contact.[11] Surprisingly, even Huguccio, who took a much more extreme position
against excommunicates' legal rights than his contemporaries, believed that debts should be repaid.[12] Only obligations requiring direct
contact with an excommunicate were suspended; thus the vassals of
an excommunicated lord must continue to pay feudal tributes even
though they were forbidden to perform their normal feudal services.

Although oaths were the crux of his arguments, Huguccio also believed that debts should be repaid even if they had not been sworn.
A decretal of Alexander III required that interest promised under
oath be paid to usurers; only after the gesture of payment would
church authorities enforce the laws by forcing the usurer to return
the money.[13] Oaths were treated with a respect often tinged with obsessive compulsion; in this, canon law only expressed the medieval
norm. But oaths also yielded a good deal of litigation for the church
courts, for debt cases of all sorts came to them under the guise of
perjury. Secular jurisdictions objected strenuously.[14] Already in 1164
the Constitutions of Clarendon prohibited the church courts from

[10] I.e., C.15 q.6 cc.3–5, discussed above in Chapter 1 at n. 105 and Chapter 3 at n. 120.

[11] Appendix 3b.

[12] Appendix 1d lines 45–51; Appendix 3a.

[13] X 2.24.6. See Appendix 3a line 12, where Huguccio cites *Cum sit Romana* to confirm that debts sworn to usurers must be repaid (cf. Appendix 1b note 9; I am indebted to Professor Charles Duggan for help in identifying this citation). Neither
this nor Huguccio's other citation (X 2.24.7) is as relevant as X 2.24.6. Under a
canon of the Third Lateran Council usurers were excluded from the sacraments
(X 5.19.3), i.e., subjected to what was just coming to be called "minor" excommunication. Huguccio is doubtless alluding to this when he says usurers are "perhaps excommunicated" (Appendix 3a lines 10–11; he believed even minor excommunicates should be subjected to legal disabilities (see Chapter 4 at n. 58). The later
papal law ruling that they were not excommunicated invalidated his analogy between
excommunicates and usurers. See the vigorous refutation by Host. below at n. 92.

[14] On France, see Fournier, *Officialités* 86; on England, Maitland, *History* II 197–
200; Flahiff, "Writ" part 1, 278 and part 2, 260; Donahue, "Roman" 660; and Woodcock, *Canterbury* 89–92.

trying debt cases merely because an oath had been given.[15] If the ecclesiastical courts were to continue to compete for this litigation, it was important to have a strong policy of enforcing sworn obligations.

But whereas Huguccio anticipated the future significance of such a policy, several canonists writing about the turn of the twelfth and thirteenth centuries still believed that debts should not be repaid to excommunicates. Alanus Anglicus wrote that even money promised under oath should be withheld.[16] To avoid interest payments and free oneself from obligation, one could register the payment and deposit it in a sacred building. Yet even debtors who withheld the money entirely, Alanus argued, would not be transgressing: as Augustine had said, one would not keep a sworn promise to return a sword to a friend who had gone mad. If an excommunicate died unabsolved, however, the money could be repaid to the heirs, since excommunicates retained control of their possessions. (In the course of his discussion Alanus had cited *Vergentis*, which decreed that even orthodox children of heretics could not inherit.) Writing a few years later, Laurentius Hispanus agreed that debtors could justify retaining their money: since the creditor's excommunication was responsible for the delay, let him suffer the consequences.[17] But Laurentius did not feel that repaying such debts was wrong if conversation was avoided.

Johannes Teutonicus reviewed the problem in the *Glossa ordinaria* on the Decretum.[18] Could one speak of a legal obligation to someone incapable of suing? Moreover, canon law obliged the faithful to "harass sinners in every possible way in order to correct them." From the Digest Johannes cited Tryphoninus's argument about the deterrent effect of burdening criminals with poverty;[19] he excised the phrase acknowledging that natural law dictated the opposite. In short, Johannes made a strong case for not repaying debts to excommunicates. Nonetheless, he concluded that "although excommunication destroys feudal obligations, it does not destroy the obligations incurred through other contracts." This conclusion was based on a new factor in the debate on contracts, Innocent III's decretal *Si vere*.

---

[15] Const. of Clarendon, c.15, in Stubbs, *Charters* 167.
[16] Appendix 3b.
[17] Appendix 3c.
[18] *Glos. ord.* C.15 q.6 c.4, v. *Constricti sunt*.
[19] I.e., Dig. 16.3.31, discussed above at n. 6.

SI VERE

Quoniam multos's principle that family members should be allowed to associate with an excommunicated *dominus* was unusually applied in *Si vere*, issued by Innocent III in 1203.[20] The Crusaders had been excommunicated for attacking the Christian city of Zara as part of their bargain with the Venetian doge Enrico Dandolo: having hired a large number of ships, the Crusaders proved heavily in debt when only a fraction of their anticipated forces turned up. Booty from the Zara invasion, the doge proposed, could pay the balance.[21]

Innocent III excommunicated all participants. But the Crusaders, never enthusiastic about the Zara detour, were repentant and obtained absolution on the condition that they return the stolen property. The Venetians were unrepentant, and the pope sent another letter excommunicating them. At first the Crusaders withheld the letter, telling the pope that it would dissolve the Crusade. But Innocent insisted that it be delivered.

The Venetians' excommunication created a predicament. The Crusaders were eager to set off for the Holy Land, and no one was more reluctant than Innocent III to delay their highly valued mission—but it could not be accomplished without the Venetians. Innocent's ingenious solution in *Si vere* was to assure the Crusaders that their contacts with the excommunicated Venetians were permissible provided they were conducted in a spirit of regret. The Venetians, the pope said, had already been paid a large part of the passage money and refused to return it.[22] Thus if the Crusaders withdrew, the Venetians would be "rewarded for their disobedience" by being released from the contract.[23] Alluding to *Quoniam multos*, Innocent noted that if a *paterfamilias* was excommunicated his family was allowed to communicate with him as usual. The excommunicated doge of Venice, Inno-

[20] *Si vere*: X 5.39.34.

[21] For details see E. H. McNeal and R. L. Wolff, "The Fourth Crusade," in R. L. Wolff and H. W. Hazard, eds., *The Later Crusades, 1189–1311*, in K. M. Setton, ed., *A History of the Crusades* (Madison, Wisc., 1969–77) II 153–86 at 161–81.

[22] Evidently the Venetians collected only about half the debt: see D. E. Queller et al., "The Fourth Crusade: The Neglected Majority," *Speculum* 49 (1974) 441–65 at 445–48.

[23] X 5.39.34.

cent proposed, stood in the relation of *paterfamilias* to the Crusaders as long as they were travelers in his ships.

What bearing did *Si vere* have on contracts? At face value it implied that one could associate with excommunicates in order to enforce their obligations. When Johannes Teutonicus initially referred to *Si vere* in his debate on contracts, his point was that however the converse question should be decided, excommunicates should certainly be forced to pay their debts.[24] But he cited *Si vere* a second time in arguing that debts to excommunicated creditors also must be repaid.

Few of Johannes's contemporaries saw *Si vere* this way. It clearly made the point that one could have any contacts with an excommunicate that served one's own advantage. Indeed, an early gloss drew the conclusion that friends need not inconvenience themselves to desert an excommunicated acquaintance immediately.[25] Since *Si vere* had emphasized that the Crusaders had to sail in Venetian ships, some commentators believed that the decretal spoke of a highly unusual case. For Vincentius Hispanus, Innocent's observation that the Venetians would not return the passage money indicated that excommunication would under other, more normal circumstances dissolve a business partnership.[26]

Johannes Teutonicus was led to his conclusion by thinking about the nature of contractual relations, rather than about the facts of the case that formed the basis of *Si vere*.[27] Only one other early commentator on *Si vere*, Laurentius Hispanus, reached the same conclusion; his reasoning was based on a quote from Ulpian's commentary on the praetorian edict: "Here . . . the praetor is fostering natural equity by guarding matters established by consent; for it is a grave thing to break one's promise."[28]

---

[24] *Glos. ord.* C.15 q.6 c.4, v. *Constricti sunt*, for both.

[25] Jo. Teut., *App.* 3 Comp. 5.21.7, v. *Excommunicatorum*, quoted in Chapter 3 at n. 22.

[26] Vinc. Hisp., *App.* X 5.39.34, v. *Induci*, Paris 3967, fol. 206ra: "Ar. excommunicatio superueniens potest inducere dissolutionem societatis, xv. q. vi. Iuratos [5], et supra de penis. Grauem [X 5.37.13]."

[27] *Glos. ord.* C.15 q.6 c.4, v. *Constricti sunt*.

[28] Laurentius Hispanus, *App.* 3 Comp. 5.21.7, v. *Et recepi*, Paris 3932, fol. 198rb: "Sed nunquid debent ei soluere? Dicunt quidam quod non. Sed debeo obligare et deponere. . . . Sic credo soluendum esse nec ei loquendum. Nam grave est fidem fallere, ut ff. de constitu. pecu. l. i. [Dig. 13.5.1] et xxii. q. vi. Iuramenti [*rect.* C.22 q.5 c.12]."

Around the same time as *Si vere*, Innocent III issued two general decretals on extrajudicial communication with excommunicates. In *Per tuas* (1203) Innocent added a second ground of appeal from excommunication—the claim that the sentence contained an intolerable error (a command entailing mortal sin)[29]—to the single ground for appeal laid down by Alexander III, that the excommunication had been imposed after and, of course, in order to impede an appeal.[30] *Per tuas* decreed, however, that the ostracism of excommunication was not to be relieved during appeal, whereas other sorts of sentences were held in abeyance while being contested.[31] Unlike other judicial sentences, excommunication was executed immediately, with no delay for appeal;[32] when there was any doubt whether people were excommunicated or not, they were to be treated as if they were.[33]

In the other decretal, however, Innocent III seemed to contradict this rule himself. *Dilectis* narrated a dispute between the bishop and the dean of Auxerre that had led to an exchange of excommunication by the bishop and interdict by the dean.[34] The dean had appealed to Rome before being excommunicated, and Innocent nullified the excommunication. In the interim, however, the archbishop of Sens had obliged the bishop of Auxerre by denouncing the dean as an excommunicate who must be publicly shunned. But some of the canons of Sens, as the decretal narrates in words attributed, of course, to Innocent III, were "led by wiser counsel." Aware that the excommunication would be nullified because it had been imposed after appeal, these canons had continued to associate with the dean. And Innocent approved: "We judge innocent the canons of Sens who continued to communicate with the dean, deferring to the appeal he made to us

---

[29] X 5.39.40. On "intolerable error" see C.11 q.3 d. p. c.101. Cf. Jo. Teut., *App.* 3 Comp. 5.21.14, v. *Intollerabilem errorem*, ed. Pennington, *Study* II.1, p. 756: "Ut si excommunicet ideo quia non furatur, uel quia est obediens suo prelato. Item error intolerabilis potest dici si expresse extra ius pronuntiat. . . ." See also *Glos. ord.* C.11 q.3 c.4, v. *Interpellat*.

[30] I.e., in *Quaesitum* (1 Comp. 1.23.2), discussed in Chapter 4 at n. 50. See also X 2.20.16.

[31] Dig. 49.7.

[32] X 5.28.53; cf. *Glos. ord.* C.11 q.3 c.31, v. *Sed Christus*.

[33] Jo. Teut., *App.* 3 Comp. 5.21.14 (X 5.39.40), v. *In aliis evitari*, ed. Pennington, *Study* II.1, p. 757: "Nam in dubiis habendus est pro excommunicato, ut supra eodem, Cum desideres [X 5.39.15]. . . ."

[34] X 2.28.55.

[before being excommunicated] rather than to the archbishop's denunciation." Contradicting *Per tuas*, *Dilectis* thus implied that communicating with appellant excommunicates was permissible.

Like *Si vere*, however, *Dilectis* had too many peculiar facts to commend itself as a statement of law. The pope had absolved the canons for communicating with the dean, which is not to say that he would have encouraged their communication if asked in advance. Moreover, *Dilectis* stressed the certainty that the excommunication was null. Also, the appeal that the bishop held in contempt was an appeal to the Apostolic See itself. At most, then, *Dilectis* offered a hint of possible circumstances for waiving *Per tuas*'s rule that even appellant excommunicates must be avoided.

For our purposes, the most important inference from these decretals of Innocent III is this: there was no question of permitting extrajudicial communication with non-appellant excommunicates. No wonder, then, that many early thirteenth-century canonists did not cite *Si vere* to support the validity of contracts with excommunicates; for the *ius commune* to all appearances dictated that excommunicates should be avoided entirely in extrajudicial affairs.

INNOCENT IV AND *SOLET*

During the first year of his pontificate, Innocent IV issued a decretal, *Solet*, that reversed Innocent III's *Per tuas* by decreeing that appellant excommunicates need not be avoided in extrajudicial matters.[35] *Solet* specified three types of ecclesiastical transactions ("in officiis, postulationibus, et electionibus") as examples of extrajudicial acts in which appellant excommunicates should henceforth be allowed to participate. But a more general clause followed—"ac aliis legitimis actibus nihilominus admittatur"—and the canonists did not limit *Solet* to ecclesiastical matters.[36] Appeals from excommunication would now conform to other judicial appeals, Goffredus de Trano

---

[35] *Solet*: VI 5.11.2; see Chapter 4 n. 93. The other problem *Solet* treated, absolution *ad cautelam*, was discussed at greater length in *Venerabilibus* (VI 5.11.7).

[36] See esp. Pet. Samp., *Lect.*, *Solet* (VI 5.11.2), v. *Et aliis*, Vienna 2113, fol. 77rb: "Scilicet in mensa, osculo"; cf. *Glos. ord.* VI 5.11.2, v. *In officiis*: "Publicis uel diuinis."

wrote, and appellant excommunicates would not be ostracized even on a direct order from the excommunicating judge.[37]

But *Solet*'s concessions give only a bare hint of Innocent IV's private views on the extrajudicial rights of excommunicates. In fact, nothing in earlier canonists' discussions foreshadowed Innocent IV's surprising views. In glosses written before he became pope, Innocent IV wrote that *Si vere* showed contracts with excommunicates were valid and must be enforced.[38] Fulfillment of such contracts after absolution entailed no sin, and in any case the "natural" penalty for illicit contracts was not nullification but a fine or a corporeal punishment: "Pacta servabo," as the familiar maxim went.[39] So far, Innocent IV's position resembled Huguccio's. But in another early gloss Innocent went much farther, arguing that even a contract knowingly negotiated during excommunication was valid and could be enforced in court by the excommunicate after he had been absolved.[40]

Innocent IV's most important argument was that the church itself would be responsible for the fraud and mendacity that would undoubtedly result from a policy of nullifying contracts with excommunicates.[41] A case recorded in the plea roll for the Dorset assizes in the summer of 1244 illustrates the accuracy of his apprehensions. Agnes of Aunestowe, fearing imprisonment as a contumacious excommunicate, had fled "from the province," appointing her bailiff, Adam of Foukland, as attorney in suits she was initiating in the county and hundred courts, presumably to recover property she had lost in the ecclesiastical court.[42] Adam, however, took advantage of her vulnerability as a fugitive excommunicate and occupied one of her tenements, claiming she had instructed him to do so by letters

---

[37] Goff. Tr., *App.*, *Solet*, v. *In iudiciis*, Fulda D. 10, fol. 7rb–va: "Item, necessitas iuris cogit nos dicere quod contra iudicem nos uitare non debeamus, quia etsi iudex a quo appellatum est mandat quod euitetur, prius dicit quod appellatione precedente nihil innouandum est, ff. de appellationibus. Peti [? cf. Dig. 49.7: "Nihil innovari appellatione interposita"]. Item, lite pendente nihil innouandum est. Ergo quousque pendet lis, an sit excommunicatus, non debet priuari communione hominum, nec aliis iuribus suis. . . ."

[38] Inn. IV, *App.* X 5.39.34, v. *Convenerit*.

[39] Ibid. On the maxim see Maitland, *History* II 196–97.

[40] Inn. IV, *App.* X 2.14.8, v. *Excommunicationem*, no. 2.

[41] Inn. IV, *App.* X 2.14.8, v. *Excommunicationem*.

[42] *Somersetshire Pleas (Civil and Criminal) from the Rolls of the Itinerant Justices (Close of 12th Century–41 Henry III.)*, ed. C. E. H. Chadwyck Healey (London 1897) 329–30.

patent. Agnes, as she testified in the Dorset suit, "did not dare return to these parts because she was excommunicated. . . ." Luckily for her, the jury upheld her claims, though Adam produced evidence that she had put him in seisin and received rent from him. Agnes recovered her tenement and was granted damages of ten marks; Adam went to prison.

Innocent IV also pointed out that the intention of the canons on excommunication was to punish excommunicates, whereas interference in private legal matters would inevitably sometimes affect others as well.[43] Of course, he warned the faithful not to enter into contracts with an excommunicate if they could obtain what they needed elsewhere with equal ease (or even with some slight inconvenience) or if by their association they would increase an excommunicate's arrogance and contempt for ecclesiastical discipline.

Other early glosses show that Innocent IV believed the ecclesiastical policy on excommunication was sometimes unrealistic and even unjust, needing reevaluation and perhaps reform. Excommunication was often used to sanction court procedures without "manifest and solemn proof" of guilt.[44] Though technically just, such excommunications were not the consequence of sin, and the church easily granted absolution in such cases. So fully was excommunication integrated into the adversary process, Innocent observed, that some litigants seemed to think they had a right to their adversary's excommunication.[45] But excommunication was a therapy, not someone's right.[46] Church authorities must prevent abuse of social pressures; a judge might have to order people to associate with an excommunicate whose sentence has been nullified on appeal, "lest he lose his friends' support."[47]

On becoming pope, Innocent IV seems to have immediately set about transforming his private aspirations into law. *Pia* and *Solet*, with their parallel mitigations for the legal status of excommunicates

---

[43] Inn. IV, *App.* X 2.14.8, v. *Excommunicationem.*

[44] Inn. IV, *App.* X 2.20.54, v. *Per exceptionem.*

[45] Inn. IV, *App.* X 5.39.40, v. *Consueuerit*, no. 3. Note the similar phrasing in *Solet* (VI 5.11.2) in response to the question whether absolution *ad cautelam* should be granted despite an adversary's objection.

[46] On this point see also Inn. IV, *App.* X 2.20.54, v. *Per exceptionem*: "Excommunicatio non est culpa, sed est medicina, uel poenitentia. . . ."

[47] Inn. IV, *App.* X 2.28.54, v. *Notorium*, no. 4.

in judicial and extrajudicial legal activities, were originally issued during his first year in office and reissued at the Council of Lyon. Also repromulgated there was *Cum medicinalis*, the famous canon Luther quoted, which incorporated Innocent IV's belief—again, already expressed in a gloss—that excommunication was not a punishment for the soul but a therapeutic censure.[48] Hence, *Cum medicinalis* goes on, ecclesiastical judges should excommunicate only to heal and should always put their sentences in writing, with a clear statement of the cause. Otherwise, superior judges would readily overturn their excommunications, and the excommunicating judges would be condemned to pay expenses with interest and suspended from entry to the church and participation in divine offices for one month—punishments by which they would learn "how grave it is to fulminate sentences of excommunication without mature deliberation." Another Lyon canon held ecclesiastical judges to issue a warning before increasing from minor to major the excommunication of persons associating with someone they had excommunicated.[49]

After the council, too, Innocent IV issued legislation reforming excommunication. Though the chief object of *Romana* (1246) was to trim metropolitan prerogatives, this famous decretal also forbade excommunication of corporate groups (*universitates*) on the grounds that innocent souls were endangered by such excommunications.[50] *Romana* also restricted the excommunicating authority of metropolitans and their officials.[51]

Thus the decretal *Solet* was only one part of a broad program of excommunication reform. Since its mitigations applied only to appellant excommunicates, moreover, *Solet* fell far short of the liberal views on extrajudicial rights that Innocent IV expressed in his *Apparatus*, where the pope clearly wished to extend these rights to all excommunicates.

Alas, evidently even *Solet* was too generous for the prelates assembled at the council. For when the decretal was reissued, the appendix to another Lyon canon, *Quia periculosum*, denied *Solet*'s con-

---

[48] *Cum medicinalis*: VI 5.11.1.

[49] VI 5.11.3; cf. X 5.39.48.

[50] *Romana. Ceterum* (VI 5.11.5), ed. Kessler, "Untersuchungen" part 1, 178–79.

[51] Esp. *Romana. Prohibemus* (VI 1.16.1 § 1), ed. Kessler, "Untersuchungen" part 1, 177. See also below, n. 56.

cessions to anyone appealing an excommunication imposed by a bishop or archbishop.[52] *Quia periculosum*, besides encroaching on *Solet*, also mitigated for bishops and archbishops the penalties simultaneously enacted in *Cum medicinalis* for unjust excommunications; these prelates would not automatically incur suspension from office or interdict unless they were specifically mentioned in the legislation.[53] Originally, *Quia periculosum* would also have exempted bishops and superior prelates from excommunication *latae sententiae* unless they were specifically mentioned in the canon that established the sentence, but the pope succeeded in deleting this exemption from the draft. According to Hostiensis, when asked why he deleted it Innocent IV replied that bishops would have thus been rendered immune from the excommunication for violence to clerics imposed by *Si quis suadente*.[54] But others, Hostiensis said, believed it was not *Si quis suadente* but one of his own *novellae*, a constitution enacting excommunication *latae sententiae* against princes or prelates who hired assassins, that Innocent IV was safeguarding by excising the word "excommunication" from *Quia periculosum*.[55]

Thus where episcopal immunity clashed with papal reforms, disagreement ensued on the details of the Lyon legislation. The bishops, anxious over the daily problems of diocesan discipline and even, in some places, over anticlerical rebellions, needed the protection of

[52] *Quia periculosum*: VI 5.11.4. The appendix is printed in Friedberg's apparatus because it was deleted from the Sextus's version; see below at n. 109.

[53] On *Cum medicinalis*'s sanctions against unjust excommunications see the text at n. 48. The relation between *Cum* and *Quia* was explained by Pet. Samp., *Lect.*, *Quia periculosum* (VI 5.11.4), v. *Et superioribus*, rec. 1, Vienna 2083, fol. 45ra; rec. 2, Vienna 2113, fol. 77rb: "Quia ideo non euadunt penam istius constitutionis, supra eodem, Cum medicinalis [VI 5.11.1], nec illius, supra, eodem titulo, Sacro [X 5.39.48; but cf. VI 5.11.3], nisi quoad hoc quod hic expresse dicitur, scilicet quod non incurrunt ipso iure suspensionis sententiam uel interdicti. Nihilominus tamen tenetur ad expensas eius quem excommunicauerunt contra formam dictorum capitulorum Sacro et Cum medicinalis, et ad interesse. Hoc autem fuit confirmatum pocius in fauorem subditorum quam episcoporum, quia periculosum erat subditis quod episcopus non posset officium suum exequi. . . ." ("Quia" may really be the lemma. MS 2113 has "immo" for "ideo.")

[54] Host., *App.*, *Quia periculosum* (VI 5.11.4), v. *Interdicti* . . . , no. 2; cf. Kuttner, "Konstitutionen" 107–8. *Si quis suadente* (C.17 q.4 c.29) is discussed in Chapter 2 at n. 1 and passim.

[55] I.e., *Pro humani* (VI 5.4.1). Cf. H. Wolter and H. Holstein, *Lyon I et Lyon II* (Paris 1966); Wolter notes that of the juridical canons of Lyon only *Pro humani* bore the phrase "with the approbation of the council" (pp. 79–80).

their own immunity from discipline. Rather than allying with them, the papacy was increasingly antagonistic: *Romana* firmly checked competition from metropolitans, and in the following year, 1247, the French clergy complained to Innocent IV that papal nuncios were treating them like slaves, excommunicating them and otherwise maligning them in favor of Mendicants.[56] Then, too, the master diplomat Innocent IV doubtless foresaw that episcopal immunity to excommunication was too valuable to be distributed wholesale: better to deal it out piecemeal in papal privileges.[57]

But Innocent IV's attempt to reform excommunication did not fail outright. The story is less straightforward than that, and the canonists' interpretation of the Lyon canons reveals a complex relationship between law and custom. Before examining their interpretation, however, it will be illuminating to consider a later attempt at reform marked by the same mixture of success and failure.

CONSTANCE AND LYON: ATTEMPTS TO REFORM EXCOMMUNICATION

"We don't care about your excommunication or set any store by it," the prelates of Toulon had been told by their parishioners.[58] The prelates and their colleagues, deliberating before the Council of Vienne in 1311, chorused an increasing lay apathy toward excommunication, which in some dioceses kept many parishioners away from the church for years.[59] Secular failure to coerce contumacious excommunicates, Mendicant outreach to those being punished by the ordinary channels of discipline, and the princely immunities to excommunication and interdict too lavishly bestowed by the Apostolic See had in the prelates' view all taken their toll on the "nerve of eccle-

---

[56] On *Romana*'s limitations of metropolitan prerogatives see Kessler's edition in "Untersuchungen" part 1, 156–82, which includes the charges of the prelates on both sides. On the grievances of the French clergy see Berger, *Innocent IV*, pp. cxci–xcii and cxciv.

[57] Hostiensis received such an indulgence in August 1248; see N. Didier, "Henri de Suse, evêque de Sisteron (1244–1250)," *RHDFE*, ser. 4, 31 (1953) 244–70 at 13 and 45.

[58] Ehrle, "Vienne" 380; see P. E. Müller, *Das Konzil von Vienne, 1311–1312* (Münster in Westfalen 1934) passim, for analysis of the gravamina discussed at the council.

[59] See, e.g., the remarks from Reims in Ehrle, "Vienne" 395.

siastical discipline."[60] Remedies for the growing contempt for excommunication tended, however, to employ more coercion—and
therefore more excommunication.[61] Few acknowledged the wisdom
of a Bourges proposal "that no sentence of excommunication be imposed for a small matter or slight contumacy . . . ," and that excommunication not be used for small debts in the church courts even
though such a restriction would impair the courts' much-used small-
claims jurisdiction.[62]

Virtually no general reform emerged[63]—though occasional echoes

[60] On secular neglect of coercion, see, e.g., the complaints from England in Ehrle,
"Vienne" 395; on the Mendicants' "abuses" see Müller, *Konzil* 702, and cf. Clem.
5.7.1 and 3.7.1; on excessive exemptions, see Müller 400, and for some examples see
Regestum Clementis papae V, ed. Monachi ordinis S. Benedicti (Rome 1885–88) I 91,
no. 479; I 205, no. 1140; II 84 no. 1873.

[61] Most remarkable was a proposal for graded punishments of contumacious excommunicates, directed specifically against violators of ecclesiastical liberties: with
each year, ineligibility for ordination was extended to another degree of relations;
withal, "transacto biennio tanquam contra suspectum de heresi inquiretur . . ."
(Ehrle, "Vienne" 416). See also next note.

[62] Ehrle, "Vienne" 416. Though seemingly at cross-purposes, this and the proposal
described in the preceding note were both submitted by Bourges. But decades later,
in 1359, the archbishop, acknowledging that his own and his predecessors' laws had
not achieved their goal, replaced the excommunications in those laws with fines; see
Vat. 9868, fol. 459r: "subjectorum nostrorum animarum periculis obviare volentes
. . . nonnullas constitutiones . . . tam a nostris praedecessoribus quam etiam a nobis
editas, excommunicationis sententiam infligentes . . . per quam anima traditur sathanae, reperierimus, in quam frequenter tam clerici quam laici ex eorum simplici-
tate et ignorantia, et quandoque inanimadvertentia, immo quod pejus est ex fre-
quenti abusu incidunt . . . , praedictas constitutiones . . . reformare curavimus,
dictam excommunicationis poenam . . . penitus amovendo. . . ." A final clause
stated that "dictas poenas excommunicatorias et quandoque pecuniarias in eleemosynas infra expressatas . . . duximus convertandas. . . ."

[63] Only checks on the Mendicants' administering sacraments to those under ecclesiastical censure made their way into the canonical compilation based on the council,
the Clementines; see Clem. 5.7.1 and 3.7.1. On the effects of excessive excommunications on parish life in the fourteenth century see Adam, *Vie* esp. 179–95,
with some impressions of the numbers of excomunicates based on visitation records,
etc. (There is summary evidence from similar records in G. G. Coulton, *Five Centuries of Religion* [Cambridge 1923–50] II 84–85 and 457.) Cf. also Toussaert, *Flandre*
443–52, with a statistical analysis of a register of excommunicates from the diocese
of Oudenburg in a much later period, 1450–54. But reports of numbers of excommunicates are hard to interpret. R. Hill found excommunication "too widely-used"
in late thirteenth-century Lincoln ("Public Penance: Some Problems of a Thirteenth-
Century Bishop," *History* 36 [1951] 214) whereas Haines thought it used less than
one might suppose in early fourteenth-century Worcester (*Worcester* 186). The sources
on which assessments must be based are often contentious.

of the Vienne discussion can be discerned in fourteenth-century synodal legislation—and the reform tracts and agendas for the Council of Constance (1414–18) contain similar laments.[64] Into the council itself Pierre d'Ailly carried a suggestion that the clergy circuit their parishes and interview their innumerable excommunicated parishioners, lecture them on obedience, and absolve them "nullis susceptis pecuniis."[65]

The Constance council failed to enact any comprehensive reform. But the German nation was particularly insistent. Bound by a 1377 constitution of Charles IV correcting the secular courts' abuse of permitting lawsuits even by publicly denounced excommunicates, the Germans pressed to obligate a new pope by conciliar reforms.[66] They did not succeed, but Martin V (1417–31) evidently shared their belief that excommunication in particular needed reform. The only Constance legislation on excommunication came in the form not of a canon but of a clause in the concordat with the German nation declaring that excommunicates should not be avoided unless or until they had been publicly condemned by judicial sentence or denounced, with the reservation that anyone notoriously guilty of violence to a cleric should be ostracized immediately.[67] This, aside from the reservation, was the doctrine unsuccessfully sponsored in the late twelfth century by Johannes Faventinus, who was unwilling to accept that

[64] See esp. Adam, *Vie* 179–85.

[65] For the proposal see Finke, *Acta* IV 572–73; on d'Ailly's attempts to enact these reforms see J. P. McGowan, *Pierre D'Ailly and the Council of Constance* (Washington, D.C., 1936) 71.

[66] The statute is in J. F. Böhmer, *Regesta Imperii VIII. Die Regesten des Kaiserreichs unter Kaiser Karl IV. 1346–1378*, ed. and rev. A. Huber (Innsbruck 1877) p. 484, no. 5789; cf. Eichmann, *Acht* 97. For the discussion of the statute at the council (sess. 19) see H. von der Hardt, *Magnum oecumenicum Constantiense Concilium* (Frankfurt and Leipzig 1700) IV 523–25; on German pressure for reform see ibid. 1419–26 (sess. 38).

[67] von der Hardt, *Constantiense Concilium* I, "Germanicae nationis et Martini V. Papae concordata," c.7, cols. 1066–67: "omnibus Christi fidelibus . . . indulgemus, quod nemo deinceps a communione alicujus . . . praetextu cujuscunque sententiae aut censurae ecclesiasticae . . . teneatur abstinere. . . . Nisi sententia . . . fuerit in vel contra personam . . . aut locum certum vel certa, a judice publicata, vel denunciata specialiter et expresse. Constitutionibus Apostolicis, et aliis in contrarium facientibus, non obstantibus quibuscunque. Salvo, si quem pro . . . manuum injectione in clerum, sententiam latam a canone adeo notorie constiterit incidisse, quod factum non possit aliqua tergiversatione celari, nec aliquo juris suffragio excusari."

those under excommunication *latae sententiae* should be avoided until they had been publicly identified and denounced.[68]

Technically the clause, headed *Ad vitanda*, was applicable only in Germany, and, with the rest of the concordat, was due to expire after five years. But Martin V made his broader intentions clear. The clause was addressed "to all Christians," and a separate provision allowed individual chapters in the concordat to be copied and circulated independently.[69] Moreover, two distinguished representatives at the council, the theologian Nikolaus Dinkelsbühl (d. 1433) and Andreas, bishop of Posen (1414–26), later told the famous theologian Antoninus of Florence that the "constitution" *Ad vitanda* had been accepted by the whole council and was a permanent law.[70] Recording this in his *Summa theologica*, Antoninus also said that Bishop Andreas had later, on a visit to the Roman Curia, asked Martin V for a dispensation to use excommunication with *Ad vitanda*'s mitigations; more than five years had passed since the council.[71] The pope replied that the council had unanimously supported *Ad vitanda*. Andreas reminded him that it was nonetheless due to expire after five years, whereupon the pope pronounced "Ego volo quod semper duret." Further consultation with the papal auditor Julianus, an eminent jurist and (Antoninus noted) later a cardinal, revealed that *Ad vitanda* was universally binding and permanent.[72] Such was the nature of a "constitution" unless it was revoked, and *Ad vitanda* had on the contrary been confirmed by the Council of Basel before its dissolution

---

[68] See Chapter 2 at n. 13.

[69] See n. 67 for the address, and for the provision see c.11 of the concordat, in von der Hardt, *Constantiense Concilium* I 1068–69.

[70] Antoninus of Florence, *Sum. theo.* 3.25.2, vol. 3, cols. 1414–16. This certainly seems to be contradicted by a third eyewitness, Peter of Pulka, who referred to *Ad vitanda* as a provision "pro natione nostra" (i.e., the German nation) in a letter of 23 March 1418; see F. Firnhaber, "Petrus de Pulka, Abgesandter der Wiener Universität am Concilium zu Constanz," *Archiv für Kunde österreichischer Geschichts-Quellen* 15 (1856) 1–70 at 70.

[71] Antoninus of Florence, *Sum. theo.* ibid., col. 1416.

[72] Ibid. It is not clear in Antoninus's account whether he himself consulted the auditor or whether he is still reporting on Bishop Andreas's visit. Whichever, this is a curiously vague way to identify the man who must be the famous Cardinal (from 1426) Giuliano Cesarini, who presided over most sessions of the Council of Basel, including the twentieth, when the reform canons (among them the one on excommunication discussed just below in the text) were passed.

(1438). So Antoninus, who attended the council in 1439, after Pope Eugenius IV had transferred it to Florence, ended his perplexing summary of the status of *Ad vitanda*. Antoninus himself had become a papal auditor in 1431; evidently even those well placed, and presumably well informed about the law, felt that assertions about *Ad vitanda*'s interpretation should be tied to as many authorities as possible. Equally baffling is a tract on excommunication written about 1427–38 by the theologian Nicholas de Plowe at the behest of Andreas's successor-but-one as bishop of Posen, which insists that the Constance "statute" did not change the existing custom that those reputed by public rumor to be excommunicated must be avoided.[73]

In fact, the Council of Basel did in January 1435 enact a canon *Ad vitandum*, whose opening sentences are almost identical to those of the clause in the German concordat.[74] But the stipulation requiring immediate avoidance was extended to anyone who had notoriously incurred excommunication. The existing custom was thus tacitly reinstated, with the extra emphasis of an observation that the canon was not intended to succor excommunicates in any way.[75] Yet the very popular *Summa* of Antoninus claimed that the Basel canon confirmed the Constance legislation. Moreover, the clause of the Constance concordat enjoyed a wide manuscript transmission, identified as a "constitution" of Martin V.[76]

Oddly enough, the confusion surrounding Martin V's reform may have been the key to its endurance.[77] Overt papal tampering with ex-

---

[73] Nicolaus de Plowe, "De excommunicatione," *TUI* 14, fol. 365ra–rb, nos. 11–12. For the date see R. Chabanne, "Nicolas de Plowe," *DDC* 6.1010, noting that this tract is evidently excerpted from a larger work on the sacraments by this still not fully identified theologian.

[74] Council of Basel, session 20, *COD* 487. The Basel canon follows the Constance clause (see n. 67) closely through "expresse," then diverges: "aut si aliquem ita notorie excommunicationis sententiam constiterit incidisse. . . ."

[75] Ibid.: "Per hoc . . . excommunicatos . . . non intendit in aliquo relevare, nec eis quomodolibet suffragari."

[76] E.g., Vat., Pal. 718, fol. 40r (the manuscript contains tracts by Antoninus of Florence and other works); and Vat. 4988 (a fifteenth-century papal chancery formulary), fol. 32v–35r.

[77] E.g., B. Hübler, *Kirchenrechtsquellen*, 4th ed. (Berlin 1902) 74, calling the Basel canon a "Generalisierung des deutschen Censur-Indults." The Constance version was adopted in the *Codex iuris canonici* (ed. P. Gasparri [Rome 1917]) c.2258 and was named as the source in *Codicis iuris canonici fontes* (by the same editor [Rome 1923–47])

communication's tabu met with consternation—but resistance was checked by befuddlement about what was said and meant. The same had been true of the Council of Lyon—but there the story is even more intriguing, because we have the pope's own glosses, from whose facets glanced a bewildering array of lights.

QUIA PERICULOSUM

Quia periculosum's appendix does not say that excommunicates appealing from episcopal sentences must be avoided in extrajudicial acts notwithstanding *Solet*'s mitigations, though it certainly so implies. What it does say is, "Let past custom be maintained in the future."[78] Bernard of Compostella, in the earliest apparatus on the Lyon constitutions, concluded that *Solet*'s concessions were denied to those excommunicated by bishops and their superiors.[79] But Innocent IV's gloss on *Quia periculosum* drew attention to *Quia*'s strange phrasing, noting that the author of *Quia*'s appendix chose his words "cautiously—for he does not wish to say that [appellant excommunicates] should be avoided in extrajudicial affairs. Rather he says, "Let past custom be observed in the future." For appellant excommunicates were never to be avoided extrajudicially, and "he that saw bare record" [John 19.35]."[80] Innocent IV's gloss thereupon acknowledges that Innocent III's decretal *Per tuas*[81] seems to show, on the contrary, that ap-

---

I 58. As E. Jombart observes ("Excommunication," *DDC* 5.615–28 at 616–17), interpretation of these canons is still uncertain. I do not follow Jombart's opinion that Martin V did not intend to better the position of excommunicates and that a clause embracing "all notorious excommunicates" must be tacitly added to the Constance canon; nor do I agree with the opinion of Jombart and others that the Constance canon is the source of the modern distinction between *vitandi* and *tolerati* excommunicates (e.g., E. Magnin, "Ad vitanda scandala," *DDC* 1.250–52; F. E. Hyland, *Excommunication. Its Nature, Historical Development, and Effects* [Washington, D.C. 1928] 42). The Constance concordat treated only one class of excommunicates, those excommunicated *latae sententiae* and not yet denounced. Still less does the Basel canon foreshadow modern usage. Morel (*Pouvoir* 189–91) notes the change introduced at Basel, but without elucidating its significance.

[78] Friedberg, apparatus 1095.

[79] Appendix 4 lines 1–14.

[80] Inn. IV, *App.*, *Quia periculosum* (VI 5.11.4), v. *Olim.* Cf. *App.*, *Solet* (VI 5.11.2), v. *Articulo*, no. 7.

[81] X 5.39.40.

pellant excommunicates must be avoided "in matters other [than their appeals]." But in fact *Per tuas* simply meant that appellant excommunicates were still to be prohibited from bringing lawsuits—or perhaps it meant that such excommunicates must still be avoided until their appeals were underway. Thus Innocent IV reconstructed the literal meaning of *Per tuas*.

In the second recension of his *Apparatus* (ca. 1253) Bernard of Compostella posed the obvious question: if appellant excommunicates had not customarily been avoided extrajudicially, what was the point of *Solet*?[82] He might have added that if *Solet* was nugatory, *Quia periculosum*'s appendix restricting *Solet* must have been doubly so.

Peter Sampson and Hostiensis agreed that the key to Innocent IV's gloss on *Quia periculosum* lay in the pope's instruction to observe existing custom, and both wrote that Innocent IV had "borne his record" on existing custom in his commentary on Innocent III's decretal *Dilectis*.[83] *Dilectis*, of course, records Innocent III's approval of the canons of Sens's continued association with the appellant and thus illicitly excommunicated dean of Auxerre.[84] In his gloss on *Dilectis*, Innocent IV concluded that one should avoid appellant excommunicates only in doubtful cases, not when the appeal was sure to succeed.[85] This gloss is scarcely the ringing testimony the comments of Peter Sampson and Hostiensis suggest. Still, Innocent IV did make one rather startling pronouncement: the canons of Sens would have been blameless even if they had elected the excommunicated dean of Auxerre to office. Though one might infer that election to office was thereby singled out as the ultimate proof that associating with appellant excommunicates was permissible, Innocent IV pointed out on the contrary that the act of election did not require communication.

Hostiensis also recommended consulting Innocent IV's commentary on *Solet* to understand the pope's reasoning.[86] Strangely, in his gloss Innocent IV wrote as if to persuade himself and others that

---

[82] Appendix 4 lines 16–18, between *uncini*.

[83] Pet. Samp., *Lect.*, *Quia periculosum* (VI 5.11.4), v. *Quod olim*, Vienna MSS 2083, fol. 45ra, and 2113, fol. 77rb: "Caute hoc dicit. Nam non uult dicere quod euitentur extra iudicium. 'Et qui uidit testimonium perhibuit' secundum papam Innocen., qui dixit quod ipse uidit et quod ⟨non⟩ uitabantur per decretalem extra de ap. Dilectis [X 2.28.55], ad fi."; and Host., *App.*, *Quia periculosum*, v. *Quod olim*.

[84] X 2.28.55.

[85] Inn. IV, *App.* X 2.28.55, v. *Inculpabiles*.

[86] Host., *App.*, *Quia periculosum* (VI 5.11.4), v. *Quod olim*.

Solet's innovations were just and necessary.[87] Perhaps the gloss was written before *Solet* was issued. In a long and difficult commentary, Innocent IV posed as an example the case of an excommunicate appealing on the grounds of official exemption from the excommunicator's jurisdiction. Should there exist a general law that appellant excommunicates be avoided—there was one, of course; *Solet* tried to change it—"then if this excommunicate should ask me whether to seek absolution, at the expense of acknowledging the excommunicator's jurisdiction and thereby permanently surrendering his church's exemption, I would advise not seeking absolution. But I would then incur major excommunication for giving this good advice." Hence derived the need for a law allowing free communication with appellant excommunicates. But such a law, Innocent IV continued to ruminate, would imply that a person could be worthy of communicating with the faithful and yet unworthy of being absolved.

And here we find one of those solutions that, revealing an ingenious intuition of a point at which law and theology merge, made Innocent IV the foremost theorist of medieval law. To allow the faithful to communicate with appellant excommunicates is to ensure that the law does the latter no injury (hence Gerald of Wales admonished Innocent III not to withhold the papal kiss from the excommunicated but appellant bishop-elect of Bangor), whereas absolution is an act of grace, of which the appellant excommunicate has not yet been proved worthy.[88]

Innocent IV's arguments here enable us to suggest why the pope, although privately believing that no excommunicates whatsoever should be avoided in extrajudicial legal transactions, began his reforms with the case of appellant excommunicates. Only here could he argue that the church was unjust to forbid communication; for the court must regard an appellant's claim as being as valid as his adversary's. Since there was no delay before a sentence of excommunication was executed, appellant excommunicates remained excommunicated throughout their appeals; but to avoid injuring them, Innocent believed, the courts must relieve the worst effect of the sentence, the ostracism.

The publication of *Solet* and the restrictive appendix in *Quia periculosum* perplexed the canonists. Looking at Innocent IV's private

[87] Inn. IV, *App.*, *Solet* (VI 5.11.2), v. *Articulo*.
[88] Ibid. no. 7.

writings—and perhaps reviewing their own experience—they argued that excommunicates could participate freely in extrajudicial legal transactions. In glosses evidently written during his pontificate, Innocent IV reiterated his view that "contracts and sales and similar transactions are valid even when one party is publicly and solemnly excommunicated. . . ."[89] Peter Sampson enthusiastically endorsed Innocent IV's academic views, writing that excommunicates could make gifts, buy, and sell.[90] Moreover, one could certainly repay debts to excommunicates, as *Si vere* and *Quoniam multos* had shown. Abbas Antiquus agreed that "all contracts celebrated by and with [an excommunicate] are valid, and both parties are given the appropriate legal actions arising from such a contract," though the excommunicate would have to postpone a lawsuit until obtaining absolution.[91]

Thus most canonists hastened to support Innocent IV's personal views. But how to reconcile these views with the Lyon constitutions? *Solet* extended these freedoms only to appellant excommunicates, and *Quia periculosum* further restricted them to those excommunicated by a prelate lower than a bishop. Matters were at a standoff. On the one hand there was a juristic tradition that all excommunicates could freely participate in extrajudicial legal acts, that they could enter into contracts and similar transactions even as beneficiaries, and that they could sue over such transactions after absolution. On the other hand, *Solet* and *Quia periculosum* considerably restricted this permission. One canonist, however, was well pleased by the Lyon legislation: Hostiensis alone opposed Innocent IV's reforms and refuted them brilliantly and vigorously.

HOSTIENSIS: AN IDEOLOGICAL APPROACH

Since the decretist period the question of contracts with excommunicates had always had a practical orientation. Huguccio, with his

---

[89] Appendix 2c lines 54–57.

[90] Appendix 2d lines 14–23. But in a gloss on *Solet*, Sampson implied that this permission was not only limited to appellant excommunicates but was also further limited by *Quia periculosum*, which, in this gloss, he did not interpret as Innocent IV did. Commenting on *Solet*'s declaration that appellant excommunicates should be admitted to extrajudicial acts, Sampson said, "Non sicut excommunicati ab episcopis uel archiepiscopis, infra eodem, Quia periculosum" (v. *Admittatur*, Vienna MSS 2083, fol. 77ra, and 2113, fol. 45ra).

[91] Appendix 2f lines 12–27.

immense influence, had endorsed the validity of obligations to excommunicates, and the retreat from his position that occurred around
the turn of the century was overwhelmed by Innocent IV's forceful
glosses. Who could disagree with the pope's statement that if the
church did not uphold contracts with excommunicates it would be
responsible for fraud and mendacity?

Hostiensis could, and did. Starting at the opposite end of the question, Hostiensis never turned his glance from the purpose of the ban
on associating with excommunicates. Withholding money from an
excommunicated creditor, as a deterrent to crime and an inducement
to absolution, was simply a detail in this broad ideological picture.

Hostiensis took on all the canonists who had argued the contrary.
Huguccio's reasoning, that since the church required repayment of
debts to usurers it should also require repayment of debts to excommunicates, was based on a false premise, since usurers were excommunicated only by minor excommunication and did not have to be
avoided socially.[92] Repayment through an agent of the excommunicated creditor was both ineffective and fraudulent. Payment to an
agent did not expunge a debt unless ratified by the creditor. More
important, it made a sham of the canons forbidding communication.
Hostiensis approved only the proposal that the debt be registered and
deposited until absolution.[93]

So much for existing debts. What if one entered into a new contract with an excommunicate? Hostiensis drew on a panoply of legal
arguments to forbid this. There could be no question of civil obligation to excommunicates, since they could not sue.[94] But one did incur
a natural obligation, for which canon law granted legal actions. Yet
canon lawyers must be guided by theological injunctions as well as by
legal ones, Hostiensis decided. "In detestation of the excommunicate," the money could be given to the poor.[95] Thus excommunicates
would be punished in a currency that as sinners they lacked—the currency of charity.

[92] Host., *Sum.* 5.59(*De sen. exc.*).16, cols. 1935–36. Cf. 5.56(*De pen. et rem.*).61,
col. 1862.
[93] Host., *Sum.* 5.59(*De sen. exc.*).16, col. 1936.
[94] Host., *Sum.* 5.59(*De sen. exc.*).16, cols. 1936–37. See Lefebvre, "Hostiensis"
1224, for Hostiensis's doctrine that a natural obligation gave rise to a legal action; and
on enforcement of nude pacts in canon law see J. Roussier, *Le Fondement de l'obligation contractuelle dans le droit classique de l'église* (Paris 1933), and Maitland, *History* II
195–203.
[95] Host., *Sum.* 5.59(*De sen. exc.*).16, col. 1937.

To epitomize an excommunicate's status in legal negotiations, Hostiensis contrasted it to that of "pupils" in Roman law: while the latter could only obligate others to themselves, excommunicates could only obligate themselves to others.[96] One circumstance alone would justify repayment of a debt to an excommunicated creditor: if there were an invasion by heretics or pagans and the excommunicate alone could defend the country.[97]

These opinions Hostiensis expressed in his *Summa* during Innocent IV's pontificate. Naturally, Hostiensis welcomed *Solet's* implicit support of his position. By conceding appellant excommunicates the right to engage in extrajudicial legal transactions, *Solet* confirmed that other excommunicates were barred from them.[98] In his gloss on *Solet*, also written during Innocent IV's pontificate, Hostiensis wrote that legal transactions benefiting excommunicates were invalid. Elsewhere, he admitted that "certain" canonists contradicted his views, but he did not directly take issue with the pope in this period.[99] Instead he systematically refuted Peter Sampson, a prominent exponent of opinions similar to the pope's. After quoting Sampson at some length, Hostiensis professed to agree with him "except in a few matters, of which I'll now speak." He went on to reject Sampson's arguments in almost every detail. Excommunicates must be excluded from all legal transactions, judicial or extrajudicial, that served their advantage.[100] Anyone who believed the contrary should read Innocent III's decretal *Si vere*, which ruled that a particular contract be upheld lest the excommunicated party (the Venetians) benefit and the other party (the Crusaders) suffer loss. When the terms were reversed, therefore, the law would never validate a contract. Once again, summing up these points in his gloss on *Pia*, Hostiensis took the opportunity to point out that *Solet* would not have singled out appellant excommunicates unless all others were excluded from extrajudicial acts.

If *Solet* was welcome, *Quia periculosum* was yet more so. Hostiensis, who had a reputation for exalting, even exaggerating, episcopal

---

[96] Host., *Sum.* 5.56(*De pen. et rem.*).61, col. 1862.

[97] Host., *Sum.* 5.59(*De sen. exc.*).16, col. 1936.

[98] Host., *App.*, *Solet* (VI 5.11.2), v. *Legitimis actibus*, no. 13.

[99] Host., *App.*, *Pia* (VI 2.12.1), v. *Actibus*, no. 6, excerpting or paraphrasing Pet. Samp.'s distinction on *Pia* (Appendix 2d lines 1–33). See also v. *Excluduntur*.

[100] Host., *App.*, *Pia* (VI 2.12.1), v. *Actibus*, no. 13.

status,[101] must have urged its adoption at the council. In his gloss, he interpreted *Quia periculosum* absolutely logically, refusing to enter into Innocent IV's semantic play.[102] *Quia periculosum*, Hostiensis wrote, showed that someone excommunicated by a bishop or archbishop must be avoided even during an appeal of the sentence as null because imposed after appeal.

These opinions, expressed during Innocent's pontificate, might have been modulated from respect for "dominus noster." Hostiensis's opposition to Innocent IV's private opinions must also have been mollified by *Solet* and *Quia periculosum*, conforming as they did much more closely to his positions than to the pope's. But by the time he wrote his lectures on the Liber Extra in the 1260s Hostiensis's comments on Innocent IV's opinions had become an acid critique. *Si vere* was the occasion for his harshest judgments;[103] he quoted Innocent IV's gloss and expressed surprise that one "expert in the law" could embrace such views and support them by legal citations that, had the pope read them more carefully, would have led him to the opposite conclusions. Perfecting the arguments he had used so effectively in his *Summa*, Hostiensis now proposed that an excommunicate's inability to enforce a civil obligation should persuade any Christian not to engage in contracts with excommunicates; the ban should function like any other legal device that destroyed a right of action, such as a prior agreement not to sue (*pactum de non petendo*). With this argument Hostiensis was even able to deflect the burden of natural obligation. Contracts entered into during excommunication were like good works performed while one was in a state of mortal sin—they were "born dead." No penance would revive them, whereas after absolution one could enforce contracts initiated before excommunication, just as the merits of good works performed before one committed mortal sin could be revived by penance.[104] Thus it should seem "just and reasonable" to any faithful Catholic that excommunicates could not effectively bind anyone by contract. Natural obligation was extinguished by the diseases of disobedience and excommunication.

---

[101] Didier, "Sisteron" 17 and 21–28 on Hostiensis's litigation to augment his episcopal rights as bishop of Sisteron (1244–50).

[102] Host., *App.*, *Quia periculosum* (VI 5.11.4), v. *Nullatenus.*

[103] Host., *Lect.* X 5.39.34, v. *Inter vos*, no. 5.

[104] Host., *Lect.* X 2.14.8, v. *Excommunicationem.*

Hostiensis continued to argue that *Si vere* could not be used to prove that excommunicates could engage in contracts. Each of the facts narrated in the decretal indicated an extenuating circumstance peculiar to the case. The Venetians refused to return the passage money, and secular authorities, chronically neglectful, would not force them to.[105] If the pope had been more strict, the Crusaders would have lost their ships and could not have obtained any elsewhere. What could be more obvious than that contracts with excommunicates were normally forbidden?[106] And rightly so; for by permitting excommunicates to obligate others the church would only make them more arrogant and less respectful of its sanctions.[107]

The clash between Innocent IV and Hostiensis was ideological. Innocent IV, as his contemporaries testified, believed that custom did not and should not require avoiding excommunicates in extrajudicial legal affairs. A law calling for a much higher standard of behavior than custom was pointless. But Innocent IV's reasoning was not merely negative. The rules on excommunication were almost obsessive, nearly ends in themselves, to be enforced even at the expense of non-excommunicates. Secular institutions, such as commerce, were inherently valuable; they should not be treated merely as hostages in the transcendent battle for salvation.

Hostiensis, on the other hand, defended the primacy of canonical injunctions. The community of the faithful should be mindful above all of Christian duties and the Christian precepts that governed it, expressed in canon law as clearly as one could wish. Faithful Christians should be prepared to contemplate a theological analogy while analyzing even so mundane a matter as a legal contract. They should take seriously the presence of an excommunicate in the community, and their relations with excommunicates should be governed not only by strictures thrown directly across their path but also by the maxims for daily life that could be extrapolated from the great general principles of law. Christians should be prepared if necessary to suffer inconvenience to enforce the prohibition against contact with excommunicates; for the faithful had responsibilities far deeper than the superficial exigencies of practical affairs.

---

[105] Host., *Lect.* X 5.39.34, v. *Induci*; and Host., *Lect.* X 5.39.34, v. *Coarctari*.
[106] Host., *Lect.* X 5.39.34, v. *Videremini*.
[107] Host., *Lect.* X 2.14.8, v. *Excommunicationem*, no. 18.

Hostiensis's charge that Innocent IV did not give sufficient weight to the laws in reaching his conclusions would be hard to refute, at least on technical grounds. At most, *Si vere* showed that faithful Catholics could associate with excommunicates to enforce contracts favoring themselves. More narrowly, *Si vere* was simply an indulgence for the Crusaders, whose mission was of such moment for the Christian community.[108] One can deduce from Innocent IV's own laws that excommunicates were normally forbidden to engage in extrajudicial legal transactions.

Yet if Hostiensis had the law on his side, Innocent IV had juristic opinion on his. Huguccio had upheld the validity of contracts with excommunicates, despite his exceptional stringency regarding the legal rights of excommunicates in court. For Johannes Teutonicus, *Si vere* applied even to contractual obligations favoring excommunicates. Innocent IV's contemporaries strongly supported his views, and Hostiensis himself recorded the pope's testimony that appellant excommunicates could by custom engage in extrajudicial legal matters. The issue was complex, with law and custom, interpretation and opinion, rapidly shifting relations with one another.

LAW AND PRACTICE: THE AFTERMATH

The fates of *Solet* and *Quia periculosum* were as curious as their origins. *Quia*'s appendix on *Solet* was excised in the redaction of the Liber Sextus of 1298.[109] Studying *Quia* when he wrote the *Glossa ordinaria* on the Liber Sextus a few years later, Johannes Andreae compared the version in the Sextus with the original *novella* and remarked, "There used to be more text here, with a declaration about the decretal *Solet*, but since it had no purpose it was excised."[110] By the time he wrote his commentary on the Liber Sextus, however, four decades later, Andreae had realized that the now-missing portion of *Quia periculosum* was not superfluous: "At one time this last part [of *Solet*] was restricted in relation to sentences of bishops by the

---

[108] Thus described by Abb. Ant., *Lect.* X 5.39.34, v. *Si vere* and v. *Convenerit*.

[109] Hence it is printed only in Friedberg's apparatus at VI 5.11.4, from the manuscripts he collated of Innocent IV's *Novellae*.

[110] Jo. An., *Glos. ord.* VI 5.11.4, v. *Habeatur*.

decretal *Quia periculosum*. But today the [restrictive] part has been excised."[111] So Innocent IV enjoyed a posthumous triumph? Possibly, or, perhaps, partially. But the Liber Sextus also contained Boniface VIII's decretal *Licet*, which declared that an excommunicate who had already been denounced must be avoided both in court and extrajudicially until successfully proving the excommunication null on appeal.[112] On the surface, *Licet* abolished any concessions *Solet* made, with or without *Solet*'s qualifications in *Quia periculosum*. But the canonists did not see *Licet* this way, or rather, they made a special effort not to. Johannes Andreae interpreted *Licet*'s phrasing to mean that an excommunicate could participate in extrajudicial matters from the moment appeal began.[113] Guido de Baysio was willing to accept that the appellant excommunicate envisaged by *Licet* should be avoided extrajudicially, but only as a special punishment for neglecting to appeal within the year allowed.[114] *Solet*'s concessions (now indeed in the Sextus's version minus the restrictions of *Quia periculosum*) were still available to other excommunicates, Guido wrote.

Licet, by focusing on the effects of denunciation, might provide a clue to practice. Perhaps the ban on extrajudicial transactions was now normally enforced not as an effect of mere excommunication but as an aggravation of an existing sentence. The denunciation parish priests used against contumacious excommunicates specifically warned the faithful to avoid trade with them.[115] This aggravation would not have been slight even if the canonists had agreed that all excommunicates were forbidden extrajudicial transactions, since the aggravation raised the penalty for communication from the usual minor to major excommunication. But perhaps in practice the ban was reserved for the contumacious, and public denunciation alerted the community that more strenuous ostracism should take effect. A case that came before the English royal court in 1304, just when

---

[111] Jo. An., *Comm.* VI 5.11.2, v. *Admittatur*: "Olim iste finis restringebatur ⟨quo⟩ad sententias episcoporum per decre. Quia periculosum. Sed illa pars hodie est sublata." I have supplied the *quo-* as necessary to the meaning, as is clear from Johannes's own correction of his earlier comments in an addition to *Glos. ord.* VI 5.11.4, v. *Habeatur*.

[112] VI 5.11.14.

[113] *Glos. ord.* VI 5.11.14, v. *Docuerit*.

[114] Guido de Baysio, *Comm.* VI 5.11.14, v. *Nullitate*.

[115] E.g. Arnulphus, *Sum.* c.10, in Wahrmund, *Quellen* I.2, p. 11; cf. Chapter 3 at n. 100.

the canonists were making their first assessments of *Licet*, may reflect the growing significance of denunciation.[116] Robert Winchelsey, archbishop of Canterbury, was summoned before the royal court at Gloucester to defend his exercising jurisdiction and his fulminating sentences of excommunication against the prior and canons of the monastery of St. Oswald's. The prior, arguing that St. Oswald's was a royal free chapel, charged that the archbishop had acted in defiance of a royal writ of prohibition and had disobeyed orders to revoke a sentence of excommunication inflicted on the prior and canons in August 1303 for resisting his visitation. For about six months afterward, the prior claimed, Winchelsey had regularly denounced the prior and canons as excommunicates and had forbidden all trade with them.[117] The monastery claimed a loss of two hundred pounds. Though loss of tithes and offerings must be taken into account here, this very considerable sum shows how grave the ban on extrajudicial legal transactions could be. The prior was unable to recoup the monastery's losses, since he failed for lack of proof that the writ of prohibition had been delivered to the archbishop.

Perhaps, then, the prohibition of extrajudicial transactions was often reserved as a penalty for contumacy in excommunication but was executed by the stiffer sanction of major excommunication when it was put into effect. In any event, the prohibition certainly remained a potential consequence of excommunication. In 1383 Wyclif complained that "worldly priests" while "cursing" the faithful for other contacts with excommunicates instructed them to repay excommunicated creditors.[118] Yet only a few years before, in 1376–77, Gregory XI had organized a boycott of Florentine merchants throughout Europe because their city lay under ecclesiastical interdict.[119] The relief ex-

---

[116] *Select Cases in the Court of King's Bench under Edward I*, ed. G. O. Sayles, SS 55 (1936), 57 (1938), and 58 (1939), III 138–44.

[117] Of course the archbishop might have forbidden trade from the start. English secular law books of the period shed little light on the question; the only one that mentions contracts with excommunicates is the bizarre *Mirror of Justices*, which forbade them (ed. W. J. Whittaker, SS 7 [1895] II, c.27, p. 73). Among French secular law books the only one I have found that mentions such contracts is a sixteenth-century commentary on Touraine customs, which stated that excommunicates were allowed contracts (*Consuetudines Bituricenses* [ed. N. Boerius], *Aurelianenses* [ed. P. Englebermeus], *Turonenses* [ed. I. Sainson] [Paris 1543] fol. 223, col. 1, comm.).

[118] J. Wyclif, "The Grete Sentence of Curs Expouned," in T. Arnold, ed., *Select English Works of John Wyclif* (Oxford 1869–71) III 267–337 at 328.

[119] Trexler, *Florence*, passim.

pressed by an anonymous diarist when the Florentines were finally informed that they "were . . . released from every excommunication and were allowed . . . to trade and sell and buy in all parts of the world"[120] reveals their greater experience of Hostiensis's "*odium excommunicati*" than of Innocent IV's warning lest "*ecclesia machinaretur fraudes vel mendacium.*"

POST MORTEM

Even contact with deceased excommunicates could result in contagion. The papal protonotary Ludovicus Pontanus (d. 1439) believed that friends who prepared an excommunicate's cadaver for burial would incur minor excommunication, though he admitted the courts had ruled the opposite.[121] In the fifteenth century Cardinal Turrecremata still believed that burial in consecrated ground should be denied even to those unjustly excommunicated.[122] On one level the famous dictum of Leo I remained in force: "Those with whom we cannot communicate while they are living we must continue to avoid after death."[123] But Innocent III had taken a more realistic approach in the decretal *A nobis*, determining that excommunicates who died repentant could be absolved *post mortem*, their heirs being forced to satisfy the courts for their wrongs.[124]

Whether an excommunicate could make amends *post mortem* through a will remained a point of debate throughout the high middle ages.[125] Late twelfth-century heresy decretals revived the Ro-

---

[120] Ibid. 107–8, quoting *Diario d'Anonimo fiorentino*, ed. A. Gherardi (Florence 1876) 373; Trexler's translation. Cf. Trexler 47 for another merchant's comment on the censure's effects.

[121] Ludovicus Pontanus, *Singularia* (Frankfurt am Main 1629) c.709, vol. 1, p. 115a.

[122] Johannes de Turrecremata, *Repertorium* C.13 q.2 c.18, v. *Nullus*.

[123] Leo I, *Ep.* 167 (to Rusticus of Narbonne) *inq.* 8, *PL* 54.1205–1206 = C.24 q.2 c.1.

[124] X 5.39.28, discussed in Chapter 2 at n. 41.

[125] One reason the question was widely debated—I have only sampled the literature—was that it evoked comparisons of ancient and current penal laws (e.g., *Glos. ord.* Inst. 1.16, v. *Interdictum*, comparing excommunicates and criminals subjected to deportation or *interdictio aqua et igni* in order to argue that excommunicates could not create valid wills; cf. *Glos. ord.* X 2.28.53, v. *Subtrahitur*). Jacobus de Belviso, "Tractatus solennis de excommunicatione," *TUI* 14, fol. 387ra–388ra, provides a good cross-section of the debate as it stood in the early fourteenth century. On medieval wills in general see M. M. Sheehan, *The Will in Medieval England* (Toronto 1963);

man penalties of confiscation and loss of testamentary rights for heretics,[126] and a canon of the Fourth Lateran Council extended the penalty to all "credentes . . . , receptatores, defensores et fautores" of heretics who remained excommunicated for a year or more.[127] Under Innocent III's *Vergentis* even orthodox children were denied the right to inherit from heretical parents.[128] As Maisonneuve has shown, *Vergentis* was a source of controversy among canon and civil lawyers since it challenged the canonists' rather complacent contrast between the rigor of Roman law and the equity of canon law.[129] Many canonists rejected a literal interpretation of *Vergentis*, and eventually Alexander IV (1254–61) created an escape clause whereby orthodox children could inherit by showing that a parent had been insane when joining a heretical sect.[130]

Although the property of excommunicates other than heretics was not confiscated, some canonists did believe that their testamentary rights should be limited or even denied.[131] Innocent IV rather un-

---

Maitland, *History* I 28 and II 115 and 331–34; and H. Auffroy, *Evolution du testament en France* (Paris 1899) 370–98.

[126] On withdrawal of heretics' testamentary rights see CT 16.5.7.pr., 9.pr., 17, 23, 25, 27, 36.pr., 40.2–6, 49, 58.4, 65.3; 16.6.4.3; Cod. 1.5.18, 19, and 22; and Nov. Val. III 18.3. On apostates: CT 16.7.1–2, 3.pr., 4 (= Cod. 1.7.3), 6, 7 (= Cod. 1.7.4). Cf. T. Mommsen, *Römisches Strafrecht* (Leipzig 1899) 604 and 608; and Maisonneuve, *Etudes* 29–36. Mere *infamia* did not entail loss of the right to make a will or to inherit, though these might be joined with *infamia* as penalties in a particular criminal statute (Greenidge, *Infamia* 165–70).

[127] Lateran IV c.3 (*COD* 234) = X 5.7.13 § 5. *Vergentis* (X 5.7.10) imposed the same penalties "after two warnings." On confiscation and withdrawal of testamentary rights as penalties for heresy see also Lea, *Inquisition* esp. I 457–509; and Shannon, *Heresy* 96–102.

[128] X 5.7.10.

[129] Maisonneuve, *Etudes* esp. 156–57, 232, 238, 281–85, and 330–50.

[130] VI 5.2.3; cf. Maisonneuve, *Etudes* 321.

[131] Most prominently Hostiensis, who believed that excommunicates should be prohibited from making wills or inheriting (*App.*, *Pia* [VI 2.12.1], v. *Actibus*, no. 10, and v. *Excluduntur*, no. 10) except as "necessary heirs," those in the testator's power, who could not reject the inheritance (*Sum.* 3.32[*De testam.*].17, col. 1047). On the basis of the second Council of Lyon, which forbade usurers to create wills, Johannes Garsias agreed; see his *App.* on c.27 (VI 5.5.2), v. *Irrita*, Vat., Pal. 629, fol. 284rb: "Quid de excommunicato—nunquid poterit condere testamentum? Et est ar. hic quod non, quia si usurarius non potest multominus excommunicatus, quia iste est penitus extra ecclesiam. Separato a communione ecclesie sacrosancte omne beneficium ex legibus descendens denegatur, aut. de privile. dotis hereticis mu. non prestandis § antepenult. [Auth. 8.10 = Nov. 109.1]. . . . Et preterea similis est deportato qui est intestabilis, ff. de testamentis. Eius qui § i [Dig. 28.1.8.1]. Et hec est oppinio Hostiensis, supra de excep. Pia." Guido de Baysio was persuaded by Garsias;

characteristically wrote that although excommunicates could create valid wills, they should not be allowed to atone for their sins through bequests "pro anima";[132] but Peter Sampson more sensibly observed that the right to make testamentary gifts, like all other extrajudicial legal transactions, should be allowed to excommunicates.[133] Later canonists largely agreed, though they reserved denial of testamentary rights for those excommunicated for serious crimes, especially if they were contumacious.[134] Although the question of wills was a popular subject of academic debate, Frederick of Siena in the mid-fourteenth century rightly called it trite.[135] In *A nobis* Innocent III had provided a more effective means for handling the *post mortem* exigencies of excommunicates: he considered the exertions of the living rather than the wishes of the dead.

---

see *Comm.* VI 2.12.1, v. *Excludatur*. Late fourteenth-century synodal statutes of Quimper forbade excommunicates to inherit; see tr. 4, c.4, Vat. 9868, fol. 503r, under the rubric "Ut excommunicati legatis careant": "sicut in provinciali statuto tractatum est, ne quicumque excommunicatione majori ligatus gaudeat aliquo legato in testamento. . . ."

[132] Inn. IV, *App.* X 5.39.34, v. *Eleemosynas*, no. 1.

[133] Appendix 2d lines 28–end.

[134] E.g., Abb. Ant., who believed that those excommunicated for associating with heretics should lose testamentary rights after a year (Appendix 2f lines 58–end), and Duranti, who wrote that only those excommunicated for heresy or other grave crimes should lose testamentary rights (*Spec.* 2.2[*De inst. ed.*] § "Compendiose," vol. 2, fol. 242ra, no. 5). Cf. Baldus, *Comm.* X 2.14.8, v. *Excommunicationem*; and Franciscus Zabarella, *Lect.* X 5.39.23, no. 27.

[135] Frederick of Siena, *Consilia* (Venice 1570) qu. 74.

VII

Excommunicates in Secular Courts

Becket's martyrdom in 1170 dramatized a new relationship between secular and ecclesiastical authorities. Bureaucratic memoranda now replaced the polemics of the Gregorian reform period as the format for working out differences and adjusting the borders between clergy and laity. Between the ecclesiastical and the secular courts, a guerrilla war was now being waged that would last until the Council of Trent. The English ecclesiastical courts, given a clear jurisdiction by William the Conqueror, began a process of slow surrender with the Constitutions of Clarendon of 1164; by the end of the thirteenth century, as Flahiff has shown, the dominance of the royal courts was so firm that the church courts, important though they continued to be, existed virtually on royal suffrage.[1] In France, jurisdiction was fragmented, and local customs, rather than royal statutes, governed the secular courts. Ecclesiastical courts had weathered the anarchy of the early middle ages, and the technical excellence and prestige their application of Roman and canon law conferred naturally sharpened their competitive edge against the lay courts.[2] The royal *parlement* had to establish its supremacy over rival secular jurisdictions even as it chal-

[1] Flahiff, "Writ" part 1, 261 and part 2, 237–40, 246, and 282–83.
[2] Bongert, *Cours* passim, esp. 38–39.

159

lenged the superiority of the ecclesiastical courts, and its eventual triumph came much later than that of the English royal courts.[3]

Competition between the two jurisdictions was balanced by the cooperation necessary in broad areas, a mutual dependency designed, sometimes in the heat of conflict, by innumerable documents recording settlements between the two jurisdictions and practiced—doubtless constantly—by their respective bureaucracies. If, for example, the outcome of the Becket controversy was that criminous clerics would be tried only in the church courts, a preliminary hearing to determine whether a defendant was indeed a cleric was held in the royal courts.[4] Conversely, the secular courts had to rely on ecclesiastical authorities for rulings on the validity of marriages or the legitimacy of children.[5]

Secular enforcement of the canon law depriving excommunicates of legal rights belonged to this sphere of negotiated cooperation. The canonists, it is true, sometimes portrayed the enforcement as proof of ecclesiastical superiority flowing from the papal power to judge any sinner, emphatically enunciated by Innocent III.[6] In effect, however, use of the exception of excommunication in the secular courts was a procedural matter, its resonance of the glorious rhetoric of papal supremacy muted by the tedium of legal process.[7] When an exception of excommunication was submitted in the secular courts, its cognizance was remitted to the episcopal court, whose letter certifying excommunication was usually accepted as full proof of the exception by the lay judge.[8] Defense counsel argued truthfully in a 1314 case in the English royal court when stating that "any letter of any ordinary

---

[3]J. R. Strayer, *The Reign of Philip the Fair* (Princeton 1980) passim, e.g., 199–206.

[4]On English procedures see Gabel, *Benefit* 88–89; on French see Fournier, *Officialités* 68–74, and Strayer, *Philip* 193–94.

[5]On marriage see Maitland, *History* II 374–85, for England, and Strayer, *Philip* 198, for France; on legitimacy see Maitland, ibid. and II 396–99, and Fournier, *Officialités* 84, for England and France, respectively.

[6]E.g., *Glos. ord.* VI 5.11.8, v. *Seculares*: "Certum est quod potestas secularis minor est ecclesiastica. . . ." Cf. Guido de Baysio, *Comm.* VI 2.12.1, v. *Ecclesiasticis*, citing Innocent III's *Novit* (X 2.1.13) to establish the church's authority to promulgate laws for the secular courts such as those on the exception of excommunication; cf. also v. *Opponantur* [*sic*].

[7]Hostiensis gives a brief description of the procedures in *App.*, *Pia* (VI 2.12.1), v. *Opponitur*.

[8]Cf. Johannes Monachus, *Glosa aurea* VI 5.11.8, fol. 406ra no. 2: "Sic enim est excommunicatio de foro ecclesiastico, quod secularis iudex habet credere iudici ecclesiastico, et expectare suam determinationem. . . ." In 1299 clerical grievances

competent to testify about excommunication is enough to put you out of court, unless you are exempted by the pope."[9]

Until 1257 there was no universal canon law explicitly decreeing that the lay courts must deprive excommunicates of their legal rights. But the canonists had begun to monitor secular endorsement of the exception of excommunication and had found it wanting. Writing during the pontificate of Innocent IV, Hostiensis lamented that the secular courts paid little heed to the exception of excommunication, despite the ancient tradition of lay guardianship of the church.[10]

Negligence was bad enough, but in France, as we have seen, anticlerical rebellions advocated overthrow of the exception of excommunication—guarantee of the civil rights of excommunicates—as part of their program.[11] It may have been the formal cessation of the

---

from the province of Tours, presented to the king by Guillaume Le Maire, the famous bishop of Angers, charged that lay courts were treating episcopal letters certifying excommunication as mere half-proofs (*Livre de Guillaume Le Maire*, ed. C. Port, *CDI* X.11 [Paris 1877] 187–569 at 356); see below for more details. Since canon law regarded one witness as only half-proof (Lévy, *Preuves* 110), canonical requirements for proving an exception of excommunication in a secular court were lower than those (discussed in Chapter 4 at n. 126) in an ecclesiastical court. See also below at n. 52.

[9]Appendix 5 case 36. "Bracton" in *De legibus* required defendants to prove the exception with episcopal letters or testimony (*Bracton*, fol. 426b, vol. 4, p. 326); at the end of the century, *Fleta* affirmed this (6.44.1, vol. 1, pp. 437–38). In the cases in Appendix 5 the royal court virtually always accepted episcopal letters as proof; occasionally, a bishop testified *in banco* (cases 17, 19, and 22). It is true that in the case (36) now being discussed in the text, the judge eventually ruled against the exception, saying the bishop's letter had not proved jurisdiction or given a definite reason for excommunication. The judge noted that when the royal court writes to a bishop, "we write clearly, and we should expect them to do the same for us . . ."; the exception of excommunication was too "heynuse" to rest on slipshod proof.

[10]Host., *App.*, *Pia* (VI 2.12.1), v. *Opponitur*, p. 16A cols. 1–2: "Et admittitur coram iudicibus ecclesiasticis. Tamen alii parum curant; tamen leges magnam vim faciunt, unde et dicitur in constitutionibus feudo. 'Hic finitur lex consuetu. regni ca. Domino guerram' [2.28]. . . . Et secundum iura authentico habet archiepiscopus potestatem concilium provinciale convocandi, ut ecclesiasticus status et sacrae regulae diligenter custodiantur . . . ut in Authen. de sanct. episcopis § Ut autem omnis ecclesiasticus. Colla. ix [tit. 15 = Nov. 123 c.10]. . . ." Hostiensis went on to cite Lombard law, etc., to the same effect. Might he have been influenced by being in England (1236–44) when abuses of the exception of excommunication were disturbing the royal courts? (See below at n. 114.) Hostiensis spearheaded opposition to royal judge William Raleigh's election to the see of Winchester; Raleigh and his clerk (later a judge) Bracton were concerned with abuses of the exception both in their judicial practice and in *De legibus*; see Chapter 5 at n. 19.

[11]On other French anticlerical movements of the same period see Morel, *Pouvoir* passim, e.g. 102 and 148. On French clerical grievances of the late 1240s, see Berger,

most famous of these rebellions that prompted the first papal statement on lay enforcement of the exception. Although Count Jean le
Roux of Brittany had sustained the anticlerical confederacy spearheaded by his father, Pierre de Dreux, for several decades, he finally
submitted to the pope in April 1256, obligating himself and his heirs
in an oath he swore to two cardinals at the Apostolic See to assure
that "excommunicates [would be] avoided throughout Brittany, both
in the courts, as plaintiffs or witnesses, or in other judicial acts, and
[extrajudicially] in public offices. . . ."[12] In exchange Jean was absolved from the excommunication he had borne since 1252.

Perhaps inspired by this seemingly triumphant settlement of a dangerous and long-standing rebellion, Alexander IV in the following
year responded in a long decretal to the French clergy's complaints
about violations of their ecclesiastical liberties.[13] *Decernimus*, the section of this decretal that dealt with excommunicates' legal rights, ordered lay judges on pain of excommunication to prevent excommunicates from being plaintiffs, advocates, or witnesses in their
courts.[14] (In a separate decretal on the Inquisition, the same pope
made it clear that lay judges who were excommunicated were also to
be barred from presiding over their courts except in heresy trials.)[15]
Though not promulgated in an official canonical collection until the
Liber Sextus of 1298, *Decernimus* had long circulated in collections of
extravagantes.[16] From the early 1260s on, the canonists cited it to support their claim that legal rights should be denied to excommunicates
in the lay courts.[17]

Innocent IV clxxv–xxx and cxci–vi, and G. von Puttkamer, *Innocenz IV. Versuch einer
Gesamtcharakteristik aus seiner Wirkung* (Münster in Westfalen 1930) 62–63.

[12] Lobineau, *Bretagne* II 401–2: "parebo, et per eos qui meae sunt jurisdictioni subditi faciam adimplere universa . . . quae in . . . preceptis Gregorii et Innocentii etc.
continentur; et inter cetera quod per totam Britanniam excommunicati vitentur, et
in judiciis, ab agendo et testificando, et aliis actibus legitimis, nec non publicis officiis, quamdiu in excommunicatione permanserint, repellantur."

[13] See VI 3.23.1 and Friedberg's apparatus for the larger decretal.

[14] *Decernimus*: VI 5.11.8.

[15] VI 5.2.6.

[16] Thus Duranti cited *Decernimus*—or rather the decretal of which it was a part—in
Spec. 2.1.13 (*De exc. et repl.*), vol. 2, fol. 120ra, no. 10: "ut in consti. Alex. IIII de
excep. Quia nonnulli."

[17] Abbas Antiquus's reference, from the early 1260s, is the first I have found: *Lect.*,
Pia (VI 2.12.1), v. *Periculum* . . . , Vat. MSS Borgh. 231, fol. 141vb, and Vat. 2542,
fol. 86ra: "Ex hac littera uidetur quod iudex secularis exceptionem excommunicationis admittere teneatur, cum enim sit periculum in communione, quia per eam a

Invariably, such claims charged secular neglect.[18] Yet other, independent evidence shows that secular lawyers and judges were well aware of the significance of the exception of excommunication. They upheld the exception more often than the canonists' generalizations imply, and they never rejected it without some consideration of its merits, as a survey of court records and other secular evidence in France and England will show.[19]

---

perceptione sacramentorum quis suspenditur, supra eodem A nobis [X 2.25.2] et de cleri. ex. c. ulti. [X 5.27.10]. Iudex reum excommunicato actori respondere cogere non debet inuitum: immo eum excludere ab agendo. Et nedum propter partis periculum, immo etiam propter suum, cum et ipse iudex incidat in minorem illi communicando. Idem et uidetur de iure ciuili per auten. de priuile. do. hereticis mulieribus non prestandis [Coll. 8 tit. 5 = Nov. 109 c.1], ubi dicitur quod illis est deneganda facultas agendi quibus communio per episcopos denegatur. Nec ualet si respondeas quod speciale est in crimine hereseos, quia semper eadem ratio prohibitionis remanere uidetur. Et hodie dicitur Alex. IIII hoc statuisse expresse [i.e., in *Decernimus*]." (Abbas was cited by Jo. An., *Comm.* VI 5.11.8.) Abbas's teacher, Peter Sampson, had first cited this *novella* in connection with lay enforcement of the canon law depriving excommunicates of their legal rights in *Lect.*, *Pia* (VI 2.12.1), Vienna MSS 2083, fol. 44ra, and 2113, fol. 75va: "Aut etiam ciuilibus, quia in foro etiam seculari est excommunicationis exceptio admittenda, ut probatur in auten. de priuil. circa medium colla. ix [*rect.* Coll. 8 tit. 5 = Nov. 109 c.1]. . . . Non putantur multi seculares iudices hoc seruare." Although he found the *novella* useful, Abbas emphasized that the policy was not restricted to excommunicated heretics.

[18] Hostiensis, cited in n. 10, seems to have been the first to register the complaint, which was echoed by Peter Sampson (quoted in n. 17). Guido de Baysio repeated it in the early fourteenth century, but his gloss is so nearly a paraphrase of Hostiensis's that it is hard to assess its value as an observation: "et admittantur a iudicibus ecclesiasticis. Seculares tamen ["cum" in ed., corrected from Vat., Borgh. 40, fol. 212va] parum curant, et tamen leges vim magnam faciunt. . . ." See also, from the 1340s, Jo. An., *Comm.* VI 2.12.1, in gl. v. *Seculari*: "dicit etiam quod licet iudices seculares de his exceptionibus non curent, tamen curare debent, cum et leges hoc ponderent. . . ." Cf. Dominicus de Sancto Geminiano's *casus*, printed with *Glos. ord.* VI 5.11.8: "Et istud non solum procedit de iure canonico sed etiam de iure ciuili, ut no. Bar. in l. Placet C. de sac. san. eccl. [Cod. 1.2.5]. Sed tamen hodie in foro seculari istud non servatur. Sed non video quomodo iudex secularis qui potest repellere actorem excommunicatum ab agendo et non repellit sed cum eo communicat possit evitare maculam peccati mortalis." Ironically, as noted in Chapter 4 n. 141, the Roman Rota rarely accepted the exception by the late fourteenth century.

[19] France and England were chosen because their medieval court records are accessible. For Germany, there is E. Eichmann's magisterial *Acht und Bann*, based mainly on law rather than practice. I know of no comparable studies for other countries. In "Individual" I 236–60 and II 97 n. 59 on 98, I cited a number of Italian communal statutes on the subject. For Spain, surprisingly, *Las Siete Partidas*, with a more extensive discussion of excommunication than any other medieval secular law book I have investigated, does not mention legal disabilities (ed. Ignacio Sanponts y Barba et al. [Barcelona 1843–44] I 9, vol. 1, pp. 472–526). In Portugal, the 1289 concordat be-

FRANCE

As several anecdotes in the memoirs of Joinville (completed ca. 1309) reveal, St. Louis was critical of church authorities' use of excommunication.[20] On one occasion, around 1263, when the French clergy petitioned the king to coerce contumacious excommunicates, St. Louis responded that he should be allowed to verify the guilt of any excommunicate he was asked to discipline.[21] To illustrate the need for royal supervision he cited (rather insultingly, it would seem) the example of the count of Brittany—Pierre de Dreux—who according to the king had been vindicated by the Apostolic See after a long struggle with the Breton clergy.[22] Had he confiscated the count's property to make him surrender, St. Louis said, he would have injured both the count and God.

Quite apart from factual errors—no incident in the life of Pierre de Dreux, not even his expedient absolutions, could be described as a papal vindication—the heroization of the notoriously anticlerical Count Pierre can only have set the prelates' teeth on edge, and they declined the king's mediocre grant as an encroachment on their own jurisdiction.[23] In another of Joinville's vignettes, St. Louis is portrayed

---

tween Nicholas IV and King Dionisius included an agreement that the king would cease granting letters "ut non uitentur tanquam excommunicati nec ut tales habeantur" to laymen excommunicated by the ecclesiastical courts and would not block the ecclesiastical courts' right to convene laymen when they were sued by clerics: see E. Melo Peixoto, *Derecho concordatario medieval portugues* (Salamanca 1979) p. 17 art. 2.

[20] See G. J. Campbell, "The Attitude of the Monarchy toward the Use of Ecclesiastical Censures in the Reign of Saint Louis," *Speculum* 35 (1960) 535–55.

[21] Jean, Sire de Joinville, *Histoire de Saint Louis*, ed. N. de Wailly (Paris 1868) c.13, pp. 22–23; cf. c.135, pp. 241–42.

[22] Ibid. On St. Louis's attitude toward Pierre de Dreux see Berger, *Innocent IV* clxxv–vii; Painter, *Peter* 49; and Pocquet du Haut-Jussé, *Papes* I 52–53.

[23] Which absolution was St. Louis meant to be alluding to? He says the count's excommunication lasted seven years, but no sequence in Pierre's anticlerical campaign corresponds to this. Pierre was absolved by authority of Honorius III in 1218 after several years of conflict with the bishop of Nantes (Pocquet du Haut-Jussé, *Papes* I 63–64), but almost immediately (1219) excommunicated again by the same pope (Lobineau, *Bretagne* II 374–76). In 1221 he submitted once again (Lobineau II 376–77). But his campaign peaked in the 1220s, and a series of episcopal censures culminated in the 1228 papal threat to free his vassals from their oaths (Lobineau II 379–81; see above). In 1230 and 1234 Pierre obtained absolution, the first time in anticipation of a royal invasion, the second to join the crusade (Painter, *Peter* 97–98). Thereafter, he seems to have been in constant disgrace. Interestingly, though modern

using the exception of excommunication against Bishop Peter of Châlons (1247–61) to reject the bishop's lawsuit against Joinville himself, whom the bishop had excommunicated in an election dispute.[24] In that familiar medieval twist in which a wish is turned against the wisher, St. Louis refused the petition on the grounds that the prelates "have laid it down between you that no excommunicated person should be heard in a lay court."[25]

Yet Joinville's undoubtedly authentic portrayal of royal ambivalence overlooks a tradition of stiff royal sanctions against contumacious excommunicates and heretics. Indeed, it might have been the harshness of the punishments in the royal statutes and the tendency of the French laws to treat excommunicates of every stripe as heretics that made St. Louis reluctant to coerce mere excommunicates at the clergy's request. Against the heretics of Languedoc, King Louis VIII (1223–26) and St. Louis himself (or rather Queen Blanche as regent) had enacted ordinances applicable to all excommunicates, not just to heretics, ordinances that, moreover, exceeded and even violated canon law. The Crusader King Louis VIII, implementing to his kingdom's profit the disinheritance of Count Raymond VII of Toulouse decreed by the Fourth Lateran Council, enacted at Bourges in April

---

historians regard Pierre as the "count" to whom St. Louis refers, a seventeenth-century editor of Breton pleas saw Pierre's son Jean as the hero of St. Louis's story (Sébastien Frain, ed., *Arrests du parlement de Bretagne*, 3d ed., rev. Pierre Hevin [Rennes 1684] 74). Yet no more in his life than in his father's was there any reconciliation that could be described, even rhetorically, as a vindication. Innocent IV affirmed Count Jean's excommunication shortly before the Council of Lyon in 1245 (Lobineau, *Bretagne* II 393–94). In 1247 Innocent informed the abbot of Buzay that he had absolved Jean (Berger, *Registres* I.2, no. 2742, p. 408; cf. idem, *Innocent IV* clxxviii, and Pocquet du Haut-Jussé, *Papes* I 143–44). Clearly Jean was soon reexcommunicated, however, since in 1256 he went to Rome for absolution.

[24] Joinville, *Histoire* c.136, ed. de Wailly 243. In the edition, it is the bishop himself whom St. Louis refuses to hear because he is excommunicated ("que vous estes excommeniés: dont je ne vous escouterai jeusques à tant que vous soiés absouz"). But it is more likely that the real irony of the story—told to illustrate the king's shrewdness—lies in the king's refusal to hear a suit that might well go against Joinville on the grounds that Joinville is excommunicated, a fact he has mentioned a few sentences before in the narrative. This is the interpretation in R. Hague, trans., *The Life of St. Louis* (New York 1955) 198–99, quoted by Campbell, "Censures" 551. In a literal translation, St. Louis tells the bishop that he will not hear the case because "you [the bishop] are excommunicated" (e.g., F. T. Marzials, trans., *Memoirs of the Crusades, by Villehardouin and de Joinville* [New York 1958] 306).

[25] Joinville, *Histoire* ibid., trans. Hague 199.

of 1226 an ordinance that adhered to the letter of Innocent III's decretal *Vergentis* by denying inheritance rights even to orthodox children of heretics, a measure found overstrong by many canon lawyers.[26] Moving south to enforce the new royal claim on Toulouse, Louis VIII at a council at Pamiers prescribed a fine of nine pounds and one penny for anyone excommunicated after three warnings, to be followed by confiscation of possessions after one year in excommunication.[27] Since canon law required that all excommunications *ab homine* be preceded by three warnings, a rule reiterated by the Fourth Lateran Council only a decade before the enactment of the royal ordinance, the very large fine prescribed by the king would, if the law were interpreted literally, accompany all except *latae sententiae* excommunications.[28] Confiscation was, of course, the canonical penalty for convicted *heretics*, and at the most a literal interpretation of the heresy canons would have applied the penalty to those excommunicated for suspicion of heresy if they failed to obtain absolution within one year.[29] Moreover, the Fourth Lateran Council of 1215 enacted strong penalties for abusive fines for absolution from excommunication, though it is true that the canon was not taken up in the official collection of 1234, the Liber Extra.[30] Gratefully quoting the

[26] Isambert, *Recueil* I 227–28. See Maisonneuve, *Etudes* 236–37, and Morel, *Pouvoir* 67–70, on the royal ordinance; on the events that preceded it see also W. L. Wakefield, *Heresy, Crusade and Inquisition in Southern France, 1100–1250* (Berkeley and Los Angeles 1974) esp. 114–29. The canonists' attitudes toward *Vergentis* were discussed in Chapter 6 at n. 2.

[27] Quoted in the 1227 Council of Narbonne, c.1, Mansi 23.21. The Pamiers council must have been in early autumn, 1226: Louis VIII died in November (Wakefield, *Heresy* 126).

[28] See X 5.39.48 for the decree of Lateran IV. Maisonneuve, *Etudes* 237 and n. 212, interprets the ordinance to mean that anyone excommunicated after three warnings (i.e., all but *latae sententiae* excommunicates) should be fined and that the possessions of contumacious excommunicates should be confiscated. Morel, *Pouvoir* 67–68, rather ambiguously sees the fine as a penalty for "l'excommunié récalcitrant" and the confiscation "en cas d'obstination."

[29] E.g., X 5.7.10. These canons were discussed in detail in Chapter 2 at n. 18 and passim.

[30] Lateran IV c. 49 (*COD* 257). See Morel, *Pouvoir* 47–48, 89–90, 97n., 108–10, and 131, on fines accompanying excommunication in France. In 1244 Innocent IV agreed to the duke of Burgundy's request to prohibit such fines in Burgundy (Berger, *Registres* I.1, p. 133 no. 779; cf. Morel 84), and *Romana* (1246) referred to abusive fines as a problem in the province of Reims (in Kessler's edition, "Untersuchungen" part 1, 165); but in *Venerabilibus* (1254), addressed to Rouen, Innocent acknowledged that "secundum patriae consuetudinem ab excommunicatis emendae huiusmodi exigantur" (VI 5.11.7, in Friedberg's appendix, 1098).

late king's ordinance in a council of 1227, the archbishop of Narbonne demurred at the steep fine (about a year's wages for a peasant) and announced that mitigations or alternative punishments would be available for those unable to pay it.[31]

Louis VIII's legislation was enacted against the backdrop of the Albigensian Crusade, and the "disrespectful laymen" of Narbonne whom the king addressed were the heretics flourishing in Langue-doc.[32] But nothing indicates that the laws were restricted to heretics or suspected heretics.[33] The same was true of the famous ordinance *Cupientes*, promulgated in Nîmes in April 1229.[34] *Cupientes* decreed that the possessions of contumacious excommunicates be confiscated after one year. The penalty was not restricted to those excommunicated for heresy, though of course *Cupientes* is deeply rooted in the heresy crisis in the south.[35]

St. Louis evidently found it expedient to work within the constraints of the legislation he inherited. *Cupientes*, as Campbell has shown, was enforced mainly against heretics.[36] In 1235, three decades earlier than the petition described by Joinville, a Council of Reims petitioned the king not to force the faithful to associate with excommunicates, and to coerce contumacious excommunicates without a preliminary royal investigation.[37] Since the existing royal ordinances would have met these needs, they must have been unknown or unused.

Also put to the king at the Council of Reims was a request that the

---

[31] Council of Narbonne, ao. 1227, c.1, Mansi 23.21. The average wage is based on the figure in Strayer, *Philip* 203. For comparison: the fine the royal ordinance imposed on all excommunicates (except those excommunicated *latae sententiae*) was about the same as that prescribed in Normandy for contumacious excommunicates after one year; see below n. 79.

[32] Mansi 23.21.

[33] Maisonneuve (*Etudes* 237) and Campbell ("Censures" 542) believe the ordinance applied to all excommunicates, though they acknowledge the significance of its context, the heresy crisis. In the 1246 Council of Béziers (c.36; Mansi 23.700–701) and in Peter Sampson's 1252 synodal statutes for Nîmes (Mansi 24.566) the fine Louis VIII prescribed at Pamiers was applied to all excommunicated after the required warning—i.e., all but *latae sententiae* excommunicates.

[34] *Cupientes*, art. 7, in Isambert, *Recueil* I 233. The text should certainly state that contumacious excommunicates are to be coerced "corporaliter" (i.e., this variant is better than the text's "spiritualiter"). Mansi has "temporaliter" (23.186).

[35] On *Cupientes* see Maisonneuve, *Etudes* passim, esp. 238–41, and Morel, *Pouvoir* passim, esp. 69–74.

[36] Campbell, "Censures" esp. 544.

[37] Council of Reims, ao. 1235, Mansi 23.365–68. Cf. Morel, *Pouvoir* 81 and 170.

exception of excommunication be enforced in the secular courts.[38] It is rather surprising to discover, therefore, that the exception of excommunication was held valid in the royal *parlement* during the reign of St. Louis. A procedural rule of 1268 proclaimed that the exception would be rejected if the defendant could not prove it immediately, "quia ita voluit rex."[39] True, the rule required immediate proof of the exception, but like *Pia*, which itself allowed only eight days for proof, these parliamentary rules were undoubtedly intended to facilitate legal processes. However grudgingly, the parliamentary rule endorsed the validity of the exception.

Unfortunately, perhaps because of the deficiencies of surviving parliamentary records, only two cases survive to document the use of the exception. One dates from 1269, when the Paris *parlement* agreed to hear an appeal from a Breton defendant, Gaufridus de Plessaico, who claimed that Count Jean le Roux's seneschal at Rennes had forced him to litigate with an excommunicated plaintiff.[40] As we have seen, two distinguished southern French canonists, Peter Sampson and the papal judge Duranti, had agreed that appeal was available to defendants whose exceptions of excommunication were rejected. Yet the motive of the royal *parlement* might have been simply to assert its supremacy over the Breton court, from which a royal route of appeal had not been firmly established, rather than to vindicate the validity of the exception.[41]

Purity of motive is also suspect in a case that came before the royal *parlement* in the Pentecost term of 1270 involving the mayor and the abbot of St. Riquier, who shared jurisdiction of the town.[42] The mayor's suit, resulting from the abbot's refusal to confirm the appointment of a sheriff, was successfully rebuffed by the abbot's exception of excommunication. But when the abbot then tried to have the mayor placed in default for delaying proceedings, the court ruled that the mayor had suffered enough by being refused admission to court.[43]

---

[38] Mansi 23.365.

[39] *Olim* I 738.

[40] *Olim* I 293–95; cf. Chapter 4 n. 105.

[41] On appeals from the Breton court, see Strayer, *Philip* 228. For the opinion expressed by Sampson and others see Chapter 4 at n. 104.

[42] *Olim* I 802, discussed by Lea, "Excommunication" 391–92.

[43] Although the royal *parlement* rebuffed this attempt, other traces of a French custom of penalizing excommunicated litigants by default come from St. Quentin a century later (1370). Three plaintiffs suing the mayor and other officials over war

Chagrined at his defeat, the mayor evidently sought an opportunity to publicize the fact that his excommunication did not reflect personal immorality. In the autumn he sued the abbot again, now over a private matter—we are not told what.[44] The abbot again submitted an exception of excommunication, as the mayor must have anticipated; he thus enabled the mayor to record that his excommunication had resulted from official duties and therefore should not bar litigation over a personal matter. The court listened to arguments on both sides; unfortunately we are not told what they were. Eventually, the court judged that the mayor was bound by excommunication even in the private capacity in which he now presented himself. The case was dismissed. A more attractive personality might have tipped the scales in the other direction and created an effective precedent for restraining the abuse of excommunication to coerce royal officials. The exception of excommunication might then have enjoyed sturdier prospects on the occasions when it was used without chicanery. (Such a resolution was eventually reached in England, where fraudulent use of the exception of excommunication might for a time have jeopardized its legitimate use as well.) But the mayor was not the appropriate medium for such a reform. Evidently proud and querulous, he was in court again later in the same year, fined for banning some men against the prohibition of the royal bailiff.[45]

These two cases, dating from 1269 and 1270, are the only examples of the use of the exception revealed in the registers of the royal *parlement*, which are now published through 1350. Many other examples might lie buried beneath such phrases as "proposing many exceptions and bars for the purpose of repelling [the plaintiff]."[46] But this seems unlikely. Forces against the validity of the exception of excommunication in the French courts were gathering strength throughout the late thirteenth century. Because of St. Louis's recalcitrance, the French bishops exploited every possible means to protect their liberties. When, in 1244, the bishop's official of Orléans tried to exact the

---

taxes tried to appoint an excommunicate as proctor. The defendants succeeded in removing the proctor and in having the plaintiffs treated as if contumaciously absent (*Archives anciennes de la ville de St-Quentin*, ed. E. Le Maire [St. Quentin 1888–1910] vol. 2, no. 620, p. 198).

[44] *Olim* I 817.

[45] *Olim* I 830. Cf. Strayer, *Philip* 226, on the eventual outcome.

[46] *Olim* III 382 (ao. 1309).

fine of nine pounds and one penny from certain excommunicates guilty of contumacy in his court, St. Louis not only refused to force the excommunicates to pay but also sent a royal bailiff to seize the church's temporalities, claiming injuries to his jurisdiction.[47] Innocent IV responded with a decretal advising the dean of Orléans that "as all laws condone the use of force to repel force," prelates who had both temporal and spiritual jurisdiction (as many of the French bishops did) could use the sanctions of either jurisdiction to defend their rights when necessary.[48] It would be disingenuous to suggest that many prelates had not long since availed themselves of this ambidexterity, but the fact remains that this decretal, allowing bishops to use excommunication to defend their temporal power, reversed a principle of canon law.[49] Perhaps the main significance of the decretal lay in the papal recognition that in the bitter power struggle in France, involving important temporal as well as ecclesiastical jurisdictions, excessive scruples would mean certain defeat for the bishops. Or worse: the second Council of Lyon (1274) promulgated a sentence of excommunication *latae sententiae* for secular authorities who contracted to kill or capture prelates or to confiscate their possessions in retaliation for excommunication or interdict.[50]

In 1274, a few months after the council, King Philip III issued a confirmation of *Cupientes*, addressing it to certain church officials of Rouen.[51] But it was a halfhearted effort: "If, before and after [the enactment of *Cupientes*], contumacious excommunicates were not coerced, we do not wish to create any innovations," the king stated. Another royal endorsement of *Cupientes*, in 1299, was equally restrained. Representing the clergy of the province of Tours, Guillaume

---

[47] Morel, *Pouvoir* 85–87.

[48] VI 5.11.6.

[49] Expressed in Gratian at C.23 q.4 c.27. Cf. Morel, *Pouvoir* passim, e.g., p. 76, on abuses related to episcopal possession of both secular and spiritual authority.

[50] VI 5.11.11. The first Council of Lyon had already enacted the penalty of excommunication for assassins (see Chapter 6 at n. 55), but this canon was partly vitiated by other Lyon legislation.

[51] Isambert, *Recueil* II no. 249, art. 1, p. 655: "scire volumus quod constitutionem domini et genitoris nostri probamus et nolumus . . . contraire. Si tamen ante et post constitutionem eamden [*sic*] non fuerint dolose excommunicati compulsi, rem novam nolumus inchoari." Morel, *Pouvoir* 135, notes that "dolose" could mean either that the excommunicates were not coerced because the excommunications were unjust, or that they were not coerced because of negligence arising from official corruption.

Le Maire, the famous bishop of Angers, charged that the secular courts were admitting excommunicates as plaintiffs and witnesses and were treating ordinaries' letters certifying excommunication as mere half-proofs of the exception.[52] Addressing his remedies to royal bailiffs in Touraine and Maine, Philip the Fair instructed royal judges to prevent excommunicates from appearing as plaintiffs or advocates.[53] It is hard to imagine that Philip the Fair, now in a calm between the papal excommunications threatened in the bulls *Clericis laicos* (1296) and *Unam sanctam* (1302), brought much enthusiasm to such a measure, which he indeed may merely have traded for clerical taxes.[54] Increasingly the royal *parlement* heard appeals of purportedly unjust excommunications and sought to force ecclesiastical absolution of royal officials excommunicated for fulfilling duties that encroached on ecclesiastical liberties.[55] On occasion, the royal *parlement* imposed an "excommunication" of its own: when, around 1345, the dean and chapter of Agde "excommunicated, aggravated, and re-aggravated" the consuls and citizens of Agde because of a demand for taxes, *parlement* came to the rescue with a prohibition of all communication and commerce with the dean and chapter.[56]

Another development jeopardizing the exception of excommunication in the royal court was a trend against the traditional Romanocanonical classifications of those unfit to participate in litigation on general moral grounds. Guillaume du Breuil's *Style du parlement du Paris* (ca. 1330) excluded all exceptions against witnesses "racione

---

[52] Port, *Livre* 356; cf. n. 8.

[53] Isambert, *Recueil* II no. 337, art. 4, pp. 720–21. The mandate is contained in Le Maire's *Livre* (ed. Port 370–72). Port notes that there are some problems in dating the mandate to 1299 if one accepts that the grievances were proposed in a council at Samur in 1300 (pp. 198–99); still, Fournier (*Officialités* 119) seems to be wrong in ascribing this grievance to the 1294 council at Samur.

[54] On Philip the Fair's excommunications see Morel, *Pouvoir* esp. 120–22. Cf. Strayer, *Philip* 247–48, on the exchange of pro-church laws for clerical taxes.

[55] Among many parliamentary cases see, e.g., H. Furgeot et al., eds., *Actes du parlement de Paris, deuxième série, 1328–50* (Paris 1920–75) I no. 2992, p. 295 (ao. 1340); no. 2662, p. 260 (ao. 1339); and no. 4492, p. 456 (ao. 1342). From the end of the century, see the remarks in Jacques d'Ablieges, *Coutumier* 4.5, pp. 611–13. On royal control over excommunication of royal officials, see F. Olivier-Martin, *L'Assemblée de Vincennes de 1329* (Paris 1909) passim, esp. 367–68; and Morel, *Pouvoir* passim, esp. 51, 80, 90, and 135.

[56] Furgeot, *Parlement* II nos. 6647–48, p. 138. For a 1342 example see Le Maire, *St. Quentin* II no. 596, p. 177.

alicujus criminis vel actus infamativi" unless there had been a conviction or confession.[57] Although du Breuil did not mention the exception of excommunication in particular, a good many such exceptions would fall short of this standard.

In 1389, moreover, *parlement* rendered a judgment strongly prejudicial to the exception of excommunication. Over strenuous objections of the bishop of Le Mans, the duchess of Anjou was allowed to reject an exception of excommunication submitted in her court on the grounds that the bishop would not agree to abide by the decision of the superior lay judge if the exception was rejected and the defendant wished to appeal.[58] This judgment challenged the exception of excommunication at its essence. Within a decade or so, Jacques d'Ablieges compiled his *Grand Coutumier de France*, a composite of royal ordinances, parliamentary rules of procedure, and Parisian customs. Excommunicates were not to be excluded from the courts either as plaintiffs or as witnesses, the *Coutumier* pronounced, and indeed all exceptions based on mere suspicion or moral unfitness were now obsolete.[59] Never a high priority on the royal agenda, the exception of excommunication seems to have passed out of use completely by the end of the fourteenth century.

But practice in the royal *parlement* is not an accurate index of practice in other French courts, even in areas within the royal sphere of influence. In exactly the same period that d'Ablieges denied the validity of the exception of excommunication, the famous *Somme rural* (ca. 1395) of Jean Bouteiller pronounced that "n'est à recevoir homme excommunié, s'il est ainsi qu'il en appare promptement par lettres de son excommuniement, autrement non."[60] French custumals in fact show a mixed reaction to the exception of excommunication, sometimes opposing the very sources on which they are based and on oc-

---

[57] Du Breuil, *Style* 50. See P. Fournier, "Guillaume du Breuil, juriste, sa vie, ses écrits," *Histoire littéraire de la France* 37.120–46 at 139–40, on du Breuil's incorporation of Romano-canonical procedural rules. His attitude toward exceptions based on immorality was not disinterested, since, as Fournier describes, he was burdened with charges of fraud and treason in two important lawsuits undertaken in the course of an unedifying career.

[58] Morel, *Pouvoir* 212–16, prints the document recording the case and discusses it at 184–85.

[59] D'Ablieges, *Coutumier* II 45, p. 389; and III 18, p. 476.

[60] I. Bouteiller, *Somme rural*, ed. L. C. Le Caron (Paris 1603) I 9, p. 42.

casion varying between one recension and the next. The most famous of all medieval French law books, Philippe de Beaumanoir's
Coutumes de Beauvaisis (ca. 1280), took no stand at all on the question
of excommunicated plaintiffs. A high royal official, successively
bailiff or seneschal of Clermont, Poitou, Vermandois, Tours, and
Senlis, Beaumanoir enforced an important royal judgment against the
bishop of Poitiers in 1288, deflecting appeals from the bishop's temporal courts away from his metropolitan, the archbishop of Bordeaux, and into *parlement*.[61] The royal brief, which Beaumanoir successfully defended at Rome, mentioned many of the abuses with
which secular authorities perennially taxed the church courts, including unjust use of excommunication against royal officials. But Beaumanoir was fair and even generous to the ecclesiastical jurisdiction.
Unlike many lay lawyers, for example, he advised that litigation on
contracts could be tried in the church courts even if both parties were
laymen, as long as both parties agreed.[62] Although silent on the subject of excommunicated plaintiffs, the *Coutumes* declared that judges,
advocates, or witnesses under aggravated sentences of excommunication were to be excluded from the courts.[63]

Beaumanoir's testimony on the status of excommunicated plaintiffs
would have been all the more welcome because his only thirteenth-
century rival, the anonymous (and despite its name unofficial) *Etablissements de Saint Louis* (1272–73), explicitly rejected the exception
of excommunication against plaintiffs even while endorsing secular
coercion of contumacious excommunicates by fines and confiscation.[64] Customs of Touraine-Anjou and of Orléans were the two main
sources for the *Etablissements*, and it has been suggested that their au-

[61] Strayer, *Philip* 243–44.

[62] Beaumanoir, *Coutumes* c.11, vol. 1, p. 165.

[63] Beaumanoir, *Coutumes* c.5 § 191, vol. 1, p. 95, on judges and advocates; and c.39
§ 1206, vol. 2, p. 121, on witnesses. In the case of witnesses, many manuscripts omit
the stipulation that the excommunication be aggravated. Although Beaumanoir did
not mention the exception of excommunication against plaintiffs, it was successfully
used in Vermandois in the much later (1370) case at St. Quentin, discussed above
in n. 43.

[64] P. Viollet, ed., *Les Etablissements de Saint Louis, accompagnés des textes primitifs et de
textes dérivés* (Paris 1881–86) I c.127, vol. 2, p. 241: "generaument tuit escomenié
sunt oï en cort laie an demandant. . . ." On secular coercion, see ibid. I c.127, vol. 2,
pp. 238–39, prescribing distraint and fines for contumacious excommunicates after a
year and a day.

thor was trained, as perhaps was Beaumanoir himself, at the famous law school of Orléans.[65] A gloss in two manuscripts of the *Etablissements* comments that the admission of excommunicated plaintiffs advocated by the author accords with "l'usage d'Orlenois."[66] In mid-century, as was mentioned, a dispute between a royal bailiff and the bishop's court at Orléans had prompted Innocent IV to uphold "the use of force to repel force," and in the bitter aftermath the abbot charged with jurisdiction over scholars deliberately refrained from excommunicating, fearing that the bailiff would seize his temporalities on the pretext of any misstep.[67]

Thus Orléans, rather than Anjou, is the likely source for opposition to the exception of excommunication. Enlisted in the anticlerical rebellion of Pierre de Dreux, Anjou might have seemed a more probable breeding ground for such attitudes.[68] The *Usage de Touraine et d'Anjou*, composed in 1246 and one of the sources for the *Etablissements*, does not mention this topic.[69] But an independent redaction of Angevin customs dating from the early fourteenth century stated that excommunicates were not allowed to plead in secular courts.[70] Hence during this early period Angevin law seems to have supported the canonical position, though Guillaume Le Maire's grievances of 1299 show that the exception was disliked and hard to enforce, and the parliamentary case already discussed shows that by 1389 the Angevin court was ready to discard the exception on principle.

In Poitou, where Pierre de Dreux's campaign had also won support, the exception of excommunication was upheld in late fourteenth-

---

[65] For references see H. Coing, ed., *Handbuch der Quellen und Literatur der neueren europäischen Privatrechtsgeschichte* (Munich 1973–) I 277 and 357.

[66] Viollet, *Etablissements*, vol. 2, p. 241 n. 4. On the text's statement that excommunicates are admitted as plaintiffs, quoted above, the gloss adds "selonc l'usage d'Orlenois."

[67] Morel, *Pouvoir* 86–87. Unfortunately another Orléans law book, *Li Livres de jostice et de plet* (ed. G. Rapetti, *CDI* V.6 [Paris 1850]), dating from the 1250s and surviving in only one manuscript, does not mention excommunicates' legal rights, though the author was very familiar with canon law.

[68] Painter, *Peter* 72.

[69] Ed. Viollet, with *Etablissements* vol. 2, pp. 1–104 as one of the sources for the *Etablissements*. On date, etc., see ibid. vol. 1, pp. 8–24.

[70] "Compilatio de usibus et consuetudinibus Andegavie," in Viollet, ed., *Etablissements* vol. 3, pp. 116–39; c.12, p. 119. (On the origins of the work see ibid. p. 116.) This compilation was also edited by A.-J. Marnier, *Anciens Usages inédits d'Anjou* (Paris 1853).

century customs.[71] Its use against witnesses, however, was forbidden by the *Vieux Coustumier* of 1417.[72] Champagne had a law book based on the *Etablissements de Saint Louis*, the *Abrégé champenois* (ca. 1278), but excommunicates were nonetheless excluded from the lay courts.[73] Reims customs dating from 1481 held the exception of excommunication valid when brought against plaintiffs or witnesses.[74] Earlier customs also required the six compurgators who supported a defendant to be "hommes tous bourgois non excommeniez," a rule enforceable *ex officio* by court officials.[75] Grievances that Reims prelates presented to the king at the Council of Namur in 1344 charged that the courts did not observe the prohibitions, but a fragmentary record surviving from the *bailli*'s court in the same year shows the court considering an objection of excommunication submitted against one of the compurgators. Unfortunately, we lose sight of the case after the defendant promised to prove the excommunication within ten days.[76] In nearby Verdun, too, the exception of excommunication was valid (if proved immediately) under customs dating from the first half of the thirteenth century, and procedural rules of the early fourteenth century stipulated that the two "bonnes gens" needed to endorse a

---

[71] See Painter, *Peter* 48–49, on the involvement with Pierre de Dreux. *Le Livre des droiz* in the late fourteenth century endorsed the exception (§ 72, ed. Beautemps-Beaupré, vol. 1, p. 352; see also n. 72). The exception of excommunication could also be used against witnesses (ibid.) and proctors if they were excommunicated when appointed (ibid. § 320, vol. 2, p. 9). As Viollet noted (*Etablissements* III 116), the redactor of these Poitevin customs used the post–1315 Angevin "Compilatio," which he might be following in endorsing the exception. The earliest source of Poitevin law, a brief gloss on the *Etablissements*, does not mention our topic ("Glose poitevine," ed. Viollet, *Etablissements* vol. 3, pp. 106–14).

[72] Filhol, ed., *Le Vieux Coustumier* 35.278, p. 116. Filhol (p. 3) dismissed the slightly earlier *Livre* (see previous note) as incomplete, but on our subject it is so detailed and systematic I think it can be regarded as an important source.

[73] "Abrégé champenois des Etablissements," in Viollet, ed., *Etablissements* vol. 3, pp. 140–87; c.33, p. 151. On the origin and use of the "Abrégé" see Viollet I 323–27.

[74] Varin, *Arch. lég.* I 816, no. [vii]. In a variation of the canon law under *Pia* (VI 2.12.1), defendants had to prove the exception immediately, as in the royal court, and plaintiffs were allowed eight days to prove absolution. These customs were redacted in 1481, revised in 1507.

[75] Varin, *Arch. lég.* I 634–35, no. [77].VII. Varin noted that the customs are probably fourteenth-century, if not earlier, since their commentator, Gérard de Montfaucon, who died in 1439, called them the "Vieil Coustumier" (ibid. 637 n. 1).

[76] For the Council of Namur see Varin, *Arch. admin.* II.2, p. 925n. The 1344 case is recorded ibid., p. 905n. on 905–6 (cf. p. 891 for the date).

plaintiff's claim be "hors d'excommunjement."[77] In an undated case incorporated into the Verdun *Livre des droits*, a plaintiff suing to recover money still owed on the purchase of his estate triumphed over the exception of excommunication submitted by his adversary when the judge pointed out that the plaintiff had sold his estate precisely for the purpose of freeing himself from excommunication.[78]

Such sales were forbidden explicitly in Normandy by the *Très Ancien Coutumier* of the turn of the twelfth and thirteenth centuries.[79] Norman customs might well have been the model for the decrees of Louis VIII and for *Cupientes*, since they ordered confiscation of excommunicates' possessions after one year; a fine of up to nine pounds was to be turned over to the bishop, sparing the excommunicated debtor his home and necessities.[80] Perhaps under English influence, the period allowed to lapse before confiscation in at least some Norman jurisdictions was only forty days. In a decretal of 1254, Innocent IV tried to prevent the archbishop of Rouen from conferring absolution *ad cautelam* too easily on those excommunicated by his suffragans and about to be coerced by confiscation of their possessions after the forty days allowed to lapse "de more Normaniae."[81] A mid-century inquest at Caux found few who had ever heard of a case of such coercion, but in 1288 the Norman exchequer's court found it necessary to forbid arrest of Christians excommunicated by the church courts because of debts to Jews.[82]

---

[77] Meijers, *Verdun* c.[LXXVI], p. 63, for the rule, which dates from before 1246 (cf. p. v for the date; this chapter is part of II b). On the fourteenth-century rule for compurgators see ibid. c.[CIII], p. 76, and for its date, 1308–13, see p. v, on section II c¹.

[78] Meijers, *Verdun*, c.[CLXXXVI] p. 104. Cf. p. v on the case.

[79] E.-J. Tardif, ed., *Coutumiers de Normandie* (Rouen 1881–96) vol. 1, p. 2, c.2 § 3: "Misericordia excommunicati, et emendatio, est versus episcopum: catalla, que habet, usque ad novem libras, preter victum suum et domus sue. Hereditas excommunicati non vendetur nec invadiabitur pro satisfactione excommunicationis." According to a fragment of a commentary by Gérard de Montfaucon (d. 1439), in Reims the usual prohibition against sale of an estate could be waived if the sale was necessary to obtain absolution from excommunication; see Varin, *Arch. lég.* I 644, no. [25].VIII.

[80] See previous note. On the background of the Norman procedure see Hoffmann, *Gottesfriede* 179.

[81] VI 5.11.7, in Friedberg's apparatus, col. 1097.

[82] See Morel, *Pouvoir* 97–99, on the inquest. For the 1288 judgment see E. Perrot, ed., *Arresta communia scacarii. Deux collections d'arrêts notables de l'échiquier de Normandie de la fin du XIIIe siècle (1276–1290. 1291–1294)* (Caen 1910) 73–74.

A 1234 case in which the exception of excommunication was used in the Norman exchequer's court has already been cited.[83] No other instances have been found, nor is the exception mentioned either in the *Ancien Coutumier* or in the *Grand Coutumier* of 1254–58.[84] An early fifteenth-century *Style* of the exchequer confined *infamia* to those excommunicated for a year or more.[85]

In Brittany, too, according to the *Très Ancienne Coutume* (1312–25), *infamia* and legal disabilities had to be grounded in definite proof or long-standing excommunication.[86] As we have seen, the anticlerical activities of Count Pierre de Dreux and his son Jean le Roux had included granting legal rights to excommunicates, and since as late as 1269 the royal *parlement* heard an appeal from a Breton charging that his exception of excommunication had been ignored by the seneschal at Rennes, Count Jean le Roux seems not to have abided by his promise in 1256 to ensure enforcement of excommunicates' legal disabilities in his courts. But the fourteenth-century *Coutume* bears no traces of the earlier hostility. With the sense of justice for which his book is famous, the author insisted that excommunicates unable to pay their debts in full be absolved on ceding what possessions they had.[87] The exception of excommunication against plaintiffs, so controversial in the thirteenth century, was not discussed, though persons infamed by judicial conviction or other public proof were forbidden to submit criminal accusations or testify.[88] Excommunicates were specifically excluded from the courts only in the capacity of proctor.[89]

Summary

Impressions, rather than conclusions, are the fruit of an investigation necessarily based on fragmentary and often negative evidence. The absence of any trace in customs or court records does not prove that

---

[83] Marnier, *Etablissements* 163; see Chapter 4 at n. 147.

[84] Tardif, *Coutumiers.* None of the late thirteenth-century cases edited by Perrot (see n. 82) mentions the exception.

[85] *Coutume, style et usage au temps des échiquiers de Normandie,* ed. L. de Valroger (Paris 1851) c.74, p. 57.

[86] Planiol, *Bretagne* c.[88], pp. 136–37.

[87] Planiol, *Bretagne* c.[334] p. 309.

[88] Planiol, *Bretagne* c.[106], p. 147; and c.[156], p. 174.

[89] Planiol, *Bretagne* c.[88], pp. 136–37.

the legal disabilities of excommunication went unenforced. In Normandy, for example, a record of the use of the exception survives in the absence of any reference in the customs; and in Toulouse an indirect but definite reference to excommunicates' inability to sue in a commentary on the customs of 1286 is our only clue to a practice on which the customs themselves are silent.[90] Many French custumals fall far short of the level of detail and precision at which reference to the exception of excommunication would be expected.[91] Moreover, in criminal trials, at least, it is obvious from surviving fourteenth-century registers that procedures were not sufficiently refined to accommodate such defenses as a matter of course.[92]

Still, enough evidence has been gathered to show that the exception of excommunication was at best controversial. Surprisingly, some secular jurisdictions were prepared to enforce the much harsher penalty of confiscation or imprisonment against contumacious excommunicates but either opposed the far milder coercion of the exception of excommunication (e.g., the *Etablissements de Saint Louis*) or simply ignored it (e.g., ordinances of the Duchy of Burgundy and of Franche-Comté).[93] Of course, secular authorities drew at least

[90] The Norman evidence is discussed above at nn. 79–85. For Toulouse, see H. Gilles, ed., *Les Coutumes de Toulouse (Consuetudines Tholose) 1286, et leur premier commentaire (Consuetudinem commentarium) 1296* (Toulouse 1969) 207. The commentary states that excommunicates are prohibited from reconvening, i.e., because they cannot be plaintiffs. Gilles suggests Arnaud Arpadelle, *doct. leg.* (1289–) and advocate, as author (pp. 25–29).

[91] E.g., without mentioning court procedures, Burgundian customs of the turn of the fourteenth and fifteenth centuries make it clear (albeit in a bizarre and possibly defective text) that excommunicates are to be avoided. The customs describe a priest threatening to excommunicate anyone who treats as a leper a man judged not to be one: "je met en escommuniement toz ces qui diront dois ore en auant que il est mesels, et les desseuroit de la compaignie nostre seignours et c[etera]" (A.-J. Marnier, ed., *Ancien Coutumier de Bourgogne* [Paris 1858] c.32, pp. 35–36).

[92] Neither of the surviving fourteenth-century criminal registers refers to excommunication; see L. Tanon, ed., *Registre criminel de la Justice de St Martin des Champs à Paris au XIVe siècle* (Paris 1877); and T. H. L. A. Duplès-Agier, *Le Registre criminel du Châtelet de Paris du 6 Septembre 1389 au 18 Mai 1392* (Paris 1861–64).

[93] The *Etablissements de Saint Louis* have been discussed earlier in this chapter. For Franche-Comté, see *Ordonnances franc-comtoises sur l'administration de la justice (1343–1477)*, ed. E. Champeux (Dijon and Paris, n.d. [introd. dated 1912]) no. 41 § 3, p. 230, an ordinance of ca. 1460 on imprisonment of contumacious excommunicates. In 1474 a similar ordinance was enacted in the duchy of Burgundy; see, by the same editor, *Les Ordonnances des ducs de Bourgogne*, R. Bourguignonne 17 (Dijon and Paris 1907) 237 § 63.

some profit from confiscation, but something more than financial incentive seems to have been at work.[94] The penalties that French authorities were required to enforce against contumacious excommunicates were very harsh indeed—so harsh that, in effect, they blurred the distinction between excommunicates and heretics.[95] It is therefore not surprising that some lay authorities were reluctant to give any support whatever to excommunication. The potential consequences were simply too dangerous. Others were willing to aid the church after an excommunicate had shown himself genuinely guilty at least of contempt for church authorities by remaining contumacious.[96]

Other harsh customs that flourished in France undoubtedly contributed to lay reluctance to penalize excommunicates. Very large fines and the custom of excommunicating whole families can only have estranged the lay community over time. In relation to the exception of excommunication itself, there are traces in France of a custom of giving a judgment in a defendant's favor as if the plaintiff were in default.[97] Canon law never contemplated such a measure, and after the promulgation of *Pia* excommunicated plaintiffs were allowed to

[94] Division of excommunicates' fines and property varied greatly from one jurisdiction to another. To mention only two of the most influential law books: the *Très Ancien Coutumier de Normandie* seems to award the entire amount to the bishop (see n. 79), whereas the *Etablissements de Saint Louis* prescribed a fine of £6 to be paid to the ecclesiastical judge and 60*s.* to the secular judge (ed. Viollet I c.127, vol. 2, pp. 239–40). For other examples see Morel, *Pouvoir* passim, and Maisonneuve, *Etudes* passim.

[95] Although, as said in an earlier chapter, the universal canon law gave no grounds for the inference that mere contumacy in excommunication gave rise to suspicion of heresy, individual French councils, like the 1310 Council of Béziers, did not hesitate to advise priests to warn parishioners that after a year "tanquam contra suspectos de fide catholica, prout justum fuerit, procedemus" (c.17, Mansi 25.364). Likewise, the thirteenth-century formulary "Curialis" prescribes imprisonment of a contumacious excommunicate after one year since "plus videtur haeresi quam fidei catholicae consentire" (c.17, Wahrmund, *Quellen* I.3, p. 9). Cf. the 1385 case in the Official's court at Paris, in which the corpse of the late Colinus Lupi was granted ecclesiastical burial notwithstanding a sentence of excommunication, since Lupi had promised to seek absolution within eight days on pain of "vehement" (i.e., sufficient for condemnation; see Lévy, *Preuves* 64–65) suspicion of heresy (Petit, *Registre* 443).

[96] Since Inquisitors sometimes used excommunication to trap heretics in errors on the articles of faith implicit in the authority to excommunicate, contumacious excommunicates may have been regarded with equanimity in many communities. See Bernardus Guidonis, *Practica inquisitionis heretice pravitatis*, ed. C. Douais (Paris 1886) 5.11, pp. 285–86.

[97] Discussed above in the text at n. 42 in relation to the 1270 case in the royal *parlement* and in n. 43 in relation to a St. Quentin case of 1370.

benefit from whatever they had managed to transact before the exception.[98] In short, French ecclesiastical authorities had partly to blame themselves for the troubled reception of the exception of excommunication in French secular law. Despite its vicissitudes, however, the exception continued to be a desideratum of the ecclesiastical program well into the sixteenth century, and as late as 1510 its retirement from the customs of Auvergne was opposed by the "gens d'Eglise," as Charles du Moulin reported—"mais tout cela est abrogé parmi nous."[99]

ENGLAND

The English evidence forms a marked contrast. In the royal courts the exception of excommunication was endorsed by jurists and faithfully upheld by judges and advocates: forty cases collected here document its use from 1196 to 1411, and a discussion in the exchequer chamber shows that it was still regarded as a valid defense in 1467.[100] Defendants successfully used the exception throughout this period, although its validity was temporarily jeopardized by frequent chicanery during the middle decades of the thirteenth century and by legal arguments of principle during the early fourteenth century.

Only in one significant point did English law differ from canon law: the exception could be used only against persons excommunicated by name and for clearly specified reasons. Canonists of the late twelfth century, among them at least one northerner, had expressed the opinion that the usual legal penalties accompanying excommunication should not result from excommunication *latae sententiae*.[101] Though quickly repressed in canon law, the doctrine commended itself to the English authors of the tract *De legibus* (now no longer to be regarded as the work of Bracton alone), whose original redaction, as

---

[98] VI 2.12.1.

[99] *Les Coutumes du haut et bas pais d'Auvergne*, with notes by Charles du Moulin, ed. C. I. Prohet (Paris 1695) 18.5, p. 169.

[100] The remainder of the text is based on Appendix 5 except where otherwise indicated. On England see W. R. Jones, "Relations of the Two Jurisdictions: Conflict and Cooperation in England during the Thirteenth and Fourteenth Centuries," *Medieval and Renaissance St.* 7 (1970) 77–210, esp. 80 on the exception of excommunication.

[101] Discussed in Chapter 4 at n. 44.

Thorne has shown, existed in the first decades of the thirteenth century.[102] Toward the end of the century this was affirmed in *Fleta*, the Edwardian epitome of *De legibus*.[103] In only one of our cases was the plaintiff originally charged with an excommunication *latae sententiae*, and the bishop who certified this excommunication carefully noted that the plaintiff had been "puplice nunciata" as a major excommunicate.[104] When Margery Blaket, with her husband, Roger, tried to sue a plea of disseisin in 1312, defendant Ralph Loveday objected that Margery had been excommunicated as an apostate nun, having left the convent of Burnham in Buckinghamshire after twenty-three years.[105] Despite the plaintiff's rebuttal that she had "precontracted" marriage in the presence of her ordinary—a claim that might be hard to prove after two decades!—the court was presented with a letter from the bishop of Lincoln confirming that "soror Margeria" had indeed been condemned by authority of the canon—that is, by excommunication *latae sententiae*—for leaving the convent "tanquam aposticando" and that she had since been publicly denounced. The case was immediately dismissed.

Although episcopal letters of proof rarely gave any more definite reason for excommunication than "contumacy" or "manifest excesses," Margery's was the only case in which the original excommunication was clearly not by judicial sentence. In a 1302 case already mentioned briefly, an exception was overturned when the plaintiffs' counsel argued that the evidence proved the plaintiffs denounced as excommunicates but not actually excommunicated. (Boniface VIII's 1298 *Licet*, as we have seen, declared denunciation sufficient for expulsion.)[106] The archbishop of Canterbury had decreed that they should be excommunicated and had had them denounced in his dio-

---

[102]*Bracton*, fol. 426b, vol. 4, pp. 325–26; on Thorne's changes see below at n. 119.

[103]*Fleta* 6.44, pp. 436–37.

[104]That is, even if the crimes for which they were excommunicated were covered by excommunications *latae sententiae*, as in many cases they were, the plaintiffs had also been expressly excommunicated by name.

[105]Appendix 5 case 35. Margery said she would prove she had precontracted marriage by summoning her ordinary, the Abbot of St. Alban's, before whom (she said) the arrangement had taken place. The court summoned him to testify, but if he did we are not told what he said; the next thing we are told is that the parties left "sine die" because of the bishop of Lincoln's testimony.

[106]Appendix 5 case 29, discussed in Chapter 4 at n. 140. *Licet* (VI 5.11.14) was also discussed in detail in Chapter 4 at n. 138 and Chapter 6 at nn. 112–14 and passim.

cese, but their ordinary claimed that they had never, in fact, been excommunicated, and so had legal standing in court.[107] Counsel successfully argued that the royal court was bound to give credence only to the testimony of the plaintiffs' ordinary, and the case, a plea of replevin, went on.

Excommunication *latae sententiae* was also insufficient grounds for invoking secular coercion of contumacious excommunicates in England, where coercion normally took the form of arrest and imprisonment after forty days rather than the usual continental punishment of confiscation. Logan found that only a tiny fraction of surviving medieval writs of signification (for arrest of contumacious excommunicates) dealt with excommunications *latae sententiae*; even in these instances the excommunicates had already been denounced at least forty days before the writ was applied for.[108] By insisting on an objective and public criterion, the English courts greatly simplified the procedures surrounding the exception of excommunication, and this might well have favored its longevity.

The exception was used in a wide range of civil and criminal pleas. Excluding for the moment those concerned with ecclesiastical matters, the other cases tabulated here involved disseisin (4 cases), land (2), debt (1), (feudal?) services (1), replevin (1), inheritance (1), dowry (1), trespass (2), and robbery (1).[109]

It may be that during the early thirteenth century the exception of excommunication was not effective in blocking criminal appeals. *De legibus* warns against the subterfuge of criminal defendants' obtaining writs to have their accusers imprisoned as contumacious excommunicates.[110] It is not clear why this rather elaborate fraud would be

---

[107] Appendix 5 case 29. In cases 10 and 18 we are also told that the plaintiffs had been denounced, though it does not seem this was required for their expulsion.

[108] Logan, *Excommunication* 43 and n. 1, and p. 75. Perhaps there is also no evidence of judicial sentences preceding the cases between 1371 and 1407 resulting from failure to pay clerical subsidies for the war (pp. 55 and 60–61).

[109] Disseisin: Appendix 5 cases 1, 12, 35, and 40; land: cases 2, 3, and 5 (case 5 is a continuation of 2); debt: case 32; (feudal?) services: case 6; replevin: case 29; inheritance: case 7; dowry and chattels: case 9; trespass: cases 37 and 39; housebreaking and robbery: case 38. The records name no plea for case 4.

[110] *Bracton* fol. 427a, vol. 4, p. 328. True, *De legibus* also warned against fraudulent writs of signification in writ of prohibition cases (*Bracton* fol. 408b, vol. 4, pp. 270–71), and Flahiff found evidence of this abuse ("Writ" part 2, 244–45). But here the more drastic step of signification might have been necessary because, as discussed below, the exception of excommunication was for a time automatically re-

deployed if the simpler device of a fraudulent exception of excommunication were sufficient to block a criminal charge—though of course prison incapacitated one's adversary completely, in this period probably for years. In any event, the one criminal plea (robbery) and two semicriminal pleas (trespass) in our survey all date from the early fourteenth century.[111] Moreover, a chance remark by an advocate in the replevin case from 1302 implies that the exception of excommunication was commonly accepted both in appeals of felony and in the gravest civil cases, those involving the writ of right. When the defense attorney submitted the exception of excommunication, the plaintiff's attorney objected that since the defendant had already "defended generally" and prayed oyer (hearing) of the writ, she should not be allowed to submit a personal exception, a defense lower in degree than the ones already attempted.[112] An advocate for the defendant objected that "if, after mise of the great assize or wager of battle, you proffer a letter of excommunication, you are allowed to do so." The argument, which was accepted by the court, indicates that the exception was considered by the royal courts even in the most serious cases; for the grand assize was for writ of right cases, and wager of battle was by now used only in writ of right cases or felony appeals.[113]

Ecclesiastical matters constitute a deceptively high proportion of our cases—just over half—because of the availability of published Curia Regis rolls for exactly the period in which the exception of excommunication was used to counter the writ of prohibition.[114] When

---

jected in writ of prohibition cases if the royal court plaintiff proved the excommunication resulted from the writ alone.

[111] Appendix 5 cases 37–39. To those can be added an example of the exception being used against the plaintiff in a late thirteenth-century homicide case, outcome unknown (Woodcock, *Canterbury* 94–95).

[112] Appendix 5 case 29.

[113] Maitland, *History* I 147 on the grand assize and II 632–33 on wager of battle.

[114] Nineteen cases involved the writ of prohibition: see Appendix 5 cases 11, 13–27, 31, 33, and 34. An additional five cases concerned ecclesiastical matters: advowson (8, 10, 30, and 36) and violence to a cleric, i.e., the plaintiff (28). (The latter crime was, of course, handled by the church courts, but clerics could also sue in the royal courts for damages [Maitland, *History* I 440].) Likewise, there are disproportionately more (twenty) clerics among the defendants, partly because of the predominance of writ of prohibition cases—since clerics were often the original plaintiffs in the ecclesiastical court, hence defendants in the writ cases—and moreover because the prelates who imposed excommunication in reaction to the writ were often sued together with the plaintiffs. (Cases 14, 19, 22, 23, and 31 definitely illustrate this, and others might also. Defendants were also clerics in cases 3, 6, 10, 11, 13, 15, 18, 20, 21, 24,

the royal writ of prohibition, in use since the 1160s, was served on an ecclesiastical court plaintiff to inhibit a suit over which the royal courts (it was alleged) might rightfully have jurisdiction, the ecclesiastical court defendant who had obtained the writ would often be excommunicated under the guise of contumacy, since naturally he now absented himself from the ecclesiastical court trial.[115] In the ensuing writ of prohibition suit, the defendant (plaintiff in the ecclesiastical court) would submit an exception of excommunication, and a letter would be produced showing that the plaintiff had indeed been excommunicated for contumacy.[116] Since the letter of certification frequently came from the ordinary in whose court the disputed suit had begun and who had himself excommunicated the (royal court) plaintiff because of the writ, these cases comprised a tangle of adversarial relationships, an effective diffusion of the hostilities between the secular and ecclesiastical jurisdictions. Confronted with what must often have seemed the most brazen challenges to their authority, the royal judges in fact treated these cases with great delicacy. In a 1220 writ of prohibition case the royal court, even while vindicating the plaintiffs' claim that the case, which concerned advowson, did belong in the royal court, sent away three knightly plaintiffs to obtain absolution because "it is the custom that excommunicates are not heard in any pleas. . . ."[117] With the courtesy that is often the hallmark of conscious superiority, the royal judges waved off the offer of the defendants (choirmaster and treasurer of Salisbury, armed with a

---

26, 30, 32, 34, and 36.) When Appendix 5 was assembled, fifteen volumes of CR rolls had been published.

[115] Flahiff, "Writ" passim, esp. part 2, 243–45.

[116] Flahiff, "Writ" part 2, 264–65.

[117] Appendix 5 case 13. This case and cases 15 and 18 turned on whether the disputed property consisted of tithes (church courts) or advowson (royal courts). As Flahiff showed, the disputes often arose because a sufficiently large amount of tithes constituted a living, hence real property, a matter for the royal courts ("Writ" part 1, 275–76, and part 2, 262). Thorne has recently shed further light on the matter: if a large enough portion of tithes were removed (which could be accomplished in the church courts) an advowson would become worthless anyway (*Bracton* vol. 3, pp. xviii–xix). Friction over this probably subsided when the exception of excommunication ceased being used fraudulently to impede writs of prohibition (see below at n. 118). But note that under c.1 of the *Articuli cleri* of 1316 the royal courts agreed not to use writs of prohibition in tithes cases unless the clerical owner sold his tithes and sued for payment in the church court, in which event the tithes were deemed to have become chattels (*Statutes of the Realm* [London 1810–28] I 1710).

papal mandate) to respond in spite of the exception "out of reverence for the king" if the court so ruled, and ignored the plaintiffs' proof that they had duly and respectfully informed the ecclesiastical judge of the writ (he would not listen) and even vainly sought absolution.

Eventually, the royal courts would come to reject almost all exceptions of excommunication resulting from a writ of prohibition, but this case and others that could be adduced show that the policy developed only gradually.[118] In the *Notebook* he helped to compile about 1227–39, Henry Bracton (d. 1268), cited four cases to show that excommunicated plaintiffs could validly replicate that they had been excommunicated because of a writ of prohibition.[119] *De legibus*, which Thorne has now shown was compiled in the first decades of the century and was successively revised by Bracton and others until about mid-century, also holds such replications valid.[120] Flahiff in his study of the writ of prohibition concluded that by mid-century it was the plaintiff himself who informed the court of his excommunication and asked for damages when excommunication arose from the writ.[121] This did not wholly curtail the use of excommunication to impede writs of prohibition, even over a period of decades.[122] The church courts still found it worthwhile to force the issue, and in the last of

---

[118] For the policy of rejecting such exceptions, which prevailed by mid-century, see Flahiff, "Writ" part 2, 245, 264–65. Several cases seem to show the policy did not develop in a straight line. In the 1220 case (13) just described, the exception delayed trial even after it was shown that the excommunication resulted from the writ of prohibition; but in another case (14) from the same term the court rejected an exception of excommunication on these grounds. In 1224 (case 17) the judges upheld an exception under the same circumstances even as they vindicated the plaintiff's writ of prohibition; perhaps, however, this was from respect for the bishop of Lincoln, who testified in person.

[119] Appendix 5 cases 13, 14, 18, and 21. On Bracton's work on the *Notebook* see Thorne's introduction to *Bracton*, vol. 3, pp. xxxiv–xxxv.

[120] *Bracton* fol. 426b, vol. 4, p. 326. See Thorne's introd., vol. 3, pp. xxx–xxxii and xl–xliv, for the dates of Bracton's revision of *De legibus* and his tenure (1247–51 and 1253–57) as royal judge.

[121] Flahiff, "Writ" part 2, 264 no. 11. It may be significant that already in our 1220 case (Appendix 5 case 13) the reason given for excluding the plaintiffs was two-pronged—not merely that the plaintiffs were excommunicated but also that they had not so informed the court. See also n. 122.

[122] Appendix 5 cases 31, 33, and 34 are all early fourteenth-century cases involving the writ. In the first two the plaintiff declared he was excommunicated and asked for damages, as described by Flahiff (see n. 121). See text and next notes on the third case.

our cases involving the writ of prohibition, from 1312, the dean of Arches as defendant unsuccessfully submitted an exception of excommunication.[123] Still, it is hard to believe that anything more than public relations motivated the royal denial in 1350–51 of a Commons petition that plaintiffs be allowed to clarify whether their suit involved disputed jurisdiction when they were challenged by an exception of excommunication.[124] Since this allowance had been usual for more than a century, the parliamentary exchange must have been an unsuccessful conciliatory gesture to placate the pope; despite such efforts, the breach soon came with the statutes of Provisors (1351) and Praemunire (1353).[125]

On the whole, the exception of excommunication probably gained more than it lost from measures taken to prevent abuses in writ of prohibition cases. Because this litigation was isolated and defined for what it was—a jurisdictional conflict in which the parties' interests were sometimes only secondary—the exception of excommunication remained untainted in principle. In fact, several cases dating from the early fourteenth century seem to show that the royal courts deliberately stanched the development of a replication that would have enabled them to function as a court of appeal from excommunication, the role increasingly assumed by the French royal *parlement* and, as the 1389 appeal from the duchess of Anjou's court shows, by other lay courts in France.[126] In writ of prohibition disputes the ecclesiastical court judge, as well as the plaintiff in the church court, was an adversary of the plaintiff, and even if the ecclesiastical judge was not actually sued, a plaintiff charged with excommunication often claimed that it had been imposed by his adversary.[127] The replication might be elided by proof that the excommunication was related to a different

---

[123] Appendix 5 case 34.

[124] *Rotuli parliamentorum* (London 1767–77) 25 EIII, vol. 2, p. 230. The review of Logan's *Excommunication and the Secular Arm* by Donald W. Sutherland, *Speculum* 45 (1971) 145–47, drew my attention to this petition (p. 146).

[125] On royal conciliation in this period, see E. B. Graves, "The Legal Significance of the Statute of Praemunire of 1353," in Charles H. Taylor and John L. La Monte, eds., *Anniversary Essays by Students of C. H. Haskins* (New York 1929) 57–80, esp. 70–74; W. A. Pantin, "The Fourteenth Century," in C. H. Lawrence, ed., *The English Church and the Papacy in the Middle Ages* (London 1965) 157–94, esp. 192; idem, *The English Church in the Fourteenth Century* (Cambridge 1955) passim, esp. 54–86; and Mollat, *Avignon* 250–68.

[126] Discussed above at n. 58.

[127] Appendix 5 cases 14, 19, 25, 31, 33, and 34 are variations on the theme that the excommunication arose from the adversarial relationship.

matter; thus in a 1231 case the defendant, the prior of Worksop, charged with excommunicating the plaintiff in retaliation for distraint of his lay fee, successfully replicated with a letter from the bishop of Coventry and Lichfield testifying that William, *quondam* archdeacon of Derby, had excommunicated the plaintiff "for his merits." [128] But as time wore on the implicitly adversarial relationship between excommunicator and excommunicate emerged as a source of prejudice. [129] In a 1302 case attorneys argued that the episcopal letter of proof was insufficient since it merely reported an excommunication recorded on the archdeacon's rolls. [130] This argument, if allowed to stand, would invalidate a good many exceptions of excommunication. [131] Worse still, the exception was rejected on the even more general grounds adduced by another attorney, who claimed that not even personal testimony from the bishop would be sufficient proof, "car issi ensuerit qe de sa malice demeyne si avereit il avantage. . . ." [132] In several other cases during the next decade the court heard similar reasoning from plaintiffs' attorneys. [133] Finally, in 1313 or 1314, the abbot

---

[128] Appendix 5 case 21. The year before, the bishop of Coventry had used a similar defense as defendant (case 19). When the plaintiff charged the bishop had excommunicated him for reasons stemming from the matter under dispute, the bishop successfully replicated that, on the contrary, he had excommunicated the plaintiff for violence to a cleric. Whether the violence arose from this dispute was not stated.

[129] In a 1241 case (Appendix 5 case 25) the defendant at first claimed the plaintiff had been excommunicated because of his writ of prohibition, then, presumably under advice of counsel, changed his charge and claimed the excommunication had been for another reason.

[130] Appendix 5 case 30.

[131] I.e., episcopal letters certifying excommunications were simply reports of action taken in one of the diocesan courts or (cf. Appendix 5 case 18) in the courts of judges delegate.

[132] Appendix 5 case 30.

[133] Appendix 5 case 33, in which the plaintiff successfully replicated that he had been excommunicated at his adversary's behest, though the latter—and the proof—claimed he had been excommunicated for contumacy. Cf. case 34, in which the dean of Arches, represented by his commissary, was sued on a writ of prohibition. The commissary produced episcopal letters showing the plaintiff had been excommunicated for contumacy. Counsel for the plaintiff argued that the defendant was merely commissary for the dean of Arches, who in turn was merely commissary for the bishop (cf. Woodcock, *Canterbury* 7). Hence the bishop's testimony should be discounted; if the writ had been brought against him directly he would not have been allowed to benefit from his own testimony. Significantly, the judge rejected the exception on different grounds, namely, that the defendant must have conducted a case in the ecclesiastical court after the writ was served, since the proof was dated after the writ.

of Battle, John of Northburne (1311–18), sued the prior of Christ-church, Canterbury, as guardian *sede vacante*, for the late Archbishop Robert Winchelsey's (d. 1313) failure to present the royal candidate.[134] The prior submitted an exception of excommunication and tried to prove it with a letter from the bishop of Rochester (dated 29 Nov. 1312) declaring that the abbot had been excommunicated "for his of-fense and [had] long been bound by a sentence of major excommuni-cation." In response, it was argued that the bishop had neither given a definite reason for the excommunication nor demonstrated his juris-diction over the abbot. Opposing counsel argued that since "contract and trespass confer jurisdiction," the bishop in whose diocese the trespass was committed could testify. The judge asked what plain-tiff's counsel would advise if the bishop's original letter of excommu-nication had stated a definite reason, even though the letter of cer-tification to the royal court did not. Plaintiff's counsel argued that even in that event the royal court could not accept the bishop's testi-mony; for if that testimony were false, the plaintiff's only remedy would be in the ecclesiastical court.[135]

Here, it seems, was an argument that went to the heart of the matter, the adversarial nature of episcopal testimony on excommuni-cation and the absence of a route of appeal for a plaintiff claiming that he was wronged by such testimony. Hence it seems significant that the judge insisted on debating the more straightforward issues of ju-risdiction and the reason for excommunication, avoiding further dis-cussion of the injustice of bishops' testifying to legal incapacity caused by a penalty they themselves were responsible for. And if the

---

[134] Appendix 5 case 36. See J. H. Denton, *Robert Winchelsey and the Crown 1294–1313* (Cambridge 1980) 272–77, on similar disputes during Winchelsey's career, though this case does not seem to be mentioned. E. Searle, *Lordship and Community. Battle Abbey and Its Banlieu 1066–1538* (Toronto 1964), briefly mentioned the case at 239 and n. 19. Northburne attended Winchelsey's memorial service (Denton, p. 15)—interesting not only because it shows the hostilities were not personal but also because it is an example of a publicly excommunicated prelate attending reli-gious services.

[135] Appendix 5 case 36. Cf. Milsom's introduction to *Novae narrationes*, ed. E. Shanks and S. F. C. Milsom, SS 80 (1963) p. cc, noting that in a writ of prohibition case in 1311, some defendants tried to elude charges on the grounds that they were charged as if they were plaintiffs in the church court, whereas they were judges. But the court refused to absolve them, saying that if it granted such concessions habitually there would be no remedy for people alleging they had been wronged by *ex officio* pro-ceedings in the church courts.

exception was eventually rejected on the grounds that the evidence was too weak, it was an extinction of a species that left the genus intact.[136] Several years later, in 1316, the *Articuli cleri* secured a royal promise not to force ordinaries to justify their sentences of excommunication or to require them to absolve excommunicates unless the excommunication prejudiced royal liberties.[137] Later cases show no difficulties with the exception, and in legal discussions in 1388 and 1467 the exception was even made the basis of arguments by analogy concerning other legal procedures.[138]

What made the exception of excommunication so resilient in England? Perhaps most important, the Constitutions of Clarendon (1164) early established that royal officials could not be excommunicated without the king's permission.[139] Thus whatever disputes arose in individual cases, precedent was set to avert the constant excommunications of royal agents that so exasperated the French *parlement*. Henry III exercised a general supervision when royal aid against contumacious excommunicates was invoked, but evidently unlike St. Louis he did not turn the matter into an issue for ideological debate.[140] Likewise, the royal courts pruned away certain complications concerning the exception of excommunication without challenging it in principle. Bureaucratic inertia did the rest.

---

[136] Appendix 5 case 36. Once admitted, the plaintiff, though presenting the royal side, immediately lost.

[137] C.7, *Statutes of the Realm* I 172.

[138] In 1388 the exchequer justices entertained an argument that an action was never valid if, of a group of defendants, not all were allowed to sue in the exchequer's court—i.e., severance should not be permitted in favor of the plaintiff who was entitled to sue there—based on Justice Clopton's analogy that if two plaintiffs sued on a writ of debt and one was excommunicated or outlawed, severance could not be made because the action had never been good (*Year Books of Richard II* vol. 5, ed. I. D. Thornley (London 1937) E 11RII, no. 3, p. 189). In the same term Clopton presided over one of our trespass pleas (Appendix 5 case 39) and accepted an exception of excommunication against the plaintiff. In 1467, the exchequer judges agreed that once proven excommunicated or outlawed, a plaintiff bore the burden to show absolution or pardon, even if the certifying letter referred to events that occurred twenty years before! (*Select Cases in the Exchequer Chamber*, ed. M. Hemmant, vol. 2, SS 64 [1948, for 1945], case 6, pp. 11–12. This partially contradicts *Fleta*'s rule that "Actiones . . . ante tempus excommunicationis institutae propterea non cadent" [6.44.1, vol. 1, p. 438].)

[139] Const. of Clarendon, c.7, Stubbs, *Charters* 165.

[140] See F. M. Powicke, *The Thirteenth Century*, 2d ed. (Oxford 1962) 465–67, for some examples; cf. also Flahiff, "Writ" part 2, 245.

One other contrast with French procedures seems important: in England there was little danger that the line between penalties of excommunication and those against heretics would be overstepped. The writ of signification, whose effects were milder, in any event, than the French confiscation, seems only rarely to have been used against those excommunicated for heresy.[141] Moreover, while Continental governments and the papacy itself adopted the death penalty for heresy during the early thirteenth century, English statute law did so only in 1401.[142] It was thus possible in England to identify excommunicates and penalize them without setting in train processes that might lead to the terrible punishments used against heretics.

But perhaps the true explanation for the endurance of the exception of excommunication in England is one that unfortunately begs the question: in the long medieval calm bracketed by Becket and Henry VIII, the secular and ecclesiastical courts vied in a genteel rivalry of attrition. Flahiff has shown that the writ of prohibition confirmed the peaceful triumph of the royal courts by the end of the thirteenth century.[143] In exchange, evidently, the exception of excommunication was allowed to thrive, assuring the ecclesiastical courts some measure of prestige to compensate their loss.

---

[141] Logan, *Excommunication* 68–70, observes that there are few surviving significations of heretics, though indeed fewer than half the surviving cases record the reasons for excommunication (ibid. 52). On the rarity of confiscation of excommunicates' possessions in England see Logan, p. 109.

[142] On the establishment of the death penalty for heresy on the Continent see Maisonneuve, *Etudes* esp. 241–57. For England, see H. G. Richardson, "Heresy and the Lay Power under Richard II," *English Historical R.* 51 (1936) 1–28; and Maitland, *History* II 551–52.

[143] Flahiff, "Writ" part 2, 282–83.

Conclusion

From among the several forms of punishment prominent in the ancient world, the church at a very early stage in its institutional development chose social and religious exclusion as its chief sanction. Severance of the relation of individual and group remained the essence of excommunication, though in other punishments entailing exclusion, such as exile or outlawry, loss of life or possessions eclipsed the rupture of social ties. Great individuals flourished in the church, but structurally it remained a simple society in which individual and group were radically interdependent.[1] The alarm greeting moral or intellectual deviation was not mere sentimentalism, as the increasingly desperate measures of the high middle ages reveal. Through baptism an individual obtained his identity from the corporate society of the church.[2] A member cut off from this source of life was "like a corpse," the withered branch cut off from the True Vine (John. 15.6).[3]

But parallel to the concept of the rebirth of the individual through society—no theme was more beloved by the conservative theologians of the twelfth century—was the concept of the group itself as an individual: the *corpus Christi*.[4] The pious metaphor of hierarchy, in which

[1] G. Piers and M. B. Singer, *Shame and Guilt* (New York 1971) 92–93.

[2] S. Freud, *Group Psychology and the Analysis of the Ego*, ed. J. Strachey, standard edition (London 1953–74) XVIII 74–76.

[3] Host., *Lect.* X 5.7.9, v. *Debitam*: "Sicut palmes, id est homo infidelis et inutilis, ac mortuus, cum in eo omnino Dei gratia sit extincta."

[4] W. Ullmann explored various aspects of this theme in many places, perhaps most fully in *The Individual and Society in the Middle Ages* (Baltimore and London 1966). Another masterly study of the theme is O. Heggelbacher, *Die christliche Taufe als Rechtsakt nach dem Zeugnis der frühen Christenheit* (Freiburg 1953).

upper members need the lower ones, expresses a profound truth: this society really was a single organism.[5] Only the new metaphysics of St. Thomas would free the individual from this dependency by emphasizing a direct existential relationship to God.[6]

Contagion was the most important negative concept for expressing relations between individual and society, as sacramental grace was the most important positive concept. Good was shared through common acts of suffrage, but evil could also be conducted through social channels.

Excommunication's tabus reflect the fragility of Christian civilization. Superseding a ban on contacts with clergy—and with laymen only in religious acts—absolute exclusion of excommunicates was enforced from the fifth century.[7] Occasional attempts to modify the tabu encountered a resistance whose spontaneity and strength betrayed deep insecurity. Optimism amid economic and demographic expansion thus accounts for the reduction of excommunication's contagion at the end of the twelfth century. Other margins were shifting. The Fourth Lateran Council reduced the marital tabus of consanguinity. It also pronounced that the unity of the Trinity did not in itself constitute an entity, the first major Christological statement since the early councils. Politically, the theocratic experiments of the eleventh century had been defeated; Becket's martyrdom commemorated the dualistic commitment of this society.[8]

Why, then, did the mitigation of the tabu take the form of a universal reduction to minor excommunication rather than the reservation of sharper sanctions for sacral contacts, as in the early church? Possibly because the expressions of dualism could not conceal the growing community of interests and outlook shared by layman and cleric, heretic and Mendicant.

The most important change in the twelfth century, however, was the

---

[5] Based on a number of passages in the Pauline epistles, esp. 1 Cor. 12.12. On exposition in twelfth-century theology, see Vodola, "Individual" I 1–15.

[6] Sum. theo. 1, q.8, esp. a.1, resp., and 3 ad 1.

[7] See Chapter 1 for details. Priests are, of course, always surrounded by more rigid tabus than laymen (cf. the observation in S. Freud, Totem and Taboo, ed. Strachey, standard edition, XIII 19).

[8] For the first see Lateran IV c.50, COD 257–58, and cf. the pioneering study by H. Schadt, Die Darstellungen der Arbores Consanguinitatis und der Arbores Affinitatis (Tübingen 1982) esp. 195–200, for reflections on the significance of this change. For the Christological statement see Lateran IV c.2, COD 231.

association of full excommunication with the sphere of law. Only the lesser sanction of minor excommunication was available in religious or spiritual transactions. No surer index could be found of the fruits already being reaped from scholastic theology. Guilt was driving out shame. Theology and canon law were to pursue wholly different courses. This was really the deathblow for excommunication. Of course the legal sanction survived through the middle ages and beyond. But divorced from the great psychological issues that now engrossed theologians, excommunication as such became a mere relic.

APPENDIXES

Early Glosses on Excommunicates' Legal Rights in Court

(a) Bazianus (d. 1197), Gloss on C.4 q.1 c.1, v. *Laicus*, Vat. 2494, fol. 104va.[1]

Cum ad agendum in propria causa quilibet admittatur, ut C. e. q. v. Omnibus et C. ii. q. i. Prohibetur,[2] nunquid excommunicatus audietur, cui nec excommunicationis causa ante absolutionem agere licet, ut ⟨in⟩ decretali Alexan. III, Quesitum,[3] nec alii loqui nisi que ad
5 eandem per excommunicationem pertinent, ut C. xi. q. iii. Cum excommunicato?[4] Item, an audietur excommunicatus contra excommunicatum? Vel coram quo iudice eum poterit conuenire? An coram excommunicato, cuius nulla est sententia vel iudicialis cognitio, ut ar. C. vii. q. i. Factus, et ar. xxiiii. q. i. Audiuimus?[5] Bar.

---

[1] On the relation of glosses in Vat. 2494 to the apparatus *Ordinaturus magister*, see A. Stickler, "Dekretapparatus 'Ordinaturus Magister Gratianus,'" *St. Gratiana* 12 (1967), 111–41 at 122; and R. Weigand, "Frühe Glossen zu D.12 cc.1–6 des Dekrets Gratians," *BMCL* 5 (1975) 35–51. On Bazianus see also, by the same author, "Bazianus- und B.-Glossen zum Dekret Gratians," *St. Gratiana* 20 (1976) 453–95, especially 488 on the siglum "Bar." for Bazianus.
[2] *Rect.* C.4 q.6 c.2; C.2 q.1 c.14.   [3] 1 Comp. 1.23.2.
[4] C.11 q.3 c.18.   [5] C.7 q.1 c.5; C.24 q.1 c.4.

(b) Anonymous apparatus *Ordinaturus magister*, recension 1 (1180–82), C.4 pr., v. *Quidam*, Bamberg, Can. 13, fol. 92va (B), and Vat., Ross. 595, fol. 118va–vb (R).[1]

Sed nunquid possum conuenire et accusare excommunicatum, cum non debeamus ei loqui? Itaque, ne crimina eius maneant inpunita, et ne fauorabilis efficiatur persona, cum omnia licerent ei inpune. Et ut ipsa exactione compellatur ad rectitudinem, ar. xxiii. q. vi. Iam
5 uero.[2] Sed non potest conuenire uel accusare excommunicatum, quia coram quo iudice? An coram excommunicato, cuius nulla est senten- tia, ar. vii. q. i. Factus, et xxiiii. q. i. Audiuimus?[3] Item, non potest conuenire uel accusare catholicum, ar. Diffinimus, quod autem ar. iii. q. v. Nullus, ar. vi. q. i. Infames, ar. ii. q. vii. Pagani, Si hereti-
10 cus, ar. xcv. di. Illud et xiiii. Miratus, et xi. q. iii. Si episcopus forte.[4] Excommunicatos cum excommunicato, ar. C. xv. q. 3. Sane. Ar. contra iiii. q. vi. Omnibus, ar. iii. q. vii § Tria. uer "Alii enim omnes," ac in extra. Tanta est labes, Licet preter, ar. xiiii. q. i. Quod debetur.[5] Erit ergo reus in causa, et non actor, ar. in extra. Quesitum.[6]
15 Item, in sacramento calumpnie faciendo erit ei copia sacrorum: sit in perditionem et detestationem sui. Quod quidam negant. Item, in crimine simonie et hereseos et lese maiestatis, et si uelit prosequi suas uel suorum iniurias ubi passim quisquis admittitur, admittetur ad ac- cusationem. Quod quidam concedunt. Sed uidetur non esse admit-
20 tendus. Et hoc in detestationem sui criminis. Quidam tamen dicunt

---

2 Itaque] Utique R   **3** liceret B   ut] in B   **4** exactione] excommunicatione R
10 xiiii *sic codd.*

---

[1] Professor Charles Duggan generously helped me with identifications, dates, and readings. On this apparatus see, most recently, R. Weigand, "Zur Handschriftenliste des Glossenapparatus 'Ordinaturus Magister,'" *BMCL* 8 (1978) 41–47.
[2] C.23 q.6 c.4.   [3] C.7 q.1 c.5; C.24 q.1 c.4.
[4] C.4 q.1 c.1; C.3 q.5 c.11; C.6 q.1 c.17; C.2 q.7 cc.25–26; D.95 c.3; *Miratus: rect.* D.93 c.2; C.11 q.3 c.4.
[5] C.15 q.3 c.4; C.4 q.6 c.2; C.3 q.7 d. p. c.1, and c.2 § 2 *infra*; *Tanta*: X 5.3.7; *Licet*: JL 14091, dating ca. 1176–77 (cf. X 2.20.15; and see S. Kuttner, "Anhang: zur De- kretale 'Licet preter solitum,'" in P. Landau, "Die Glossen der Collectio Chelten- hamensis," *BMCL* 11 [1981] 9–28 at 27–28); *Quod*: C.14 q.1 c.2.
[6] 1 Comp. 1.23.2.

quod in predictis casibus debeat cogi ab ecclesia ut reddat se idoneum ad predicta facienda, uel satisfaciendo uel promittendo firmiter se postea satisfacturum, ar. de cons. di. ii. Hii qui.[7]

Item, si iuraui soluere ei tali die debitum, tenebor iuramento ei
25 soluere? Videor ei non esse obligatus propter iusiurandum, ar. xv. q. vi. Nos, Iuratos.[8] Sed melius est ut religione iurisiurandi persoluam ei debitum, ar. in extra. Sicut Romana.[9] Et est casus necessitatis iste, sicut et permissus ut non tenear ei loqui, ar. xi. q. iii. Quoniam.[10] Possum ei per alium uel alii pro eo debitum soluere.

---

23 de cons. *om.* B   **26** religione] religionem *codd.; emendavi ex rec. 2 in* Salzburg, Stiftsbibl. St. Peter a.XII.9, fol. 92vb   **28** tenear] teneat B

---

[7] *De cons.* D.2 c.20.   [8] C.15 q.6 cc.4–5.
[9] X 2.24.8, excerpted from *Sicut Romana*, which dates 1173–74. The decretal itself reads "sub religione."
[10] C.11 q.3 c.103.

(c) *Quaestiones Barcinonenses* III (1170s), nos. 9 and 10, Barcelona, Arch. Corona de Aragón, S. Cugat 55, fol. 55rb.[1]

[9.] Queritur an excommunicatus possit quem conuenire uel accusare. Et uidetur quod accusare non posset. Nam omnes tales infames sunt, ut xxxii. q. v. Preceptum.[2] Et etiam heretici sunt, ut iiii. q. i. c. ii. Et ideo sunt ab accusatione repellendi, ut ii. q. vii. Laicos[3] et iiii. q. i. c. i.

5 Item, nullus excommunicatus est audiendus in causa ante absolutionem suam, ut in decretali Quia quesitum.[4] Similiter non ciuiliter quem conuenire potest, quia in omni causa debet sacramentum de calumpnia prestari nec est aliquis audiendus. Sed excommunicatus iurare non debet quia non debet ei copia sacrorum fieri. Non enim
10 debemus margaritas ante porcos ponere nec sanctum dare canibus [cf. Matt. 7.6], ut di. xlii. Etiam mandatis.[5] Et quia qui semel peierauit uel suspectus habetur ultra non in sua uel alterius causa iurator existet, ut xxii. q. v. Paruuli.[6]

[10.] Sed quid si suam suorumque iniuriam prosequatur—nonne
15 potuerit accusare? Videtur quod possit. Nam omnes illi qui iuri communi ratione infamie ab accusatione repelluntur in hoc casu sunt audiendi, ut ii. q. i. Prohibentur, et in decretali Licet preter solitum.[7] Item, uidetur dicendum si de enormibus quem accusare uoluerit excommunicatus quod sit audiendus, ut ii. q. i. Imprimis et xv. q. iii. c.
20 iiii. Sane, et in decretali Tanta est labes.[8]

In primis dic quod nec ciuiliter nec criminaliter potest quem conuenire excommunicatus ante absolutionem suam. Utrum autem debeat audiri suam uel suorum iniuriam prosequens ante absolutionem uel in enormibus uario modo soleunt sapientes respondere. Ego
25 tamen crederem non admittendos.

---

9 sacrorum] sacramentorum *cod.*   **11–12** peierauit] deierauit *scr.; emendaui ex* C.22 q.5 c.14, *Parvuli:* "qui semel periuratus fuerit."

---

[1] See, most recently, J. Brundage, "Some Canonistic Quaestiones in Barcelona," *Manuscripta* 15 (1971) 67–76. The date comes from the references to *Licet*, ca. 1176–77 (see n. 7, and Appendix 1b n. 5) and *Quaesitum*, ca. 1171–79 (see n. 4, and Chapter 4 at n. 50).
[2] C.32 q.5 c.21.   [3] C.2 q.7 c.3.
[4] 1 Comp. 1.23.2 (with variant incipit).   [5] *Rect.* D.43 *In mandatis* (2).
[6] C.22 q.5 c.14.
[7] C.2 q.1 c.14; JL 14091, on which see Appendix 1b n. 5.
[8] C.2 q.1 c.7; C.15 q.3 c.4; X 5.3.7.

(d) Huguccio, *Summa* (1188–90) C.4 q.1 c.2, v. *Ostenderint,*
Admont 7, fol. 187ra–rb (A), and Vat. 2280, fol. 139rb–va (V).

Deficientibus accusatoribus per purgationem, patet ex premissis
quod excommunicatus non potest accusare regulariter. Sed nunquid
non recipietur in aliis casibus in quibus quilibet admittitur, ut in iniuria sua uel suorum, et in criminibus exceptis, ut ii. q. i. Prohibentur,
5 et infra eadem, q. ult. Omnibus?[1] Dico quod non. In nullo enim casu
potest aliquem accusare. Non catholicum, ar. hic i. et ii. et C. ii. q.
vii. Pagani et iii. q. v. Nullus et vi. q. i. Infames.[2] Item, generaliter
dico quod non potest accusare uel conuenire ciuiliter aliquem. Non
excommunicatum, quia excommunicatus cum excommunicato non
10 debet participare.
   Et preterea, coram quo iudice? An coram excommunicato, cuius
nulla est sententia, ar. vii. q. i. Factus et xxiiii. q. i. Audiuimus?[3]
Item, nec a iudice nec ab alio est communicandum nisi in his que
spectant ad eius correctionem, ut xi. q. iii. Excommunicatos, Cum
15 excommunicato.[4] Sic ergo excommunicatus in nullo casu potest
agere criminaliter uel ciuiliter. Nec potest esse accusator in causa, ut
in extra. Quesitum.[5]
   Sed nunquid potest accusari uel conueniri ciuiliter, cum non debeamus ei participare? Sic generaliter, ne crimina eius remaneant
20 inpunita. Et ne uideatur ex delicto consequi emolumentum, et ne
fauorabilis efficiatur persona cum omnia licerent ei impune, et ut ipsa
exactione compellatur ad rectitudinem, ar. xxiii. q. vi. Iam uero.[6]
Erit ei copia sacrorum: tunc in prestando sacramentum de calumpnia
sic ut eis obligatus uerum non taceat. Vel si tacuerit fit ei ad maiorem
25 cumulum sue perditionis. Sed si excommunicatus conueniatur nonne
poterit excipere et ita agere? Resp., poterit quidem opponere exceptionem facti, scilicet negando se debere, introducendo testes, defen-
dendo se. Sed si uelit opponere exceptionem de iure, scilicet quod
uelit aliquid obicere in personam accusatoris uel actoris uel testis, et

---

13 nec] si A   communicandum] excommunicandum A   **18** conuenire A
22 exactione] ex accusatione(?) A

---

[1] C.2 q.1 c.14; C.4 q.6 c.2.
[2] C.4 q.1 cc.1–2; C.2 q.7 c.25; C.3 q.5 c.11; C.6 q.1 c.17.
[3] C.7 q.1 c.5; C.24 q.1 c.4.   [4] C.11 q.3 cc.17–18.
[5] 1 Comp. 1.23.2.   [6] C.23 q.6 c.4.

30 uelit probare, non debet audiri. Item, si uult reconuenire eum iuxta
regulam illam, scilicet, cuius in agendo, etc., in extra. Miramur et in
auten. Et consequenter,[7] non est audiendus. Sibi imputet cum possit
se reddere aptum ad hoc. Generaliter enim dicit Alexan. quod excommunicatus non potest esse actor in causa, ut in extra. Quesitum.

35 Item, ubi excommunicatus non potest conuenire, poterit dare procuratorem ad causam, presertim filium, qui sine peccato participat ei?
Dico quod non, cum is intelligatur agere cuius mandato agitur, ut in
extra. Mulieres.[8] Preterea, principalis persona et non procurator debet prestare sacramentum de calumpnia, ad quod non admittitur ex-

40 communicatus si uelit agere. Preterea, hec omnia fiunt in penam illius, ut facilius conuertatur, ut xi. q. iii. Audi et xxiii. q. vi. Iam
uero.[9] Quod autem ei communicatur cum accusatur uel conuenitur
non obuiat regule ecclesiastice, quod talis communicatio est in illis
que spectant ad eius correctionem.

45 Sed ecce mutuauit michi xx. soli. Teneor ei reddere dum est excommunicatus, presertim si iuraui me redditurus ei tali die? Credo
quod sic. Nec pecco communicando ei in hoc, quia uidetur esse causa
necessitatis, ut xi. q. iii. Quoniam.[10] Vel possum ei per alium uel alii
pro eo debita soluere, non communicando ei. Sed uidetur obuiare xv.

50 q. vi. Nos, Iuratos.[11] Mihi uidetur uerum quod nullus sit obligatus
excommunicato. Sed hoc ibi melius determinabitur.

Et hec uera sunt generaliter de excommunicato, id est, de anathe-
matizato. Sed de excommunicato, id est, tantum a communione sacramentorum et non fidelium separato, dico quod repellitur ab accusa-

55 tione regulariter et a testimonio, ut aperte colligitur ex hoc capitulo.
Sed non prohibetur agere ciuiliter uel accusare in causa propria uel
suorum. Et in criminibus exceptis: tali enim licite loquimur.

Item, si dubitetur utrum quis sit excommunicatus, licite stabit in
causa, etiam ut de hoc ipso cognoscatur, ar. ff. Si quis in ius uocatus

60 non ierit.[12]

---

36 sine peccato participat] si non participatur A   57 tali enim *om.* A   59 etiam]
et V

---

[7] 1 Comp. 2.4.3; Nov. 96.2, *post* Cod. 7.45.14.
[8] 1 Comp. 5.34.7.   [9] C.11 q.3 c.21; C.23 q.6 c.4.
[10] C.11 q.3 c.103.   [11] C.15 q.6 cc.4–5.
[12] Dig. 2.5.

Sed ecce, de excommunicatione constat, uel forte ipse accusat me, et ego excipio quod ipse est excommunicatus uel fuerit, et ipse replicat contra me quod iniuste sit uel fuerit excommunicatus, est audiendus? Distingo, si uolo repellere quia olim fuit excommunicatus,
65 quamuis postea fuerit absolutus, est audiendus si uult replicare et probare se iniuste fuisse excommunicatum, quo facto non repelletur ab accusatione. Si uero uolo eum repellere quia adhuc est excommunicatus, et ipse uelit replicare se iniuste fuisse excommunicatum, non est audiendus, quia excommunicatio iniuste facta tenet et ligat,
70 dummodo sit a iudice suo et ante appellationem. Nec ante absolutionem est audiendus in causa si uelit agere, ut in extra. Quesitum.

(e) Huguccio, *Summa* C.4 q.1 d. a. c.1, v. *De prima*, Admont 7, fol. 186vb (A), and Vat. 2280, fol. 139ra (V).

Hic intitulatur questio i., scilicet an in excommunicatione constitutus ualeat accusare. Et sine distinctione dicendum est quia non potest, siue iuste siue iniuste sit excommunicatus, dummodo excommunicatio teneat, ar. infra eadem questione c. i. et ii. et xxxii. q. v. Pre-
5 cipit.[1] Set illa questio pocius fuit tractanda, scilicet an post reconcilationem possit accusare. Et quidem in hac questione Io. et R. sic distinxerunt: si fuit excommunicatus pro crimine et pro contumacia non potest preterquam in exceptis casibus ubi omnes admittuntur nisi restituatur in integrum. Si pro sola contumacia, quia forte nolebat
10 facere quod precipiebatur ei, si per annum perseuerauerit in illa contumacia non potest siue restituatur siue non. Sed uerba fuerunt ista. Dico ergo secure et precise quod semel excommunicatus iuste siue pro crimine et pro contumacia siue pro contumacia sola, et siue per annum in contumacia perstiterit siue non, de cetero accusare non
15 potest.

Quod multipliciter probatur. Talis criminosus antea fuit a tempore baptismi et nunc. Ergo hoc solum sufficit ut repellatur ab accusatione, ar. vi. q. i. Qui crimen.[2] Item, contumacia in ueteri testamento morte mulctabatur, ut xi. q. iii. Absit.[3] Sed quecumque in ueteri tes-
20 tamento morte mulctabantur nunc repellunt a promotione, ut di. liiii. Multos.[4] Ergo contumacia nunc repellit a promotione. Ergo et ab accusatione. Qui enim promoueri non potest nec accusare uel testificari, saltem contra clericos, ut ii. q. vii. Ipsi, Testes.[5]

Item, quicumque post baptismum fuit criminosus repellitur a pro-
25 motione, ar. di. xxv. Primum et di. xlviii. Quoniam et di. l. Illud et i. q. vii. Si quis omnem.[6] Ergo olim contumax repellitur a promotione. Ergo et ab accusatione et testimonio.

Item, peccatum contumacie iudicatur grauius omni alio peccato,

---

8 omnes *add. marg.* V[2]

---

[1] C.4 q.1 cc.1–2; C.32 q.5 c.19.   [2] C.6 q.1 c.6.
[3] C.11 q.3 c.14.   [4] D.54 c.23.
[5] C.2 q.7 cc.38–39.
[6] D.25 c.6; D.48 c.1; D.50 c.66; C.1 q.7 c.2.

quia grauius punitur. In ecclesia enim nulla est maior pena quam ex-
30 communicatio, ut xi. q. iii. Nichil et xxiiii. q. iii. Corripiantur.[7] Sed
excommunicatio est pena contumacie tantum, nec debet infligi nisi
contumaci tantum, ut ii. q. i. Nemo et xi. q. iii. Nemo et xi. q. iii.
Nemo episcoporum et di. xlv. Set illud et xxiiii. q. iii. Tam sacerdotes.[8] Ergo contumacia est grauius peccatum quam aliquod aliud.
35 Quis enim dubitat sceleratius esse commissum quod grauius est uin-
dicatum, ut xxiiii. q. i. Non afferamus.[9] Si ergo aliquod peccatum repellit a promotione uel accusatione uel testimonio, hoc ergo multo
fortius. . . . [several lines of similar arguments omitted].

Sed in multis locis a sensu contrario colligi uidetur quod excom-
40 municatus post absolutionem possit accusare et testificari, ut infra
eadem c. i. et ii. et supra iii. q. iiii. Beatus et vi. q. i. Illi et xxxii. q. v.
Precipit.[10] Sed dico quod in his locis et similibus non ualet argumentum a sensu contrario, quia contradicit iuri etiam scripto, ut vi. q.
i. Illi.[11]

45 Et omnibus premissis rationibus et generaliter dico argumentum a
sensu contrario non debere sumi nec ualere sumptum, ex quo iuri uel
constitutioni alii contradicit, ut xxxiii. q. ii. Quicumque, Ad-
monere.[12] Vel dico quod in omnibus talibus locis subauditur maxime.

---

[7] C.11 q.3 c.33; C.24 q.3 c.17.
[8] C.2 q.1 c.11; C.11 q.3 cc.31 and 41; D.45 c.17; C.24 q.3 c.14.
[9] C.24 q.1 c.21.
[10] C.4 q.1 cc.1–2; C.3 q.4 c.2; C.6 q.1 c.3; C.32 q.5 c.19.
[11] C.6 q.1 c.3. [12] C.33 q.2 cc.7–8.

Appendix 2

Later Glosses on Legal Rights

(a) Goffredus de Trano, *Apparatus* (1243–45), *Pia* (VI 2.12.1), v. *Duraturis*, Fulda D.10, fol. 8vb.[1]

Sed quare ualet quod cum excommunicato fit in iudicio, cum aliter excommunicatus rescriptum impetrare non possit, ut supra de rescr. Dilectus,[2] nec procurator esse in iudicio etiam absolutus ex mandato sibi facto tempore excommunicationis, ut supra de prob. Post ces-
5 sionem,[3] nec sententia ab excommunicato lata ualeat, ut infra de sen. et re iud. Ad probandum?[4] Respondeo ad singula: excommunicatus agere non potest si excipiatur, et ideo nec litteras impetrare, ut C. si nupt. ex. rescr. pe. l. ii.[5] Procurare non potest quia per hoc assumit negotium alienum. Sententia ab eo lata non ualet quia sententia inni-
10 titur auctoritati iudicis. Et hec eadem ratio est quare scriptura ab ex- communicato confecta non ualet, ut iii. q. iiii. Nullus,[6] quia scriptura sumit auctoritatem ex persona scribentis. Secus autem in excomm- municato qui in iudicio petit quod ei forsitan debebatur, nec fuit ex- ceptum. Sed si excipiatur et probetur, absoluetur reus ab obserua-
15 tione iudicii, non ab eo quod petebatur, ut ff. de iudiciis l. Non idcirco § Cum postea.[7] G.

---

[1] Cf. Kessler, "Untersuchungen" part 2, 307 and 358–59.
[2] X 1.3.26.   [3] X 2.19.7.
[4] X 2.27.24.   [5] Cod. 5.8.2.
[6] C.3 q.4 c.6. [7] Dig. 5.1.44.

(b) Bernard of Compostella, *Apparatus*, *Pia* (VI 2.12.1), v.
Duraturis, recension 1 (1246–53), Vat. MSS Vat. 1365, fol.
588vb–589ra (Va), and Ottob. 1601, fol. 260va–vb (Vb); recension
2 (1253–54/55), Vat. MSS Vat. 3980, fol. 104rb–va (Vc), and
Borgh. 268, fol. 132rb–vb (Vd). Passages Bernard added in
recension 2 are in *uncini*.

Sed mirum uidetur quod ualet quod fit cum excommunicato, cum
alias excommunicatus rescriptum impetrare non possit, supra[1] de
rescr. Dilectus,[2] nec procurator constitutus tempore excommunicationis admittitur in iudicio licet postmodum absoluatur, arg. supra
5 de probat. Post cessionem,[3] nec sententia publice excommunicati
tenet, infra de re iudi. Ad probandum.[4] Et excommunicatus a quolibet actu legitimo exclusus est ipso iure, et extra ecclesiam est. Et ita
per consequens si non potest agere non potest impetrare litteras ad
agendum, arg. C. si nupt. ex rescr. peta. l. ii.[5]
10 Ad primum respondeo: hec uera sunt si excipiatur contra ipsum.
Alias ualebit iudicium quod cum eo actum est, sicut dici consueuit de
procuratore cuius mandatum a domino reuocatum est, quod cum eo
actum est ualet si reuocatio ad iudicem uel ad aduersarium non per-
uenit, supra de proc. Mandato,[6] secundum quod ibi notatur, et supra
15 de rescr. Ex parte decani.[7] ⌐Quia impetrare non dicitur actus legitimus, quia etiam mulier et seruus possent litteras impetrare pro se et
pro alio. Tamen non posset esse procurator seruus uel mulier. Et decretalis illa Dilectus non obstat, quia littere ille nulle fuerunt tacito de
re iudicata a qua non fuerat appellatum, C. sent. rescin. non pos. l.
20 Impetrata.[8] Et rescriptum non sumit auctoritatem ab impetrante sed a
delegante.⌐
Ad secundum simili modo potest responderi. Vel aliter: cum sit excommunicatus, officium procurationis non cadit in ipsum, nec ali-

---

6 Et] Ad primum respondeo Vab   **10** Ad primum respondeo] Et Vab   **14** secundum quod] sed Vb

---

[1] Va always has "extra" for "infra" or "supra"; for the significance see Kessler, "Untersuchungen" part 2, 320–30.
[2] X 1.3.26.   [3] X 2.19.7.
[4] X 2.27.24.   [5] Cod. 5.8.2.
[6] X 1.38.13.   [7] X 1.3.33.
[8] Cod. 7.50.3.

quod aliud officium, ⌜quia per hoc assumit officium alienum.⌝ Ad
25 illud quod dicitur quod sententia publice excommunicati non tenet
licet post sententiam excommunicatio detegatur, et ea que fiunt cum
excommunicato ualent licet postea excommunicatio probetur, respondeo in iudice secus est, quia defectus est ibi in iurisdictione, quia
iurisdictio non cadit in excommunicatum. Et ita sententia eius nulla
30 est, cum nullam habeat iurisdictionem. Et eius scripta non tenent
cuius auctor dampnatus est, iii. q. iiii. Nullus, et infra de heret. Fra-
ternitatis et c. Excommunicamus § Credentes.[9] ⌜Et sententia nititur
auctoritate iudicis. Sed cum iudex excommunicatus nullam habeat
iurisdictionem eius sententia nullam habet rei iudicate auctoritatem.
35 Secus in rescripto impetrato ab excommunicato, ut dictum est.⌝ Et
hec est ratio que assignari consueuit, quod sententia lata cum falso
procuratore potest haberi rata a partibus, sed sententia excommunicati non ualet nec conualescere potest propter defectum iurisdic-
tionis, infra de immun. ec. Aduersus § Quia uero,[10] ubi de hoc. Sed in
40 excommunicato qui petiit in iudicio quod sibi forsitan debebatur nec
fuit exceptum secus est. Si excipiatur et probetur absoluitur reus ab
obseruatione iudicii, sed non absoluitur ab eo quod petebatur ab
ipso, ff. de iudi. Non idcirco § Cum postea,[11] quia hec exceptio dila-
toria est, supra eodem titulo, Exceptionem.[12] ⌜Sed decretalis illa Ex-
45 ceptionem innuit quod processus habitus non ualet. Et hic ualet processus habitus ante oppositam exceptionem. De hoc notatur in
decretale predicta Exceptionem. Dic ut ibi in glossa que incipit Etiam
§ i.[13] Et sic uidetur quod littere impetrate ab excommunicato ualeant
eo absoluto. Per hanc enim decretalem non distinguitur utrum op-
50 ponatur excommunicatio lata tempore impetrati rescripti an post impetratum rescriptum. Et ita non refert quandocumque impetrator dicatur excommunicatus dummodo fuerit absolutus. Ad hoc optime
facit supra de off. dele. Prudentiam § vi.[14] Et sic uidentur correcta
illa iura que uidebantur dicere quod rescripta impetrata per excom-
55 municatum non ualebant. Alias necesse est dicere quod loquitur de

---

45 ualet[1]] ualeat Vc

---

[9] C.3 q.4 c.6; X 5.7.4; X 5.7.13 § 5. [10] X 3.49.7, *nunc indiv.*
[11] Dig. 5.1.44.1. [12] X 2.25.12.
[13] *Glos. ord.* X 2.25.12, v. *Condemnandus.* [14] X 1.29.21, *nunc* § 3.

excommunicatione lata post rescriptum impetratum uel quod loquitur in iudice ordinario. Sed satis uidetur consonare rationi ut quod
dicitur in hac decretale locum habet in quolibet iudice ordinario uel
delegato. Et illa decretalis Prudentiam intelligenda est in hoc casu. Et
60 sic ualebit rescriptum impetratum ab excommunicato postquam
fuerit ab excommunicatione absolutus, ut dictum est. Et iudicium
quod cum ipso actum est tenet ante probatam exceptionem excommunicationis, ut dicitur in littera. Et sic rescriptum impetratum ab
excommunicato non est ipso iure nullum. Et si contrarium inueneris
65 notatum illud reducas ad hoc quod hic dicitur.⌐

---

56 uel] et Vc

(c) Innocent IV, *Apparatus, Pia* (VI 2.12.1), v. *Duraturis*, recension 1 (1246–51), Fulda D.10, fol. 4vb–5ra (F); recension 2 (1251–54), edition of 1570, Venice, p. 355a–b (Ed.), and Vat. 1443, fol. 158rb–va (V). Passages added in recension 2 are in *uncini*. There are two glosses on the lemma.

Sed quare ualet quod cum excommunicato fit in iudicio, cum alias excommunicatus rescriptum impetrare non possit suo nomine, ut supra de rescr. Dilectus,[1] nec procurare in iudicio etiam absolutus ex mandato sibi facto tempore excommunicationis, ut supra de prob.
5 Post cessionem,[2] nec sententia ab excommunicato lata ualeat, ut infra de sen. et re iud. Ad probandum?[3] Respondeo ad singula. Excommunicatus agere non potest si excipiatur, et sic nec litteras impetrare, ut C. si nup. ex rescr. pe. l. ii.[4] Item, procurare non potest, quia per hoc assumit negotium alienum. Et sententia ab eo lata non ualet, quia
10 sententia nititur auctoritate iudicis. Et hec eadem ratio est, quia scriptura ab excommunicato confecta non ualet, iii. q. iiii. Nullus,[5] quia scriptura sumit auctoritatem ex persona scribentis. Secus autem statutum est in excommunicato qui in iudicio petit quod ei forsitan debeatur, nec fuit exceptum. ⌜Et hoc ideo quia in culpa fuit qui non
15 excepit, et propter fauorem rerum iudicatarum et uim iudiciorum, et quia modicum prodest excommunicato sententia et modicum interest rei. Quia⌝ et si excipiatur et probetur, absoluetur reus ab obseruatione iudicii, non ab eo quod petebatur, ut ff. de iud. l. Non idcirco § Cum postea.[6] ⌜Aliqui tamen dicunt quod hodie auctoritate huius de-
20 cretalis tenebit quicquid fit in iudicio siue actor sit excommunicatus, siue rescriptum cuius auctoritate processum est sit per excommunicatum impetratum, siue etiam iudex excommunicatus sit. Et dicunt iura que contradicunt per hanc decretalem sublata. Verumtamen

---

3 absoluto Ed.   **5** ualet FEd.   **6** respon. Ed.   **9** sententia] factum V*ac*   **10** nititur] utitur Ed. innititur V   auctoritati V   **11** confecta] lata F*ac*   **12–13** statutum est *om.* F   **13** petiit FV   **13–14** debebatur FV   **15** et uim iudiciorum *om.* V*ac et om. adhuc* uim   iudiciorum] indiciorum Ed.   **17** et] Sed F *om.* V   **20** fit] fiet V   **21** auctoritatis V   **23** Verumtamen] Videtur tamen V

---

[1] X 1.3.26.   [2] X 2.19.7.
[3] X 2.27.24.   [4] Cod. 5.8.2.
[5] C.3 q.4 c.6.   [6] Dig. 5.1.44.1.

alii dicunt quod non est presumendum quod papa tot iura uoluerit
25 uno uerbo tollere. Item, quod non reuocatur, quare stare prohibetur,
C. de inof. test. l. Si quando, C. de test. l. Omnium.⌐[7]

v. *Duraturis*: In iudiciis constat, quod quicquid facit excommunicatus antequam probetur excommunicatus ualet, ut hic. Idem dicimus
extra iudicium. Nam si sit notarius excommunicatus, non tamen sen-
30 tentialiter dampnatus, et faciat instrumentum, ualebit, licet aliqui
dicant contra. ⌐Arg. pro eis supra, de proc. Consulti.[8] Sed alii respondent illam decretalem loqui de illis qui prestant scilicet auctoritatem
his que dicuntur in instrumentis. Hic autem loquitur de illis qui prestant auctoritatem in instrumento, scilicet quod fit autenticum, et non
35 in his que dicuntur uel fiunt in instrumento. Item pro eis est iii. q. iiii.
Nullus.

Sed ipsi respondent quod ibidem loquitur de scripturis quas faciunt excommunicati non ratione publici officii sed proprio motu.
Item, loquitur ibi de dampnatis, hic loquitur de toleratis.⌐

40 Dicimus etiam quod instrumentum ualebit, etiam si testis excommunicatus sit ibi inscriptus, dummodo instrumentum non sit suspectum. Sed si esset suspectum, non daretur fides instrumento per
testem nunc suspectum uel excommunicatum, licet satis dici possit
quod si nunc esset absolutus, quamuis eo tempore quo fuit inscriptus
45 esset excommunicatus, quod bene nunc per suum testimonium dat
fidem instrumento. Sed non econtra: scilicet, si nunc excommunicatus esset, sed tempore inscriptionis erat absolutus, quia tunc per
suum dictum non dat fidem instrumento, sed suspectum est quia excommunicatus est. Aliqui tamen contradicunt.

50 Sed hec est differentia inter ea que aguntur extra iudicium et ea

---

29 notorius F   29–30 non—dampnatus *om.* F   30 ualebit] tunc *praem.* F
32 praestant] putant V alias prestant *add. marg. al. man.*   scilicet *om.* V   34 in
om. V   37 ipsi] illis V   39 de dampnatis] in condemnatis Ed.   42 instrumento]
in *praem.* V   43 nunc] non Ed. V*ac*   suspectum—uel] *om.* FV   possit] posset
FV   44–45 absolutus, quamuis—esset excommunicatus *om.* V*ac*, et *om. adhuc* inscriptus   46 instrumento] in *praem.* V   48 instrumento] in *praem.* V   50–52 ea
que—ut instrumenta] ea que aguntur ⟨in iudicio et⟩ extra iudicium. Quia extra
iudicium non ualent ⟨ea que aguntur extra [*sic*]⟩, ut instrumenta F [Bracketed sections added by a different hand.]

---

[7] Cod. 3.28.35; 6.23.19.   [8] X 1.38.15.

que aguntur in iudicio: quia ea que aguntur in iudicio ualent, et ea que aguntur extra iudicium non ualent, ut instrumenta et huius-modi que fiunt ex officio publico, si est sententialiter dampnatus. Licet aliqui contradicant. Si autem sint talia que non aguntur ex of-
55 ficio publico, ut emptio, contractus, et huiusmodi, illa ualent etiam si publice et solempniter sit excommunicatus, ut not. supra de dol. et contum. Veritatis, et infra eodem t. Exceptionem.[9] Ea autem que aguntur in iudicio similiter ualent, licet actor sit sententialiter excom-municatus, dummodo sibi in presenti actione excommunicatio non
60 obiciatur, nec iudex eum repellet. Secus tamen uidetur si iudex sen-tentialiter esset uel alias publice excommunicatus, quia tunc etiam si non obiciatur iudici excommunicatio, non ualet quod agitur, infra de sen. et re iud. Ad probandum.[10]

Ratio diuersitatis est, quia magis uerentur partes obicere iudici
65 quam aduersariis, et quia magis afficitur sententia excommunicatione iudicis quam partium. In spiritualibus autem quid obtineat, ut in electione et huiusmodi, no. de ele. Cum Wintonien. et c. Illa et c. Nihil.[11]

---

53 que fiunt ex officio publico] que facit ex officio et publico instrumento F   fiunt] facit V   55 etiam si] etsi FV   57 autem *om.* F   62 non ualet quod agitur] tamen ualet quod agit F tamen non ualet V   64 obicere] opponere F   65 et *om.* Ed.   afficit Ed.   excommunicationis F*pc*   67 de] supra *praem.* F

---

[9] X 2.14.8; X 2.25.12.   [10] X 2.27.24.
[11] X 1.6.25, 39, and 44.

(d) Peter Sampson, *Distinctiones* (1246–50/51), *Pia* (VI 2.12.1), v. *Communibus*, Vat., Pal. 656, fol. 144ra–rb (V), partially edited from Leipzig, Stadtbibl. MS 249, in Kessler, "Untersuchungen" part 2, 379 (L).

Nota quod quidam sunt actus publici ut tutela et cura, ut Institu. de tutel. circa prin.[1] Quidam ciuiles, ut iudicare, arbitrium ferre, ff. de iudiciis. Cum pretor, iii. q. vii § Tria, supra de arbitris. Dilecti.[2] Et hec ideo quia arbitria redacta sunt ad instar iudiciorum, ff. de ar-
5 bitris. l. 1.[3] Quidam uero communes, ut procuracio, agere, testimonium ferre, ut hic et supra de testibus. Licet ex quadam.[4] Et ideo dicuntur communes quia inter ciuiles et publicos reperiuntur. Et a talibus scilicet communibus excommunicati in iudicio repelluntur, supra de probacio. Post cessionem.[5] Ergo multo forcius ab aliis, scili-
10 cet a publicis et ciuilibus, infra de re iudi. Ad probandum, supra eodem, Exceptionem.[6] Unde circa hoc sic distingue. Refert enim utrum excommunicatus faciat aliqua in iudicio de predictis a quibus prohibetur, et tunc non ualent, ut hic et supra eodem, Exceptionem et c. A nobis.[7] Vel extra iudicium. Et tunc subdistingue, quia aut facit
15 tanquam privata persona aut tanquam persona in publico officio constituta. In primo casu non prohibetur excommunicatus, quia uendere potest cum ab eo licite ematur. Et possit ab eo exigi quod debetur, et ei dari possit, infra de sen. ex. Si uere, et c. Inter alia. xi. q. iii. Quoniam multos.[8] Ergo multo forcius illud donare possit, et ualet
20 donacio facta per ipsum, infra de dona. Inter dilectos.[9] Unde illi qui excommunicatis participant quantum ad eorum salutem licite recipiunt elemosinas, alias ecclesias, ab eisdem, infra de sen. ex. Cum uoluntate.[10] In secundo uero casu prohibetur excommunicatus publice ab eis que fuerint extra iudicium, ut puta tabellio. Non enim

---

Several obvious errors in V have been silently corrected.   **11** distingue] distinguendum est L   **12–13** a quibus—non ualent] quia tunc a talibus prohibetur L **14** tunc subdistingue] sic distingue L

---

[1] Inst. 1.13.
[3] Dig. 4.8.1.
[5] X 2.19.7.
[7] X 2.25.12 and 2.
[9] X 3.24.8.

[2] Dig. 5.1.12; C.3 q.7 d. p. c.1; X 1.43.4.
[4] X 2.20.47.
[6] X 2.25.12.
[8] C.11 q.3 c.103.
[10] X 5.39.54.

25 ualent pendente tali excommunicatione instrumenta per eum facta,
infra de hereticis, Excommunicamus § Credentes.[11] Hiis premissis
patet solucio cuiusdam questionis de qua consueuit dubitari, scilicet,
utrum excommunicatus possit condere testamentum. Et dicendum
est quod sic, cum donare possit, ut probatum est. Et testamenti factio
30 in donacionibus et in legatis constat. Nam legatum est quedam donacio a defuncto relicta, et ab herede prestanda, Institu. de lega. circa
prin.[12] Et sic excommunicatus ea potest, maxime que ad eius spiri-
tus [?] salutem, ut dixi. Sed per factionem testamenti eius salus procre-
atur, cum per hoc bona eius in pios usus distribuantur. Et heredibus
35 maxime litigia euitentur, unde in talibus ei licite participatur, infra de
sen. excommuni. Cum uoluntate, etc. Responso.[13]

---

[11] X 5.7.13 § 5.   [12] Inst. 2.20.1.
[13] X 5.39.54 and 43.

(e) Peter Sampson, *Lectura* (1250s), *Exceptionem* (X 2.25.12), v. *Condempnandus*, Vienna MSS 2083, fol. 27vb (Va), and 2113, fol. 48rb (Vb).

Sed quare fit hec condempnatio, cum non intersit actoris huius exceptionem prius fuisse propositam? Quia nichilominus ualerent ea que cum ipso acta sunt, per nouam constitutionem eodem titulo, Pia.[1] Unde non uidetur reus in expensis condempnandus, cum non
5 fecerit actorem in uanum laborare. Dicas ad hoc quod hec decretalis hodie stare possit, quod habeat locum usque ad § Excommunicatus, cum iudex erat excommunicatus, et tunc interesset actoris si exceptio excommunicationis non proponatur in initio cause, quia non ualet que coram iudice tali agitur, infra de sen. et re iudi. Ad probandum.[2]
10 Unde reus presumitur malitiose exceptare. Hoc dicas tunc subticuisse quare condempnatur actori in expensis in § Excommunicatus.[3] Et mutat casum, et loquitur quando actor erat excommunicatus. Inno. papa IIII. posuit casum similiter, et bene, ut concordet iuri nouissimo, quia cum iudex assignasset terminum ad proponendas excep-
15 tiones dilatorias, reus primo proposuit contra rescriptum, et succubuit secundo contra partes iudicis, et succubuit et sic de multis aliis. Ultimo proposuit exceptionem excommunicationis contra actorem, cum iam fecisset ipsum maliciose fatigari laboribus et expensis. Certe condempnatur modo in expensis quas fecit quia ante non proposuit huius exceptionem.

1–2 actoris—propositam] actoris an huius exceptio fuisset proposita Va   **6** possit] posset Vb; non *praem. codd.*   **10** subticuisse] conticuisse Va   **12–13** Innocentius III Va   **14–15** exceptores Vb   **16** secundo contra—et succubuit *om.* Vb   **19** modo *om.* Va   non *om.* Vb

---

[1] VI 2.12.1.   [2] X 2.27.24.
[3] In fact, it is the section preceding "Excommunicatus" that prescribes this.

(f) Abbas Antiquus (Bernardus de Monte Mirato), *Distinctiones* (early 1260s), *Pia* (VI 2.12.1), v. *Communibus actibus*, Vat. MSS Vat. 2542, fol. 97va–vb (V), and Borgh. 231, fol. 162ra–va (Vb).

Appellatione communium actuum intelligo omnem actum qui sine communione alterius procedere nequeat. Quod eo manifeste apparet quia excommunicato prohibitum est ne loquatur alicui uel quocumque modo alio participet. Et peccat si contrafecerit, infra de cleri. ex.
5 mi. Illud,[1] uer. "Excommunicato non uitare multo magis quam non uitari periculosum existit: non uitare siquidem, cum in eo sit, sine delicto excommunicatus non potest," etc. Cum igitur sine delicto non possit communicare alii ergo omnis actus quem nisi communicet alteri exercere non potest est ei interdictus, nisi esset talis actus per
10 quem absolutionem suam procuraret, qui ei concessus est infra de sen. ex. Cum uoluntate.[2]
     Verum licet excommunicatus peccet communicando alii credo tamen contractus omnes ab eo et cum eo celebratos firmitatem habere, et eis ultro citroque competere debitas actiones. Unde ex contractu
15 cum eo habito conueniri potest ne uideatur de sua contumacia commodum reportare, infra de sen. ex. Si uere.[3] Et ipse potest agere ex eodem. Sed tunc demum cum fuerit absolutus; ante enim sibi actio denegatur, supra de iudici. Intelleximus.[4] Quod autem ex contractu celebrato excommunicatione durante post absolutionem agere ualeat,
20 et quod ipse contractus ad eius utilitatem ualeat, ex eo probatur quod processus iudicialis cum actore excommunicato habitus bene tenet, licet ei sit agere interdictum, ut patet supra. Ex illo processu ad anteriora proceditur cum fuerit absolutus, ut expresse dicitur in hac constitutione. Unde cum parificentur iudicium et contractus, quia in
25 iudicio bene contrahitur, ff. de peculi. Licet § Si filius fa.,[5] sicut tenet

---

5 excommunicatum V   **15** contumacia] malicia V   **16–17** ex eodem] de eadem V
21 iudicialis *om.* V   actore *om.* V   **25** bene] quod V quasi Vb*pc*   sicut] Unde
praem. Vb*ac*

---

[1] X 5.27.5; Friedberg 830.   [2] X 5.39.54.
[3] X 5.39.34.   [4] X 2.1.7.
[5] Dig. 15.1.3.13, but § 11 should have been cited.

iudicium et ex eo proceditur absolutione optenta, sic debet tenere contractus et ex eo post absolutionem agi potest.

Porro hoc de illis contractibus intelligo quos excommunicatus cele-
brat proprio nomine. Nam aliud dico esse si tanquam prelatus ec-
30 clesie quid alienat, quia illa alienatio est irrita ipso iure, supra de do. et con. Veritatis[6] in fi., quia ipso iure postquam excommunicatus est ei est saltim quoad alienationem rerum ecclesiasticarum administratio interdicta, ut in eadem colligitur decretale . . . [several lines on ecclesiastical matters omitted].
35 Actus publici ut tutela et cura, Insti. de tutela. in prin.,[7] et ciuiles actus ut iudicare, ff. de iudi. Cum pretor et iii. q. vii § Tria, et supra de arbi. Dilecti,[8] excommunicatis publice sunt adeo interdicti, ut quecumque ab ipsis acta fuerint in premissis ipso iure non habeant fir-
mitatem, infra de re iud. Ad probandum, infra de immu. ec. Aduer-
40 sus.[9] Et ideo dico quod si tanquam tutor uel curator uel tanquam iudex alicui alienanti auctoritatem seu decretum prestiterit non ha-
beat eius auctoritas uel decretum ipso iure aliquam firmitatem si erat publice excommunicatus, quia excommunicatus publice non potest ratione tutele uel cure uel publici officii auctoritatem prestare, ut pro-
45 batur supra de procu. Consulti.[10] Per quam decretalem non credo ualere aliquod instrumentum per tabellionem publice excommuni-
catum confectum, cum talis instrumenti auctoritatem prestare non possit, ar. predicta decretalis Consulti, et melius iii. q. iiii. Nullus.[11] Item actus iudiciales quos si quis in iudicio prosequitur nomine alieno,
50 ut est postulare, procurationis officium exercere, testimonium per-
hibere, et prosequi populares actiones, ut est, secundum canones, crimina alterius denunciare ad penitentiam peragendam, excommunicatus publice prosequi si contra eum excipiatur non potest, supra de proba. Post cessionem,[12] que de procuratore loquitur, per
55 quam de aduocato intelligo illud idem, et de testi. Veniens ii.[13] in fi.,

---

26 procedet Vb   **27** potest *om.* Vb   **28** Porro *om.* V   **30** alienet V   **41** auctoritate Vb   **44** officii] iudicii V   **47** auctoritate Vb

---

[6] X 2.14.8.   [7] Inst. 1.13.1.
[8] Dig. 5.1.12; C.3 q.7 d. p. c.1; X 1.43.4.
[9] X 3.49.7.   [10] X 1.38.15.
[11] C.3 q.4 c.6.   [12] X 2.19.7.
[13] X 2.20.38.

que de teste loquitur, et supra de iudi. Exhibita, et de accusa. Dilecti,[14] que loquitur in popularibus actionibus.

An autem excommunicatus testari ualeat ab aliquibus dubitatur. Et
cum testamentum non aliud sit quam disposicio qua quis distribuit
60 quid de rebus suis "post mortem suam fieri uelit," ff. de test. l. i.,[15] et
excommunicato non sit suarum rerum administratio interdicta siue
distributio, credo quod testari possit nisi in casu, scilicet, quando
stetit in excommunicatione per annum qua ligatus fuerat quia erat de
credentibus, defensoribus, receptoribus, siue fautoribus heretico-
65 rum, infra de hereti. Excommunicamus i. § Credentes.[16] Item, credo
quod ualeat heredis institutio si heres fuit institutus; cum enim possit
acquirere ex contractibus, ut probatum est supra, quare non possit ex
causa acquirere, non uideo rationem nisi in casu prealle. § Credentes,
per quam § uidetur posse utram questionem terminari. Cum enim
70 excommunicato pro facto heresis testandi prohibeat factionem uel
facultatem, et ne ad cuiusque successionem accedat si satisfacere con-
tempserit infra annum, ita quod extunc penis teneatur predictis, sequitur per locum ab oppositis quod predictis penis non sit obnoxius
infra annum. Item facit pro solutione utriusque questionis regula
75 generalis quod quilibet potest condere testamentum et heres institui
qui expresse non prohibeatur, ut ff. qui testa. fa. pos. Si queramus, et
ff. de her. insti. Non minus.[17]

---

60 quid *om.* V   **62** potest V   **63** fuit V   **70–71** uel facultatem *om.* Vb
71 ne] non V

---

[14] X 2.1.19; X 5.1.20, with a variant incipit.
[15] Dig. 28.1.1.   [16] X 5.7.13 § 5.
[17] Dig. 28.1.4; 28.5.31.

Early Glosses on Contracts with Excommunicates

(a) Huguccio, *Summa* (1188–90) C.15 q.6 c.4, v. *Fidelitatem,*
Admont 7, fol. 268rb–va (A), and Vat. 2280, fol. 210vb (V).

Sed nunquid in hoc casu uassalli debent subtrahere omnem seruitium
domino excommunicato, scilicet ut interim non soluant ei censum
uel tributum uel pensionem, uel si quid aliud ei debent ratione fidelitatis uel feudi? Et uidetur quod sic ar. hic. Et ut sic cogatur ad recti-
5 tudinem, ut xxiii. q. i. Iam uero.[1] Preterea: in nullo communicandum
est excommunicato nisi in his que spectant ad eius correctionem, ut
xi. q. iii. Excommunicatos, Cum excommunicato.[2] Sed dico quod
uassalli tenentur ei soluere talia, scilicet tributa et pensiones et huiusmodi, presertim si iuramento ad hoc sunt obligati. Nam et usure que
10 ex toto sunt indebite iubentur persolui usurario scelerato et forte excommunicato si iuramento sint promisse, ut in extra. Ad audientiam,
Cum sit Romana.[3] Quod ergo seruitium debent ei negare? Dico quod
non debent eum uisitare uel ei curiam facere uel cum eo conuersari in
equitando, in eundo, in cibo, potu, et in omnibus huiusmodi debent

---

10 iubentur] uidentur V

---

[1] C.23 q.6 c.4. [2] C.11 q.3 cc.17–18.
[3] X 2.24.7 and (?) X 2.24.8, the latter excerpted from *Sicut Romana*. See Appendix
1b n. 9.

15 ab eo abstinere sicut ab aliis excommunicatis. Non facient ei exerci-
tum, non ibunt cum eo ad bellum, non defendent eum, non auxilia-
buntur ei et huiusmodi. De debitore dico quod siue iurauerit siue non
tenetur excommunicato reddere debitum. Sed non tenetur ei ob hoc
communicare, quia potest reddere per alium uel priuatum uel eccle-
20 siam. Si tamen reddat ei in propria persona non peccat sic communicando ei, quia uidetur esse casus necessitatis, ut xi. q. iii. Quoniam.[4]

---

[4] C.11 q.3 c.103.

(b) Alanus Anglicus, *Apparatus Ius naturale* C.15 q.6 c.5, v.
Persolvere, recension 1 (ca. 1192), Paris B.N. 3909, fol. 39rb;
recension 2 (ca. 1202), Paris B.N. 15393, fol. 155r, upper margin.
Text Alanus added in recension 2 is in *uncini*.

Pari ratione creditori excommunicato non tenetur debitor soluere
⌐licet iurauerit se soluere, de hereticis. Vergentis.⌐[1] Sed si debitum sit
usurarium uel sub pena promissum consignetur et deponatur, et sic
usure non current nec pena committetur, ⌐ut ff. de mino. Ait pretor
5 § i. et ff. de usuris. Pecunie § ult. et l. Cum quidam § Si debitores et
C. e. t. Si per, etc.⌐[2] Et creditori cum fuerit absolutus soluetur secundum Baz. Vel eius heredi si excommunicatus moriatur. Quamuis
enim excommunicatio similis sit aqua et igni interdictioni, cuius loco
successit deportatio, que bona adimit, C. de penis. Deportatorum,[3]
10 tamen excommunicatus res suas non amittit. ⌐Perpetuo posset etiam
dici quod cum ei debitum soluere non liceat nec iuramentum trans-
greditur nec pena committatur si apud se quod debet usque quo absoluatur creditor retinuerit licet dies statutus aduenerit, ar. xxii. q. ii.
Ne quis, ff. qui satisda. co. l. ult., ff. de usuris pecunie in fi.⌐[4]

---

7 Bas. Paris 3909   **10** admittit Paris 15393

---

[1] X 5.7.10.
[2] Dig. 4.4.7.1; 22.1.9.1; ibid. 17.6; Cod. 4.32.9.
[3] Cod. 9.47.8.   [4] C.22 q.2 c.14; Dig. 2.8.16; 22.1.9.1.

(c) Laurentius Hispanus, *Glossa Palatina* (ca. 1210) C.15 q.6 c.4, v. *Constricti sunt*, Vat. MSS Pal. 658, fol. 56ra, and Reg. 977, fol. 157va. (On the *Palatina* see Chapter 4 nn. 59–60.)

Sed quid si principi excommunicato tributum debeo uel pecuniam cuilibet excommunicato sub pena uel iuramento ad certum diem soluendam—numquid ei soluam? Videtur quod sic, quia quedam necessitas incumbit soluendi, ar. xxiii. q. vi. Iam uero et xi. ⟨q. iii.⟩
5 Quoniam multos.[1] Debeo ergo ei soluere secundum B. Et sibi non loquitur. Vel dic quod non debeo ex quo per eum stat et ei debet nocere mora, ff. de periculo et com. Si per uenditorem.[2] Vel consignetur et deponatur in sacram edem pecunia.

---

[1] C.23 q.6 c.4; C.11 q.3 c.103.
[2] Citation has not been identified with certainty; cf. Dig. 18.6.18, second sentence.

Appendix 4

Gloss on Avoiding Excommunicates

Bernard of Compostella, *Apparatus, Quia periculosum* (VI 5.11.4), v. *Extendatur*, recension 1 (1246–53), Vat. 1365, fol. 590rb (Va); recension 2 (1253–54/55), Vat. MSS Borgh. 268, fol. 138ra–rb (Vb), and Vat. 3980, fol. 112rb (Vc). The addition Bernard made in recension 2 is in *uncini*. The incomplete copy of recension 2 in Vat., Ottob. 1601 (cf. Appendix 2b) does not include this gloss.

Nota quod ista constitutio Solet,[1] supra eodem titulo, ubi dicitur quod excommunicati post appellationem legitimam et cum sententia intollerabilem errorem continet non sunt extra iudicium euitandi, non extenditur ad sententias episcoporum, archiepiscoporum et alio-
5 rum superiorum, set obseruatur secundum quod ante constitutionem illam Solet obseruabatur. Olim sic obseruabatur quod si aliquis dicebat se excommunicatum post appellationem legitimam uel quod in sententia intollerabilis error esset expressus euitabatur in iudicio et extra iudicium, sed in his duobus articulis admittebatur ad proba-
10 tionem, eodem titulo, Per tuas,[2] secundum quod ibi notatur, et xi. q.

---

4 archiepiscoporum *om.* Va 6 Olim sic obseruabatur *om.* Vb 9–10 proba-
tionem] earum *add.* Vac

---

[1] VI 5.11.2. [2] X 5.39.40.

iii. Si episcopus forte.[3] Et ita in sententiis episcoporum et superiorum adhuc idem debet seruari non obstante illa constitutione Solet, que locum habet in sententiis et aliorum prelatorum et aliorum iudicum delegatorum. Et sic episcopi in hoc sunt priuilegiati fauore pon-

15 tificalis officii, supra de priuile. Quod nonnullis,[4] et in eo quod in ista constitutione dictum est in prima parte. ⌜Dominus papa dicit quod nunquam uitabantur extra iudicium, sed secundum hoc nichil statutum fuit per decretalem Solet.⌝

---

13 et[1] *om.* Vac   aliorum *om.* Va   **14** delegatorum *om.* Va   **15** supra] extra Vc
et *om.* Va   **17** uitabantur] mittebantur   Vb secundum] sine Vb

---

[3] C.11 q.3 c.4.   [4] X 5.33.25.

Exceptions of Excommunication in English Courts

Source	Date	Parties	Reason for Excommunication	Proof	Replication	Exception Succeed? / Outcome
1 T 7RI; *CRR* I 127; cf. *CRR* III 147	1196	Hugo of Kenebell vs. Gilbert Martell	Contumacy	Letters of judges (delegate?) to abp. of Canterbury	None	Yes; "assisa remanet"
2 M 2J; *CRR* V 335	1200	Agnes le Angevin & husb., William Burdun vs. William of St. Patricius	Not given	Bp. of Lincoln's mandate to justiciar	None	Yes, but plaint.'s husb. takes over; see case 5
3 E 2J; *CRR* I 462	1201	Adam of Areblastr' vs. prior of Derhurst	Not given	Letters of bp. of Worcester & a dean	None	Yes; unknown
4 T 4J; *Pl. Ab.* 267	1202	Prior of Pontefract vs. Galferus of Nevill	Not given	Letters of abp. of York	None	Yes; unknown
5 H 4J; *CRR* II 181	1203	William Burdun vs. William of St. Patricius (see case 2)	Not given	Letters of abp. of Canterbury	None	Yes; unknown (day appointed, CRR II 307)

Source	Date	Parties	Reason for Excommunication	Proof	Replication	Exception Succeed? / Outcome
6 T 8J; *CRR* IV 182	1206	Simon le Bret & Magnus of Watercroft vs. William, dean of Hogestorp	Def.: Contumacy Plaint.: Theft of animals	Letters of bp. of Lincoln	Excom. was for theft of animals, now returned	Yes; unknown
7 M 9J – M 4–5HIII; *CRR* V 79–80, 123, 171, 183–86; VII 108–9, 180, 246; VIII 173, 184; IX 381–82, 385 (Exception against a fideiussor)	1204–20	Alicia Clement vs. Jordan of Newton	Apostasy & contumacy	Letters of judges delegate, etc.	Substantive: Fraud Other: Absolution	Yes; see Chapter 4 "Two Cases"
8 M 9J – T 10J; *CRR* V 83, 280, 293; *Pl. Ab.* 59	1207–8	Abbot of Pipewell vs. Hamo of Bidun	See case 7	See Chapter 4 "Two Cases"	Absolution	Yes; see Chapter 4 "Two Cases"
9 H 15J; *CRR* VII 88	1214	Matilda Martel vs. Walter of Martun	Disobedience of husb. & desertion	Testimony of bp. of Lincoln	None	Yes; unknown
10 M 16J; *CRR* VII 266	1214	Abbot of Sherborne vs. bp. of Salisbury	Grave excesses (plaint. had been denounced as excom.)	Letters of unidentified bp.	None	Yes; unknown

11 M 3–4HIII; CRR VIII 66	Beatrix de Munfichet vs. Robert, archd. of Huntingdon	Def.: Sacrilege Plaint.: Writ of prohibition[a]	Letters of bp. of Lincoln	Excom. resulted from writ of prohibition	Yes; unknown
12 M 3–4HIII; CRR VIII 158 (Exception against a def.)	Gilbert de Gaunt vs. William, ct. of Albamarl'	Presence at tournament	Not given	None	No; unknown
13 T 4HIII; CRR IX 52–53; NB III 349–50, no. 1388 (cf. Flahiff, "Writ" part 2, 265 n. 13)	Robert Morin & al. vs. W., precentor, & A., treasurer of Salisbury	Contumacy	Not given	(1) Writ of prohibition ignored (2) Plaints. sought absolution	Yes; unknown
14 T 4HIII; CRR IX 78–79; NB III 358, nos. 1402–3 (cf. Flahiff, "Writ" part 2, 264 n. 9)	Richard Scot vs. Peter FitzPeter (& vs. bp. of Worcester)	Contumacy	Letters of excommunicator, bp. of Worcester	Excommunicator was adversary	No; plaint. won on writ of prohibition dispute; trial began M 4–5HIII (CRR IX 380–81)
15 E 5HIII; CRR X 28; & M 5–6HIII; CRR X 179	Ralph de Tivill vs. Nicholas de Trailly, clerk	Contumacy	Letters (of judges delegate?)	Excom. resulted from writ of prohibition	No; unknown
16 E 5HIII; CRR X 52	William Heirun vs. Adam of Wudeton & Robert of Charteray	Manifest delict	Letters of bp. of Salisbury	None	No; defs. fined & told to get plaint. absolved

Source	Date	Parties	Reason for Excommunication	Proof	Replication	Exception Succeed? / Outcome
17 M 8–9HIII, pl. 2831; *CRR* XI 569	1224	John Bec vs. Robert de Hinges	Contumacy	Testimony of bp. of Lincoln	None	Yes; unknown: plaint. won on writ of prohibition dispute
18 M 9–10HIII, pl. 1318; *CRR* XII 269; *NB* III 526–27, no. 1680 (cf. Flahiff, "Writ" part 2, 264 n. 5)	1225	John FitzRobert vs. Philip de Adern, clerk	Writ of prohibition? (plaint. had been denounced as excom.)	Letters of abp. of York referring to letters of judges delegate	None	No; def. won on writ of prohibition dispute; plaint. fined
19 M 14–15HIII, pl. 579; *CRR* XIV 114	1230	Thomas Corbet vs. Alexander, bp. of Coventry	Plaint.: Enclosing animals in disputed fief Def.: Violence to a clerk	Def. was excommunicator	Def. was excommunicator	Yes; unknown
20 M 14–15HIII, pl. 893; *CRR* XIV 180 (cf. pl. 198 & 354)	1230	John of Colerne vs. prior of Bradenstock	Not given	Letters of bp. of London	Plaint. absent	Yes; plaint. fined for contumacy; def. went "sine die"
21 M 14–15HIII, pl. 1358; *CRR* XIV 287. *NB* II 428 no. 552 (cf. Flahiff, "Writ" part 2, 265 n. 13)	1231	Adam de Creteling vs. Robert, prior of Worksop	Plaint.: Imprisoning prior (distraint) Proof: "For his merits"	Letters of bp. of Coventry saying archd. of Derby excommunicated plaint.	None	Yes; def. went "sine die"; plaint. told to get absolution

Reference	Date	Parties	Cause	Testimony		Outcome
22 M 17–18HIII, pl. 358; *CRR* XV 77	1233	Drogo of Stanton vs. Walter of Stanton, Hugo, archd. of Bath, & Thomas, his official	Contumacy	Testimony of bp. of Bath	None	No; day given in H 18HIII, for which no roll survives
23 E 20HIII, pl. 1556; *CRR* XV 399–400	1236	Hervicus Belet vs. Master Galfridus, official of Colchester	Plaint.: Land dispute Def.: Manifest excesses	Letters of bp. of London	None	No; day given in T 20HIII, & def. told to get plaint. absolved
24 E 20HIII, pl. 1761; *CRR* XV 445	1236	Robert of Henham vs. Roger, dean of Wyham, & Philip of Hobrig	Not given	Letters of bp. of London	None	No; day given in T 20HIII, & def. told to get plaint. absolved
25 25 HIII; *Pl. Ab.* 108 (cf. Flahiff, "Writ" part 2, 264 n. 9)	1241	Attorney for William, chaplain of Neuton vs. Master Adam of Kaukeberg	Plaint.: Writ of prohibition Def.: (1) Writ of prohibition (2) "Another reason"	Unidentified letters	Excom. was at def.'s behest	No; license to compromise
26 KB 26/123, m. 9d, from Flahiff, "Writ" part 2, 265 n. 13	1242	Unknown. Def. unidentified prior	Unknown	Letters of bp. of Norwich	Unknown	Yes; def. went "sine die"
27 KB 26/139, m. 22, from Flahiff, "Writ" part 2, 265 n. 13	1250	Unknown	Unknown	Unknown	Unknown	Yes; unknown

Source	Date	Parties	Reason for Excommunication	Proof	Replication	Exception Succeed? / Outcome
28 KB 27/33, m. 10d, from Flahiff, "Writ", part 2, 265 n. 13	1277	Unidentified chaplain *vs.* two unidentified men	Unknown	Letters of bp. of Norwich	None	Yes; plaint. sued again with new writ & was again repelled by excep. of excom.
29 M 30EI; YB EI, RS 31.1.3, pp. 40–43[b]	1302	"A." & "B." *vs.* Maud de Mortimer	Not given	Letters saying abp. of Canterbury decreed plaints. should be excommunicated & had them denounced	(1) Def. already pleaded generally (2) Plaints. not excommunicated, though denounced	No; unknown, but trial continued
30 Cornish Eyre, 30 EI, YB EI; RS 31.1.3, pp. 268–79	1302	William, prior of Budlegh *vs.* bp. of Worcester	Not given	Letters of bp. of Worcester based on archd.'s rolls	(1) Archd. could not certify royal court (2) Bp. could not either, because party	No; unknown
31 M 31EI, YB EI; RS 31.1.3, pp. 454–57	1303	Henry Child *vs.* Master Roger of Felthorpe (bp.'s official) & parson of Pike	Writ of prohibition	Letters of unidentified bp.	Testimony from adversary	No; unknown

	Date	Parties	Charge	Letters	Exception	Outcome
32	M? 32–33EI; SS 48, no. 263, pl. 221[c]	1304	Peter of St. Marius, clerk of Walter, bp. of Coventry & royal treasurer vs. prior of Bermondsey & abbot of Chertsey	Not given	Letters of bp. of Winchester	None	Yes; def. went "sine die"
33	E 3EII, YB EII 3; SS 20, pl. 45, pp. 134–35[d]	1310	John Baret vs. William Sparewe	Plaint.: At def.'s behest Def. & proof: Contumacy	Letters of unidentified bp.	Excom. was at def.'s behest	No; case continued
34	T 5EII, YB EII 12; SS 33, case 37, p. 237[e]	1312	John le Suter of Breadstreet vs. dean of Arches & al.	Contumacy	Letters of abp. of Canterbury	Testimony from adversary (i.e., dean was bp.'s commissary)	No; unknown. Judgment that writ of prohibition was not transgressed
35	T 5EII, de banco roll, no. 193, YB EII 12; SS 33, pp. 213–14	1312	Roger & Margery Blaket vs. Ralph Loveday & al.	Apostasy	Letters of bp. of Lincoln saying plaint. was excommunicated & had been denounced	Substantive, namely, plaint. had precontracted marriage	Yes; def. went "sine die"
36	YB EII 8; SS 29, pp. 161–67[f]	1314	Abbot of Battle vs. prior of Christchurch, Canterbury	Contumacy	Letters of bp. of Rochester	(1) No proof of excommunicator's jurisdiction (2) Proof vague	No; plaint. lost
37	M 12EII; Pl. Ab. 332	1318	Not given	Not given	Not given	None	Yes; trial ended

Source	Date	Parties	Reason for Excommunication	Proof	Replication	Exception Succeed?/Outcome
38 KB E 7EIII; *Sel. Cases EIII* 5; SS 76, no. 32, pp. 72–74[g]	1333	Richard of Bockmer of Coventry *vs.* John of Birmingham of Lichfield	Manifest contumacy & offenses	Letters of bp. of Coventry	None	Yes; on 15 June plaint. showed letters of absolution and was given writ to re-attach def.
39 E 2RII, YB RII, no. 13, p. 229[h]	1388	Not given	Not given	Unidentified letter	None	Yes; def. went "sans iour"
40 M 13HIV, *Sel. Cases Excheq.* 1; SS 51, no. 6, p. 15[i]	1411	Lewes & Hawise Cardycan *vs.* William Brentyngham & al.	Not given; but see p. 15 n. 1, saying patent rolls, 14 HIV, mention pardon of Lewis Cardycan of Wales, chaplain, for breaking into church	Letters of bp. of Winchester	None	Yes; at next session plaint. showed letters of absolution and had def. re-attached

[a] Theft of ecclesiastical chattels was an ecclesiastical crime during peace but a secular crime, under royal jurisdiction, during war; see Flahiff, "Writ," part 2, 263.

[b] *Yearbooks of the Reign of King Edward the First,* ed. and trans. A. J. Horwood, 30–31 Edward I, RS 31.1.3 (1863).

[c] *Select Cases in the Exchequer of Pleas,* ed. H. Jenkinson and B. E. R. Formoy, SS 48, for 1931 (1932).

[d] *Year Books of Edward II,* vol. 3, ed. F. W. Maitland, SS 20 (1905) 134–35. S. F. C. Milsom mentions the case in his introduction to *Novae narrationes,* ed. E. Shanks, SS 80 (1963) p. cc n. 5.

[e] *Year Books of Edward II,* vol. 12, ed. W. C. Bolland, SS 33 (1916) 237. Mentioned by Milsom (see note *d*) ibid.

[f] *Year Books of Edward II,* vol. 8, ed. W. C. Bolland, SS 29 (1913) 161–67.

[g] *Select Cases in the Court of King's Bench under Edward III,* vol. 5, ed. G. O. Sayles, SS 76, for 1957 (1958) 72–74.

[h] *Yearbooks of Richard II,* vol. 5, ed. J. D. Thornley, Ames Foundation (London 1937) 229.

[i] *Select Cases in the Exchequer Chamber before All the Justices of England,* ed. M. Hemmant, vol. 1, SS 51 (1933).

Who Wrote Abbas Antiquus's Lectures on the Liber Extra?

Authorship of the published lectures on the Liber Extra that begin "Interpretatur vigilans et bene vigilavit" has long been disputed.[1] Though the editions, and many manuscripts, attribute the work to Abbas Antiquus (the nickname of Bernard, abbot of Montmajour, d. 1296), the oldest manuscripts name Abbas's teacher, Peter Sampson. Pontal recently reinvigorated Sampson's claims. Only by emendation or addition, she points out, do the oldest manuscripts favor Abbas.[2]

Other evidence confirms that the two authors collaborated so closely that it is easy to confuse their works.[3] Several manuscripts have mixed recensions of lectures on the Liber Extra. Vienna N.B. 2113 seems to contain the standard version of Sampson's Extra lectures enlarged by glosses of Abbas, while in Lincoln Cathedral Li-

---

[1] I used the 1588 Venice edition, vol. 1 of *Perillustrium doctorum . . . in libros Decretalium aurei commentarii*, ed. A. Amicius. Coing, *Handbuch* I 378, cites a 1510 Strasbourg edition.

[2] O. Pontal, "Quelques remarques sur l'oeuvre canonique de Pierre de Sampzon," *Annuarium historiae conciliorum* 8 (1976) 126–42, esp. 134–38 and 141–42.

[3] For further evidence of mixtures of the two authors' works see Kessler, "Untersuchungen" passim (e.g., part 2, 380; part 3, 60) and J. F. von Schulte, *Die Geschichte der Quellen und Literatur des canonischen Rechts* (Stuttgart 1875–80; repr. Graz 1956) II 130 n. 4 on 131. Cf. also the ambiguous reference in Jo. An., *Nov*. VI 5.11.8, v. *Non potest*: "Pe. et Abb. in distinctionibus."

brary 167 the balance seems to be reversed.[4] Comparing incipits and explicits for the five books of the Liber Extra:

		Vienna 2113	Lincoln 167
I.	incipit	Abb. Ant.	Abb. Ant.
	explicit	Pet. Samp.	Abb. Ant.
II.	incipit	Pet Samp.	Pet Samp.
	explicit	X 2.30.9 (*Sua*), v. *Impetratas*: "Supra in forma communi."	
III.	incipit	Pet. Samp.	Pet. Samp.
	explicit	Pet. Samp.	Pet. Samp.
IV.	incipit	Pet. Samp.	Pet. Samp.
	explicit	Pet. Samp.	Pet. Samp.
V.	incipit	Pet. Samp.	Pet. Samp.
	explicit	X 5.41.11 (*Indignum*): "Pone casum per decre. s. de symonia. Ex diligenti [X 5.3.17]. p."	

Obviously Abbas extensively revised Sampson's Extra lectures. Nonetheless a number of references seem to show that he wrote his own commentary on the Liber Extra as well and that the disputed lectures are indeed his. Abbas himself referred to his own lectures on the Liber Extra in his commentary on Innocent IV's *Novellae*, citing an exegesis of *Pia* that he wrote in a gloss on *Exceptionem*.[5] The long gloss on *Exceptionem* in the disputed lectures certainly seems to be what is meant. Another witness is a late thirteenth-century French author of questions edited by Meijers; these cite an opinion of "abbas

---

[4] Vienna N.B. 2113, as will be clear below, seems to contain Sampson's Extra lectures enlarged by glosses of Abbas. Lincoln Cathedral Library MS 167, as described by Professor S. Kuttner in files at the Institute of Medieval Canon Law, School of Law, University of California, Berkeley, contains the lectures of Abbas on the Liber Extra, contaminated by glosses of Sampson. The latter manuscript is identified as the Extra lectures of Sampson in R. M. Wooley, ed., *Catalogue of the Manuscripts of Lincoln Cathedral Library* (London 1927) 127. In fact, the Extra lectures end on fol. 212ra; Sampson's lectures on Innocent IV's *Novellae*, probably recension 1, follow on fol. 212rb–216rb.

[5] Abbas Antiquus, *Lect.*, *Pia* (VI 2.12.1), Vat., Borgh. 231, fol. 141va: "Hec decretalis bonam habet arengam siue prefationem. Et ideo singulariter ipsam exponam in quacumque, supra eodem Exceptionem [X 2.25.12]," for which see *ed. cit.*, fol. 83va–vb.

Montis Maioris" (Montmajour), which can be confirmed in the disputed lectures.[6] A second anonymous witness, author of lectures on
the Liber Extra and some of Innocent IV's *novellae* in Vat., Borgh. 228
(dating, I believe, from the late thirteenth century), cites an opinion
Abbas and his teacher, Sampson, shared ("prout dicebat magister
suus").[7] In the disputed lectures the opinion is indeed attributed
to Sampson ("ut dicebat"). Slightly later, in the 1320s and 1330s,
Johannes Andreae quoted teachings of Abbas that can likewise be
confirmed in the disputed lectures.[8] (The author of the Borgh. 228
lectures and Johannes Andreae both refer to glosses on canons not included in the standard version of Sampson's lectures, which end at X

[6] E. M. Meijers, *Responsa doctorum Tholosanorum* (Haarlem 1938) 84, confirmed in
the disputed lectures, X 1.29.12, v. *Scripsissemus, ed. cit.*, fol. 36ra.
[7] Vat., Borgh 228, fol. 156ra–170va, X 5.12.10, *quaestio*, v. *Pallium*, fol. 161va: "Sed
pone cepi latronem. Nunquid possum tradere curie seculari? Dic quod non, si possum aliter res meas recupere, i. e. Tua nos [X 5.12.19], secundum Abbatem, prout
dicebat magister suus P. de Samp.," for which see the disputed lectures, X 5.12.10, v.
Ipse, ed. cit., fol. 139rb: "Ad gl. in hoc ubi dicit "capere" et ipsum potest tradere
iudici saeculari, si aliter nequeat sua recupere, ut dicebat m. P. de Sam. Et ad hoc
facit inf. eo. Tua [X 5.12.19]." Vat., Borgh. 228 contains six sets of commentaries,
one each for Books 1–4 of the Liber Extra, and two for Book 5. Only the second on
Book 5 cites the Liber Sextus (1298), I believe. The earlier ones—if they are by one
author—can be dated by a reference to the second Council of Lyon (1274) on fol.
2va. Only Books 1–2 have glosses on Innocent IV's *novellae*, embedded, and thus
unnoticed in A. Maier, ed., *Codices Burghesiani Bibliothecae Vaticanae* (Vatican City
1952) 280–81. On the first folio a later hand inscribed "Lectura Petri Boneti. . . ."
This must be the "P. Boneti" whose glosses occur in the margins of the Liber Extra
in Vat. 1390, perhaps the "Petrus Bo." whose glosses were added to Hostiensis's Lectura in Vat. 2545. Details that might help identify: abundant references to usages of
the Roman Curia in Book 3; mention of "fratres Tolose" (fol. 169va); and a note on a
question on marriage already described as "fatuous": "Et per istam questionem re-
pulsus fuit quidam Bononie a doctoratu" (ibid.).
[8] Jo. An., *Nov.* X 5.39.40, v. *Non debet*: "Melius poterant probare secundum Abb.,
quia cum nullus excommunicetur nisi pro contumacia, xi. q. iii. Nemo [41], et contumax non auditur appellans, ii. q. vi. Sunt quorum [41 § 11]. Ergo appellare non
potest. Dicit Abb. absoluendum, ut no. de offi. or. Ad reprimandam [X 1.31.8]."
See the disputed lectures, X 5.39.40, v. *Separatus, ed. cit.*, fol. 149va: "Melius tamen
illud posset hoc ar. probare nullus excommunicatur nisi pro contumacia, 11. q. 3
Nullus [42], inf. eo Sacro [X 5.39.48]. Sed contumax non auditur appellans. Sed
solve ut no. sup. de offi. ordi. Ad reprimandam [X 1.31.8]." Two other brief glosses
on the same chapter are signed "Ab." and can be confirmed with glosses on the same
lemmata (*litis* and *accipiat*) in the disputed lectures; a third gloss (v. *emendetur*),
though it has no siglum in Andreae's *Novellae*, reproduces a gloss in the lectures.

5.3.32.)⁹ Finally, from the mid-fourteenth century comes a reference to Abbas in lectures by Jean de Jean, abbot of Joncels (d. 1361); Gilles has already confirmed this citation in the disputed lectures.¹⁰

Not a watertight case for Abbas, but perhaps it shifts the burden of proof. In any event we cannot insist on a unique author—not for many medieval legal works, and certainly not for the works of these two authors. But if we are looking for the man who took credit and responsibility for the disputed lectures among his near contemporaries, the preferred candidate seems to be Abbas.

---

⁹ On X 5.3.32 in Vienna B.N. 2113 there is a gloss that ends "de crimine excepto etiam suspectum et grauiter infamatum. Et tunc ualet" (v. *Civiliter*, fol. 71rb). Lincoln Cath. Libr. 167 has two glosses on this canon. One has the same *explicit* as the standard version of Sampson's Extra lectures (in Vienna N.B. 2083); the other has the same *explicit* as the gloss just quoted in Vienna B.N. 2113, signed "p." (fol. 208va–209ra). Other evidence of Sampsonian glosses beyond X 5.3.32: on X 5.39.48 (v. *Personis*) the printed lectures, i.e., those, as I believe, of Abbas, refer to "magister meus" for an opinion that corresponds to one expressed in a gloss (see Chapter 4 n. 133) on this chapter in Vienna B.N. 2113: "Dicit Inno. quod sufficit una. Et inducit ad hoc supra de test. In omni [X 2.20.4], quia probatio admonitionis factae sit per testimonium admonentis et alterius, ut ibi dicitur. Magister meus tamen dicebat esse cautius saltem esse duos praesentes in admonitione . . ." (*ed. cit.*, fol. 150ra, no. 2). Two manuscript copies of Abbas's (i.e., the printed) lectures expand the citation of "magister meus" to "magister p." and "magister p. de sam.," respectively (Vat., Borgh. MSS 231, fol. 136ra, and 260, fol. 107va).

¹⁰ H. Gilles, "Jean de Jean, Abbé de Joncels," *Histoire littéraire de la France* 40.53–111 at 79.

Manuscripts Cited

All manuscripts are Latin. Only the works actually cited are mentioned here.

Admont
 Stiftsbibl. 7 (Huguccio's *Summa*)

Arras
 Bibl. munic. 271 (Johannes Faventinus's *Summa*)

Bamberg
 Staatsbibl. Can. 13 (*Apparatus Ordinaturus magister*)
 Staatsbibl. Can. 20 (Vincentius Hispanus's *Apparatus* on Comp. 3)
 Staatsbibl. Can. 45 (Canonical *quaestiones*)

Barcelona
 Arch. Corona de Aragón, S. Cugat 55 (Canonical *quaestiones*)

Cambridge
 Gonville and Caius Coll. 331 (Robert Courçon's *Summa*)
 Gonville and Caius Coll. 676 (Glosses by various authors on Decretum)

Fulda
 Landesbibl. D.7 (Canonical *quaestiones*)
 Landesbibl. D.10 (Innocent IV's *Apparatus* and Goffredus de Trano's *Apparatus* on Innocent IV's *Novellae*)

Lincoln
 Cathedral Library 167 (Abbas Antiquus's *Lectures* on the Liber Extra, mixed with glosses of Peter Sampson; cf. Appendix 6.)

London
 British Library, Royal 11.C.VII (Tancred's *Apparatus* on Comp. 1)
 Lambeth Palace 244 (Robert Winchelsey's Register)

Paris

    B.N. 3909 (Alanus Anglicus's *Apparatus Ius naturale*)

    B.N. 3932 (Laurentius Hispanus's *Apparatus* on Comp. 3)

    B.N. 3967 (Vincentius Hispanus's *Apparatus* on the Liber Extra)

    B.N. 15393 (Alanus Anglicus's *Apparatus Ius naturale*)

Salzburg

    Stiftsbibl. St. Peter a.XII.9 (*Apparatus Ordinaturus magister*)

Vatican, Bibliotheca Apostolica (In the notes, manuscripts in the *Vaticani* fond are cited simply as "Vat.")

    Barb. 1626 (Vincentius Hispanus's *Apparatus* on the Liber Extra)

    Borgh. 40 (Guido de Baysio's *Commentary* on the Liber Sextus)

    Borgh. 71 (Johannes Faventinus's *Summa*)

    Borgh. 228 (Anonymous lectures on the Liber Extra and Innocent IV's *Novellae*)

    Borgh. 231 (Abbas Antiquus's *Lectures* on the Liber Extra and on Innocent IV's *Novellae*)

    Borgh. 260 (Abbas Antiquus's *Lectures* on the Liber Extra)

    Borgh. 261 (Damasus's *Quaestiones*)

    Borgh. 264 (Tancred's *Apparatus* [*Glos. ord.*] on Comp. 3; Johannes Teutonicus's *Apparatus* on Comp. 4)

    Borgh. 268 (Bernard of Compostella's *Apparatus* on Innocent IV's *Novellae*)

    Chig. E.VII.207 (Johannes Teutonicus's *Apparatus* on Comp. 4)

    Ottob. 1601 (Bernard of Compostella's *Apparatus* on Innocent IV's *Novellae*)

    Ottob. 2524 (Vincentius Hispanus's *Apparatus* on the Liber Extra)

    Pal. 624 (Decretum)

    Pal. 629 (Johannes Garsias's *Apparatus* on the canons of the second Council of Lyon)

    Pal. 656 (Peter Sampson's *Distinctiones*; Damasus's *Quaestiones*)

    Pal. 658 (*Glossa Palatina*)

    Pal. 718 (Concordat of the Council of Constance)

    Reg. 977 (*Glossa Palatina*)

    Ross. 595 (*Apparatus Ordinaturus magister*)

    Ross. 596 (Innocent IV's *Apparatus*)

    Vat. 1365 (Bernard of Compostella's *Apparatus* on Innocent IV's *Novellae*)

    Vat. 1377 (Tancred's *Apparatus* on Comp. 1 and on Comp. 3; Johannes Teutonicus's *Apparatus* on Comp. 4)

    Vat. 1378 (Vincentius Hispanus's *Apparatus* on Comp. 3)

    Vat. 1390 (Liber Extra)

    Vat. 1439–43 (Innocent IV's *Apparatus*)

    Vat. 2280 (Huguccio's *Summa*)

    Vat. 2494 (Gloss by Bazianus)

    Vat. 2509 (Johannes Teutonicus's *Apparatus* on Comp. 4)

    Vat. 2542 (Abbas Antiquus's *Lectures* on Innocent IV's *Novellae*)

    Vat. 2545 (Hostiensis's *Lectura*)

    Vat. 2644 (Nicolaus de Gangio's tract on indulgences)

    Vat. 2647 (Egidius de Fuscarariis's *Ordo*)

Vat. 3980 (Bernard of Compostella's *Apparatus* on Innocent IV's *Novellae*)

Vat. 4988 (Concordat of the Council of Constance)

Vat. 5711 (Papal formulary)

Vat. 6769 (Vincentius Hispanus's *Apparatus* on the Liber Extra)

Vat. 9868 (French synodal statutes)

Vienna

N.B. 2083 (Peter Sampson's *Lectures* on the Liber Extra [fol. 1–43] and on Innocent IV's *Novellae* [fol. 43–45])

N.B. 2113 (Peter Sampson's *Lectures* on the Liber Extra mixed with glosses of Abbas Antiquus [fol. 2–74; cf. Appendix 6] and on Innocent IV's *Novellae* [fol. 74–77])

N.B. 2197 (Goffredus de Trano's *Apparatus* on the Liber Extra)

Sources Cited

Abbas Antiquus [Bernardus de Monte Mirato]. *Lectura.* Vol. I of *Perillustrium doctorum . . . in libros Decretalium aurei commentarii,* ed. A. Amicius, 3 vols. Venice 1588.

d'Ablieges, Jacques. *Le Grand Coutumier de France.* Ed. E. Laboulaye and R. Dareste. Paris 1868. Reprint. Aalen 1969.

Adam, P. *La Vie paroissiale en France au XIVe siècle.* Paris 1964.

Alexander of Hales. *Glossa in quatuor libros Sententiarum Petri Lombardi.* Ed. Collegium S. Bonaventurae. 4 vols. Bibliotheca Franciscana Scholastica Medii Aevi 12–15. Quaracchi 1951–57.

Amanieu, A. "Antonin (Saint)." *DDC* 1.632–33.

Antoninus of Florence. *Summa theologica.* 4 vols. Verona 1740.

Arnold, T., ed. *Select English Works of John Wyclif.* 3 vols. Oxford 1869–71.

Artonne, A., et al. *Répertoire des statuts synodaux des diocèses de l'ancienne France du XIIIe à la fin du XVIIIe siècle.* 2d ed. Paris 1969.

Auffroy, H. *Evolution du testament en France.* Paris 1899.

Autenrieth, J. "Bernold von Konstanz und die erweiterte 74-Titelsammlung." *Deutsches Archiv für Erforschung des Mittelalters* 14 (1958) 375–94.

———. *Die Domschule von Konstanz zur Zeit des Investiturstreits.* Stuttgart 1956.

Badian, E. *Publicans and Sinners.* Ithaca, N.Y., 1972.

Baldus de Ubaldis. *In Usus feudorum commentaria.* Lyon 1585.

———. *Super Decretalium volumen commentaria.* Lyon 1551.

Basdevant-Gaudemet, B. "Les Sources de droit romain en matière de procédure dans le Décret de Gratien." *RDC* 27 (1977) 193–242.

Bateson, M., ed. *Records of the Borough of Leicester (1103–1603).* 3 vols. In *Records of the Borough of Leicester (1103–1835),* 7 vols. London 1899–1901, Cambridge 1905–23, and Leicester 1965–74.

de Beaumanoir, Philippe. *Coutumes de Clermont en Beauvaisis*. Ed. A. Salmon. 2 vols. Paris 1899–1900.

Beautemps-Beaupré, C. J., ed. *Le Livre des droiz et des commandemens d'office de justice*. 2 vols. Paris 1865.

Berengarius Fredoli. *See* Vernay.

Berger, E., ed. *Les Registres d'Innocent IV*. 4 vols. in 8. Bibliothèque des Ecoles françaises d'Athènes et de Rome. Paris 1884–1920.

——. *Saint Louis et Innocent IV*. Vol. 2.1 of *Les Registres*. [q. v.; also published separately, Paris 1893.]

Bernard of Pavia. *Summa Decretalium*. Ed. E. A. T. Laspeyres. Regensburg 1860. Reprint. Graz 1956.

Bernardus Guidonis. *Practica inquisitionis heretice pravitatis*. Ed. C. Douais. Paris 1886.

Bernardus de Monte Mirato. *See* Abbas Antiquus.

Bernhardus de Bisgneto. *Conclusiones sive decisiones . . . causarum auditorum*. 3 vols. Rome 1475. [Unpaginated.]

Bertram, M. "Angebliche Originale des Dekretalenapparats Innocenz' IV." *MIC* C-7, 41–47. Vatican City 1985.

von Bethmann-Hollweg, M. A. *Der Civilprozess des gemeinen Rechts*. 6 vols. Bonn 1868–74. Reprint. Aalen 1959.

Bisson, T. N. "The Organized Peace in Southern France and Catalonia, ca. 1140–ca. 1233." *American Historical R.* 82 (1977) 290–311.

Blumenthal, U.-R. *Der Investiturstreit*. Stuttgart 1982.

Böhmer, J. F. *Regesta Imperii VIII. Die Regesten des Kaiserreichs unter Kaiser Karl IV. 1346–1378*. Ed. and rev. A. Huber. Innsbruck 1877.

Boerius, N., ed. *Consuetudines Bituricenses*. Bound with P. Englebermeus, ed., *Consuetudines Aurelianenses*; and I. Sainson, ed., *Consuetudines Turonenses*. Paris 1543.

Bolland, W. C., ed. *Year Books of Edward II* Vols. 8, 12. SS 29, 33. 1913–16.

Bongert, Y. *Recherches sur les cours laïques du Xe au XIIIe siècle*. Paris 1949.

Boswell, J. *Christianity, Social Tolerance, and Homosexuality*. Chicago and London 1980.

Du Boulay, F. R. H. "The Fifteenth Century." In C. H. Lawrence, ed., *The English Church and the Papacy in the Middle Ages*, 195–242. London 1965.

Bourke, V. J. *See* Miethe.

Boutaric, M. E., ed. *Actes du parlement de Paris*. 2 vols. Paris 1863–67.

Bouteiller, I. *Somme rural*. Ed. L. Charondas Le Caron. Paris 1603.

Brentano, R. "Three Thirteenth-Century Italian Cases in Ecclesiastical Courts." *MIC* C-1, 311–19. Vatican City 1965.

——. *York Metropolitan Jurisdiction*. Berkeley and Los Angeles 1959.

Brett, M. *The English Church under Henry I*. Oxford 1975.

du Breuil, Guillaume. *Style du parlement de Paris*. Ed. H. E. Lot. Paris 1877.

Brommer, P. "Die bischöfliche Gesetzgebung Theodulfs von Orléans." *ZRG Kan. Abt.* 60 (1975) 1–120.

Brundage, J. A. *Medieval Canon Law and the Crusader*. Madison, Wisc., 1969.

——. "Some Canonistic Quaestiones in Barcelona." *Manuscripta* 15 (1971) 67–76.

Buisson, L. *Potestas und Caritas: Die päpstliche Gewalt im Spätmittelalter.* Forschungen zur kirchlichen Rechtsgeschichte 2. Cologne 1958.

Burn, A. R. *The Romans in Britain: An Anthology of Inscriptions.* 2d ed. Columbia, S.C., 1969.

Cabié, R., ed. *La Lettre du pape Innocent Ier à Décentius de Gubio (19 Mars 416).* Bibliothèque de la RHE 58. Louvain 1973.

Campbell, G. J. "The Attitude of the Monarchy toward the Use of Ecclesiastical Censures in the Reign of Saint Louis." *Speculum* 35 (1960) 535–55.

Cannon, W. B. "'Voodoo' Death." *American Anthropologist* 44 (1942) 169–81.

Caspar, E., ed. *Das Register Gregors VII.* 2 vols. *MGH Epp. Sel.* 10. Berlin 1920–23. Reprint. 1967.

Ceruti, A., ed. *Statuta communitatis Novariae, anno 1277 lata.* Novara 1879.

Chabanne, R. "Nicolas de Plowe." *DDC* 6.1010.

Chadwyck Healey, C. E. H., ed. *Somersetshire Pleas (Civil and Criminal) from the Rolls of the Itinerant Justices (Close of 12th Century–41 Henry III.).* London 1897.

Champeux, E., ed. *Les Ordonnances des ducs de Bourgogne.* R. Bourguignonne 17. Dijon and Paris 1907.

———, ed. *Ordonnances franc-comtoises sur l'administration de la justice (1343–1477).* Dijon and Paris 1912[?].

Cheney, C. R. "The Diocese of Grenoble in the Fourteenth Century." *Speculum* 10 (1935) 162–77.

———. *English Bishops' Chanceries, 1100–1250.* Manchester 1950.

———, and M. G. Cheney. *The Letters of Pope Innocent III (1198–1216) concerning England and Wales.* Oxford 1967.

Cheney, M. "The Compromise of Avranches of 1172 and the Spread of Canon Law in England." *English Historical R.* 56 (1941) 177–97.

Cironius, Innocentius. *Paratitla in quinque libros Decretalium.* Ed. J. A. de Riegger. Vienna 1761.

Clement V. *Regestum Clementis papae V.* Ed. Monachi ordinis S. Benedicti. 9 vols. in 8. Rome 1885–88.

de Clercq, C., ed. *Concilia Galliae A. 511–A. 695. CCL* 148A.

Coing, H., ed. *Handbuch der Quellen und Literatur der neueren europäischen Privatrechtsgeschichte.* Munich 1973–.

Connolly, R. Hugh, ed. *Didascalia Apostolorum. The Syriac Version Translated and Accompanied by the Verona Latin Fragments.* Oxford 1929.

Corpus iuris canonici . . . una cum glossis. 3 vols. Venice 1525–28. [Used for *Glossa ordinaria* citations.]

Corpus iuris civilis. Ed. G. Kroll, P. Krueger, T. Mommsen, and R. Schoell. 3 vols. Berlin 1868. Reprint. 1954.

Corpus iuris civilis cum glossa ordinaria. 5 vols. Lyon 1549–50. [Used for *Glossa ordinaria* citations.]

Coulton, G. G. *Five Centuries of Religion.* 4 vols. Cambridge 1923–50.

Cross, F. L. "History and Fiction in the African Canons." *J. of Theological St.* 12 (1961) 227–47.

Dareste, R. *See* d'Ablieges.

Daube, D., "*Collatio* 2.6.5." In *Essays in Honour of the Very Rev. Dr. J. H. Hertz*, ed. I. Epstein et al. London 1943.

———. "'Ne quid infamandi causa fiat.' The Roman Law of Defamation." *Atti del Congresso internazionale di diritto romano e di storia del diritto*, ed. G. Moschetti, 4 vols., III 413–50. Milan 1951–53.

Dauvillier, J. *Les Temps apostoliques, Ier siècle.* Histoire du droit et des institutions de l'église en occident 2. Paris 1970.

Dekkers, E. *Clavis Patrum Latinorum.* 2d ed. Sacris erudiri 3. Steenbrugge 1961.

Denholm-Young, N. "The Tournament in the Thirteenth Century." In *Studies in Medieval History Presented to Frederick Maurice Powicke*, ed. R. W. Hunt et al. Oxford 1948.

Deusdedit. *See* von Glanvell.

Dictionary of the Middle Ages. Ed. J. Strayer. New York 1982–.

Didier, N. "Henri de Suse en Angleterre (1236?–1244)." In *Studi in onore di Vicenzo Arangio-Ruiz*, 4 vols., II 333–51. Naples 1952.

———. "Henri de Suse, évêque de Sisteron (1244–1250)." *RHDFE*, ser. 4, 31 (1953) 244–70.

———. "Henri de Suse, prieur d'Antibes, prévôt de Grasse (1235?–1245)." *St. Gratiana* 2 (1954) 597–617.

Dolezalek, G. "Die handschriftliche Verbreitung von Rechtsprechungssammlungen der Rota." *ZRG Kan. Abt.* 58 (1972) 1–106.

Donahue, C. "The Policy of Alexander the Third's Consent Theory of Marriage." *MIC* C-5, 251–81. Vatican City 1975.

———. "Roman Canon Law in the Medieval English Church: Stubbs vs. Maitland Reexamined." *Michigan Law R.* 72 (1974) 647–716.

Doskocil, W. *Der Bann in der Urkirche, eine rechtsgeschichtliche Untersuchung.* Munich 1958.

Douglas, M. *Purity and Danger: An Analysis of the Concepts of Pollution and Taboo.* London 1966.

Duggan, C. "The Reception of Canon Law in England in the Later-Twelfth Century." *MIC* C-1, 359–90. Vatican City 1965.

———. "The Significance of the Becket Dispute in the History of the English Church." *Ampleforth J.* 75 (1970) 365–75.

Duggan, L. G. *Bishop and Chapter. The Governance of the Bishopric of Speyer to 1552.* New Brunswick, N.J., 1978.

Dumézil, G. *Archaic Roman Religion.* Trans. P. Krapp. 2 vols. Chicago and London 1970.

Duplès-Agier, T. H. L. A., ed. *Le Registre criminel du Châtelet de Paris du 6 Septembre 1389 au 18 Mai 1392.* 2 vols. Paris 1861–64.

Eckhardt, K. A. *See* Lehmann.

Ehrle, F. "Ein Bruchstück der Acten des Concils von Vienne." *Archiv für Literatur und Kirchengeschichte des Mittelalters* 4 (1888) 361–470.

Eichmann, E. *Acht und Bann im Reichsrecht des Mittelalters.* Paderborn 1909.

Elze, R. "Stephanus Polonus und Johannes Andreae. Eine bologneser Quaestion von 1270 und ihre Wiedergabe in der Novella in Sextum." *St. Gratiana* 12 (1967) 293–308.

———. *See also* Vogel.

Englebermeus, P. *See* Boerius.

Eschmann, I. T. "Studies on the Notion of Society in St. Thomas Aquinas. I: St. Thomas and the Decretal of Innocent IV *Romana Ecclesia. Ceterum.*" *Medieval St.* 8 (1946) 1–42.

Esmein, A. "Débiteurs privés de sépulture." In *Mélanges d'histoire du droit. Droit romain*, 245–68. Paris 1886.

———. *Le Mariage en droit canonique.* 2 vols. Paris 1898.

d'Espinay, G., ed. *La Coutume de Touraine au XVe siècle.* Tours 1888.

Evans-Pritchard, E. E. *Nuer Religion.* New York and Oxford 1956.

Febvre, L. "L'Application du Concile de Trente et l'excommunication pour dettes en Franche-Comté." Parts 1, 2. *R. Historique* 103 (1910) 225–47; 104 (1910) 1–39.

Federicus Petrucius Senensis. *Consilia.* Venice 1570.

Feine, H. E. *Kirchliche Rechtsgeschichte.* 4th ed. Cologne and Graz 1964.

Festus. *De verborum significatu quae supersunt cum Pauli Epitome.* Ed. W. M. Lindsay. Leipzig 1913.

Filhol, R., ed. *Le Vieux Coustumier de Poictou.* Bourges 1956.

Finke, H., et al., eds. *Acta Concilii Constanciensis.* 4 vols. Münster in Westfalen 1896–1928.

Firnhaber, F. "Petrus de Pulka, Abgesandter der Wiener Universität am Concilium zu Constanz." *Archiv für Kunde österreichischer Geschichts-Quellen* 15 (1856) 1–70.

Flahiff, G. B. "The Use of Prohibitions by Clerics against Ecclesiastical Courts in England." *Medieval St.* 3 (1941) 101–16.

———. "The Writ of Prohibition to Court Christian in the Thirteenth Century." Parts 1, 2. *Medieval St.* 6 (1944) 261–313; 7 (1945) 229–90.

Fleta . . . subjungitur . . . Joan. Seldeni ad Fletam dissertatio. 2d ed. 2 vols. London 1685.

Formoy, B. E. R. *See* Jenkinson.

Les Fors et costumas de Bearn. Pau 1715.

Foucault, M. *Madness and Civilization: A History of Insanity in the Age of Reason.* Trans. R. Howard. London 1967.

Fournier, E. "L'Accueil fait par la France du XIIIe siècle aux décrétales pontificales: leur traduction en langue vulgaire." In *Acta congressus iuridici internationalis . . . Romae . . . 1934.* 5 vols., III 247–67. Rome 1935–37.

Fournier, P. "Le Décret de Burchard de Worms—ses caractères, son influence." *RHE* 12 (1911) 451–73.

———. "Etudes critiques sur le Décret de Burchard de Worms." *RHDFE*, ser. 3, 34 (1910) 41–112, 213–21, 289–331, and 564–84.

———. "Guillaume du Breuil, juriste, sa vie, ses écrits." *Histoire littéraire de la France* 37.120–46.

————. *Les Officialités au moyen-âge.* Paris 1880.

Fowler, L. "Recusatio Iudicis in Civilian and Canonist Thought." *St. Gratiana* 15 (1972) 717–85. *See also* Fowler-Magerl, L.

Fowler, W. W. "The Original Meaning of the Word *Sacer*." *J. of Roman St.* 1 (1911) 57–63.

Fowler-Magerl, L. *Französische und spanische vor-Gratianische Kanonessammlungen.* Universität Regensburg, Juristische Fakultät. Manuscript computer indices. *See also* Fowler, L.

————. *Ordo Iudiciorum vel Ordo iudiciarius. Begriff und Literaturgattung.* Ius commune, Sonderheft 19. Frankfurt am Main 1984.

Frain, Sébastien, ed. *Arrests du parlement de Bretagne.* 3d ed. Rev. Pierre Hevin. 2 vols. in 1. Rennes 1684.

Fransen, G. "Colligite fragmenta: La Summa Elnonensis." *St. Gratiana* 13 (1967) 85–108.

————. "Les 'Questiones' des canonistes." Parts 2–4. *Traditio* 13 (1957) 481–501; 19 (1963) 516–31; 20 (1964) 495–502.

————, ed. *Summa "Elegantius in iure divino" seu Coloniensis.* Adlaborante S. Kuttner. 2 vols. *MIC* A-1. New York 1969 and Vatican City 1978.

Freud, S. *Group Psychology and the Analysis of the Ego.* Vol. 18 of *Works*, ed. J. Strachey, standard edition, 24 vols. London 1953–74.

————. *Totem and Taboo.* Vol. 13 of *Works*, ed. Strachey.

Fuhrmann, H. *Einfluss und Verbreitung der pseudoisidorischen Fälschungen.* 3 vols. MGH Schriften 24. Stuttgart 1972–74.

————. *See also* Seckel.

Funk, F. X., ed. *Didascalia et Constitutiones Apostolorum.* 2 vols. Paderborn 1905. Reprint. Turin 1970.

Furgeot, H., et al., eds. *Actes du parlement de Paris, deuxième série, 1328–50.* 2 vols. and index vol. Paris 1920–75.

Gabel, L. C. *Benefit of Clergy in England in the Later Middle Ages.* New York 1928. Reprint. 1969.

Gaius. *Institutiones.* Ed. F. de Zulueta. 2 vols. Oxford 1946–53.

Garnsey, P. *Social Status and Legal Privilege in the Roman Empire.* Oxford 1970.

Gasparri, P., ed. *Codex iuris canonici.* Rome 1917.

————, ed. *Codicis iuris canonici fontes.* 9 vols. Rome 1923–47.

Gaudemet, J. *La Formation du droit séculier et du droit de l'église aux IVe et Ve siècles.* 2d ed. Paris 1979.

Génestal, R., ed. *Plaids de la Sergenterie de Mortemer, 1320–1321.* Caen 1923.

van Gennep, A. *The Rites of Passage.* Trans. M. B. Vizedom and G. L. Caffee. Chicago 1960. [Originally published Paris 1909.]

Gilchrist, J., ed. *Diuersorum Patrum sententie siue Collectio in LXXIV titulos digesta.* *MIC* B-1. Vatican City 1973.

————. "Gregory VII and the Juristic Sources." *St. Gratiana* 12 (1967) 3–37.

————. "The Reception of Pope Gregory VII into the Canon Law (1073–1141)." Parts 1, 2. *ZRG Kan. Abt.* 59 (1973) 35–82; 66 (1980) 192–229.

———. "'Simoniaca haeresis' and the Problem of Orders from Leo IX to Gratian." *MIC* C-1, 209–35. Vatican City 1965.

Gilles, H., ed. *Le Coutumes de Toulouse (Consuetudines Tholose) 1286, et leur premier commentaire (Consuetudinem commentarium) 1296.* Toulouse 1969.

———. "Jean de Jean, abbé de Joncels." *Histoire littéraire de la France* 40.53–111.

Giraldus Cambrensis. *De iure et statu Menuensis ecclesiae distinctiones VII.* Ed. J. S. Brewer. RS V.21.3.

von Glanvell, V. W., ed. *Die Kanonessammlung des Kardinals Deusdedit.* Paderborn 1905. Reprint. Aalen 1967.

Goebel, J. *Felony and Misdemeanor.* Introd. by E. Peters. Philadelphia 1937. Reprint. 1976.

Göller, E. *Die päpstliche Pönitentiarie von ihrem Ursprung bis zu ihrer Umgestaltung unter Pius V.* 2 vols. in 4. Rome 1907–11.

Goffredus de Trano. *Summa super titulis Decretalium.* Lyon 1519. Reprint. Aalen 1968.

Gommenginger, A. "Bedeutet die Exkommunikation Verlust der Kirchengliedschaft?" *Z. für katholische Theologie* 73 (1951) 1–71.

Graham, R., ed. *Registrum Roberti Winchelsey, Cantuariensis archiepiscopi, A.D. 1294–1313.* 2 vols. Canterbury and York Society 51, 52. Oxford 1952–56.

de Grave, S. *See* Meijers.

Graves, E. B. "The Legal Significance of the Statute of Praemunire of 1353." In Charles H. Taylor and John L. La Monte, eds., *Anniversary Essays by Students of C. H. Haskins,* 57–80. New York 1929.

Greenidge, A. H. J. *Infamia. Its Place in Roman Public and Private Law.* Oxford 1894.

Gregory VII. *See* Caspar *and* Jaffé.

Guido de Baysio. *In Sextum Decretalium commentaria.* Venice 1577.

———. *Rosarium.* Venice 1577.

Guillaume Le Maire. *See* Port.

Hageneder, O. "Exkommunikation und Thronfolgverlust bei Innozenz III." *Römische historische Mitteilungen* 11 (1957–58) 9–50.

Hague, R., trans. *The Life of St. Louis.* New York 1955.

Haines, R. M. *The Administration of the Diocese of Worcester in the First Half of the Thirteenth Century.* London 1965.

von der Hardt, H. *Magnum oecumenicum Constantiense Concilium.* 6 vols. in 4. Frankfurt and Leipzig 1700.

Havet, J. *L'Hérésie et le bras séculier au moyen âge.* 2 vols. Paris 1896.

von Hefele, K. J., and H. Leclercq. *Histoire des conciles d'après les documents originaux.* 11 vols. in 22. Paris 1907–52.

Heggelbacher, O. *Die christliche Taufe als Rechtsakt nach dem Zeugnis der frühen Christenheit.* Paradosis. Beiträge zur Geschichte der altchristlichen Literatur und Theologie. Freiburg 1953.

Hein, K. *Eucharist and Excommunication. A Study in Early Christian Doctrine and Discipline.* Frankfurt am Main 1973.

Helmholz, R. H. *Marriage Litigation in Medieval England.* Cambridge 1974.

Hemmant, M., ed. *Select Cases in the Exchequer Chamber.* Vols. 1, 2. SS 51, 64. 1933, and 1948 for 1945.

Herde, P., ed. *Audientia litterarum contradictarum*. 2 vols. Tübingen 1970.

———, ed. *Marinus von Eboli, "Super revocatoriis" und "De confirmationibus."* Quellen und Forschungen aus italienischen Archiven 42–43 (Rome 1964). [Also published separately, Tübingen 1964.]

Hevin, Pierre. *See* Frain.

Hilgard, A., ed. *Urkundenbuch zur Geschichte der Stadt Speyer*. Strasbourg 1885.

Hill, R. "Public Penance: Some Problems of a Thirteenth-Century Bishop." *History* 36 (1951) 213–26.

Hinschius, P., ed. *Decretales Pseudo-Isidorianae et Capitula Angilramni*. Leipzig 1863. Reprint. Aalen 1963.

———. *System des katholischen Kirchenrechts*. 6 vols. Berlin 1869–97. Reprint. Graz 1959.

Histoire littéraire de la France. Paris 1733–.

Hockaday, F. S. "The Consistory Court of the Diocese of Gloucester." *Transactions of the Bristol and Gloucestershire Archaeological Society* 46 (1924) 195–287.

Hödl, L. *Die Geschichte der scholastischen Literatur und der Theologie der Schlüsselgewalt*. Part 1. Beiträge zur Geschichte der Philosophie und Theologie des Mittelalters 38. Münster in Westfalen 1960.

Hoffmann, H. *Gottesfriede und Treuga Dei*. MGH Schriften 20. Stuttgart 1964.

Holstein, H. *See* Wolter.

Holtzmann, W. *Papsturkunden in England*. 3 vols. Berlin 1931–35, Göttingen 1952. Reprint, vols. 1–2. Göttingen 1970.

Honorius III. *Regesta Honorii papae III*. Ed. P. Pressutti. 2 vols. Rome 1895. Reprint. Hildesheim and New York 1978.

Horborch, Guilhelmus. *Decisiones novae*. Rome 1472. [Unpaginated.]

Horwood, A. J., ed. *Year Books of King Edward the First. 30–31 Edward I.* RS 31.1.3.

Huber, A. *See* Böhmer.

Hübler, B. *Kirchenrechtsquellen*. 4th ed. Berlin 1902.

Huizing, P. *Doctrina Decretistarum de excommunicatione usque ad Glossam ordinariam Joannis Teutonici*. Rome 1952.

———. "The Earliest Development of Excommunication *Latae Sententiae*." *St. Gratiana* 2 (1955) 279–320.

Hyland, F. E. *Excommunication. Its Nature, Historical Development, and Effects*. Catholic University of America, Canon Law St. 49. Washington, D.C., 1928.

Isambert, F. A., ed. *Recueil général des anciennes lois françaises*. 29 vols. Paris 1822–23.

Jacobi, E. "Der Prozess im Decretum Gratiani und bei den ältesten Dekretisten." *ZRG Kan. Abt.* 3 (1913) 223–43.

Jaffé, P., ed. *Gregorii VII epistolae collectae*. Bibliotheca rerum Germanicarum 2. Berlin 1865.

———, ed. *Monumenta Bambergensia*. Bibliotheca rerum Germanicarum 5. Berlin 1869.

Jenkinson, H., and B. E. R. Formoy, eds. *Select Cases in the Exchequer of Pleas*. SS 48. 1932 for 1931.

Johannes of Freiburg. *See* William of Rennes.

Johannes Monachus. *Glosa aurea . . . super Sexto Decretalium . . . cum additionibus D. Philippi Probi.* Paris 1535. Reprint. Aalen 1968.

Johannes Teutonicus. *See* Pennington.

Johannes de Turrecremata. *In Gratiani Decretorum primam (–tertiam) partem commentarii. Repertorium.* Venice 1578.

Johnson, C., ed. *Registrum Hamonis Hethe.* 2 vols. Canterbury and York Society 48. Oxford 1948.

Joinville. *See* de Wailly.

Jombart, E. "Excommunication." *DDC* 5.615–28.

Jones, W. R. "Relations of the Two Jurisdictions: Conflict and Cooperation in England during the Thirteenth and Fourteenth Centuries." *St. in Medieval and Renaissance History* 7 (1970) 78–211.

Jourdain, C. "Les Excommunications pour dettes." *R. des Sociétés savantes,* ser. 6, vol. 6, part 2 (1877) 75–82.

Kaser, M. "Infamia und Ignominia in den römischen Rechtsquellen." *ZRG Kan. Abt.* 73 (1956) 220–78.

Keeney, B. C. *Judgment by Peers.* Cambridge, Mass., 1949.

Kehr, F. *Italia pontificia.* 10 vols. in 8. Berlin 1906. Reprint. 1961–65.

Kelly, J. M. *Roman Litigation.* Oxford 1966.

Kelly, J. N. D. *Early Christian Doctrines.* Rev. ed. New York 1978.

Kempf, F. *Papsttum und Kaisertum bei Innocenz III.* Miscellanea historiae pontificae 19. Rome 1954.

———. "Ein zweiter Dictatus Papae?" *Archivum historiae pontificae* 13 (1975) 119–39.

Kessler, P.-J. "Untersuchungen über die Novellen-Gesetzgebung Papst Innocenz' IV." Parts 1–3. *ZRG Kan. Abt.* 31 (1942) 142–320; 32 (1943) 300–383; 33 (1944) 56–128.

Knaake, J. K. F., et al., eds. *D. Martin Luthers Werke.* Weimar 1883–.

Knowles, D., et al. *Heads of Religious Houses, England and Wales, 940–1216.* Cambridge 1972.

Kober, F. *Der Kirchenbann nach den Grundsätzen des canonischen Rechts.* 2d ed. Tübingen 1863.

Kuttner, S. "Anhang: Zur Dekretale 'Licet preter solitum.'" In Landau, "Die Glossen" [q.v.] 27–28.

———. "Decretalistica." *ZRG Kan. Abt.* 26 (1937) 436–70.

———. "Johannes Teutonicus." *Neue deutsche Biographie* 10 (1974) 571a–573a.

———. "Die Konstitutionen des ersten allgemeinen Konzils von Lyon." *St. et documenta historiae et iuris* 1 (1940) 70–131.

———. *Repertorium der Kanonistik.* St. e testi 71. Vatican City 1937.

———. "Wer war der Dekretalist 'Abbas antiquus'?" *ZRG Kan. Abt.* 26 (1937) 471–87.

———, and E. Rathbone. "Anglo-Norman Canonists of the Twelfth Century." *Traditio* 7 (1949–51) 279–358.

———. *See also* Fransen.

Landau, P. *Die Entstehung des kanonischen Infamiebegriffs von Gratian bis zur Glossa ordinaria.* Forschungen zur kirchlichen Rechtsgeschichte und zum Kirchenrecht 5. Cologne 1966.

―――. "Die Glossen der Collectio Cheltenhamensis." *BMCL* 11 (1981) 9–28.

―――. "Lucius III und das Mietrecht in Bologna." *MIC* C-5, 511–22. Vatican City 1976.

―――. *See also* Kuttner.

Landgraf, A., ed. *Commentarius Cantabrigiensis in Epistolas Pauli e Schola Petri Abaelardi.* Notre Dame Publications in Medieval St. 2. Notre Dame, Ind. 1937–45.

―――. "Grundlagen für ein Verständnis der Busslehre der Früh- und Hochscholastik." *Z. für katholische Theologie* 51 (1927) 161–93.

―――. "Sunde und Trennung von der Kirche in der Frühscholastik." *Scholastik* 5 (1930) 210–47.

Latko, E. F. *Origen's Concept of Penance.* Quebec 1949.

Lattimore, R. *Themes in Greek and Latin Epitaphs.* Urbana, Ill., 1962.

Lea, H. C. "Excommunication." In *Studies in Church History,* 2d ed., 235–521. Philadelphia 1883.

―――. *A History of Auricular Confession and Indulgences.* 3 vols. Philadelphia 1896. Reprint. New York 1968.

―――. *A History of the Inquisition of the Middle Ages.* 3 vols. Rev. ed. London and New York 1906. Reprint. New York 1958.

Le Bras, G. *L'Immunité réele.* Paris 1920.

Leclercq, H. *See* von Hefele.

Lefebvre, C. "Hostiensis." *DDC* 5.1211–27.

―――. "Sinibalde dei Fieschi." *DDC* 7.1029–62.

Lehmann, K., ed. *Consuetudines feudorum.* Rev. K. A. Eckhardt. Bibliotheca rerum historicarum, Neudrucke 1. Aalen 1971.

Le Maire, E., ed. *Archives anciennes de la ville de St-Quentin.* 2 vols. St. Quentin 1888–1910.

Lerner, R. E. "An 'Angel of Philadelphia' in the Reign of Philip the Fair: The Case of Guiard of Cressonessart." In W. C. Jordan et al., eds., *Order and Innovation in the Middle Ages. Essays in Honor of Joseph R. Strayer,* 343–64. Princeton 1976.

Le Roy Ladurie, E. *Montaillou. The Promised Land of Error.* Trans. B. Bray. New York 1978.

Lévy, J. P. *La Hiérarchie des preuves dans le droit savant du moyen-âge.* Paris 1939.

Liebermann, F., ed. *Die Gesetze der Angelsachsen.* 3 vols. Halle 1903–16.

Litewski, W. "Les Textes procéduraux du droit de Justinien dans le Décret de Gratien." *St. Gratiana* 9 (1966) 65–109.

Little, L. K. "Formules monastiques de malédiction aux IXe et Xe siècles." *R. Mabillon* 58 (1975) 377–99.

―――. "La Morphologie des malédictions monastiques." *Annales. Economies, sociétés, civilisations* 34 (1979) 43–60.

Lobineau, G. A. *Histoire de Bretagne.* 2 vols. Paris 1707.

Logan, F. D. *Excommunication and the Secular Arm in Medieval England.* Pontifical Institute of Medieval St., St. and Texts 15. Toronto 1968.

Ludovicus Pontanus. *Singularia.* 2 vols. Frankfurt am Main 1629.

Luibhéid, C. "Theodosius II and Heresy." *J. of Ecclesiastical History* 16 (1965) 13–38.

Lydford, John. *See* Owen.

McGowan, J. P. *Pierre D'Ailly and the Council of Constance.* Washington, D.C., 1936.

McKeon, P. R. *Hincmar of Laon and Carolingian Politics.* Urbana, Ill., 1978.

McLaughlin, T. P., ed. *The Summa Parisiensis on the Decretum Gratiani.* Toronto 1952.

McNeal, E. H., and R. L. Wolff. "The Fourth Crusade." In R. L. Wolff and H. W. Hazard, eds., *The Later Crusades, 1189–1311,* 153–86. Madison, Wisc. 1969. [Vol. 2 of K. M. Setton, ed., *A History of the Crusades,* 4 vols.]

Magnin, E. "Ad vitanda scandala." *DDC* 1.250–52.

Maier, A. *Codices Burghesiani Bibliothecae Vaticani.* St. e testi 170. Vatican City 1952.

Maisonneuve, H. "Le Droit romain et la doctrine inquisitoriale." In *Etudes d'histoire du droit canonique dédiées à Gabriel Le Bras,* 2 vols., I 931–42. Paris 1965.

———. *Etudes sur les origines de l'inquisition.* 2d ed. L'Eglise et l'état au moyen-âge 7. Paris 1960.

Marinus of Eboli. *See* Herde.

Marnier, A.-J., ed. *Ancien Coutumier de Bourgogne.* Extrait de la RHDFE, 1857. Paris 1858.

———. *Anciens Usages inédits d'Anjou.* Paris 1853.

———. *Etablissements et coutumes, assises et arrêts de l'échiquier de Normandie au treizième siècle (1207 à 1245).* Paris 1839.

Marzials, F. T., trans. *Memoirs of the Crusades, by Villehardouin and de Joinville.* New York 1958.

Maskell, W. *Monumenta ritualia Ecclesiae Anglicanae.* 2d ed. 3 vols. Oxford 1882.

May, G. "Die Anfänge der Infamie im kanonischen Recht." *ZRG Kan. Abt.* 47 (1961) 77–94.

———. "Anklage- und Zeugnisfähigkeit nach der zweiten Sitzung des Konzils zu Karthago vom Jahre 419." *Theologische Quartalschrift* 140 (1960) 163–205.

———. "Die Bedeutung der pseudoisidorischen Sammlung für die Infamie im kanonischen Recht." *Österreichisches Archiv für Kirchenrecht* 12 (1961) 87–113, 191–207.

———. "Die Infamie im Decretum Gratiani." *Archiv für katholisches Kirchenrecht* 129 (1959–60) 389–408.

Meijers, E. M., and S. de Grave, eds. *Le Livre des droits de Verdun.* Haarlem 1940.

Melo Peixoto, E. *Derecho concordatario medieval portugues.* Salamanca 1979.

Miethe, T. L., and V. J. Bourke. *Thomistic Bibliography 1940–1978.* Westport, Conn., and London 1980.

Milsom, S. F. C. *See* Shanks.

Mirbt, C. *Die Publizistik im Zeitalter Gregors VII.* Leipzig 1894.

Mollat, G. *The Popes at Avignon.* 9th ed. Trans. J. Love. London 1963.

Mommsen, T. *Römisches Strafrecht.* Leipzig 1899.

Monaldus. *Summa de iure canonico.* Lyon 1516.

Moore, R. I. *The Origins of European Dissent.* London 1977.

Mordek, H. *Kirchenrecht und Reform im Frankenreich: Die Collectio Vetus Gallica . . . Studien und Edition.* Beiträge zur Geschichte und Quellenkunde des Mittelalters 1. Berlin and New York 1975.

Morel, M. *L'Excommunication et le pouvoir civil en France.* Paris 1926.

Morice, H. *Mémoires pour servir de preuves à l'histoire ecclésiastique et civile de Bretagne.* 2 vols. Paris 1742–46.

du Moulin, Charles. *See* Prohet.

Moulin, L. "Sanior et maior pars." *RHDFE*, ser. 4, 36 (1958) 491–521.

Müller, P. E. *Das Konzil von Vienne, 1311–1312.* Vorreformationsgeschichtliche Forschungen 12. Münster in Westfalen 1934.

von Mülverstedt, G. A., ed. *Regesta Archiepiscopatus Magdeburgensis.* 3 vols. and index vol. Magdeburg 1876–99.

Munier, C. "Canones Conciliorum Africae qui in Gratiani Decreto citantur, cum indicatione fontium." *MIC* C-5, 3–10. Vatican City 1976.

———, ed. *Concilia Africae A. 345–A. 525. CCL* 149.

———, ed. *Concilia Galliae A. 314–A. 506. CCL* 148.

———, ed. *Les Statuta ecclesiae antiqua.* Bibliothèque de l'Institut de droit canonique de l'Université de Strasbourg 5. Paris 1960.

———. "La Tradition littéraire des canons africains (345–525)." *Recherches augustiniennes* 10 (1975) 3–22.

Myrc, John. *Instructions for Parish Priests.* Ed. E. Peacock. Early English Text Society 31. London 1868.

New Catholic Encyclopedia. 15 vols. New York 1967.

Nicholas, B. *An Introduction to Roman Law.* Oxford 1962.

Nicolaus de Tudeschis. *See* Panormitanus.

Nörr, K. W. "Päpstliche Dekretalen und römisch-kanonischer Zivilprozess." In W. Wilhelm, ed., *Studien zur europäischen Rechtsgeschichte*, 53–65. Frankfurt am Main 1972.

Noonan, J. "The True Paucapalea." *MIC* C-6, 157–86. Vatican City 1980.

———. "Who Was Rolandus?" In K. Pennington and R. Somerville, eds., *Law, Church, and Society. Essays in Honor of Stephan Kuttner*, 21–48. Philadelphia 1977.

Oakley, T. P. "The Cooperation of Medieval Penance and Secular Law." *Speculum* 7 (1932) 515–24.

———. *English Penitential Discipline and Anglo-Saxon Law in their Joint Influence.* New York 1923.

Ochoa Sanz, J. *Vincentius Hispanus. Canonista boloñés del siglo XIII.* Cuadernos del Instituto jurídico español 13. Rome and Madrid 1960.

Olagnier, P. *L'Infamie légale du comédien.* Paris 1899.

Olivier-Martin, F. *L'Assemblée de Vincennes de 1329.* Paris 1909.

Oost, S. I. *Galla Placidia Augusta.* Chicago and London 1968.

Owen, D. M., ed. *John Lydford's Book.* London 1974.

Painter, S. *The Scourge of the Clergy. Peter of Dreux, Duke of Brittany.* Baltimore 1937.

Panormitanus [Nicolaus de Tudeschis]. *Commentaria in quinque libros Decretalium.* Lyon 1534 [I–V, except II.1], 1522 [II.1].

Pantin, W. A. *The English Church in the Fourteenth Century.* Cambridge 1955.

————. "The Fourteenth Century." In C. H. Lawrence, ed., *The English Church and the Papacy in the Middle Ages*, 157–94. London 1965.

Paucapalea. *Summa über das Decretum Gratiani.* Ed. J. F. von Schulte. Giessen 1890. Reprint. Aalen 1965.

Pennington, K. "The French Recension of Compilatio tertia." *BMCL* 5 (1975) 53–72.

————, ed. *Johannis Teutonici Apparatus glossarum in Compilationem tertiam* I. *MIC* A-3. Vatican City 1981.

————. *A Study of Johannes Teutonicus' Theories of Church Government.* 2 vols. in 3. Ann Arbor, Mich., Xerox Microfilms 1975.

————, and R. Somerville, eds. *Law, Church and Society. Essays in Honor of Stephan Kuttner.* Philadelphia 1977.

Perella, N. J. *The Kiss Sacred and Profane.* Berkeley and Los Angeles 1969.

Perels, E. "Die Briefe Papst Nikolaus I." Part 1. *Neues Archiv für ältere deutsche Geschichtskunde* 37 (1911–12) 537–86.

Perrot, E., ed. *Arresta communia scacarii. Deux collections d'arrêts notables de l'échiquier de Normandie de la fin du XIIIe siècle.* Bibliothèque d'histoire du droit normand, ser. l, 1. Caen 1910.

Peter the Chanter. *Summa de sacramentis et animae consiliis.* Ed. J.-A. Dugauquier. 5 vols. Analecta medievalia Namurcensia 4, 7, 11, 16, and 21. Louvain 1954–67.

Peter Lombard. *Sententiae in IV libris distinctae.* Ed. Collegium S. Bonaventurae. 3d ed. 2 vols. Spicilegium Bonaventurianum 4, 5. Quaracchi 1971–81.

Petit, J., ed. *Registre des causes civiles de l'officialité épiscopale de Paris, 1384–7. CDI* V.6.a. Paris 1919.

Philippus Probus. *See* Johannes Monachus.

Piergiovanni, V. *La Punibilità degli innocenti nel diritto canonico dell'età classica.* 2 vols. Milan 1971–74.

Piers, G., and M. B. Singer. *Shame and Guilt.* New York 1971.

Pillius, Tancredus, Gratia. *Libri de iudiciorum ordine.* Ed. F. C. Bergmann. Göttingen 1842. Reprint. Aalen 1965.

Planiol, M., ed. *La Très Ancienne Coutume de Bretagne.* Rennes 1896.

Plöchl, W. M. *Geschichte des Kirchenrechts.* 5 vols. 2d ed. Vienna and Munich 1960.

Pocquet du Haut-Jussé, B.-A. *Les Papes et les ducs de Bretagne.* 2 vols. Paris 1928.

Pontal, O. "Quelques remarques sur l'oeuvre canonique de Pierre de Sampzon." *Annuarium historiae Conciliorum* 8 (1976) 126–42.

————. *Les Statuts synodaux français du XIIIe siècle. CDI*, sér. in 8, vol. 9. Paris 1971.

Port, C., ed. *Livre de Guillaume Le Maire. CDI* X.11, 187–569. Paris 1877.

Poschmann, B. *Paenitentia secunda. Die kirchliche Busse im ältesten Christentum bis Cyprian und Origenes.* Bonn 1940. Reprint. 1964.

Powicke, F. M. *The Thirteenth Century.* 2d ed. Oxford 1962.

Prohet, C. I., ed. *Les Coutumes du haut et bas pais d'Auvergne.* With notes by Charles du Moulin. Paris 1695.

von Puttkamer, G. *Innocenz IV. Versuch einer Gesamtcharakteristik aus seiner Wirkung.* Münster in Westfalen 1930.

Quasten, J. "Apostolic Constitutions." *New Catholic Encyclopedia* 1.689–90.
———. "Didascalia Apostolorum." *New Catholic Encyclopedia* 4.1967.
Queller, D. E., et al. "The Fourth Crusade: The Neglected Majority." *Speculum* 49 (1974) 441–65.

Rapetti, G., ed. *Li Livres de Jostice et de Plet. CDI*, ser. 1, V.6. Paris 1850.
Rathbone, E. "Roman Law in the Anglo-Norman Realm." *St. Gratiana* 11 (1967) 253–69.
———. *See also* Kuttner.
Raymond of Peñafort. *Summa Sancti Raymundi de Peniafort . . . cum glossis Ioannis de Friburgo*. Rome 1603. Reprint. Farnborough 1967.
Regino of Prüm. *Libri duo de synodalibus causis*. Ed. F. G. A. Wasserschleben. Leipzig 1840. Reprint. Graz 1964.
Reik, T. *Masochism in Modern Man*. Trans. M. H. Beigel and G. M. Kurth. New York 1941.
———. *Ritual. Psycho-Analytic Studies*. 2d ed. Trans. D. Bryan. New York 1946.
Richard of Middleton. *Super quatuor libros Sententiarum Petri Lombardi questiones*. 2 vols. Brescia 1591.
Richardson, H. G. "Heresy and the Lay Power under Richard II." *English Historical R.* 51 (1936) 1–28.
Richter, J. "Stufen pseudoisidorischer Verfälschung." *ZRG Kan. Abt.* 64 (1978) 1–72.
Robert, U. *Testaments de l'officialité de Besançon, 1265–1500*. 2 vols. *CDI* III.38. Paris 1902–7.
Robert of Flamborough. *Liber poenitentialis*. Ed. J. J. F. Firth. Pontifical Institute of Medieval St., St. and Texts 18. Toronto 1971.
Roffredus Beneventanus. *Quaestiones Sabbatinae*. Avignon 1500. Reprinted as vol. 6.3 in M. Viora, ed., *Corpus glossatorum juris civilis*. Turin 1968.
Rogé, P. *Les Anciens Fors de Béarn*. Toulouse 1907.
Rolandus. *Die Summa Magistri Rolandi*. Ed. F. Thaner. Innsbruck 1874. Reprint. Aalen 1962.
Rose, H. J. *Religion in Greece and Rome*. New York 1959.
Rotuli parliamentorum. 6 vols. and index vol. London 1767–77.
Roussier, J. *Le Fondement de l'obligation contractuelle dans le droit classique de l'église*. Paris 1933.
Rudolfus de Liebegg. *Pastorale novellum*. Ed. A. P. Orbán. *CCLM* 55.
Rufinus. *Summa Decretorum*. Ed. H. Singer. Paderborn 1902. Reprint. Aalen 1963.
Runciman, S. *A History of the Crusades*. 3 vols. Cambridge 1951–54.
———. *The Sicilian Vespers*. Cambridge 1952.
Russo, F. "Pénitence et excommunication. Etude historique sur les rapports entre la théologie et le droit canonique dans le domaine pénitentiel du IXe au XIIIe siècle." *Recherches de science religieuse* 33 (1946) 257–79, 431–61.

Sainson, I. *See* Boerius.
Salatiele. *Ars notarie*. Ed. G. Orlandelli. 2 vols. in 1. Milan 1961.

Sanponts y Barba, I., et al., eds. *Las Siete Partidas*. 4 vols. Barcelona 1843–44.

Sayers, J., *Papal Judges Delegate in the Province of Canterbury 1198–1254*. Oxford 1971.

Sayles, G. O., ed. *Select Cases in the Court of King's Bench under Edward I*. 3 vols. SS 55, 57, 58. 1936, 1938, 1939.

Schadt, H. *Die Darstellungen der Arbores Consanguinitatis und der Arbores Affinitatis*. Tübingen 1982.

Schieffer, R. *Die Entstehung des päpstlichen Investiturverbots für den deutschen König*. MGH Schriften 28. Stuttgart 1981.

von Schulte, J. F. "Beiträge zur Literatur über die Dekretalen Gregors IX., Innocenz IV., Gregors X." *Sitzungsberichte der Bayerischen Akademie, Wien* 68 (1871) 55–127.

———. *Die Geschichte der Quellen und Literatur des canonischen Rechts*. 3 vols. in 4. Stuttgart 1875–80. Reprint. Graz 1956.

Schwartz, E., ed. *Acta Conciliorum oecumenicorum*. 4 vols. in 13. Berlin and Leipzig 1914–74. [Vol. 4.1 ed. J. Straub (1971); vol. 4.3.1 (index) ed. R. Schieffer (1974).]

Scullard, H. H. *From the Gracchi to Nero*. 5th ed. London and New York 1982.

Shanks, E., and S. F. C. Milsom, eds. *Novae narrationes*. SS 80. 1963.

Shannon, A. C. *The Popes and Heresy in the Thirteenth Century*. Villanova, Pa., 1949.

Sheehan, M. M. *The Will in Medieval England*. Pontifical Institute of Medieval St., St. and Texts 6. Toronto 1963.

Singer, M. B. *See* Piers.

Smith, J. T., ed. *English Gilds*. Early English Text Society 40. London 1870.

Somerville, R. "The Council of Pisa, 1135: A Re-Examination of the Evidence for the Canons." *Speculum* 45 (1970) 98–114.

———. *See also* Pennington.

Statutes of the Realm. Ed. A Luders et al. 11 vols. and indices. London 1810–28.

Stephan von Doornick [Stephen of Tournai, Stephanus Tornacensis]. *Die Summa über das Decretum Gratiani*. Ed. J. F. von Schulte. Giessen 1891. Reprint. Aalen 1965.

Stickler, A. M. "Il decretista Laurentius Hispanus." *St. Gratiana* 9 (1966) 461–550.

———. "Jean de Faenza." *DDC* 6.99–102.

———. "Der Schwerterbegriff bei Huguccio." *Ephemerides juris canonici* 3 (1947) 201–42.

Strayer, J. R. *The Reign of Philip the Fair*. Princeton 1980.

Stubbs, W. *Select Charters*. 9th ed. Rev. H. W. C. Davis. Oxford 1913.

Sutherland, D. W. Review of *Excommunication . . .* , by F. D. Logan. *Speculum* 45 (1971) 145–47.

Tancred. *See* Pillius.

Tanon, L., ed. *Registre criminel de la Justice de St Martin des Champs à Paris au XIVe siècle*. Paris 1877.

de Tarde, H. "La Rédaction des coutumes de Narbonne." *Annales du Midi* 85 (1973) 371–402.

Tardif, A. *La Procédure civile et criminelle aux XIIIe et XIVe siècles*. Paris 1885.

Tardif, E.-J., ed. *Coutumiers de Normandie*. 2 vols. in 3. Rouen 1881–96.

Taylor, L. R. *Party Politics in the Age of Caesar.* Berkeley and Los Angeles 1949.

Tellenbach, G. *Church, State and Christian Society at the Time of the Investiture Contest.* Trans. R. F. Bennett. New York 1970.

Teulet, J. B. A. T. *Layettes du trésor des chartes.* 5 vols. Paris 1863–66.

Thiel, A. *Epistolae Romanorum pontificum* I. Braunsberg 1867–68. Reprint. Hildesheim and New York 1974. [No more published.]

Thomas Aquinas. *Scriptum super libros Sententiarum.* Ed. P. F. Mandonnet and M. F. Moos. 4 vols. Paris 1929–47.

———. *Summa theologiae.* Vols. 4–12 of *Opera omnia,* Leonine edition, 12 vols. Rome 1882–.

Thornley, I. D., ed. *Year Books of Richard II,* vol. 5. London 1937.

Thouzellier, C. *Catharisme et Valdéisme en Languedoc.* 2d ed. Louvain and Paris 1969.

Tidner, E., ed. *Didascaliae Apostolorum, Canonum ecclesiasticorum, Traditionis Apostolicae, Versiones Latinae.* Texte und Untersuchungen zur Geschichte der altchristlichen Literatur 75. Berlin 1963.

Toussaert, J. *Le Sentiment religieux en Flandre à la fin du moyen-âge.* Paris 1963.

Tractatus ex variis iuris interpretibus collecti. 17 vols. and index vol. Lyon 1549.

Trexler, R. C. *The Spiritual Power. Republican Florence under Interdict.* St. in Medieval and Reformation Thought 9. Leiden 1974.

Turner, C. H., ed. *Ecclesiae Occidentalis monumenta iuris antiquissima.* 2 vols. Oxford 1899–1939.

Turner, V. W. *The Ritual Process: Structure and Anti-Structure.* London 1969.

Ullmann, W. *The Growth of Papal Government in the Middle Ages.* 2d ed. London 1962.

———. *The Individual and Society in the Middle Ages.* Baltimore and London 1967.

———. *The Medieval Idea of Law as Represented by Lucas de Penna.* London 1946.

———. "The Significance of Innocent III's Decretal 'Vergentis.'" In *Etudes d'histoire du droit canonique dédiées à Gabriel Le Bras,* 2 vols., I 729–42. Paris 1965.

Valentini, V., ed. "Il 'Tractatus de tabellionibus' di Baldo degli Ubaldi." *St. Urbinati* 18 (1965–66).

de Valroger, L., ed. *Coutume, style, et usage au temps des échiquiers de Normandie.* Paris 1851.

Varin, P., ed. *Archives administratives de la ville de Reims.* 3 vols. in 5. *CDI* II.13. Paris 1839–48.

———, ed. *Archives législatives de la ville de Reims.* 4 vols. *CDI* II.14. Paris 1840–52.

Vernay, E., ed. *Le "Liber de excommunicatione" du Cardinal Bérenger Frédol.* Paris 1912.

Vetulani, A. "Gratien et le droit romain." *RHDFE,* ser. 4, 25 (1946–47) 11–48.

Viollet, P., ed. *Les Etablissements de Saint Louis, accompagnés des textes primitifs et de textes dérivés.* 4 vols. Paris 1881–86.

Vives, J., ed. *Concilios visigóticos.* España cristiana, Textos 1. Barcelona and Madrid 1963.

Vodola, E., "*Fides et Culpa*: The Use of Roman Law in Ecclesiastical Ideology." In B. Tierney and P. Linehan, eds., *Authority and Power. Studies in Medieval Law and Government Presented to Walter Ullmann on His Seventieth Birthday.* Cambridge 1980.

———. "Hostiensis." "Innocent IV." "Interdict." In J. Strayer, ed., *Dictionary of the Middle Ages.* Forthcoming.

———. "Legal Precision in the Decretist Period." *BMCL* 6 (1976) 55–63.

———. "The Status of the Individual within the Community according to Ecclesiastical Doctrine in the High Middle Ages." 2 vols. Ph.D. dissertation, Cambridge University, 1975.

Vogel, C. "Composition légale et commutations dans le système de la pénitence tarifée." Parts 1, 2. *RDC* 8 (1958) 289–318; 9 (1959) 1–38, 341–59.

———. "Les Sanctions infligées aux laïcs et aux clercs par les conciles gallo-romains et mérovingiens." *RDC* 2 (1952) 5–29, 171–94, 311–28.

———, and R. Elze, eds. *Le Pontifical romano-germanique du dixième siècle.* 3 vols. St. e testi 226–27, 269. Vatican City 1963–72.

Wahrmund, L., ed. *Quellen zur Geschichte des römisch-kanonischen Processes im Mittelalter.* 5 vols. Innsbruck 1905–28. [vols. 1–4]; Heidelberg 1931 [vol. 5].

de Wailly, N., ed. *Jean, sire de Joinville, Histoire de Saint Louis.* Société de l'histoire de France 44. Paris 1868.

Wakefield, W. L. *Heresy, Crusade and Inquisition in Southern France, 1100–1250.* Berkeley and Los Angeles 1974.

Waley, D. *The Italian City-Republics.* London 1969.

Wasserschleben, F. W. H., ed. *Die Bussordnungen der abendländischen Kirche.* Halle 1851.

Watkins, O. D. *A History of Penance.* 2 vols. London 1920.

Watson, A. *Roman Private Law around 200 BC.* Edinburgh 1971.

Weber, R., ed. *Biblia sacra iuxta Vulgatam versionem.* 2 vols. Stuttgart 1975.

Weigand, R. "Bazianus- und B.-Glossen zum Dekret Gratians." *St. Gratiana* 20 (1976) 453–95.

———. "Frühe Glossen zu D.12 cc.1–6 des Dekrets Gratians." *BMCL* 5 (1975) 35–51.

———. "Magister Rolandus und Papst Alexander III." *Archiv für katholisches Kirchenrecht* 149 (1980) 3–44.

———. *Die Naturrechtslehre der Legisten und Dekretisten.* Munich 1967.

———. "Zur Handschriftenliste des Glossenapparatus 'Ordinaturus magister.'" *BMCL* 8 (1978) 41–47.

West, F. *The Justiciarship in England 1066–1232.* Cambridge 1966.

Whittaker, W. J., ed. *The Mirror of Justices.* SS 7. 1895.

William of Rennes. *Apparatus in Summam S. Raymundi.* Printed with misattribution in *Summa Sancti Raymundi de Peniafort . . . cum glossis Ioannis de Friburgo.* Rome 1603. Reprint. Farnborough 1967.

Winchelsey, Robert. *See* Graham.

Wolff, R. L. *See* McNeal.

Wolter, H., and H. Holstein. *Lyon I et Lyon II.* Histoire des conciles oecuméniques 7. Paris 1966.

Woodcock, B. L. *Medieval Ecclesiastical Courts in the Diocese of Canterbury.* Oxford 1952.

W. S. W. "Original Documents." *Archaeological J.* 3 (1846) 343–47.

Wyclif, John. *See* Arnold.

Zabarella, Franciscus. *Lectura super tertio (–quinto) Decretalium.* Lyon 1517–18.

Zeliauskas, J. *De Excommunicatione vitiata apud Glossatores (1140–1350).* Pontificium Athenaeum Salesianum, St. et textus historiae juris canonici 4. Zurich 1967.

General Index

259

Index of Manuscript Citations

Index of Biblical Citations

Index of Legal Citations

Citations within glosses are not included unless they are of special interest. Decretals discussed by name in the text are also in the general index.

Designer: Janet Wood
Compositor: G & S Typesetters, Inc.
Text: 11/13 Bembo
Display: Bembo
Printer: Braun-Brumfield, Inc.
Binder: Braun-Brumfield, Inc.